ROY PAUL NELSON
University of Oregon

Articles
and Features

HOUGHTON MIFFLIN COMPANY

Boston   *Dallas   Geneva, Illinois
Hopewell, New Jersey   Palo Alto   London*

To Chris, Robin, Tracy, and Bryan

Printed in the U.S.A.

Library of Congress Catalog Card Number: 77-85340

ISBN: 0-395-25517-1

Credits

Preface

College-level courses in Magazine Article Writing, Magazine Writing, Article and Feature Writing, Newspaper Feature Writing, or just plain Feature Writing serve students best, probably, when they allow plenty of time for in-class exercises and the exchange and criticism of articles and features written outside of class. The value of a textbook covering the fundamentals of the craft lies in its freeing instructors from some of the lecturing to devote more class time to lab and seminar aspects of their courses.

This book, based on an instructor's experience with Magazine Article Writing courses conducted each year since 1955 and a career in freelancing to both magazines and newspapers that dates to the 1940s, attempts to cover material instructors might be expected to cover early in the term or semester. Updating the material, elaborating on it, arguing with it, instructors may find that the book helps them get their students off to early starts on their major projects.

Assuming that the students already have some training in nonfiction writing, from either Mass Communications or English departments, and an interest in placing or selling what they write, the book establishes what articles and features are, tells how ideas come about, examines the various markets for both staff writers and freelancers, and then takes the students through the various steps in research, writing, and marketing. Numerous short excerpts, packaged as invitingly as possible, illustrate points made in the text.

The book tries not to make the mistake of overselling students on their potential for publication; neither does it paint a picture that is too bleak.

The book recognizes a close relationship between the article written for a magazine and the feature written for a newspaper but offers one chapter on newspapering near the end to spell out some differences. The importance of writer-supplied illustrations and the need often for a light touch in writing, even when the subject is serious, prompt two chapters not always found in books of this kind.

Professors Byron T. Scott of Ohio University, Everette Dennis of the University of Minnesota, and John English of the University of Georgia looked over the first draft of the book, and their responses resulted in numerous changes and considerable reshuffling. The writer hopes that this final version comes a little closer to being the book any one of these three perceptive critics might have written.

RPN

CONTENTS

CHAPTER 1

INTRODUCTION

Magazines generally call them "articles"; newspapers call them "features" or "feature stories." In either medium they bring to nonfiction the touch of fiction. In the major magazines today, novelists as well as journalists write them, but what they produce is still journalism. The readers get facts, not fantasy.

If you think of short stories as novels in miniature, you can think of articles and features as nonfiction books in miniature. They deal with events, movements, trends, and processes, but with an emphasis on people. Typically, articles and features narrow in on individuals.

In the magazines, articles are everything. Short stories, which once shared the stage with articles, no longer interest most editors. In the newspapers, features play an important but secondary role to news stories. Newspapers tend to regard features as change-of-pace material, but the differences between magazine articles and newspaper features become less distinct each year. Some newspapers turn feature writers loose on major assignments and give them as much time to develop their features as writers for major magazines take. If the papers can't publish the material in a single issue, they let it spread over several issues.

Magazines and newspapers grow alike in other ways. We have magazines now that come out looking like newspapers, printed on oversize sheets, with narrow columns and with column rules. Communicators call them "magapapers." Regular-format magazines use signatures (sets of pages) printed on newsprint. We have newspapers with fewer, wider columns per page, printed in offset to better show off their photography, with lots of color, using titles rather than headlines, and putting some of the content into small magazine-size inserts. *The Christian Science Monitor* calls attention to the phenomenon in an *Advertising Age* ad directed to media buyers in agencies. "It's a Newspaper . . . in Format. It's a Magazine . . . in Audience," reads the ad's headline. Another newspaper that reads more like a magazine is *The Wall Street Journal*.

The temptation is to rank the article ahead of the feature, especially if the comparison involves a piece of writing appearing in an 8,000,000-circulation magazine to, say, one appearing in a 2,000-circulation weekly newspaper. But you could also pick an item from a 1,500,000-circulation daily newspaper and compare it to something appearing in a trade or specialty magazine reaching only 5,000 subscribers. The feature could make the article look amateurish.

Not that size necessarily makes a difference. Writing talent can be found anywhere — out in a remote part of the country as well as in a posh office in Manhattan. This book will show you samples of the work of writers of obvious talent, many of them attached to prestigious publications, true, but some doing their writing for obscure newspapers and magazines.

To simplify the discussion, the book will use "article" throughout except in the chapter devoted exclusively to newspaper features. At most mentions of articles in other chapters, you can substitute "feature" without obscuring the meaning.

• COURSES IN ARTICLE AND FEATURE WRITING

W. C. Fields, probably the most innovative juggler the world had ever seen, made the mistake, on an English tour, of reading a piece on Indian juggling by William Hazlitt, the esteemed essayist and critic who had died some years before Fields was born. On stage, Fields attempted to put what he learned into practice. As his biographer Robert Lewis Taylor tells it, "He tossed several balls and hats into the air and concentrated heavily on precision, mathematics, coordination, muscle control, breathing, relaxed nerves, and things in Latin. All about him balls and hats tumbled to the floor." This phenomenon of Fields "juggling like a man with arthritis" went on for several performances, and at one point, Fields decided he had had it. In desparation he pushed what he had learned from Hazlitt aside,

"You know the rules, Mr. Lorton. No dogs in the classroom. . . ."

and soon he was back to his true form. "I was almost put out of business by a well-meaning corpse," he said later.[1]

Some writers already contributing to magazines and newspapers might find instruction in article and feature writing inhibiting. "The centipede, when asked with which foot he started to walk, became paralyzed," observed Franz Schoenberner in *Confessions of a European Intellectual*. But other writers might find new ideas and even inspiration in formal course work. This book attempts to serve those writers, but in large part it directs itself to writers who have not tried to contribute articles and features to magazines and newspapers, or who, having tried, have not found success in placing their work. Perhaps they will see here some of the reasons editors did not buy.

With increased interest in the more creative aspects of journalism and the feeling now on college campuses that courses should be directed toward practical goals, Articles and Features courses usually fill early during registration periods. These courses draw students who

[1]Robert Lewis Taylor, *W. C. Fields: His Follies and Fortunes*, Doubleday & Company, Inc., Garden City, N.Y., 1949, p. 98, 99.

"I won't be in class Thursday. . . . Will I miss anything important?"

have had some experience in reporting classes as well as students with work in short story writing. The Reporting students usually need to spend the first few weeks loosening up, allowing their personalities to come through in their writing, giving up their strict adherence to objectivity for a more subjective approach, and learning to rely as much as possible on writing techniques used by novelists, playwrights, essayists, and poets. The Short Story Writing students need to learn to work with facts, including statistics and quotations, without sacrificing literary flair.

Articles and Features courses also appeal to students from disciplines that do not put their emphasis on writing. Some of the most productive students in the courses turn out to be majors in the sciences or social sciences or from the professional schools who want to write from their specialties.

Students from whatever discipline often enter courses as amateurs and leave as professionals, their work during the term or semester having impressed editors sufficiently to earn acceptance and payment. One of the attractions of this activity is that writers can do their work at home, at their own pace, choosing their own subject to explore and write about.

• WHO WRITES ARTICLES?

Writers produce articles under one of two arrangements: as staff writers or as freelancers. For a newspaper, writers normally work as staff writers or reporters. Newspaper editors expect their writers to turn out news stories as well as features. For a magazine, writers work either as staff writers or as freelancers. A number of magazines, once excellent outlets for freelancers, have removed themselves from the writing market because of the high cost of looking at unsolicited manuscripts. Their material is either staff-written or supplied by regular contributors. Some magazines, including many company magazines (or "house organs," as they are sometimes called), some trade journals, and the three newsweeklies, never were much of a market for freelancers. But enough magazines, including those with some staff-written content, remain open to outside contributions to make freelancing, at least on a part-time basis, an attractive possibility. And even the newspapers, especially those with locally produced magazine sections, welcome contributions from outside.

It is easy for an enthusiastic instructor or textbook writer to oversell freelancing to students. New specialized magazines come along every month to take the place of the big general-circulation magazines that died because they failed to change with the times. In order to survive, most of these new magazines need contributions from freelancers. Despite widespread opinion that the market for freelancers is dying, those who sell to the magazines; especially those who concentrate on the medium and small ones, know that the possibilities are still there.

"No kidding?! I do a little writing myself. . . ."

But with all the competition for editors' checks, freelancing can be discouraging. Some students never do catch on to what makes a salable article. And some who do sell find that it takes dozens of tries before they finally get a notice that they have made it.

That letter from an editor advising of a sale can move even the most stolid student. One of the students in a feature writing class years ago had spent some time between high school and college attending special classes for stutterers and with almost miraculous results. It was the subject he chose to write about. When, one day midway into the term, he came into the classroom excitedly waving his check, someone who apparently had missed the reading of the manuscript in class asked what the article was about. The answer carried to the far corners of the room: "How I c-c-c-cured my st-st-stuttering."

• The Writer's Gender

In its early years, *Esquire*, as a magazine for men, refused to run articles with feminine bylines. That famous piece in the October 1936 issue, "Latins Are Lousy Lovers," carried no byline, but its author was Helen Lawrenson, who, after the restriction was lifted, became one of the magazine's most frequent contributors. In those antifeminine days the magazine ran some articles and stories by women who used initials rather than first — or given — names. The late Arnold Gingrich reflected on all this in a column in the December 1975 issue, an issue carrying seven articles by women: Grace Paley, M. F. K. Fisher, Jean Stafford, Joan Didion, Nora Ephron, Julia Child, and Eudora Welty.

A few ruggedly male, adventure-oriented magazines continue to discourage women writers or at least ask them to hide their gender, and some of the militant feminist magazines say *No* to male writers; but in general the sex of the writer no longer means much to either editors or readers. More than ever before, women occupy editorial positions on magazines. In the company-magazine category, probably half the editors are women.

Nor is it likely that any article would be rejected — or accepted — on the basis of the minority status of the writer. It is generally true, though, that not many members of minority groups occupy high editorial positions on magazines or newspapers.

"I think your mother sold her article."

• Helps for Writers

Freelance writers, probably more than other groups, are subject to well-meaning and maybe not-so-well-meaning help — from literary agents who charge "reading fees," subsidy publishers who expect writers to pay for costs of publication, and writers of books who promise that "Anyone who can write a clear sentence can easily learn to make $10,000 — $20,000 — $50,000 or more a year!" One such book, *How to Make Big Money Free-lance Writing*, in a section preceding the chapters of short-cut advice, was sure it would "stir up considerable controversy among teachers, editors, and a few purist writers." *Yawn*.

More useful to freelancers are the various writing courses offered by educational institutions, either on location or by correspondence, and the advice available in writers' magazines like *Writer's Digest* and *The Writer* and the market guides these magazines publish.

For help on insurance stories, call State Farm.

When you need facts or opinions on auto, home-owners, life or boat insurance, try State Farm. Our public relations staff of former newsmen understands news deadlines. If we have the facts at hand, we'll give them to you right away. If we don't, we'll talk to an expert and call you back. When you need opinion or comment, we'll find a corporate executive for you to interview.

If you need detailed written material and you don't have time to wait for the mail, we can send it to you immediately by telephone facsimile transmission.

More and more news people are calling State Farm for facts on insurance-related topics. Call our public relations department at 309-662-2521 or 662-2063.

STATE FARM INSURANCE COMPANIES
Home Offices: Bloomington, Illinois

STATE FARM INSURANCE

Figure 1.1 One of a series of State Farm Insurance Companies advertisements run in *Editor & Publisher* and other magazines for journalists. The ads point out that the Chicago-based organization will supply facts or opinions to journalists and freelance writers working on stories or articles about insurance or the insurance business. Writers may ask to be put on a mailing list to receive regular mailings from State Farm, including the newsletter *Advisory*. Other companies and trade associations maintain similar services for writers.

• WHY WRITE ARTICLES?

"Fortunately, fairly early in my life at the typewriter, I was able to write for big magazines," says Roger Kahn. He cites some advantages of article writing over book writing: "No shark-toothed reviewers loitered there and, since magazines do not pay royalties, sales figures were someone else's concern. With diligence, which I possessed a-plenty, and the right touch, I could reach great numbers of people, and, from time to time, move some deeply. When I found this gift, magazine writing became not only a vocation but a passion."[2]

[2] Roger Kahn, *How the Weather Was*, New American Library, New York, 1975, p. xiii.

"His first article sale."

People write articles for a variety of reasons. For the satisfactions Kahn talks about. Because they like to teach or entertain. To make money. But not for fame. Readers — most of them — pay little attention to the names of the authors of articles they read, even of articles that change their lives.

Maybe the best reason for writing articles is that you learn so much in the process. As Horace Walpole said, "I never understand anything until I have written about it."

• THE ARTICLE WRITER AS ARTICLE READER

You can't expect to write articles without reading them. Reading them not only shows you how to write them; it gives you ideas for other articles to write. And much of the information going into your own articles can come from articles written by others. Steve Lorton, who writes for *Sunset* out of that magazine's Seattle office, looks upon himself as a sponge soaking up everything he reads and sees and experiences. As he expresses it, the writing process for him consists of "wringing out the sponge."

There is no place in journalism for the person who merely wants to write. What the media need are people who have something to say. The world of magazines and newspapers is no more impressed by people who "love to write" than the rest of the world is impressed by people who love to talk.

• THE DEVICES OF FICTION

As a piece of journalism, the article contains facts and ideas. To present them to readers, though, article writers make use of the devices of fiction. For one thing the writers give plots to their articles but call the plots "themes." For another, the writers create suspense. Instead of giving their stories away in the first paragraphs, as news writers do, article writers hold off until later. But they make sure to start off with information or effects that attract and hold the attention of readers.

Any literary form will do for articles: straight telling, playful telling, a drama, even poetry. Some writers have used a series of letters, similar to what fiction writer Ring Lardner used so successfully in *You Know Me Al*, that hilarious collection of semiliterate notes to a friend back home from a bragging bushleaguer who made the big leagues. Some have used the "open letter" device, in which the article reads as though it had been written to a famous person or to a powerful group. Theodore H. White used the device in *New York* (Nov. 10, 1975) to urge the Democratic majority in Congress to come to New York City's rescue during a financial crisis.

> Gentlemen:
>
> I write to you from New York City where we face disaster. Last week President Ford. . . .

Article writers using the devices of fiction are not afraid to mix and match, using facts as well as ideas, description as well as action, dialogue as well as instruction. And all of it builds to a climax, as in a short story.

"I dropped 'Magazine Article Writing.' The instructor didn't like my poems. . . ."

The material may come to the reader sequentially; or it may move back and forth, from the present to the past, from the important to the unimportant. Because dialogue and narrative — the stuff of novels and short stories — tax readers least, article writers use them generously. The dialogue (not to be confused with ordinary quotations) consists of a series of conversational exchanges between persons, set off with quotation marks, or, on rare occasions, it consists of one person's thoughts, with or without the marks.

The trick is to use these devices without distorting the facts and ideas, which are the mainstay of the articles. Some confusion is bound to result. While journalists have been busy appropriating the devices of fiction, fiction writers have moved into the journalists' territory, not only writing journalism but also putting real people into the settings of their novels and short stories. The historical novel is a case in point. And in *Ragtime*, E. L. Doctorow put well-known early-20th-century figures into imaginary settings. Did these people really do the things he says they did? "What's real and what isn't?" Doctorow answers. "I used to know but I've forgotten. Let's just say that *Ragtime* is a mingling of fact and invention — a novelist's revenge on an age that celebrates nonfiction."

• THE "NEW JOURNALISM"

Along with all the other ferment, the 1960s brought an uninhibited, sometimes artful kind of nonfiction called the "new journalism," which made use of the devices of fiction and more. The movement attracted novelists as well as journalists, including Truman Capote, Tom Wolfe, Jimmy Breslin, Norman Mailer, Gay Talese, Studs Terkel, and Nicholas von Hoffman. Capote, a novelist, wrote one of the first pieces, *In Cold Blood* (Random House, 1966), a book about a mass murder in Kansas, and called it a "nonfiction novel" because the story was real but it read like fiction. The *In Cold Blood* style spawned many imitators. While novelists switched to journalism, journalists switched to novels, causing writer Seymour Krim to wonder: "Why do . . . [journalists] still think the novel is the Higher Form, when they have in their hands a much greater power, that of writing about people with real names with more freedom today than a novelist had with his characters 30 years ago?"

It didn't have to be a book to be part of the "new journalism." It could be a shorter piece, probably unedited and rambling and highly personalized, appearing in *Esquire* or *New York* (the old New York *Herald Tribune* magazine section restarted as an independent magazine in 1968), or *The Village Voice*, or in some other magazine or alternative newspaper or, toward the end of the 1960s, in some regular newspaper. One of the most interesting new publications to grow out of the 1960s was *Rolling Stone*, described by Prof. Lauren Kessler of Linfield College as "the first publication to both chronicle and influence the entire rock culture . . . . It gave an honest and searching account of one of the deepest social revolutions of our times." In the 1970s the magazine broadened its base to become "a showcase of investigative 'New Journalism.' "[3] By 1976 King Features Syndicate was

[3]Lauren Jeanne Kessler, *Cosmic Debris: An Anecdotal History of Rolling Stone Magazine from November 1967 to September 1974*, unpublished thesis, School of Journalism, University of Oregon, Eugene, March 1975, pp. 11, 126, vii.

offering *Rolling Stone* material to daily newspapers. The Register and Tribune Syndicate was already distributing *Mother Earth News* material. And everybody, it seemed, wanted to become a "new journalist."

Unfortunately, it took more than enthusiasm and commitment to a cause to produce "new journalism" that people would want to read. It took talent. And to handle all the affectations of style typical of the "new journalism," a writer first had to understand correct usage. A writer also had to be willing to conduct research. "New journalism" was not just off-the-top-of-the-head writing, as some young writers thought.

Nor could "new journalism" techniques be applied to all the subjects writers had to cover. Some of the more mundane aspects of life could better be reported in a more traditional manner. Many college-level newspapers solved that problem by denying coverage to routine events.

Not everyone was impressed by the "new journalism." "There is nothing new about the new journalism," was a common complaint. What was Lillian Ross's *New Yorker* profile of Ernest Hemingway, published way back in 1950, if it wasn't "new journalism"? To other critics, the "new journalism" was not journalism.

In 1968 Arnold Gingrich, whose *Esquire* had been a leader in developing the "new journalism," observed that "Never has there been less editing of manuscripts. Never has there been more half-baked stuff published than there is today. There is an utter lack of discipline in writing now." Another critic, John Leo, said that, in doing a piece of writing under the "new journalism" banner, "The author orchestrates details and scenes like a novelist, heaping up great piles of carefully selected trivia, brand names, and long quotes, driving toward some cosmic sociological point."[4]

Syndicated columnist Smith Hempstone saw the "new journalism" combining with general disillusionment after Watergate to create "a vogue of smart-guy cynicism, a chic of rudeness, that is almost sadistic. The object [among reporters] seemingly is less to obtain information than to inflict hurt." Hempstone points out that Jan Morris, writing in the British magazine *Encounter*, calls this phenomenon "predatory journalism."

[4]John Leo, "The Life and Times of Gay Talese," *Commonweal*, Oct. 17, 1969, p. 66.

Prof. John W. English of the University of Georgia acknowledges some excesses among the new journalists but says ". . . they were able to shake up the snoremongers of traditional journalism at a time when the competition for media moments was never greater. Not only did the bylines of NJ celebs help sell magazines, but they also offered readers zing, life, humanized prose and new depth of reality and truth that was both intellectually and emotionally exciting." One of the academicians to first recognize the impact of the "new journalism" was Everette E. Dennis, who, as a visiting professor at the University of Oregon, launched a course to examine its techniques and influence. Dennis gathered writing from that class into a book, *The Magic Writing Machine*. Later, in collaboration with Prof. William L. Rivers of Stanford, he brought out his *Other Voices*, one of several books by various authors analyzing the movement or bringing together some of its writings. Tom Wolfe himself put together *The New Journalism* for Harper & Row. Wolfe, a pop sociologist with a Ph.D., gained fame as a "new journalist" in the mid-1960s with his two-part New York *Herald Tribune* article attacking the editorial staff of *The New Yorker*. The literary world, at least as it involves magazines, was stunned. Fault the esteemed *New Yorker* and that agreeable man who runs it, William Shawn? It was unheard of. Later Wolfe shook up the "limousine liberals" with his attack in *New York* on the "Radical Chic," which became part of a follow-up book. One of his recent books, *The Painted Word*, pokes fun at the world of modern art. In a review of that book, Robert Hughes of *Time* refers to Wolfe as "the Bugs Bunny of American journalism."

Those who analyzed the "new journalism" tended to agree on what it included: nonfiction books and articles with the moving quality of Capote's *In Cold Blood*; left-leaning articles and features appearing in alternative journals like the San Francisco *Bay Guardian* and the various city journalism reviews; propagandistic pieces found in shrill journals of advocacy like *Ramparts*; new- and far-left propaganda and pornography or near-pornography as found in the underground press; and "precision journalism" that makes use of the tools of the social scientist to measure political and social change.

The "new journalism" saw a few writers mixing fact and fiction in a ratio that made readers wonder if it was essentially fiction they were reading, with a little fact thrown in. Some writers made use of the "composite character," a person who appeared real but who was actually a combination of several persons, put together to make the story move along more quickly and more dramatically. And if a few facts were wrong, names misspelled, and quotes garbled or manufactured, it didn't matter much to some of the "new journalists." It was truth these writers were after, and truth was something different from accuracy. In the "new journalism," objectivity became a dirty word. There is no such thing as true objectivity, the "new journalists" argued, so why try to achieve it?

Not only did writers who considered themselves "new journalists" drop all pretenses of objectivity; they sometimes became participants in the news. Some of this activism spilled over into newspapers. Prof. J. K. Hvistendahl of South Dakota State University, in a 1970 article exploring trends in American journalism, saw this activism as a fourth revolution in journalism. The others had been:

1. the revolution freeing the press from government control, resulting in the First Amendment to the Constitution;
2. the coming of objectivity as press associations began supplying papers across the country with national and international news; and
3. interpretive reporting, in which reporters put the news "in perspective" and commentators and columnists on radio and on editorial pages added to our understanding of the news.

The new revolution involved "The Reporter as Activist," and the evidence gathered by Hvistendahl included the facts that *Time* employees — 500 of them — had taken time off from work to attend an antiwar discussion; Chicago reporters had founded the *Chicago Journalism Review* (no longer published) to criticize their own papers; and reporters everywhere were demanding more participation in deciding their papers' editorial policies.

As Hvistendahl saw it, college newspapers led the way to activist journalism. Some were no longer newspapers, he pointed out; they were one big editorial page or propaganda mill, with, in some cases, news confined to a single column. He quoted one young reporter as having said, in defense of this practice, "The American press is always last to recognize the disease, but is first to report the funeral."[5]

[5]J. K. Hvistendahl, "The Reporter as Activist: A Fourth Revolution in Journalism," *The Quill*, February 1970, pp. 8–11.

Whether activists or not, writers tended to play major parts in their stories. "I" is an important pronoun in the "new journalism." After Norman Mailer produced his personality sketch of Jimmy Carter for *The New York Times Magazine*, one reader, David I. Wells, wrote, "Now that you have run an article about Norman Mailer, perhaps you ought to consider doing one on Jimmy Carter!"

Hunter S. Thompson of *Rolling Stone* in the 1970s introduced a variation of the "new journalism" called "gonzo journalism." Thompson says he got the name from Bill Cardosa, editor of the *Boston Globe* Sunday magazine. It is "some Boston word for weird, bizarre," Thompson says. "But to me it means intense, demented involvement. I use it very often to contrast with 'Professional Journalism,' which I guess I don't have too much respect for."[6] Prof. Dennis, now of the University of Minnesota, thinks Thompson coined the term "to put down the increasing tendency toward definition of the New Journalism. As far as I can determine, gonzo is a kind of one-man psychodrama in which the journalist (if you can call him that) interacts with the event, source, etc. Pure gonzo is the 'fear and loathing' material, especially that related to the 1972 campaign."[7]

• "New Journalism" Today

Although it confined itself mostly to magazines like *Esquire* and *New York* and the underground and alternative press, the "new journalism" undoubtedly influenced the content of more traditional publications, including daily newspapers. In the 1970s, articles in general-circulation magazines and features in newspapers, especially in special sections and locally edited magazine sections, carried many of the trappings of the "new journalism."

Thomas R. Kendrick, editor of the "Style" section of the Washington *Post*, a section covering people, the arts, leisure, consumer affairs, books, entertainment, fashion, food, home design, gardening, travel, television, and social and cultural trends, thinks that journalism these days "is in flux. Still, this is a less turbulent time than the decade past, one with an emphasis on evolution, on assimilation, on sorting out

[6] Peter A. Janssen in *Columbia Journalism Review* reported in 1974 that a Hunter Thompson piece in *Rolling Stone* typically draws 500 letters.
[7] Letter to the author from Everette E. Dennis, July 14, 1975.

techniques and approaches that help build credibility from those that damage."

In Kendrick's view, "there never was a 'New Journalism' in the sense of a phenomenon without literary or journalistic antecedents. There were scores from Daniel Defoe to H. L. Mencken, Ernest Hemingway to John O'Hara. But there definitely was, and is, a 'New Journalism' in terms of the number of journalists influenced by its various facets, the breadth and intensity of their assaults on traditional conventions of 'objectivity.' "[8]

Because of the confusion over what the "new journalism" really is, Kendrick prefers the term "personal journalism" for the material appearing in "Style." Such material bears the personal imprint of the writer and focuses on the "human dimension" of social change.

Kendrick admits that personal journalism in newspapers is riskier than the same journalism in magazines. In an introduction to an anthology of "Style" articles put together by the Washington Post Writers Group, he points out that the stories and features, "fine as they are, provide clues to what can happen under the pressures of newspaper space and deadlines: a blur in focus or loss of context, a tired adjective or strained simile, a rough transition or absent fact, a simple error or slip to bias."[9]

• THE ETHICS OF NONFICTION

Every society sets up a system of ethics and, within that system, any number of subsystems. The ethics of one subsystem, say the law profession, may come in conflict with the ethics of another, say the journalism profession (or "trade," if you prefer). "Many of the ethical questions that trouble the journalists' working hours (and often haunt their dreams as well) would tax a Solomon," says Prof. John L. Hulteng of Stanford University. "Few are clearcut and uncomplicated. And in reaching these decisions, the journalists . . . are pretty much on their own, without detailed ground rules to guide them."[10]

[8] Thomas R. Kendrick, "Introduction," *Writing in Style* (Laura Longley Babb, editor), Houghton Mifflin, Boston, 1975, p. ii.

[9] *Ibid.*, page v.

[10] John L. Hulteng, *The Messenger's Motives*, Prentice-Hall, Inc., Englewood Cliffs, N.J., 1976, p. 2.

Journalists generally expect each other to avoid lying, making up facts, handling information carelessly, advocating violence, dealing in pornography, stealing others' writing and creative efforts, violating rights of privacy, misrepresenting themselves to get a story, interfering with fair trial, tearing down reputations unnecessarily and maliciously, keeping other journalists from getting the story, giving preferential treatment to friends, going out of the way to nail enemies, accepting gifts from people they write about, or using the medium for self-promotion.

Some of this conduct is covered in media codes, like the American Society of Newspaper Editors' Canons of Journalism promoting truthfulness, accuracy, impartiality, fair play, responsibility, decency, and independence. The Society's code, adopted in 1973, emphasizes truth, responsibility, freedom, accuracy, objectivity, and fair play. Directly or indirectly it asks newspeople to refuse to accept gifts and favors, to avoid secondary employment and political involvement, to question material received from public relations sources, to insist on access to public records, and to protect confidential sources. Other organizations in journalism have also developed codes. But codes "are vague, mostly unenforceable, and many reporters have never read one," says Michael T. Malloy, writing in *The National Observer*. Even if the codes had teeth, they would do little to correct press abuses. A code of ethics or conduct tends to be no better than what the least moral members of the group can tolerate. And it could be argued that codes in journalism sponsored by media groups evolve not so much for moral as for practical and public relations reasons — to keep government agencies from interfering. Of course, that is no small service.

Where reputation, fair trial, and ownership of literary property are concerned, the law and the courts come into play. Where other aspects enter in, peer pressure plays a role. So do the journalism reviews that began in several cities during the 1960s, the press councils, and the ombudsman idea tried by some newspapers. But ethical conduct in journalism is largely a matter of following one's conscience or listening to one's God.

• Truth and Fairness

Boiling down media codes, court decisions, and journalistic conduct generally applauded by critics and readers, you come up with two key words: truth and fairness. Journalists can be late, arrogant, careless, lazy, stupid, vulgar, dull, and obtuse and possibly get away with it; but they cannot be liars and they cannot be unfair. Not and operate ethically.

Truth mostly concerns readers; fairness mostly sources and people written about. Writers can offer readers well-documented facts that happen to point to something other than the truth. The selection of facts may be faulty. And if writers report what people say, without disputing it or putting it into context, their use of facts may mislead readers.

Being fair is as hard as being truthful. Whatever writers produce could help some people and hurt others. Writers cannot avoid that — not if they want to write material worth reading. As journalists, they court controversy. They name names. They praise when they feel it's deserved; they criticize when they feel it's due. Sometimes, just by praising one person, a writer indirectly criticizes another.

Writers who want to be fair may find it instructive to put themselves in the place of people they write about and imagine their own reactions.

Writers dealing with controversial subjects should remind themselves that they enjoy an advantage over nonwriters who defend or represent opposite sides: writers have mass media at their disposal. Further, they have communications skills their protagonists may not have. These advantages suggest that writers should make an effort to present both — or all — sides before narrowing in on preferred plans or solutions.

• Special Ethical Problems for Freelancers

Article writers — those who freelance — enjoy an advantage over reporters and staff writers in that they can choose their subjects and thus help promote only people, ideas, and movements they identify with, and attack only those they oppose. But freelance writers face some special ethical problems, too — ethical problems added to those all writers of nonfiction face. For instance: How clear should freelancers make it to their interviewees, people who give up valuable time to answer questions, that the articles are to be written on speculation — that they may never see print? If writers freelance in off hours from regular writing jobs, do their articles involve any expense to the regular employers? And how much selling of background, previous credits, and research conducted can freelancers engage in without stretching the truth?

The chapters on research and writing may suggest other ethical problems to you. But before getting to those chapters, you will want to familiarize yourself with the various kinds of articles that can be written, processes that result in ideas for articles, and the range of publications using them. The next three chapters treat those matters.

CHAPTER 2

Article and Feature Categories

Professional writers deal with subjects they can react to and subjects they know from experience will interest editors and readers. These writers give little thought to the categories their articles happen to fall into. If what a professional writer produces turns out to be a narrative in first person or a how-to-do-it piece, or a combination of the two, or something else — fine. Let the academics give it a name. Let them draw up their list of categories. If it holds little interest for professional writers, such a list can help beginning writers by pointing to the wide range of forms nonfiction takes in magazines and newspapers. It can also serve as an idea stimulator for beginners who do not know yet what they might write that would interest editors.

If what a writer gathers during the research phase doesn't seem appropriate for one kind of article, maybe it would be appropriate for another. The writer does not want to emulate the New York drama critic who, so the story goes, saw Harry K. Thaw shoot Stanford White but failed to report it to his paper. His was the only paper in town that missed the story. Why had he not pursued his lead? Because, it turns out, when he investigated the principals he found that none of them was connected with the theater.

The nature of the material the writer uncovers, the kind of thing the writer likes to do, the editor's predilection — all these influence what kind of an article it should be. And although an article may combine elements of several categories, it should fit *mainly* into one. The set of categories that follows covers most of the forms today's nonfiction takes in magazines and newspapers.

Figure 2.1 To illustrate a personality sketch or interview article, some editors like to consider a series of closeups, showing the subject with various expressions or in various moods. Sometimes the editors run the photographs same size, all in a row, to make readers feel that they are watching a motion picture. Susan Pogany, managing editor for *University of Oregon Health Sciences Center News*, took these shots (verticals and horizontals) of Dr. Lewis Bluemle, then president of the Center, now president of Thomas Jefferson University, Philadelphia.

• THE PERSONALITY SKETCH

Nearly all magazines, including trade journals, run personality sketches. You find them at their best in *The New Yorker*, which calls them "profiles," a term that has become generic. Expanded to book length, a personality sketch becomes a biography.

That people like to read about people was demonstrated anew in the 1970s when Time, Inc., launched *People* weekly and proved to a skeptical magazine industry that general-audience publications can still make it in a TV age. The personality sketches in *People* are a special breed: shorter than normal, and gossipy. When the late L. E. Sissman saw an early issue of the magazine, he noted: "The publishers of plump, stately *Fortune* and wisecracking, fiftyish *Time* have brought forth upon this continent a new abomination, conceived in avarice and dedicated to the proposition that there's one born every minute."[1] And *People* spawned *Us*.

Personality sketches can do more than merely satisfy the curious and titillate the bored. They can teach as well as inspire, and they can deal with other than famous people. All that is required of the subjects is that they be interesting.

Charles Ferguson, a *Reader's Digest* editor, told writer André Fontaine, "Before you can start to write a profile you've got to complete this sentence: 'John Smith is the man who . . . .' "

Most often a personality sketch praises the subject. This is because writers tend to pick out for interviewing persons they can identify with. But the sketch, even though it generally admires the subject, will be more believable if it takes a warts-and-all approach. "He hates prejudice, the family hour, censorship, and low ratings, but not necessarily in that order," said *The National Observer*'s John H. Corcoran, Jr., of Norman Lear, the indefatigable program creator, and we understand Lear a little better.

See how C. S. Lewis's father comes alive in this excerpt from Lewis's *Surprised by Joy*:

> The first and simplest barrier to communication was that, having earnestly asked [about a son's school life], he did not "stay for an answer" or forgot it the moment it was uttered. Some facts must have been asked for and told him, on a moderate computation, once a week, and were received by him

---

[1] L. E. Sissman, "Innocent Bystander," *The Atlantic*, June 1974, p. 29.

Figure 2.2 Like other company-magazine editors, Lionel L. Fisher of *Paper Times*, published by Boise Cascade, Portland, takes many of his own pictures. To show the subject of one of his interviews, Dave Field, Fisher decided to shoot him in Times Square, New York, surrounded by people, rather than at his desk at Fawcett Publications, where Field works as production director (Fawcett buys paper from Boise Cascade). It is easy enough in a caption to help the reader spot Field. Fisher uses the words, "with necktie, center." The fact that a person in the foreground directs his eyes at Field helps, too. Fisher pressed the shutter at just the right moment.

each time as perfect novelties. But this was the simplest barrier. Far more often he retained something, but something very unlike what you had said. His mind so bubbled over with humor, sentiment, and indignation that, long before he had understood or even listened to your words, some accidental hint had set his imagination to work, he had produced his own version of the facts, and believed that he was getting it from you. As he invariably got proper names wrong (no name seemed to him less probable than another) his *textus receptus* was often almost unrecognizable. Tell him that a boy called Churchwood had caught a field mouse and kept it as a pet, and a year, or ten years later, he would ask you, "Did you ever hear what became of poor Chickweed who was so afraid of the rats?"[2]

[2]C. S. Lewis, *Surprised by Joy*, Harcourt Brace & World, New York, 1955, p. 121.

Sometimes personality sketches take the form of exposés. Writers damn their subjects by quoting them directly — or pick up much of their information from others. Whatever the pictures to be portrayed, writers find that interviewing only the subjects of the sketches results in unbalanced assessments.

Not only are personality sketches fun to read; they are fun to write. Writers make new friends in the process. They get the chance to use almost any literary device. For some sketches, writers can act as anthologists, as when they interview poets and include in the articles samples of the poets' works.

• THE INTERVIEW PIECE

Maybe singling out one kind of article and calling it an "interview piece" is a mistake, because most articles are based to some extent on interviewing. Certainly the personality sketch is. But some articles depend solely on interviewing, and what they present to readers is only what comes out of the interview. Often, the article takes a Q. and A. form instead of a literary form. You see samples of the form each week in *U.S. News & World Report* and each month in *Playboy*.

A magazine carrying interview pieces or personality sketches in Q. and A. form has its own style of introducing each of the quotes. Maybe *Q.* followed by *A*; maybe the author's name followed by the respondent's name; maybe the magazine's name followed by the respondent's name. *Johns Hopkins Magazine* simply runs the question in boldface type,[3] the answer in regular face. No Q.s, no A.s, no names in the text.

Interview pieces differ from personality sketches in that they stress what interviewees say, not what they are or what they do. Typically, interview pieces result from writers seeking out experts and asking them to respond to a series of questions prompted by social upheavals or news events. Ordinarily, the writers or conductors of interview pieces handle their material objectively, no matter how outrageous the answers to questions. Personality sketches tend to be more subjective. The subjectivity can be subtle, as when the writer without comment contrasts actions to the words spoken by the interviewee.

[3] You indicate boldface type on a manuscript with a wavy underline, italic type with a straight underline.

Figure 2.3   For a Eugene (Oreg.) *Register-Guard* "Oregon Life" section feature at Christmastime, freelancer Duncan McDonald decided to see what elderly shut-ins in the area had to look forward to. Some had very little. One of his subjects was a 79-year-old widow, Little Bell Kirk, who lived alone in a two-room cabin. The wood stove was her only source of heat. To show that she was "dominated by her environment," McDonald used a wide-angle lens to take in more of the small cabin and to capture the visual sweep from the sign on the wall across the woodpile and dog to the woman.

Figure 2.4   Duncan McDonald photographed Little Bell Kirk a year earlier for his *West Lane News*. This photograph serves as a study in both texture and composition. To make the several textures stand out, McDonald caught his subjects in front of a dark doorway. The composition is triangular, the slant of the cane complementing the slant of the dog's back.

Figure 2.5 The lead photo for a picture story produced by Duncan McDonald for the weekly *West Lane News*, Veneta, Oregon, a 3,000-circulation weekly which he owned and edited. McDonald wanted a short depth of field and some blackness in the background to make the head stand out and yet show it in context, so he took the picture with a portrait lens and shot from just the right angle. The 75-year-old subject, Oral Spotts, a local farmer, handyman, and rockhound, was being displaced, and before moving out he invited people over to pick items from his rock collection, which he couldn't take with him.

Of course it is impossible to report what a person believes about a subject without also revealing something of his personality. Digby Diehl's excellent Q. and A. pieces in the defunct *West* magazine of the Los Angeles *Times* are a case in point. Take this one exchange from his interview with another Lear, William — inventor of the car radio, eight-track stereo tape, the automatic pilot, a small private jet airplane, and about 150 other items.

Q. You mentioned that you first determine a need and then create a solution. Could you describe your process of inventing more fully?

Lear: I can't do my kind of creating by sitting in a room with a piece of paper. My kind of inventing can only be done when I am surrounded by a lot of people with a lot of know-how. I gather a maze of information and pick out the salient things and discard the unimportant things. I always keep the goal in mind and I insist on solving the problem with the least cost. The subconscious plays an important part in this creative process.

Some engineers came to me with a part that needed to be smaller. They said it couldn't be any smaller and I said that it could be a quarter in size. I told them that they weren't going to arrive at the answer by sitting down and figuring out the possibilities. I said, "I want you not to think about it at all and come back in 30 days and show me that it can be made one quarter of that size." They asked me how they could do it without thinking about it, and I said, "You've got a subconscious mind that's a computer. You feed in all the information that you can possibly provide. Then, just let it alone and you'll come back in 30 or 60 days with the answer." They went out unsure, but I'll guarantee you they came back with the answer.

• THE NARRATIVE

Probably the most popular way of beginning an article is to start out with a story, then move on to the heavy stuff. A narrative article never leaves the story. The article *is* a story.

The narrative can be written in first or third person. If in first, it represents some adventure the writer experienced. If in third person, it represents the experience of someone else, either from the present or the past.

The first-person narrative is a favored form for hunting and fishing magazines, travel magazines, and magazines specializing in real-life adventure. The third-person narrative form works well for adventure and historical pieces. Readers of either of these forms get vicarious satisfaction from them. They may also get information that helps them enjoy or avoid similar experiences.

The narrative, whether in first or third person, along with the confession (we're coming to that), comes as close as nonfiction writers get to short-story writing. Any fictional device can be utilized to tell the story, but the story itself must be factual. The same dedication to research and accuracy that goes into other kinds of articles also goes into narratives.

• THE ESSAY

Essayists you studied in lit classes — people like Francis Bacon, Samuel Johnson, Charles Lamb, Ralph Waldo Emerson, and Oliver

Wendell Holmes — produced short, highly organized, single-minded treatises written with great flair and often reflecting the personalities of the writers. The literary form lives on in the magazines of today. A difference between the literary essay and the magazine essay is that the latter cannot assume that the reader is automatically interested in the subject. The magazine essay must do more of a selling job within the first few paragraphs to capture and hold reader attention.

Essay articles, like essays themselves, cover topics ranging from the profound to the trivial. It is possible to break them down into five subcategories.

• The Information Piece

This form of essay is an extension of the news story. The writer takes a detached view of the subject, even when dealing with one that is controversial. But unlike the news story, the information piece is not bound by time. Neither is it written in an inverted pyramid form, as the news story is. An editor can't simply cut off the last few paragraphs to make the piece fit a layout. Like any article, the information piece moves along to a calculated ending.

The writer of an information piece becomes a teacher. It could be argued that most of our education after we leave school comes from writers of information pieces appearing in the newspapers and magazines.

For *Yankee* (March 1976), James J. Canavan wrote "Business Is Blooming," an information piece about raising carnations at Tewksbury, Massachusetts. The reader learns that Tewksbury is "the undisputed Carnation Capital of the world."

> In fact, this is where it all began, more than 100 years ago. It was then that Marcellus A. Patten moved his small greenhouse to Tewksbury, and on the same site three generations of the family have grown these famous flowers and shared their exquisite beauty with people from all corners of the world. Wherever carnations are grown today, 95% of the original plant cuttings came from the Patten greenhouses.

Often information pieces deal with practical rather than controversial matters. Information pieces are the main fare of magazines like *Sunset* and *Changing Times*.

• The Opinion Piece

On a newspaper it would be an editorial. On a magazine it could be an editorial — a few magazines run editorials — but it would more likely be a full-length signed piece that would probably but not necessarily represent the thinking of the editors. You find opinion pieces most readily in opinion magazines like *The New Republic, The Nation*, and *National Review*. You also find them in what we've come to call the quality magazines, especially *Harper's* and *The Atlantic*. While most writers of opinion pieces have impressive academic credentials and academic position, it is not unusual for a newspaper person or even a student to crack the opinion-magazine and quality-magazine market.[4]

The purpose of an opinion piece is to sway readers to a point of view, usually after examining the alternatives. Pure propaganda does not have — or should not have — a place in magazines and newspapers except in the advertising columns. The opinion piece tries to reason with readers. See how Jeanine Holly, then an English major at Oregon, does it in a short essay on a controversial topic[5] submitted to the campus newspaper.

MOVEMENT RISKS CREDIBILITY

The English language cannot be taken literally 100 per cent of the time.

When my roommate said she just lost her head over a guy, I didn't rush out to help her find it. When a friend said, "Guess who I bumped into yesterday?" I didn't quickly scan him for cuts and bruises. When my dad looked at my car and said I got a real lemon, I didn't offer him a slice.

Likewise, when I say, "Mankind is facing extinction," I am not excluding women from this fate. And when I attend a meeting and see that the chair"man" is a woman, I don't presume she is just filling in for the real chair"man" while he copes with the flu or attends his father's funeral.

I am outraged and somewhat embarrassed by the offshoot of the Women's Movement which is trying to reform the English language.

I am outraged, first, because I have enough difficulties communicating major ideas without having to consciously assess every word that I'm using to convey those ideas. And, secondly, our language is awkward enough

---

[4]Students and just-graduated students at Oregon have sold to *The New Republic, The Nation, The Progressive, Commonweal, The New Leader, National Review, America*, and *Harper's*, among others.

[5]Chapter 13 further discusses the topic.

without throwing in more stumbling blocks like "s/he" (How do you pronounce it?). Our language is drab enough without taking away some of our historical "spine-tinglers" like "mankind," "countrymen," "fellowman," etc.

I am embarrassed because the Women's Movement, whose ideas I can largely support, is risking its credibility by projecting sexism where no sexism exists. I am embarrassed because, being a supporter of the movement's major philosophy, I am also expected to support this incredible snipe hunt. I am outraged because, last week, two of my professors had to waste valuable class time to defend their usage of the English language. Moreover, I am concerned because I see current and would-be advocates of the basic movement being alienated by this side issue.

Sexism lies in the person who uses the word, not in the word itself. The word is merely a symbol, a reflection of the speaker. Educate the speaker and the words will follow suit. Erase sexism in the mind and you automatically erase sexism in the word without having to change the word itself. "Mankind," to the nonsexist, becomes figurative and translates to mean, all of the people of the world. But to the sexist, it means only the male population — even if the term used is "personkind."

Let's stick with reforming the people instead of the language. We Oregonians know we can't keep it from raining just by using suntan lotion. And we can't keep our society from being sexist just by eliminating sexist words. Instead of eliminating words, let's expand them with our new awareness. Let's leave the physical qualities of the word intact as a reminder of how far we've come.

When I was a kid, I made lots of snow"men." Some of them were moms, some were dads and some were lions.

Those who still find themselves threatened by a mere word must remember this application of an old joke: "First of all, you have to be smarter than the word."

Jeanine Holly

• The Interpretive Piece

Somewhere between the information and the opinion piece lies the interpretive piece. The "new journalism" built interest in interpretive journalism, but interpretive journalism has been around a long time. The leading pre-World War II reporting textbook was called *Interpretive Reporting*.

An interpretive piece goes beyond an information piece in that it puts the information into perspective. It may answer the traditional who, what, when, where, why, and how questions; but it puts its emphasis on *why*.

An interpretive piece stops short of the opinion piece in that it does not make an overt call for action. It may not even point to the best solution from among those offered. It takes a person of restraint and keen insight to write a good interpretive piece.

A plea to magazines to devote more of their space to interpretation came recently from Merrill Panitt, editorial director of Triangle Magazines (*TV Guide*, *Seventeen*): "Considering the ephemeral nature of television, and the audience's [short] attention span, it behooves magazines to turn more to what television does poorly and magazines do well. And what they do well is interpret; their strength is in the realm of depth and background and ideas. They aren't as effective as they once were in telling what happened, but they now have the opportunity to capitalize on their unique ability to explain why it happened."[6]

Mary Ann Meyers wrote an interpretive essay for *Pennsylvania Gazette*, an alumni magazine, when she covered the recruitment activities of Campus Crusade for Christ on campus at the University of Pennsylvania. She concentrated on the program to "hustle Jews," as one critic described it, and because at the start she focused on one Jew named David (not his real name), she called her article "The Story of David." After the first case history, she cited another, partly for contrast (it involved a woman student, also Jewish, but with a different background), partly to show the extent of the recruitment activities. One case showed the despair of the parents and relatives over the conversion, the other the potential despair (the convert had not yet told her parents because "I think . . . [they] would go berserk"). From the case histories, Meyers moved to background material on both the national organization and the local chapter. She explained fully the hard-sell nature of the program.

To do her article, she interviewed people, read books and articles, and accompanied a Crusader on her rounds on campus. The latter activity allowed Meyers, deep into her article, to use pure dialogue. A short segment follows:

Susan the Crusader: What, in your opinion, is man's basic problem?

Woman: Isolation. Death. No matter how much people reach out to one another they are destined to be permanently dissatisfied. Always alone. Is this for a course?

Susan: No. I'm doing it on my own. Does your philosophy of life provide a solution for these problems?

[6]Merrill Panitt in a speech to the Western Region Convention of the American Association of Advertising Agencies, Maui, Hawaii, Oct. 14, 1975.

After showing a couple of these encounters through dialogue, Meyers dealt with the question of whether or not Jews should be proselytized on campus. She also explained, from a sociological perspective, the presence of evangelism on campuses in the seventies. And all the while, except perhaps for using the word "simplistic" midway in the article, she remained the disinterested observer. Only in the final paragraph did she really enter into the discussion:

> It seems possible, then, in light of this analysis, to suggest that students turn to Campus Crusade in a search for community. They may look to it for techniques for attaining "significant relationships," not the least important of which, surely, is a significant relationship with God. The irony, of course, is that the spontaneous experiences for which they yearn are often engineered; they must try to touch each other with memorized words, and, if they are Jews, sometimes sever the most binding of human ties.[7]

It was the right approach for an article on so sensitive a subject, going to alumni, informing them of what's happening on campus. For some other market, Meyers might have been much more argumentative.

• The Inspirational Piece

Reader's Digest and most religious magazines run articles in this subcategory, but not to the exclusion of other kinds of articles. Occasionally you will find an inspirational piece in a magazine better known for its skepticism or criticism.

Writers of inspirational pieces may draw on their own experiences or the experiences of others. The articles may deal with such attributes as faith, determination, perseverance, and patience.

The inspirational piece, along with the humorous piece, can be written off the top of the head, but both can profit from research before writing. The trick, in writing an inspirational piece, is to keep it from sounding preachy.

• The Humorous Piece

Perhaps the most elusive article or feature for editors of newspapers and magazines is the one written in a genuine humorous vein. "Humor is hard to come by at any time," says William Shawn, editor of *The New Yorker*. "Funny people are rare."

[7]Mary Ann Meyers, "The Story of David," *Pennsylvania Gazette*, November, 1974. p. 19.

So valuable is humor to article and feature writing that this book will devote most of a later chapter to the subject. If you have a humorous touch, by all means develop it. And if you choose to write other than humor pieces, you will find that your humorous touches will be allowed — encouraged, even — in your more weighty pieces. But make sure your humor does not embarrass you. Let it cool for a week. Put it to the test of outsiders. Your close friends will not be your best critics.

Humor in writing varies from the gentle to the biting. It depends often on the inventiveness of the writer.

James A. Baar in a short piece in [*More*] in January 1976, in response to the trend toward truth in packaging, came up with a rating system to measure reporters' performances. Instead of stars, Baar suggested little typewriter symbols. Baar's system would work like this:

4 Typewriters: Highly knowledgeable in field

3 Typewriters: Knowledgeable in some field

2 Typewriters: Not very knowledgeable but often accurate

1 Typewriter: Spells well

Baar worked out similar systems for rating politicians and businessmen.

Time did something similar when, for its Jan. 12, 1976 issue, it rated the soap operas on afternoon TV. Four teardrops meant a program was a real tear-jerker.

Magazines like to run light-hearted pieces that treat annoyances readers share. Slant is important here. The readers of a literary magazine face different annoyances from, say, those faced by the readers of a hunting and fishing magazine. A short piece by Robert Sylwester on committee meetings, to cite one example, was well-suited for "The Phoenix Nest" section of *Saturday Review* (December 25, 1965). "One problem that besets most of us is that of occupying ourselves constructively during dull meetings," Sylwester began. What followed was a set of stratagems, like:

Listen carefully as your fellow committee members bleat on, but every twenty seconds write down the word that is being said right then. In ten minutes you will have written thirty words if you haven't dozed off. Try to arrange these words in sentences that make more sense than what is being said in the discussion . . . . Your fellow committee members will be impressed when they see that you are writing down some of the things they are saying.

Another suggestion involved the tabulation of various letters used in the wording of reports distributed to committee members, noting which letters are most often used, and working out formulas to compare the use of letters in current reports with the use in earlier reports. The findings could be sent in later to "learned journals," Sylwester pointed out.

After offering his several suggestions, Sylwester ended with a promise to turn to another "equally pressing" problem: "how to cope with boors who appear uninterested and inattentive when *you* are speaking or presiding at a meeting."

• THE EXPOSÉ

The exposé underlines the difficulty of separating news from features and articles. A team of two feature writers for the Washington *Post* broke the story on the Wayne Hays–Elizabeth Ray affair, but two regular reporters for the paper broke the earlier Watergate story. That story evolved over a long period. At first the paper underestimated its importance, but as Robert Woodward and Carl Bernstein unraveled it, it became big enough to help topple a President.

Things got sticky as the stories began appearing. Sources willing to be quoted insisted on anonymity. The editors grew more nervous. The *Post* was clearly out on a limb. Every fact was checked and rechecked. "As matters turned out," Professor John L. Hulteng reports, "virtually all of the stories held up; one did contain an inaccuracy, but the overall score constituted a pretty solid average, considering the stakes."[8]

Hulteng cites Edward Jay Epstein's observation that it was the investigative agencies of government that really assembled the evidence and leaked it, but adds: ". . . on balance, not much can be taken away from the achievement of the two *Post* men. They dug when others settled for handouts; they persisted when others went off to what

[8]John L. Hulteng, *The Messenger's Motives*, Prentice-Hall, Inc., Englewood Cliffs, N.J., 1976, p. 95.

seemed to be more exciting stories; and they made highly effective use of secret leads that came to them."[9]

There is plenty of precedent in this country for what Woodward and Bernstein did. It started in earnest in the magazines at the turn of the century when writers told of corruption in industry and government circles. Theodore Roosevelt, although he could have been expected to identify with these writers, called them "muckrakers." As muckraking ran its course in magazines — and helped build circulations — it moved to newspapers. As it spread, muckraking became less responsible. In *The Messenger's Motives*, John L. Hulteng saw a similar deterioration as enthusiasm to get onto the Watergate story gained momentum.

Students of the press can point to any number of social reforms and judicial triumphs brought about by exposés. They still have a place in today's media, especially big-city dailies, alternative papers, and city magazines. The city magazine with the best reputation for exposés is *Philadelphia*, which, in one exposé, revealed that a reporter for the Philadelphia *Inquirer* had used his position to threaten businesses with bad publicity if they didn't pay off and, in another, revealed that local politicians had mismanaged Bicentennial celebration funds. There were others.

Exposés can prove dangerous to those who engage in them. Phoenix *Republic* reporter Don Bolles, on the trail of a story of corruption in Arizona, lost his life in 1976 after a bomb exploded in his car. In an unprecedented move by the newspaper fraternity, a number of investigative reporters from around the nation, members of Investigative Reporters and Editors, Inc., converged on Phoenix and carried on Bolles's investigation. Their work, financed by the newspapers and private donations, led to a series of widely syndicated stories in 1977. It was one of the most discussed series ever prepared, and the fact that so many people — 36 reporters from 27 news organizations — participated in the research and writing made it all the more unusual. Some important people were implicated, and the threat of libel was real. A team of lawyers went through the material to weed out information and charges that the reporters could not fully document. However, that did not prevent some suits from being filed.

[9]*Ibid.* p. 96.

Considering libel-suit threats, advertiser reaction, and time and energy involved, exposés can be expensive to publishers. They must be closely supervised. Freelancers, unknown to editors, are not likely to draw the assignments.

Exposés have some relationship to opinion and information essays, but, because they narrow in on a specific target or individual, they probably deserve this special categorization.

• THE CONFESSION

When we think of the confession we think, usually, of the pieces published by *True Story*-type magazines edited for women of the lower middle and blue-collar classes. Despite the "true" in the titles of these magazines, the pieces are more fiction than fact, although in many cases they are triggered by events that actually happened. Perhaps a bit of gossip starts the writer on a story — or a news item does. Only rarely is a confession autobiographical, and then it is highly embellished. Some writers make a living turning out confessions. Obviously they could not have endured all the tragedy and drama they write about.

One thing to remember about writing for the confession market is that the reader typically has less education than the reader of magazines like *McCall's* and *Ladies' Home Journal*. A college setting ordinarily would not be appropriate for the story.

But ". . . You cannot write down to a confession reader," cautions Jean Jackson, who sells regularly to that market. She adds: ". . . If you feel a cut above the confession reader; if you believe, even without saying it aloud, that you're 'better' than she is, you won't write a passable confession. You will not be able to get inside a confession heroine, reason as she would reason, muddle your way through problems as she would. . . ."[10]

More so, perhaps, than other kinds of articles, the confession adheres to a formula, generally expressed this way: "Sin, suffer, and repent." Jean Jackson suggests that the order can change. "Sometimes she sins and suffers anyway, in spite of repenting for pages in between."

[10]Jean Jackson, "What Makes a Salable Confession?" a chapter in *The Writer's Handbook* (A. S. Burack, editor), The Writer, Boston, 1975, p. 313.

An out-of-order SSR sequence can result in a better story. "If you can arrange your plot so that the heroine sees the light first, but has already, by her actions, set the wheels of tragedy in motion and cannot stop them, your story will probably be bought at a higher rate, or, at least, be featured on the front of the magazine that buys it."[11]

Jean Jackson points out that in the confession the heroine realizes she is taking the wrong course but can't help herself. While the heroine may not be likeable, the reader sympathizes with her because the reader understands that, in the same circumstances, she might act the same way.

Written usually in first person, clearly, and in an emotional style, the confession for *True Story* and similar magazines runs longer than the typical magazine article — up to 7,000 words. The pay often is better than average, but of course there is no recognition because there are no bylines.

The confession idea extends to regular magazines read by the middle classes. Here the articles branch out from the semisensational, love-gone-wrong themes; as legitimate articles, they more properly fall under the journalism umbrella. Like any other articles, these confessions are bylined. A typical title: "I Was a Little League Umpire." The writer "confesses" tactics used to get along with irate parents who object to wrong calls on their child players. Confessions for middle-class and more sophisticated markets can be tongue-in-cheek, but often they are deadly serious, as when a person who was convicted of a crime or who lived through some personal problem takes to the typewriter afterwards to tell the world about it.

The late Charles W. Morton nicely satirized middle-class-magazine confessions in " 'I Was a _____er,' " a piece he did for *The Atlantic Monthly*.

> The swear-off article seems to be holding its own in the slick magazines [he began], and hardly a week goes by without bringing into print a good, solid confession by a former addict of something or other.
> The author has been taking aboard too much of the stuff, and it's high time to call a halt. Those who wish to convert such an experience into marketable prose will find it helpful, therefore, to stick to standard form and avoid untested versions, however attractive.

There followed a series of vignettes familiar enough to readers of swear-off articles. The article's start in a doctor's office, the patient's

[11]*Ibid.*, p. 314.

surprise that he is so easily found out by the doctor, and that classic exchange: "And if I do [continue to use the stuff]?" "In that case, I give you _____ months to live. Possibly _____. But no more." The article then retraces the patient's background that set the stage for his addiction, goes into his attempts to overcome it, and ends with his salvation following his son's "Gee, Dad" accusation.

> That was ten years ago [Morton comments at the end of his reprinted typical article]. Not only did the author break himself of the _____ habit, but he also manages to sell an article or two every year about how he did it.[12]

• THE HOW-TO-DO-IT PIECE

"The majority of people . . . are only interested in their own lives," John Braine wrote in *Writing a Novel*, "and the great issues of the day leave them cold. They only hope to get through life with the minimum of trouble and the maximum of pleasure." If you have some advice people can use to improve their mental, physical, emotional, or financial state, or if you have access to such advice, you may have the makings of a magazine article or newspaper feature.

If your advice involves artistic, athletic, culinary, or construction advice, no doubt you will go through the steps yourself before attempting to describe them in an article.

You had better decide to do the article *before* you do the job, if for no other reason than that you will want to take pictures of the project in progress. Deciding after the fact to write the article seldom results in a sale. Your memory will prove unreliable, just as it will when you decide, after a trip, that a travel article is a possibility. Readers will discover the holes in your article.

You can forget about a literary style when writing a how-to piece. Just write clearly. That's harder to do than some people think. Certainly the people who write the instructions that go with assemble-it-yourself purchases haven't solved the problem.

A how-to-do-it could be written more as an information piece than as an instructional piece, in which case it would be a how-it-was-done. For instance, after a Presidential debate, a writer might tell how all the equipment was set up to televise the event and explain why an audio

[12]Charles W. Morton, *A Slight Sense of Outrage*, J. P. Lippincott Company, Philadelphia, 1955, pp. 121–125.

failure occurred at the end. The how-to-do-it category would also make room for the what-to-do article ("Things Children Can Do on a Rainy Day"), the where-to-do-it article ("Fishing Spots They Don't Want You to Know About"), the when-to-do-it article ("Spend Your Summer in Florida"), and the why-do-it article ("New Reasons to Quit Smoking").

• THE ANTHOLOGY

One way to break into the book-publishing world is to gather together a series of chapters, stories, articles, essays, or poems, get permissions if the material isn't in the public domain, write an introductory chapter for the collection, and introduce each of the selections. Similar activity can lead to a magazine article.

In doing this kind of an article, you become more of an editor than a writer. Your contribution lies in what you pick out and how well you tie it all together.

You start with a theme. Say it's what the greats have said about love. You submit your anthology to a magazine in time for publication before Valentine's Day.

Unlike a book-length anthology, an anthology for a magazine uses excerpts short enough in most cases not to require reprint permissions. Typically, you would write a few paragraphs of introduction, to develop your theme, then turn the reader loose among your selections. After the introduction, each paragraph could stand by itself. Transitions would not be a problem.

Perhaps you would contribute a summary paragraph at the end. Your anthology could present quotations, anecdotes, recipes — anything appropriate to the market.

Rolfe Hillman did a one-page anthology for one of the last issues of *Lithopinion* (Spring 1975): a collection of definitions from *The Devil's Dictionary* by Ambrose Bierce. Hillman wrote a three-paragraph introduction and added an author's note after one of the definitions. He selected words that were appropriate to Watergate and the Nixon resignation, even though the definitions were written 69 years before. A sample Bierce definition:

> **Conservative,** *n.* A statesman who is enamored of existing evils, as distinguished from the Liberal, who wishes to replace them with others.

An anthology need not consist of the works of others. Writers can use their own assorted paragraphs. The Sylwester humor piece could be considered an anthology. Ron Abell in his column in *Willamette Week*, Portland, did an anthology of tongue-in-cheek suggestions for work projects for the unemployed. Abell came up with eight ideas to match the WPA and CCC of the 1930s. One of Abell's suggestions:

> *Car pushers*. Here's a fantastic way to save precious gasoline and reduce smog. Large work gangs could be placed at all city intersections. Their job: To push automobiles by hand to the next intersection, where another gang takes over. They push one direction in the morning, the other way in the afternoon. That way, at quitting time they end up where they started. They get healthful exercise and motorists get to use their cars without expending fuel. . . .

(Earlier, in a column for another newspaper written during a shor tage of electricity, Abell had suggested that readers remove the light-bulbs from their refrigerators and substitute lighted candles.)

• THE FILLER

To fill in blank spaces at the bottoms of columns and to add light touches to pages heavy with serious news and information, publications developed fillers: short, timeless pieces of prose that could be stored against the times they were needed. On magazines, fillers play a lesser role than in the past, mainly because art directors, now working with editors, think that fillers intrude. They interrupt the visual flow. Even the newspapers, now that they have adopted six-column formats, use fewer boxes or brights.

Still, enough publications continue to use filler material to make the filler important enough for special attention. You can consider the filler an article in miniature. Take almost any of the article categories described in this chapter and envision it in one- or two- or three-paragraph form. Fillers most commonly fall into the narrative, information essay, humorous essay, and how-to-do-it categories.

• Magazine Fillers

Many writers receive their first national exposure by placing fillers with magazines that have set up special sections to receive them. The original *Saturday Evening Post* originated several of these special sections, including, after World War II, the popular "Post-War Anecdote," a weekly feature, which paid what was then a handsome price: $100. This writer's first magazine sale was there, with this anecdote:

> APA-165 wasn't exactly the smoothest ship afloat, and whenever we hit rough water the old Effingham did some real pitching and rolling. Of course, most of the crew members were used to it, but our Army passengers, leaning against the rails, took it pretty seriously.
>
> Just out of Manila Bay one morning with a shipload of dischargees, we ran into unusually choppy seas. Our course was taking us through the outskirts of a minor typhoon. While the deck force was busy securing loose gear, a soldier with a green complexion stumbled from his post at the rail and made his way across the dipping forecastle to a boatswain's mate who was snatching a bit of sleep in one of the gun tubs.
>
> "Say," the transient asked miserably, "does it ever get any rougher than this?"
>
> The rated man, a regular with at least a dozen nautical years salted away, rubbed his eyes and looked around.
>
> "Why," he exclaimed, "are we under way already?"[13]

The value of writing fillers like this is that you train yourself to boil down stories — true stories — to their essentials. You put nothing into the stories that doesn't contribute to the punch lines. And you learn to handle dialogue.

The new *Saturday Evening Post* continues to buy fillers, including items for its "Perfect Squelch" section. And so do many other magazines in both general-circulation and specialized categories. Perhaps the favorite target these days is *Reader's Digest* with its several carefully spelled out filler departments. Contributions to this magazine come in so fast that it is not able to return unusable ones, even when the writers include stamped, self-addressed envelopes. In 1975 *Reader's Digest* was getting an average of 50,000 humorous fillers each month, and publishing as few as 100 of them. "50,000 Laughs a Month," said a headline in a *Digest*-sponsored ad in *Advertising Age* meant to impress media buyers in agencies. "It's Enough to Make You Cry!"

But fillers for magazines do not confine themselves to special sections. Nor do all magazines that use them run special instructions in each issue on how to prepare them. A filler — or short article — comes in unexpectedly, it strikes the editor just right, and the author makes a sale. Student Ruth D. Currey writes a three-paragraph personality sketch, "How Late Is Late in Life?", about a man who started a new career at 65, and sells it to *Family Weekly*. Student Shirley Papé

[13]Copyright 1948 by *The Saturday Evening Post*. Reprinted by permission.

has an idea about how mothers can get back into shape following childbirth, and sells a one-paragraph filler to *Baby Talk*.

Some magazines allow fillers to approach full-scale articles in length. For other magazines, the filler is nothing more than a reprinting of a blooper in print that some reader spots and sends in.

Magazines dealing with mechanics, crafts, or homemaking buy how-to or helpful-hint fillers. These are no-nonsense single paragraphs written by persons with inventive minds. Typically they contain a topic sentence followed by two or three sentences of elaboration. "Clothes can be sprinkled with a fine and even spray using a brush rather than a bottle with a sprinkler top. Just. . . ." "To keep gift-tie and ribbons from Christmas or birthday packages neat and crisply re-usable, try this: Take an empty wax paper box, and. . . ." That sort of thing.

The writer's magazines and market guides list the magazines that buy fillers. Magazines that seem to be most interested, besides *The Saturday Evening Post* and *Reader's Digest*, include *Catholic Digest* (an excellent filler market), *Ebony, Guideposts, Lady's Circle, McCall's, Modern Maturity, Parent's Magazine, Playboy, The New Yorker, Seventeen, Sports Afield, Sunday Digest, True Romance,* and *Woman's Day*. Less familiar markets include *The American Field* (fillers on trials for bird dogs), *American Fruit Grower* (commercial fruit growing and selling), *American Vegetable Grower* (commercial vegetable growing and selling), *Expecting* (pregnancy), *Hardware Age* (hardware-store management), *The Jeweler's Circular-Keystone* (jewelry-store management), *Motor Boating & Sailing* (boating and water sports), *Small World* (Volkswagen owning), *Today's Christian Mother* (Christian homemaking and child rearing), and *Yankee Magazine* (New England living).[14]

• Newspaper Fillers

As a reporter for United Press, this author was surprised to find that, when his bureau at Salt Lake City listed several candidates for the trunk wire each day, the New York office often ignored important local stories that staffers at the bureau thought held some national interest and instead asked the bureau to move one of its fillers (called "boxes," "brighteners," "brights," or "brites" by newspaper people).

[14]This is a very arbitrary and incomplete list. Furthermore, it is subject to change. Magazines constantly adjust their contents. Some die. New ones come along. For current information, see *Writer's Digest, The Writer, Writer's Yearbook,* and *Writer's Market*.

Set narrow-measure and run in the newspapers with ruled lines all around (hence "boxes"), they were useful in keeping headlines for side-by-side stories from "tombstoning" (appearing to run together) and in providing a change of pace for columns of heavy or dull prose. The wire services still move these short, short stories.

Typically, they originate with reporters or feature writers on newspapers, there to be picked up by a wire service and sent to members or clients. For instance: In Hays, Kansas, a man initiates a "paternity" suit, charging that a neighbor's dog leaped a fence and mated with his dog, causing her to give birth to six unwanted mixed-breed puppies. The angry dog owner wants $110, plus postnatal expenses and "puppy support." The neighbor then initiates a counter suit, asking a $200 stud fee plus $100 for "incidentals." He also argues, somewhat inconsistently, that the mother dog had "previous suitors," so paternity is in question. The judge refuses to award damages to either party.

Not an earth-shattering story, but it was amusing enough — and easy enough for readers to identify with — to make the AP wires early in 1976. (The quoted phrases belong to an AP writer.)

The newspaper filler can't tell you a great deal about the personality of the person or persons involved in the story. It must move along single-mindedly to its O. Henryish conclusion. Read enough newspaper fillers and you will be able to figure out after the first paragraph how each one ends.

To take up just a few lines of space left over at the bottoms of columns, some newspapers run one- or two-sentence informational fillers without headlines.

A Lexington, Kentucky city ordinance forbids carrying an ice cream cone in your pocket.

Here's one from the Joplin (Mo.) *Globe*:

The region around Hilo, on the island of Hawaii, calls itself the "Orchid Capital of the World," *National Geographic* says. During a busy week, the city flies a million blossoms to the other Hawaiian Islands, the Far East and the United States mainland.

Fillers like this can be written by staff members from published sources or by people at the feature syndicates or press associations, but often they are written by PR persons working for companies and organizations and sent to newspapers as a public service and perhaps to get free mention in the news columns.

The National Association of Manufacturers sends weekly newspapers a free bi-weekly clip sheet of fillers. The following informational/how-to filler is typical of the offerings:

> A penny doesn't buy much these days, but it can insure your family's safety on the road, according to the Tire Retread Information Bureau.
>
> The condition of a tire's tread is crucial for automobile safety. To check the tread of your tires try the penny test.
>
> Insert the head of a penny upside down into the tire tread. If the tip of the head shows, your tread rubber is low and it should be turned in. Tires with low tread are 44 times more likely to blow out during highway driving than those with proper tread.

But the local angle is always best, especially for a weekly newspaper. Roberta Taussig, working for the Bluffton (Ohio) *News*, had a knack for finding the pleasantly offbeat happening in her town and telling the story with a light, sure touch. The following narrative filler serves as an example:

> When Mrs. James Kinn accepted a bag full of lily bulbs a few months ago, she decided it was too late to set them this year and left them lying in a brown paper sack in her garage.
>
> The lilies, however, disagreed with her diagnosis, and early this week she found that they had taken it upon themselves to put forth shoots and enthusiastic sprays of pink flowers.
>
> "I don't know how they did it," Mrs. Kinn said, somewhat confusedly. "They had no water, no dirt, no sunshine — nothing. I half expected they'd all dry up and die."
>
> The *News'* horticultural consultant, K. D. Herr, informs us that the blossoms are only about a week overdue, which is pretty good for shoots fighting their way out of a paper bag.
>
> Oh, yes. The bulbs that showed themselves so startlingly vigorous were Surprise Lilies.

* **Sidebars**

To keep the story line simple and the theme uncluttered, and to keep the length of an article within bounds, magazines and newspapers sometimes run sidebars: short items listing sources, giving definitions, providing addresses, or doing some other yeoman service. On a newspaper, a sidebar may be a spin-off from a major news story, covering some local angle or singling out one of the persons in the news and telling that person's side of the story. In the old days, a sidebar often was a tear-jerker.

Sidebars directly relate to articles, but, like any fillers, they can live a life of their own. Sometimes the sidebar proves to be more valuable than the main article. Once this author sent a first person narrative/how-to article to *Writer's Digest* on a book collaboration experience. A sidebar went along to describe the kinds of collaborations writers engage in. *WD* rejected the article but bought the sidebar. Another time he did a personality sketch/how-to article about a tree farmer for *Sunset*, including a sidebar mentioning the lumber industry's help to tree farmers and listing some addresses. *Sunset* rejected the article but bought the sidebar and used some of the photographs that were taken to go with the article.

When you have a sidebar to go with an article, you would type it in the same form as the article itself, starting it on a new page and giving it a heading. The magazine might set it in a different typeface and width from the main article, and use it as if it were a piece of art, but that does not affect your method of presentation.

• THE COLUMN

Probably every newspaper reporter and magazine writer has entertained the notion of one day owning a weekly newspaper, teaching journalism in college, writing a book, or writing a column. Of the four goals, column writing is probably the least attainable — if what you have in mind is a syndicated column like James Reston's, Art Buchwald's, or Jack Anderson's. But if your column is to appear only locally, or in a specialized magazine, getting started may not be so much of a problem.

If you have column-writing ambitions, you would first want to establish yourself as an authority on some subject of continuing interest or as a writer with a dependable light touch or a person of deep and commanding convictions. You would also need to convince an editor that you can be relied on to turn out 750 to 1,000 words on a regular basis. Before anyone can become a columnist, James Kilpatrick says, he will need "plenty of experience as a reporter." Looking back on his own background, Kilpatrick also believes editorial writing helps. At one time sports writing, with its stylistic freedom and flights into fancy, was considered good training ground for columnists. James Reston was once a sportswriter. So was the late Westbrook Pegler.

Figure 2.6 When record-reviewer Debby Begel was asked to supply a picture to go with her "Hi Notes" column in *Bay Area Lifestyle*, San Francisco, she decided against the expected listening-with-headphones kind of pose and settled instead for this one. And yes, she really does smoke cigars. *Bay Area Lifestyle* is an alternative monthly for singles. Begel writes another column for the publication on Bay Area music spots and night clubs.

Political columnists, who came on the scene years ago when newspaper editorial writers became less personal and more corporate, are known for the intensity of their feelings and the firmness with which they make their points. "The newspaper columnist, even more than the reporter, has an obligation to be a grouchy, suspicious, nasty, introspective monk, a horrid, raggedy thing no faction would care to capture," Nicholas von Hoffman suggests.[15]

[15]Nicholas von Hoffman, "Grumbling Off for a While," *Montana Journalism Review*, 1975, p. 59.

A syndicated column is likely to be more opinionated and probably more elegantly phrased than the unsigned editorial appearing across the page from it. Some would argue it is more reckless, too.

Probably the most respected and durable political columnist was the late Walter Lippmann. It was the depth of his thinking rather than the sparkle of his prose that impressed people. von Hoffman observed that Lippmann "wrote like an astronaut dancing the 'Nutcracker Suite' in a space suit."

As readers, we have a tendency to place political columnists on a liberal–conservative spectrum. We put von Hoffman, along with Walter Lippmann, Joseph Kraft, Gary Wills, and Tom Wicker on the left. We put the late David Lawrence and Westbrook Pegler, James Kilpatrick, William Buckley, and George Will on the right, with Jack Anderson and Evans and Novak somewhere in the middle. There are few surprises in the stands they take, but there are some. both von Hoffman and Lippmann have (had) conservative streaks, especially in fiscal matters.

Three of the most popular humor columnists are Art Buchwald, Russell Baker, and Erma Bombeck. Buchwald likes to satirize recent news events or cultural phenomena. His column on Andy Warhol's art in the spring of 1965 was prompted by the refusal of Canadian authorities to let 80 crates painted by Andy Warhol go through customs as works of art. To prove the authorities wrong, Buchwald told of his own experience of leaving a bag of groceries by mistake at an art gallery and winning first prize with it. The judges and others described what it was about the bag of groceries that impressed them.

> "Notice how the bottle of Heinz catsup is leaning against the can of Campbell's pork and beans."
> "I'll never know how he was inspired to put the Ritz crackers on top of the can of Crisco," a lady said to her escort.
> "It's pure genius," the escort replied. "Notice the way the Del Monte can of peaches is lying on its side. Even Warhol wouldn't have gone that far."

Russell Baker's columns deal mostly with urban life. He is frequently compared with Art Buchwald, but Baker is more cerebral, more abstract. Still, he ". . . was brought up on Lardner, Benchley, Stephen Leacock, Perelman, E. B. White, and a few others too humorous to mention," Groucho Marx wrote in a letter to the editor of *The New York Times Book Review*.

Bombeck deals with more mundane matters than either Buchwald or Baker. Women readers especially appreciate the frustrations catalogued in "At Wit's End." For instance:

> ... I have a horror of leaving this world and not having anyone in the entire family know how to replace a toilet tissue spindle [she writes].
>
> It's an awesome thought to have four grown people wandering around in a daze saying, "I thought she told you how," and another saying, "If I knew she was sick I'd have paid attention."

Bombeck pointed out that replacing the toilet tissue spindle was only part of the problem at home. So, she said, she had put together a "survival manual" to cover any emergency when she was away. It contained household hints on such subjects as "Turning on Stove" (". . . Do not put food directly on burner, but put it in a pan first.") and "Operating a Clothes Hamper" (". . . Bending from the waist, you

Figure 2.7 In a unique piece of art included in an ad meant to promote itself as an advertising medium, *Esquire* presented four of its front-of-the-book columnists who served "as the lively and entertaining *antipasto* to the feast of the main editorial sandwich." The ad's headline read: "DICK AND NORA, JOHN AND JOAN." Dick Joseph, now deceased, was travel editor; Nora Ephron wrote about the media; John Gregory Dunne and Joan Didion wrote about the West Coast. The art involving the writers is by Jill Krementz; the photo is by Kenn Mori. (©*1976* Esquire *magazine.*)

simply pick up a sock, a pair of pants, or a towel, lift the lid of the hamper and feed soiled clothes into it. The Good Fairy will take it from there.")

Syndicates offer several hundred columns to newspaper editors. Besides the political and humor columns, there are columns on love, religion, sports, finances, health, astrology, and just about any subject you can think of. Probably the best chance of landing a syndicate contract is to come up with a column that deals with a subject just capturing the public fancy — as CB radio did — and for which there is now no column offered.[16]

Placing a column with a local newspaper or specialized magazine is a more realistic goal yet. One who has done both is Richard Lipez, whose work appears in the Amherst (Mass.) *Record* and *The Progressive*, the midwestern monthly of opinion launched early in the century by the La Follettes. In *The Progressive* for April 1976, Lipez set up an imaginary "Let's Face It" TV interview program with a presidential aspirant. An excerpt:

Q. . . . Senator, you were asked in New Hampshire whether you favored restoration of capital punishment, and you replied that you supported a "partial death penalty." Could you elaborate on that?

A. Yes, I could. Death is an extreme remedy that is considered unpleasant by some segments of our society, but we have to remember that certain people have it coming. However, I am a mainstream moderate on this, as well as on quite a few other issues, so while I do not entirely favor the outright killing of criminals, I would support a law for putting criminals in very critical condition. . . .

To get a newspaper column started you'd probably work for the newspaper first as a reporter or feature writer. To get a syndicated column started you'd probably work first as a newspaper columnist. To get a magazine column started you'd contribute articles to the magazine first and develop a specialty.

Here's how Bill Tarrant, once a journalism student, then a businessman, sportsman, and mayor of Wichita, got started. After writing five novels and three volumes of poetry, only to have them rejected, and after trying to launch a newspaper column, only to have it fail, Tarrant "took inventory. I'd tried every medium except magazines.

---

[16]The usual contract calls for splitting the income 50–50 between the syndicate and the writer.

So, called a notable and got his consent for a New Journalism cameo. Wrote it. Sent it to *Field & Stream*. On June 6, 1973 I found a check in my road box. . . ."[17] Two months later he sold another article to *Field & Stream*. A month later he sold a third. The articles dealt with dogs and decoys. "From the first line of those stories it was apparent that a new and powerful writer had shown up on the outdoor scene," says Jack Samson, editor of *Field & Stream*. "Bill's description was bright, tight, and accurate; his dialogue was written in an altogether different style and was terse and alive and his sense of composition was excellent. He said things the way no other writer in his field had done before. . . ."[18] So Samson called Tarrant and asked him to be gun dog editor of the magazine. That meant a monthly column.

The first one, "And I Do Not Walk Alone," appeared in February 1974, and Tarrant immediately showed he was not simply going to tell hunting or dog stories and deal only with dog-training and hunting techniques. A sample set of paragraphs from inside that first column (we come onto it after four paragraphs have set the stage) shows his approach:

> I've walked cross country in deep snow — late at night — and had the companionship of a dog I didn't need to ask to come along.
>
> I've sat alone in a sad house and cursed my fortune while the dog curled at my feet had a faith in tomorrow I could not find.
>
> I've been hours late getting out a dog's feed pan and never heard a complaint.
>
> I've yelled in rage to clear a room of man and beast only to note a few minutes later one black nose and two bright eyes poke around the door jamb to scent the spell of the room. I but shifted in my chair and the rascal was in my lap. The men who cleared the room? They may never come back.
>
> I've picked up dogs with broken bones and taken them to a vet. No pain could make the dog cry out to his benefactor.
>
> I've seen children calmed at night with a dog on their pillow. There could be no better pacifier, no finer protector. I might sleep through whatever befell the child, or shy from the power of an intruder. The dog could do neither.
>
> I've seen dogs break ice to retrieve a duck, stand on point with a thorn in a pad, go down a 70 percent grade to corral a sheep, chase a car cross town to be part of a family outing, sniff out a warehouse while a policeman crouched outside with drawn pistol, lick a sick man's feet, kiss a crying child's cheek, stare beseechingly at a mother's worried face, raise an arm of a man dead tired who'd worked too hard to make ends meet.

[17]Letter to the author from Bill Tarrant, Sept. 22, 1976.

[18]In the Introduction to Bill Tarrant's *Best Way to Train Your Bird Dog*, David McKay, New York, 1977.

I've seen men bury their dogs and not be able to stand up to leave the grave. And I've seldom known a man to mention a dog's parting.

Yes, there is a God, He's dog spelled backwards. I like to think that's the way He intended it. To come as the least of all of us to do the most.[19]

In this and his succeeding columns, Tarrant manages to go far beyond merely talking about dogs and hunting; he expresses his philosophy of life and writes with a flair not to be expected, perhaps, in a gun dog column. His monthly feature takes him around the world for subject matter and in 1977 led to publication of *Best Way to Train Your Bird Dog* (David McKay, New York). He has other books in the works.

• THE REVIEW

Each year American publishers bring out 40,000 new books or new editions of existing books.[20] Although only about 10 percent of new books are reviewed (there just aren't enough reviewing media), a major way for readers to find out about books they may be interested in is to read the reviews in magazines and newspapers.

Among magazines, the major review organs — for the general public — are *The New York Times Book Review* (a Sunday magazine section of the New York *Times*), *The New York Review of Books*, *Saturday Review*, *Time* and *Newsweek*, and the opinion and quality magazines and the quarterlies. In addition, most specialized magazines run reviews of books that deal with their specialties.

Most big-city papers and some smaller papers run locally produced or syndicated reviews. *Publishers Weekly*, *Library Journal*, and other trade magazines and newsletters run reviews for the benefit of libraries and bookstores, to help them with their ordering.

It used to be that the only pay you would get from many magazines and newspapers for a review was the book itself. *The Christian Century* sweetened the pot by sending an additional book from among those it decided not to review. Now most publications pay for reviews — and at a word rate similar to what they pay for articles. *The New Republic* pays from eight to ten cents a word. But because reviews are shorter than regular articles — almost never more than a few hundred words

---

[19] Reproduced by permission of *Field & Stream*.

[20] A new edition is different from a new printing. It represents a rewriting and updating. A new printing represents only the putting of the plates back on the press for an additional run. Typically, a book goes through several printings before it goes into a new edition. So a new edition is a new book.

— the pay is minimal. And a review, properly written, can take as long to do as a full-length article.

The best way to get started as a reviewer is to go ahead and do some sample reviews and send them to an editor with the request that you be put on a list of potential reviewers. When a book comes along that you can handle, the editor may send it to you, giving you a deadline and a word limit.

You can watch the announcements of forthcoming books in *Publishers Weekly* and notify an editor that you would like to review the book when it comes out. There may come a time in your writing career, especially if you develop a specialty, when the book-review editor will seek you out.

Some writers make deals with local newspapers to act as book-review editors/reviewers on a freelance basis, using newspaper stationery to request books from publishers. Once established, you can get a listing in *Literary Market Place*. Publishers will automatically send you books to review.

Lucas Longo makes a convincing case (in *The Writer*, July 1975) for starting with small, local markets and working your way up to bigger or specialized markets. With his queries to the better markets he included copies of his earlier reviews. Eventually he was able to sell the editor of a weekly newspaper in Brooklyn on running a book-review column. "At first I received no money. Today I am paid fifty dollars for every column." Part of his sales pitch to the editor was a promise that the column would bring in advertising revenue from bookstores in the area — and it did.

You can take four different approaches in reviewing a book. One is to simply report it, as though you were writing a news story. This is a recommended approach only if you feel inadequate to really analyze the work. But in that case maybe you shouldn't be reviewing it.

Another approach is to interpret the book and to put it into context with other books. To do this you would have to be well read in the area the book covers. You would have to know the literature.

A third approach — the most common and useful one — is to judge the book. Your review becomes very subjective. You react to what the book says. This does not preclude you from also reporting on what it contains and putting it into context.

A fourth approach is to use the book as a stepping off point for your own essay. This is a luxury only a review medium like *The New York Review of Books* will allow.[21] Such an approach may not be fair to the book writer, and certainly it does not meet the generally accepted function of a review: to help readers make up their minds.

When you judge a book you should take into account how well the author has accomplished what he set out to accomplish. The Preface will lay down the author's goals.

As you judge the author's style and the book's content, you should bear in mind the book's intended audience. A student for a book-review assignment wrote indignantly of an author's simple style and of the elemental information he presented. Of course his style was simple, his information elemental; his publisher was Franklin Watts, producer of juveniles. The student had picked out a thin book with large type to review and then criticized the book for not being slanted to a college audience.

Knowing about publishers can help you make a preliminary judgment about a book under review. The only way to know about publishers is to notice the imprint whenever you read a book. Eventually you'll come to know that an Alfred A. Knopf book, to name a prestigious imprint, means material on a loftier plane than material offered, say, by Lyle Stuart, Inc. Some middle-size and small publishers promote a point of view that becomes discernible as you study their books. Arlington House, for instance, issues books with a conservative or ultraconservative slant; Beacon Press issues books with a liberal slant. Some houses specialize, as TAB Books does with its radio and TV materials, Richards Rosen Press with its books for teenagers, Watson-Guptill with its art-instruction books, Dover Publications with its technical and semitechnical paperback reprints.

The way to learn how to write reviews is to study the current ones in the magazines. One of the best lessons on book reviewing available to you is to follow a given book through its many reviews to see how various reviewers handle the assignment. You would not want to do this, however, with a book you intend to review yourself. Reading other reviews or even the book jacket (except for information about the author) will color your own review and rob it of its originality. Sydney Smith, the English clergyman and essayist, pretended to carry this advice to its extreme: "I never read a book before reviewing it; it prejudices one so."

---

[21] The *NYRB* is an opinionated, highly literary, rambling journal born of a newspaper strike when the *Times* (with its review) was not published. Philip Nobile wrote a whole book about the *NYRB: Intellectual Skywriting*. Someone once suggested the review ought to be called the *New York Review of Each Other's Books*.

Typically, a review of a nonfiction book would contain these elements:

1. A blurb above the review giving the author's name, book title, place of publication, name of publisher, year of publication and (sometimes) number of pages and price.
2. An opening or lead designed to catch the reader's attention.
3. A brief description of the aim and scope of the book.
4. Some information about the author. If you can't get enough from the jacket, turn to *Contemporary Authors, Contemporary Journalists, The Writers Directory*, or some other directory of writers or to a regional or specialized who's-who book. If the author is important enough, his biography will be included in *Who's Who in America* or *Current Biography*.
5. A statement of the thesis or theme of the book.
6. Some paragraphs covering the author's main contention.
7. Comparison of the book with previous books on the subject.
8. Discussion of the book's shortcomings.
9. Discussion of the book's merits.
10. Summary of the value of the book.

The material would not necessarily appear in this order, nor would all of it be covered for all reviews. And reviews of works of fiction would take a slightly different tack.

In reviewing a novel you would deal with the author's plot and characters and discuss the validity of his theme. You would tell part of the story, but not enough to give away the ending.

In reviewing a novel, you have an additional problem: how to determine whether what is said by either the story-teller or a character in conversation actually reflects what the author feels. Allen Drury, author of *The Promise of Joy*, rightly objected to a *Time* critic's saying: "Drury describes the Chinese variously as 'yellow hordes,' 'pagan hordes' and 'mongrel hordes.'" He, personally, did not use these descriptions, he told *Time* in a letter. They were used by a demagogue in the story, then picked up by the media that play a role in the novel. "I describe this process step by step, as the media's panjandrums reluctantly but inexorably leave sanity behind and begin hysterically to raise the bugaboo of 'the yellow peril.'

"I never resort to such terms myself. I am, in fact, consistently sympathetic to the Chinese throughout. It is only the media I portray as going overboard."

Book reviews should be written in present tense ("the author says") and, if possible, third person, although an honest "I" is better than the stuffier "this reviewer."[22] A few direct quotations from the book may help show the author's style and document his bias or originality, but paraphrasing, considering your limited space, may be more useful to your reader. You do not need footnotes in a review any more than you do for other kinds of articles.

Be wary of phrases like "must reading" and "long-needed." You are not a PR person. You are not being paid to sell the book. And if you think you have really come up with something in this lead, "Every so often there comes along a book . . . ," forget it. All too often reviewers have used it.

Don't worry a lot about typos. Every book has them. Concentrate instead on the information and ideas or on the story. Tell what is good and bad about the book — and why. Give special attention to the why.

As with other articles, you would tailor the review to the needs and interests of the audience. Ed Zern shows how in a tongue-in-cheek review of *Lady Chatterley's Lover* in *Field & Stream*:

> This fictional account of the day-by-day life of an English gamekeeper is still of considerable interest to outdoor-minded readers as it contains many passages on pheasant raising, the apprehension of poachers, ways to control vermin, and other chores and duties of the professional gamekeeper. Unfortunately, one is obliged to wade through many pages of extraneous material in order to discover and savor these sidelights on the management of a midland shooting estate.

A favorite reviewer's trick is to adopt the style of the book's author in the writing of the review. Hence, a review of an Ernest Hemingway novel uses tough-guy prose. A review of an Ann Landers book is written as though in answer to a letter.

A student reviewing the textbook for a Magazine Article Writing class some years ago used an acrostic to spell out STINKS because the author of that textbook used the acrostic device throughout to lay down his writing rules. "The S stands for silly rules. . . ."

In a column in *Esquire* about Theodore White, Nora Ephron uses the White style to make a point:

> . . . And to understand what has happened to Theodore H. White, which is the story of this column, one would have to go back to earlier years, to the place where it all started.
> *Time* magazine.

[22]But "I" is a luxury not usually accorded the writers of textbooks.

That was where it all started. At *Time* magazine. Not everything started at *Time* magazine — Theodore H. White developed his infuriating style of repeating phrases over and over again later in his life. . . .

When Max Rafferty, the one-time ultraconservative school superintendent for California, brought out his *What They Are Doing to Your Children*, Fred M. Hechinger reviewed it for *The Reporter* (another defunct magazine) and started out this way:

Should a satirist attempt to parody the style of Dr. Rafferty, he might well come up with a paragraph like this:

"If, as the example of California now gives promise, the errors and follies of an entire generation can now be terminated, and a whole new, brightly dawning day can now be ushered in, then truly this greatest profession of them all will go forward, hand in hand with the children whom it exists to serve and to love, and we will pass through the great iron door of the future, with America's destiny in our keeping, to lead proudly yet with humility, and in the most profound and meaningful sense, to sin no more."

There would be only one flaw: the paragraph actually *is* vintage Rafferty, fresh from *What They Are Doing to Your Children*. . . .

Some publications encourage their reviewers to deal only with good books, films, plays, etc., because just covering them attaches importance to them. A mention — any mention — in *The New York Times Book Review* can send sales soaring.

The inclination on the part of reviewers, though, is to attack what they review. It is the rare reviewer who doesn't think he could do a better job than the author under consideration. Besides, it's more fun to put down than to praise. Some literary and performing-arts putdowns that might inspire you:

"The covers of this book are too far apart." — *Ambrose Bierce*.
"This book fills a much-needed gap." — (allegedly) *Jacques Barzun*.
"The author was careful to leave no stomach unturned." — *Robert Benchley*.
"Mr. Henry James writes fiction as if it were a painful duty." — *Oscar Wilde*.
"This is not a novel to be tossed aside lightly. It should be thrown with great force." — *Dorothy Parker*.
"No Leica." — *Dorothy Parker* again, this time in response to the play *I Am a Camera*.
The dancing resembled "a troop of hikers trying to extinguish a campfire." — *Jay Cocks*, in a review of the musical *At Long Last Love*.
The acting is "on a par with the clean parts of a dirty movie." — *Gene Shalit* in a broadcast review of a grade-B picture.

Once Heywood Broun called an actor, Geoffrey Steyne, the worst on the American stage. The actor sued — but lost. The next time Broun reviewed a play with this actor in it, Broun didn't mention him until the last sentence, when he said: "Mr. Steyne's performance was not up to its usual standard."

In a review in *New York* (March 29, 1976) praising honky-tonk country singer Gary Stewart, Nik Cohn badmouths your typical C & W fare. He talks about the "Muzak vacuities of John Denver and Olivia Newton-John."

> True, there was a would-be resistance movement in Austin, led by Waylon Jennings and Willie Nelson, but that, in its own way, was just as fake as Nashville and even more tiresome. A bunch of cosmic cowboys, in beards and bandanas, scratching their armpits onstage and spouting mock profundities. It was a shrewd enough image, sufficiently picturesque to fool the rock-Establishment critics. Yet the music was drab beyond description, and the pretensions quite grotesque.

Mike O'Brien of the Eugene (Ore.) *Register-Guard*, in a review of the X-rated movie *Sandstone*, called it "the most boring film . . . since your Aunt Sarah's movies of her trip to Sedalia, Ohio." His ending:

> What it all boils down to is that any heavy breathing you might hear in "Sandstone" has nothing at all to do with passion.
> It's the sound of people in a deep, deep sleep.

The principle of "fair comment" as it has come up in the courts suggests that, as long as the reviewer deals with his subject's writing or performance and not with his private life, he is in little danger of committing libel. Book authors and performers, by putting what they write into print or up on stage, are asking for it. They look for applause. They should be willing to endure the boos.

But don't be surprised if, as a reviewer turning out a damning report, you find yourself quoted in the ads. It is no big challenge to an advertising person to reach into your review to find the one statement that praises, however faintly, and blow it up and out of context.

As a reviewer you would no doubt be easier on local and admittedly amateur talent than you would on professionals. What good is served by tearing into the earnest, unpaid performers on stage at the Very Little Theater or at the high school?

Numerous ethical problems present themselves to book review editors and reviewers. To start with: Who should get the book to review? Someone known to have an opposite point of view? Or someone known to have a similar point of view? And should the book go to someone who has written a similar book? Can he be trusted to give the book's author a fair hearing? Or will the reviewer be concerned that the new book will cut into his own sales?

Should the book go to someone who has never written a book? Herbert Gold quotes Saul Bellow as saying of a critic: "Over every one of his reviews stands a secret invisible headline — *"I have written three unpublished novels."*[23]

And what about the reviewer who finds that the book assigned him was written by a friend? Novelist George V. Higgins (*A City on a Hill*), when he encounters that problem, mentions the friendship in the review so the reader can be on the lookout for any bias.

Ethical problems aside, many of the persons who review books simply are not up to the task. They read but do not understand. A British critic, reviewing Mark Twain's *The Innocents Abroad* when it came out, said, perfectly seriously, that the book was worthless as a travel guide and full of exaggerations.[24]

Most journalists have a chance sometime in their careers to review books. It is less likely they will be called on to do other reviewing: of movies, plays, television programs, dance recitals, the ballet, concerts, the opera, art exhibits, recordings, architecture, restaurants, consumer items.

Film reviewing — and reviewing the performing arts — are more difficult than book reviewing in that you can't as easily check back to see how a sentence or scene goes. In film reviewing, you may also want to deal with the quality of projection, the temperature in the theater, the cost of the candy bars, the quality of the popcorn, even the stickiness of the floor.

• OTHER CATEGORIES

Whatever additional categories you can think of probably involve subject matter rather than form. For instance: The Travel Piece. What is it if not a how-to-do-it, narrative, or essay? Still, The Travel Piece deserves singling out because of its unique appeal both to readers, who want to find out about places they may visit, and to writers, who want to share their experiences. A few publications, like *Travel*, devote themselves solely to travel pieces. Others combine travel pieces with

[23]Herbert Gold, "Reviewmanship and the I-Wrote-a-Book Disease," *The Atlantic*, June 1970, p. 115.

[24]Robert Lewis Taylor, *W. C. Fields: His Follies and Fortunes*, Doubleday & Company, Garden City, New York, 1949, p. 87.

Figure 2.8 Photographer Duncan McDonald calls this an "enterprise shot," referring to its universal appeal and its potential for any number of markets. For instance, it could be sold to a stock-photograph house. The picture is beautifully composed, haunting, timeless. McDonald took it when the two girls — Gael, on the left, who is French, and Vanessa, an American — had experienced difficulty communicating with each other.

other articles. Some specialize in a particular kind of travel (by car, by trailer), some appeal to a single age or income level, some concentrate on a particular part of the world. Among the best markets for travel pieces are the magazine for customers issued by the car manufacturers. Often a magazine interested in travel pieces wants accounts of trips that their readers can duplicate. This means that exact names, prices, and other details should be featured.

Probably the Historical Piece needs singling out, too. Again, it is already covered by the list. It fits into the Personality Sketch, Narrative, or Essay categories. But it is another highly popular form, if not among major magazines then among adventure-oriented and regional magazines and among the newspapers. Probably more regional history than national history is written by journalists. Local newspaper readers enjoy looking back, and feature writers, especially for anniversary or progress issues, like to dig through the files for material

A young artist at work in Korea, Steve Lorton, assistant editor of *Sunset,* took this photograph — and many others — on assignment in the Far East. Lorton's article dealt with Korea as a place for *Sunset* readers to visit. "Surprised and excited travelers are returning from Korea claiming they've discovered the Orient. Once known only as an impoverished, war-torn country, Korea has emerged in the 1970s as a thriving, modern nation."*(Photo by Steven R. Lorton. Courtesy of* Sunset *Magazine.)*

The markets in Korea, *Sunset* Magazine explains in a travel piece, offer carefully graded produce like these trays of chestnuts. To capture this scene, writer-photographer Steve Lorton uses natural light to spotlight the kneeling figure, and shoots from an angle that puts the produce in the foreground, where it can be "read." (*Photo by Steven R. Lorton. Courtesy of* Sunset *Magazine.*)

that shows the origins of towns, regions, industries, and institutions or that tells about early leaders and memorable characters.

If in looking over the above list you don't find some newspaper-feature category brought out in a Reporting class, you may discover it under a different name. One category not on the list is "Human Interest Story," because "human interest" takes in too much territory. The human interest story, as the newspaper person sees it, can involve people (lovable children, beautiful women, tragic figures, hoodlums, sex objects, tough little old ladies, retired gentlemen with quotation marks around "retired," women who do what used to be exclusively men's jobs, men who keep house, benefactors, weirdos, alcoholics, reformed alcoholics, clergymen who are regular fellows, religious fanatics, idealists, people who reach 100 who drink and smoke, people who reach 100 who neither drink nor smoke, celebrities, people who stumble onto fortunes or who win prizes), animals, universal longings (love, success, happiness, pleasure, fame, money, power, adventure, peace of mind), and fears (death, illness, war, loss of job, loss of money, rising prices, rejection, breakup of marriage, impotency). The human interest story can tug at our heartstrings or make us laugh — or both. In his book on feature writing, Daniel R. Williamson called human interest stories "studies in human nature."[25]

You can see that just about any one of the eleven basic articles described in this chapter can be — should be — a "human interest story."

Another newspaper term, "the news feature," describes what is essentially an informational essay or a narrative. "The color story," which provides description to go along with a hard-news story, could be an informational essay, personality story, or sidebar. "The seasonal story" can fit almost anywhere: it can be a personality sketch of a local Santa Claus, a narrative about a shopping trip, an essay on the origins of St. Patrick's Day, a how-to-do-it piece on preparing the Thanksgiving turkey, an anthology of anecdotes about tricks played years ago by Halloween pranksters.

At any rate, there you have them — the categories into which most articles and features fit. Keep them in mind as you move to the next chapter to consider ideas that grow into articles.

[25]Daniel R. Williamson, *Feature Writing for Newspapers*, Hastings House, Publishers, New York, 1975. p. 116.

CHAPTER 3

The Article Idea

Sometimes an idea occurs to you suddenly. It is a natural because it involves a field you are familiar with. You know where to go for anecdotes and additional facts. Everything falls into place. Sometimes. More often you search out an idea. You stay constantly on the alert for some subject you can handle. Perhaps you overhear a remark at a reception that starts you to thinking. (Who is the originator of the income tax idea?) Or at a ball game. (How does one get to be an umpire?) In class. (Are first-borns over-achievers?) Waiting in line in a cafeteria. (What foods do certain personality types go for?) Lying in bed, trying to get some sleep. (Is there a retired person in this town who was once well known and who might make a good subject for a personality sketch?)

Like fiction, nonfiction ordinarily needs conflict to sustain reader interest. Your article can pit people against people, or against nature, or against society, or against fate, or against themselves.

Try to deal with your readers' needs. Help your readers earn more money or improve their health or sex life. Calm their fears — or scare them into some form of action. Appeal to their sense of pride. Help them realize their ambitions. Show them how to gain prestige or power. Make things easier for them. Or more pleasant. Arouse their curiosity. Don't be afraid to resort to emotion or sentiment.

"I've learned that people will read about anything that relates to the body — heat, cold, sex, health, beauty, ugliness," says Harry Golden. "The body is an object, an idea, easy to relate to. As I say, however, this knowledge is practical, so basically practical that any cub reporter who doesn't learn it on his first story had better turn in his Smith-

Corona and his press card. When a fire wipes out a family, you write about tears, not antiquated fire laws."[1] "It is an axiom of the magazine business," says L. J. Davis, "that people love to read about how miserable they are, how stupid their neighbors, how venal their public servants."[2]

Find a superlative, if you can. The fastest, biggest, smallest, longest, shortest: no doubt people will want to hear about it. The success of *The Guinness Book of World Records* shows that.

• IDEAS THROUGH OBSERVATION

In one of the early books on feature writing, Walter A. Steigleman told of the small-town writer "who thought he was a globe trotter when he boarded an excursion boat in Boston for the overnight ride to New York," going on deck in the morning to discover, as the boat entered the New York harbor, that it was not Bedloe's Island and its Statue of Liberty you first see, as he had always believed, but the top of a gas tank in Brooklyn. It was enough of a revelation to spur him to do an article exploding a myth.[3]

"Actually, pros don't *get* ideas; they *recognize* them," says article- and song-writer Paul Vandervoort II. "Ideas are everywhere and anywhere," he adds. "Anything a writer can see, hear, smell, touch, or taste may be the nucleus of a good idea." Vandervoort's bank in Burbank starts a single-line system by which customers are served on a first-come, first-served basis, and he sells an article about it to *Banking*. He becomes annoyed by noise in a hospital, and he sells an article on the problem to *Hospital Topics*. Having a fluency in the Spanish language, he does an article on foreign-language advertising by jewelers and sells it to *Jeweler's Circular-Keystone*. Whenever a new Burbank mayor is elected, Vandervoort notes the official's former hometown and occupation and does articles based on this information: an arti-

---

[1] Harry Golden, "How to Live with a Chair You Hate," *Saturday Review*, June 17, 1967, p. 14.

[2] L. J. Davis, "Is Prose Dead? Not to E. B. White," *The National Observer*, Dec. 18, 1976, p. 19.

[3] Walter A. Steigleman, *Writing the Feature Article*, The Macmillan Company, New York, 1950, pp. 136, 137.

"Remember that article I wrote that you thought was boring?"

cle about a dentist-mayor went to *Tic*. a dental publication; an article about a shoemaker-mayor went to *Master Shoe Rebuilder*; an article about an ex-Omaha bandleader-mayor went to the Omaha *World-Herald*.[4]

• IDEAS THROUGH EXPERIENCE

Ideas can come through your own experience or the experience of someone you know. Let's say that, while driving through a small town with your family, you are stopped and notified that you are "Tourists of the Week." Some Chamber of Commerce types give you free motel

[4]Paul Vandervoort II, "How to Get an Article Idea," *The Writer*, May 1976, pp. 15–17.

"Do we want a story about this gentleman's childhood in Idaho and do you have a key to the men's room?"

accommodations, free meals, free merchandise; and someone from the local paper takes your picture and interviews you. Such experience makes you wonder about similar promotions by chambers of commerce, junior chambers, and service clubs. You decide you could do an article about a single, unique program sponsored by a local Rotary Club and sell it to *The Rotarian*. Or you could do a "roundup" article about scattered civic promotions (that could involve a lot more work) and sell it to a magazine with a more general — but business-oriented — audience.

When Ron Sproat was out of a job he noticed an ad in *The Village Voice*: "Writers, Staff/Free lance, must be prolific. Must spell, punctuate, and type rapidly." It turned out the job was for a porno publisher. Sproat took it, even though it was not something he wanted to do and it meant producing 40 pages a day ("I didn't think I could *type* 40 pages a day. . . ."). He knew that what he wrote was "thoroughly miserable" and wondered if his fellow writers there were turning out prose as bad as his. He had his answer when he glanced over at what his neighbor had just typed. It read: "He glared at her through clenched teeth."

A month of this was all he could take, but the time was not completely wasted. It occurred to Sproat afterwards that people might want to know how under-the-counter novels are written. So he put together a first-person account of his month-long career as a pornographer and sold a piece to *New York*: "The Working Day in a Porno Factory" (March 11, 1974, pp. 37–40).

• IDEAS THROUGH READING

Perhaps the most fruitful sources of ideas are periodicals and other printed or written materials.

• Newspapers

A careful reading of a single issue of any daily newspaper should yield at least a dozen ideas. They'll pop up from the front-page stories, the inside stories, the editorials, the columns, the features, the ads (including classifieds), the regular departments (such as sports). As presented in the paper, the stories often have nothing more than local interest, but the magazine-article writer will see angles that can be developed for national interest.

You see an AP item in the newspaper about "an apparent attack of food poisoning" at Gaithersburg, Maryland, sending 31 persons from a birthday party to hospitals. "Officials said the illness may have been caused by staphylococcus germs, possibly in a chicken and rice casserole served at the party." Forget this particular story, but is there the germ of an *idea* here? How about an article on what to watch out for in preparing a picnic lunch?

A UPI story tells about a fellow in a nearby city who has started up a business that puts things together for people who buy them elsewhere in cartons. He is especially busy around Christmas. The story is short, but long enough to convince you that he is worth interviewing for a Christmas feature next year.

Another story deals with a blind piano-tuner who also heads up a country-and-western music combo. Surely there are some angles there for an article for a national magazine.

Another story, illustrated, deals with a fellow who does big wood sculptures using a chain saw. Maybe the company that makes the chain saw has a house organ.

On the business page a story talks about expansion plans for a paint manufacturing plant. Maybe a trade journal article?

Reporter Brad Lemley for *The Oregonian* tells you about a young man who opens a Better Beef and Bible store. Beef and Bibles? A strange combination, and one that may be of interest to a grocers' or butchers' magazine as well as a magazine, like *Publishers Weekly*, going to bookstore owners. It may also yield an article for a religious magazine.

In writing any of these, you would do your own interviewing and research, of course. And your angle more than likely would be quite different from that of the original news story or feature.

• Magazines

As idea stimulators, magazines would probably serve you differently from newspapers. Seeing an article about a handicapped person who starts up a successful business, you may decide to do an anthology describing a number of persons who also have overcome handicaps. Of course no one of these would get the in-depth treatment the original got. It is possible to do this kind of article by working exclusively from secondary — published — sources.

Seeing a personality sketch about a famous person, you may find one of several traits only briefly hinted at. Presuming you have access to the person, you may want to do your own article, for a different market, stressing that trait. Perhaps the original article mentions a religious experience. You do an article on the person's relationship to his God and sell it to a religious or denominational magazine.

You can either expand on the original article, or move in and concentrate on just one of its aspects. If it is an argumentative piece that stimulates your thinking, you may want to take issue with it. You probably wouldn't present your article specifically as a reaction to the original — that would limit its sales potential — but you might quote from it briefly, as well as from similar articles, to show how wrong other writers have been on the subject.

If it is a piece in a technical, trade, or professional journal, you can give it a broader audience by doing something for a general-interest magazine, newspaper, or wire service. A UPI reporter saw an article in a medical journal circulated in the Hartford, Connecticut area, and took notes and interviewed the physician-author, who had come up with the interesting idea that Satchel Paige's "Six Rules for a Long Life" were a forerunner of the preventative medicine doctors were practicing in the 1970s. Paige is an ageless baseball pitcher. You remember his rules. "Avoid fried meats which angry up the blood." was one of them. "Don't look back. Something may be gaining on you." was another. The UPI story repeated the rules and indirectly quoted Dr. Joseph Ungar's appraisal of them in light of today's medicine.

• Books

It is impossible to read a provocative book without finding ideas on every page for further development. In discussing a prevailing notion in some quarters that the apocalypse is near, Malcolm Muggeridge in *Jesus: The Man Who Lives* (Harper & Row, 1975, pp. 94, 95) observes:

> The truth is that famines and pestilences and wars and rumours of wars have been the constant lot of mankind. Crisis is not the exception, but our permanent condition; and awareness of this, as Dr. Johnson said of waiting to be hanged, wonderfully concentrates the mind. To believe that men living in time can know lasting peace, prosperity, and contentment is far more fallacious and demented than to expect the end of the world in the near future.

Does that stimulate your thinking?

Karl and Anne Taylor Fleming's *The First Time*, a set of sexual confessions that titillated buyers of nonbooks in 1975, might trigger first-time ideas in other areas of human experience. In an era so given to bad taste, there might even be an article idea in this: confessions from oldtimers detailing their *final* sexual encounters. A lead article for one of those periodicals for geriatrics? O.K. O.K. Then how about something for the *National Enquirer*?

Stan Bettis, a former Magazine Article Writing student who writes regularly about the outdoors, discovered a book by Zane Grey describing a boat trip Grey took many years ago with his son down the treacherous Rogue River in Oregon. Bettis decided to take the trip, with his father, to see if he could find Grey's landmarks. They proved remarkably accurate. The market he had in mind was *Saga*, which bought his article, but he sold variations of the article to *Better Camping*, *Outdoors* (a company magazine published by Mercury outboard motors), and a locally edited newspaper magazine section as well.

Don't overlook the output of the world's largest publisher, the U.S. Government Printing Office, Washington, D.C., which sends out leaflets, booklets, and hardbound books on every conceivable subject at cost, on request. (Examples: *An Assessment of Attitudes Toward Music*, 85¢; *Everything You Always Wanted to Know About Shipping High-Level Nuclear Wastes*, 70¢; and *How to Buy Food*, $4.45.) The general public is largely unaware of what's available; to writers, the material — all of it is in the public domain — is a godsend. Your library will have copies of some of the materials published by GPO, along with an index to help you trace them down. You can get on a GPO mailing list to be notified of the availability of selected publications. No charge.

Going down the entries in the index of a book — even a textbook — can also stimulate your thinking and suggest a topic for developing into an article.

Knowing that writers are constantly on the alert for article ideas, some professional and trade organizations publish helpful booklets. The American Bar Association Section of Criminal Justice, for instance, issues a twenty-six-pager called *How to Measure the Quality of Criminal Justice: Story Ideas*. An example: "*Right to counsel. How good is it?* Examine how lawyers are assigned to indigent defendants. . . ." There follows some background questions and advice for contacting sources.

• Theses

Working with master's theses and Ph.D. dissertations, you can enjoy the satisfaction of unearthing well-buried ideas and information and offering them, with proper credit, to a wide audience. The persons who presented them originally probably disdained the process of popularization. To a considerable degree, an article writer is a popularizer.

• THE WRITER AS READER

It should not be necessary to give writers pep talks on generating ideas. Writers should be bubbling over with ideas. The problem should not be "What shall I write about?" but "How can I possibly find the time to develop all the ideas I have?"

The trouble with many young writers is that not enough has happened to them to allow them to draw from their experience. And they do not read widely enough to develop ideas from the media. What remains as idea sources are their powers of observation. These are not enough.

Students should not expect to sell to the magazines unless they first read them. They should read magazines — all kinds of magazines — not only to stimulate the idea-generating process but also to find out what sells these days and to pick up information from published articles to use in their own. Magazines often are better research sources than books because they are current. Professional writers, working on several articles at a time, clip and copy as they read and stuff their findings into the several folders they have set up to receive research materials.

• THE IDEA AND THE MARKET

You don't really have an idea unless you also have a market in mind for the article. A good idea to one editor could be useless to another.

Which of the thousands of magazines will you write your article for? The time to make the decision is before you begin writing, even before you begin researching.

A danger is that you will aim too low. When several businessmen without permission erect a pre-stressed concrete cross, wired for lights, on public property on a hill at the edge of town, you see an article in it for *The Christian Century*, a magazine you know to be interested in issues concerned with separation of church and state. The article sells as a sort of narrative, "The Case of the Midnight Christians," and you learn later that *Saturday Evening Post* editors see it and assign a writer to do a similar story. From the standpoint of pay, obviously, you underestimated the article's potential.

On the other hand, you can aim too high. You are most likely to do this with an essay article. While you are submitting your article to the top magazines and seeing it rejected, the idea loses currency and you become discouraged. Only with the passing years will you learn to evaluate an idea for its correct market level. Even then you may be in for some surprises.

• THE SLANT

"Slant," to an article writer, means the emphasis given to those aspects of the story most likely to interest readers. It does not mean distorting the story or making it into a piece of propaganda. An article "slanted" to a particular audience in fact may be entirely free of controversy.

The more important you are as a writer, the more willing a magazine is to accept your slant, even though the slant may not exactly conform with what the editors want. When the old *Saturday Evening Post* asked C. S. Lewis to write an article on the right to happiness, he wrote back to say he would attempt the article, but he warned: "I may fail. . . . It would be impossible to discuss 'the right to happiness' without discussing a formula that is rather sacred to Americans about 'life, liberty and the pursuit of happiness.' I'd do so with respect. But I'd have to point out that it can only mean 'A right to pursue happiness by legitimate means,' i.e., 'people have a right to do whatever they have a right to do.' Would your public like this?" It was a fine distinction and one that the *Post* could accept.

• NARROWING THE FOCUS

A magazine editor once complained to writer Max Gunther that most writers submitting ideas to the magazine "don't think their ideas down to a narrow enough focus. The stuff is all too broad, too general. They've got to learn that magazines aren't encyclopedias." The first step toward developing an idea sense is to distinguish between an *idea* and a *subject area*. Too often the student settles for the latter.

A subject area is too big, too vague to be covered in a single article. You can't, in 1,500 to 3,000 words, deal intelligently with "Education in the United States," or "The Pollution Problem." You must, instead, move in on a single school devoted to training handicapped children. Or you must deal with subteen theft rings or with the group of grass-seed growers in the valley who burn off their fields each summer to "sanitize" them. And your base, even then, may be too broad.

Do not settle on "Driver Safety" as your idea. Instead, consider the premise that accidents are more the result of vehicle construction than driver error. Ralph Nader did this for his article in *The Nation* that grew into the book *Unsafe at Any Speed*.

Do not try to deal with so amorphous a topic as "The Oregon Coast." Narrow it down to "How You Can Spend a Weekend at the Coast for Less than $10," as one student did, selling what he wrote to a locally edited Sunday magazine. Do not write about "Jogging." Do as Bruce Handler did when, on his first try at writing an article, he sold a piece to the now defunct *This Week* magazine (for $500) on "New Hope for Heart Attack Victims." Or take the opposite view some now are taking: that "Jogging Can Kill You."

You shouldn't feel that narrowing the focus geographically necessarily limits the article's potential nationally. The local angle may be worth national attention because the story is typical or instructive or just plain interesting. Anyway, the focus does not have to be geographic. It can be subjective. Instead of writing about vegetable gardening (to cite one example), you can write about raising vegetables in a window box.

• DEVELOPING A THEME

As your idea evolves you might want to formalize it by reducing it to a sentence or two. You will be developing a theme. You should keep the theme in mind as you conduct your research and do your writing. As the weeks go by, it is easy to lose sight of what it was you were trying to say. You may want to refer to your stated theme several times while researching and writing the article, but you should be willing to change your theme as your research leads you to other conclusions.

As an exercise, you might want to pick out some articles by others and figure out the theme — the idea — behind them. Going through the 40th anniversary issue of *Esquire* (October 1973), for instance, you might settle on articles by Helen Lawrenson ("Latins Are Lousy Lovers"), Nora Ephron ("A Few Words About Breasts"), and Malcolm Muggeridge ("The Totemization of Sir Winston Churchill"). You would conclude that Lawrenson set out to explode a myth about Latin men. Ephron, you would find, makes the point that, no matter what anyone says, small breasts are an embarrassment to women. And Muggeridge, you would see, puts Winston Churchill into perspective as a not entirely admirable public figure. "Few men of action have been able to make a graceful exit at the appropriate time. . . . Power-addiction, like any other, becomes in the end incurable."

• HANGING IT ON A NEWS PEG

A news story answers who? what? where? when? why? and how? questions but usually none of them in any depth. An article is likely to take one of the questions — especially a who?, why?, or how? question — and thoroughly explore and answer it.

There had been news stories announcing the death of a once popular comic strip in 1973 and the death a few weeks later of another, but the why was only touched on. So the editor of the "Opinion" section of the Sunday Los Angeles *Times* asked this author, who had written previously on the subject, to do a 3,500-word feature putting speculation about the strips into some kind of context. Note how the opening ties the feature to the news:

> To borrow an oft-repeated line from the incredulous general in Beetle Bailey: "Now what?" First they kill off Terry and the Pirates, a comic strip so important that conversation from one of its characters once found its way into the Congressional Record. Then they announce that Smilin' Jack is getting his.
>
> To borrow another line from any number of comic-strip characters: "What the —?" What's happening to the strips?
>
> What's happening simply is that the adventure strips are going under. Humor strips are taking over. Of the 34 comic strips and panel cartoons run in the Los Angeles *Times*, for instance, only four can be classified as "adventure." And the adventure that is there is mostly soap opera.
>
> The villain (as always) is television, which offers up its adventure in a much less demanding form. You don't have to move your lips to follow the action on the screen.
>
> But there are other reasons for the plight of the adventure strips. . . .[5]

The feature detailed the reasons, then went back and traced the history of comic strips, from before the turn of the century, concluding that they have completed their cycle: from humor to adventure and back to humor.

What happens to the comic strips is not likely to seriously affect the lives of people, so not many publications rushed into print with interpretive articles on the subject. The Los Angeles *Times*, then, had an exclusive of sorts (although the feature was also digested and syndicated). But on news items with greater significance, especially when new angles continue to develop over a period of several weeks, all varieties of publications get on the bandwagon with their own interpre-

---

[5]Reprinted by permission of the Los Angeles *Times*.

Long Lines, published for employees of the Long Lines Department of American Telephone & Telegraph Co., took some 400 photographs when CBS staged its Ask President Carter call-in program in early 1977. This one by Ken Haas was one of several used to illustrate Mike Zeaman's article, "Connecting America with the President." You see it exactly as Haas turned it in to the editor, its black frame showing. The editor cropped it slightly to fit, eliminating the figure at the far right. The caption singled out senior operations clerk Phyllis Clarke, shown compiling call-volume data for later analysis "as network managers take note of the percentage of IMA (ineffective machine attempts) on the network's No. 4ESS machines."

tations. Bandwagon articles are all right provided they get into print before the public tires of the subject. And to really interest an editor, such ideas should promise points of view at least slightly different from the ones expressed in all the previous articles.

• COURTING CONTROVERSY

Whatever your point of view, it is possible, provided you present it convincingly, to find an audience for it among the thousands of periodicals that take freelance work. Your first inclination will be to match your ideology with a publication having a similar ideology, but you need not feel so limited. Many editors, out of a sense of fairness or simply because they know controversy builds circulation, are willing to give space to an unpopular point of view.

One of the values of the "My Turn" column in *Newsweek* is that it departs often from the safely liberal line of the remainder of the magazine. D. Keith Mano, novelist, film critic (for *Oui*), and columnist (for *National Review*), provides an example with "Cruel Lib," a gainsaying of the several liberation movements. Most writers for the popular press put these movements on a pedestal. Not Mano. Starting with two true stories — one about a man who turns gay and finds, because he is unattractive, that he is as out of place there as he was before as a straight; the other about a housewife who gives up her husband and children to, among other things, make "lopsided ashtrays at a Wednesday night ceramics class" and then ends up with a drinking problem — Mano then declares:

> It is an unattractive human truth, but every now and then someone should put it on record: most people — Christians used to acknowledge this fact without embarrassment — most people are not particularly talented or beautiful or charismatic. Set free to discover "the true self," very often they find nothing there at all. Men and women who determine "to do their own thing" commonly learn that they have little of note to do.

Yet, according to Mano, these people are "harassed" and "shamed" by liberation groups into giving up their traditional roles for more glamorous ones. "But there are times when it's more healthful to be frustrated than to have one's mediocrity confirmed in the light of common day."[6]

Mark Harris, who wrote the movie *Bang the Drum Softly*, came up with this idea: that following the news is a waste of time. He sold "The Last Article" to *The New York Times Magazine* (Oct. 6, 1974). It started off like this:

> I seldom read a newspaper, and you shouldn't read one, either; I seldom watch television; seldom pick up a popular magazine, though I read *Time* magazine almost every week when I lived in Hiroshima in 1957–'58. Last year a San Francisco professor said to me: "But how would you know about Watergate?" Come on, Leonard (I replied), a man or a woman of instinct knows about Watergate from history, from literature.

His friend could not accept the idea. People don't like to be told not to read newspapers, Harris pointed out. They are addicted to news-

---

[6]D. Keith Mano, "Cruel Lib," *Newsweek*, Sept. 8, 1975, p. 11.

papers and don't want anyone "tampering" with that addiction. They consider reading newspapers "a civic duty."

As the article progressed, Harris pointed out that "The news that really matters will reach us; if it really matters it forces itself upon us." And "We have permitted the world of the journalist to become more real to us than the world of our senses." And ". . . if you *must* buy a newspaper, don't read it. Save it. Read it in 10 years. You'll see how much you could have skipped. . . ."

Editors welcome controversy even when the controversy is contrived or inconsequential. Dave Anderson came up with a pleasantly arguable idea: that people who play in golf tournaments do best when they are not feeling up to par. They slow their tempo. Preoccupation with their illnesses relieves them somewhat from the pressure of the matches. When you feel lousy, Anderson concluded, double the bets. When your opponent shows up with an ailment, be wary. Illustrating his thesis with a collection of anecdotes involving sick match winners, Anderson produced "Beware the Ailing Golfer" for the February 1967 issue of *True*.

• SETTLING FOR THE MUNDANE

An article doesn't have to be controversial to sell. It may contain rather routine information, brought out clearly — that's the key word: *clearly* — by a writer willing to do some homework before sitting down to the typewriter. To write an article for *TWA Ambassador* and *Reader's Digest*, James McCrohan went through a directory of radio stations to find interesting and appropriate combinations of call letters. (Call letters start with "W" east of the Mississippi River and with "K" on the other side.) Among McCrohan's discoveries: WCAR in Detroit; KFOG in San Francisco, and WSUN in St. Petersburg. He also discovered WACO in Waco, Texas, a part of the country that ordinarily would have "K" stations. But, McCrohan told his readers, this one was established before the FCC drew up its W–K guidelines.

The idea can even be dull, provided the writer rewards the reader with interesting prose. "There are no dull subjects," H. L. Mencken said, "there are only dull writers."

Fred Dickenson came home one day to find that an electric-dishwasher overflow had completely soaked a hard-to-get Manhattan telephone directory. What to do to salvage it? Dickenson tried several procedures (including baking it) before finding one that worked. His

"How to Iron a Telephone Book" was good enough not only to make *The New Yorker* but also to appear in *The Informal Essay*, an anthology published by W. W. Norton.

> If you have been putting off ironing your telephone book, [he began] you need no longer hesitate. I can tell you how it's done. I recently ironed the Manhattan Directory — all eighteen hundred and thirty-six pages. This stimulating adventure had its beginning when. . . .

His advice included the fact that:

> The heat dial of the iron should be set for Cotton. Rayon is not hot enough, and Linen is apt to scorch around the edges, particularly if you get to watching for lady chiropractors, Arabian delicatessens, and the like.
>   Begin at the back. For some reason, it helps to think of yourself as on page 1836, rather than on page 1. . . .
>   . . . It is impossible to iron a wet telephone book quickly and still maintain a high standard of workmanship. There is no use trying to iron more than one page at a time. . . .

• WHEN FICTION ENTERS THE PICTURE

An idea for a light-hearted piece is likely to lead the article writer into the land of fiction. Maybe Rick Wolff really *did* go to a baseball game with a woman doctor, but surely the doctor's reading mental-disease symptoms into a coach's signals was part of the license a humor writer enjoys. The doctor is talking:

> ". . . He keeps touching parts of his body. First, he'll touch his cap, chest, shoulder, belt and . . . oh, my . . . his genitalia. Now I ask you if that behavior is not antisocial.
>   ". . . Listen to the man. He's talking incoherently, muttering to himself and keeps mumbling the same phrases. 'Humbabe, humbabe . . . .' "

Wolff, author of *What's a Nice Harvard Boy Like You Doing in the Bushes?* (Prentice-Hall, 1975) was able to sell the piece to the sports section of the New York *Times* (July 11, 1976, p. 25).

Some fiction can be included in a magazine article provided the reader is not fooled into thinking the fiction is fact. More about this later.

• IDEAS IN SEASON

Rare is the editor who can let Thanksgiving, Christmas, Valentine's Day, or the Fourth of July go by without an article in some way celebrating the occasion. "I receive over 200 manuscripts a week and only use a few," Darlene McRoberts of *Sunday Digest* told writer Clinton E. Parker, "but am always in need of good seasonal material." Seasonal articles at *Sunday Digest* "get special attention."

The *World Almanac* and other almanacs list the many holidays. If you want to do an article about a holiday, you should find a new angle and get your article off to the editor some months before the holiday arrives. *Better Homes and Gardens* likes seasonal material submitted a whole year in advance.

Research material, starting with encyclopedias, is abundant. Writer Parker, doing an article on "The Man Who Made Thanksgiving Possible" for *Pen* magazine, found 14 books on Thanksgiving listed in the 1974 edition of *Subject Guide to Books in Print*.[7]

Sometimes the seasonal feature writes itself. When Rep. M. G. Snyder (R–Ky.) sent out a letter to constituents in December 1975 saying that if Santa Claus were subject to the same federal regulations as everyone else, he would have "to retain a lawyer or receive executive clemency if he is to make his traditional Christmas visit on time," UPI got ahold of a copy and quoted liberally from it. It made a good pre-Christmas feature.

Some of Santa's transgressions, according to Rep. Snyder, are that he flies without certification by the Civil Aeronautics Board and without filing a flight plan, that he fails to equip his vehicle with seat belts and fit his reindeer with emission control devices, that he engages in unfair competition with the U.S. Postal Service, that he violates the Sherman Antitrust Act by maintaining a strict monopoly in his field, that he breaks Labor Department minimum wage and safety regulations (for instance, his toy shop elves don't wear hard hats). Representative Snyder in his letter further stated that Santa might be suspected of administering an unauthorized drug to make Rudolph's nose light up and that he probably does not declare as taxable income the cookies and milk left him at his various stops.

"It does give one pause to think and wonder just where our multitude of laws and regulations are taking us," the congressman wrote in good Republican tradition. It was a line good enough to serve as the ending for the UPI feature.

---

[7]Clinton E. Parker, "'Tis the Season for Seasonal Articles," *Writer's Digest,* December 1975, p. 44.

• SELLING JUST THE IDEA

It is possible to sell the raw idea to a magazine. *Playboy*, for instance, pays up to $250 for ideas. When he was a student, Jeff Clausen, now a company magazine editor for Crown Zellerbach Corporation, submitted an article to *Reader's Digest* on the dangers of hitchhiking. The magazine rejected the article as being too local but agreed to pay him $200 if it later ran an article on the subject. It did, and Clausen got his check.

But idea selling is rare in magazine and newspaper journalism. Editors would rather see completed manuscripts.

• WHEN COLLABORATION IS IN ORDER

You may come up with an idea that for one reason or another you can't develop alone. Then you turn to some kind of literary collaboration.

If one writer does the research (or provides all the information) and another writer does the actual writing, the byline will carry both names. Occasionally, for a double-bylined article both writers will research and write — perhaps in the interest of hurrying its completion. Often a double byline involves a husband–wife team.

A double-byline article can also result from an editor's accepting a manuscript based on a good idea but poorly researched or written. The editor turns it over to a staff writer for reworking.

When a writer comes up with an idea that depends upon a single interviewee's telling pretty much the whole story, the writer might make it an as-told-to article. The first byline names the interviewee. The second byline, which starts with the words "as told to," names the real writer. How the proceeds are divided depends upon what kind of deal the writer makes with the interviewee. If the interviewee stands to gain from the publicity, he may agree to relinquish any claim to payment made by the magazine.

In an as-told-to article, the real writer may merely polish a dictated or roughly written manuscript or he may actually pull the story from his collaborator through interviewing techniques. (This does not mean that every article based on interviewing is a true collaboration or carries two bylines.)

Another kind of collaboration involves the ghost-written article. This teams a celebrity or authority with a real writer willing to work anonymously. The real writer's reward is a percentage (if not all) of the payment. It should come as a shock to no writing student that behind any article or book by a politician or show business personality there lurks — a ghost.

Whether it is a co-written article, an as-told-to article, or a ghost-written article, the idea for it can come from the real writer or from the collaborator.[8]

• WRITER'S BLOCK

Writing can become an obsession. John Creasey at last count had written some 500 books, most of them mystery novels. Georges Simenon, after *his* 500 books (no wonder it's Georges rather than George), said, "When I don't write, I am sick." He once produced what *Time* (in 1965) called a "quite readable novel" in 25 hours. Isaac Asimov who, by age 55 (1975), had written 159 books and thousands of magazine articles and stories, grinds out 10,000 awesomely well chosen words every single day.

Financial considerations alone can be enough to keep a writer at work, Bruce Barton told how he operated: ". . . Picture me sitting at breakfast in the morning. As I sip my coffee, my wife across the table glances down at the floor and observes, 'Bruce, we really need a new dining room rug. This one is wearing through.' Right there I have the inspiration to write another article."

Writers like these apparently escape the ravages of Writer's Block. Other writers are not so lucky. They become bored. They grow lazy. They begin to tire. Their imagination fails them. They lose confidence.

Some writers convince themselves that conditions need to be just right before they can produce. They must be in the proper mood.

Novelist George Sand (1804–1876) scoffed at writers who produced only when they felt inspired. She sat down at her table each night at 10 and wrote 30 pages — in longhand; she wrote before the invention of the typewriter — and didn't stop until 5 in the morning.

"I am persuaded that most writers, like most shoemakers, are about as good one day as the next," says John Kenneth Galbraith,[9] the

---

[8]Part of the foregoing appeared in a different form in the author's "Kinds of Literary Collaboration," *Writer's Digest*, October 1968, p. 53.

"Why don't you write about me?"

economist who, though he stands tall in the field of the "dismal science," writes with a fine literary flair.

But even the most prolific writers face an occasional block. "There is no sense in trying to bull your way through when you're stuck on a passage — it means that somehow the facts don't fit," says Theodore H. White, the *Making of the President* man. "You have to knock off and go to bed, and if the subconscious doesn't arrange the facts, then you're nowhere."[10]

Novelist Joyce Carol Oates says her method for fighting Writer's Block is "to turn to something else, and in a short while a solution will suggest itself to me and I will try it." She adds: "Writer's block, I'm convinced, is a temporary paralysis of the imagination caused by the conviction, on an unconscious level, that what the writer is attempting is in some way fraudulent, or mistaken, or self-destructive."[11]

More often than not Writer's Block comes not because of some writing difficulty but because the idea behind the article is flawed.

Sprightly writing is useful. Adequate research is essential. But the idea is what really counts. Without a good idea to start with, one that will interest a sufficient number of readers, one that will keep the writer enthusiastic through weeks or months of work, all else in article writing is in vain.

[9]Quoted in "The Writing Life," *Writer's Digest*, March 1976, p. 5.

[10]Quoted in "They Say . . ." *The Writer*, February 1976, p. 3.

[11]Quoted in "The Writing Life," *Writer's Digest*, February 1976, p. 5.

CHAPTER 4

THE MARKET

Staff writers on newspapers and magazines don't agonize over markets. They understand their publications well enough to avoid certain subjects and concentrate on others. They do not have to talk price with each piece they produce. And they know that whatever they write will almost surely make it into print.

Freelancers are not so lucky. Every article represents a separate marketing problem. Every article faces a chance of total rejection. All those hours spent reading and interviewing and traveling and writing and rewriting and mailing can come to — nothing.

To further discourage the writer, the rejection occurs often without so much as a personal letter from the editor. By far the biggest percentage of rejected manuscripts come back with printed forms that go something like this: "Thank you for giving us a chance to consider the enclosed material. We are sorry to say it doesn't meet our current needs. . . ."

"Doesn't meet our current needs." What vagueness! And yet, not meeting needs is precisely what is wrong. The writer has not studied the magazine to determine what it is likely to run.

With so many manuscripts to consider and reject, few editors can afford to do anything more than send printed forms. Some editors have tried sending forms containing assorted printed reasons for rejection ("Overstocked at present," "Too localized," "Not in keeping with our editorial policy," "We have run similar material in the past," "We do not run poetry," etc.) and putting a check mark in front of those that apply, but that practice is not very helpful, either. Besides, it might encourage the writer to ask for elaboration.

When the manuscript shows promise that the writer may develop into someone who could write for the magazine, the editor may send a typed letter explaining why the manuscript was rejected and encouraging further submissions. When the manuscript really comes close to meeting the magazine's needs, the editor may suggest revising and resubmission.

One editor, Art Spikol of *Philadelphia Magazine*, was able to say in 1976 that he never sends out a rejection slip. All writers get letters, "and often I actually have something to say to them."

Of course, a letter can be more devastating than a printed form. Morton Walker, physician-turned-writer, tells of an editor of a medical magazine who, weary of the impossible manuscripts submitted to him, wrote back to one hopeful writer, "I cannot use your paper. You have written on it!"[1]

Perhaps the freelancer should count himself lucky that someone even bothered to read the article. Going through the "slush pile" has grown so expensive and the rewards so few that many editors have announced through the writer's magazines that they no longer look at unsolicited manuscripts.

The plight of the freelance writer has itself provided the nucleus of an idea for an article in *Publishers Weekly*. To console the freelancer, Margaret Bennett "announced" an Acceptance-of-the-Month Club. People were to buy memberships as Christmas gifts for their writer friends. "Each membership costs you little more than the price of the acceptance checks plus postage and a bribery fee for the participating editors." The year's membership started at Christmas with "A glowing acceptance from *Holiday* for a 5,000-word lead story on the writer's uniquely quaint and charming home town" and continued with acceptances each month. For instance, in May:

> This month of spring flowers brings an acceptance from the most cultivated hothouse variety magazine of them all — the *New Yorker*. Editor Shawn purchases a sensitive, introspective, symbolic short story about the author's miserable childhood. Shawn politely and deferentially requests the author's permission to remove the concluding three paragraphs, because they give the story a point and are, therefore, contrary to the *New Yorker*'s editorial policy.[2]

[1]Morton Walker, "The Medical Markets: What's Up, Doc?" *Writer's Digest*, January 1976, p. 19.

[2]Margaret Bennett, "The Acceptance of the Month Club," *Publishers Weekly*, Dec. 7, 1970, pp. 22, 23. Margaret Bennett is a pseudonym for two California freelance writers.

"His book was just rejected by a subsidy publisher."

• GETTING THE FEEL OF THE MARKET

As a freelancer, you stand a better chance of selling nonfiction (articles and features) than fiction (short stories), and you find a larger group of markets among the magazines than among newspapers and syndicates. This chapter will concentrate on magazines as a market for freelance writers.

• What's Not in a Name?

A writer cannot assume that a magazine's name really defines its perimeters. *The Iron Worker* name, for instance, does not tell you that you have a company magazine (published by the Lynchburg Foundry in Virginia) for customers and opinion leaders interested in "Virginia-related articles about American history" (for which it pays up to $600).

You cannot tell from the name *Liberty* that you have a magazine published by the Seventh-day Adventists to promote separation of church and state. And what is the non-reader of skin magazines to make of the name *Genesis*? Someone in the subsidiary-rights department of David McKay, the book publisher, obviously misjudged the magazine (it sounded like a religious magazine to him, he said) when he sold an excerpt from then Senator Walter F. Mondale's book *The Accountability of Power*. According to the Senator's lawyer, Mondale found "publication of his work in this magazine abhorrent and offensive to himself, to his family and his constituents," and so the Senator sued his publisher.[3] *Genesis* drew attention to itself later when it filed a $1,000,000 libel suit against Mondale and hired Elizabeth Ray, the nontypist friend to Congressmen, to cover the 1976 Republican Convention as a reporter.

• Magazine Directories and Writers' Magazines

Any number of directories of magazines carry information that can help familiarize freelancers with the various markets. *Writer's Market*, which is published yearly by *Writer's Digest* and has more than 4,000 listings, proves to be the most useful. But the writer should not conclude that this book exhausts the market possibilities. The listings here depend upon editors' willingness to fill out forms supplied by the publisher. Some editors don't want to be bothered. Some are not on *Writer's Market*'s list of contacts. Still, the book is a good starting point. It lists names of publications and editors, addresses, intended audiences, editorial policies, kinds of articles wanted, lengths preferred, pay rates, the rights that are purchased, and other information.

The Writer's Handbook, published (less frequently) by *The Writer*, also carries market information.

A vital supplement to the directories is the monthly *Writer's Digest* magazine, with its current market lists, and the other important writer's magazine, *The Writer*. *Writer's Yearbook*, also published by *Writer's Digest*, is useful, too. *Folio* magazine, though published for magazine editors and managers rather than freelancers, is useful in that it discusses industry problems.

[3]"Sen. Mondale Seeks Damages from McKay for Excerpt," *Publishers Weekly*, April 26, 1976, p. 18.

You can also find information about markets by reading the "Publisher's Editorial Profile" for each entry in *Standard Rate & Data Service*.

• Reading the Ads

You can pick up additional information about magazines by reading the ads they place in advertising magazines like *Advertising Age*. Those ads tell media buyers in agencies things about the subscribers that the article writer will find useful, too. "For every dollar you spend in *Co-ed* you reach more heavy users of grooming products than in any other teenage magazine," says one full-page ad in a 1976 issue of *Advertising Age*. *Ladies' Home Journal* "puts a woman's world of information and ideas into her hands every month — from mothering to movies and from crafts to best sellers," says another. "Today's new breed of sportsmen," says *Field & Stream* in an ad in the same issue of *Advertising Age*, "are better educated, have higher incomes, and more of them than ever before are younger and hold white-collar positions."

Direct-mail advertising to media buyers in agencies carries additional information.

• Magazines at First Hand

The best way to study magazines as markets is to study the magazines themselves; better yet, to become a regular reader.

You should pay attention not only to what the magazines run in their editorial columns but also to the nearby ads. You can bet that the agencies placing the ads found out all they could about the people who would be reading them and tailored the copy to appeal directly to those readers.

You will find additional hints about the readers and what interests them in the published letters to the editor.

The masthead, which accompanies the table of contents, yields helpful information. From the masthead you would pick the *editorial offices* address to write to, not the business, circulation, printing, or advertising offices, which may be in other cities. You would also select a person's name to write to — the name of the editor — so you don't have to write to simply "The Editor." Sometimes the masthead offers special instructions to writers. *R/C Modeler*, a hefty magazine for people who like to fly radio-controlled model airplanes, says: "Editorial contributions are welcomed by R/C Modeler Magazine, but cannot be considered unless guaranteed exclusive. Manuscript must be accompanied by return postage and any material accepted for publication is subject to such editorial revision as is necessary, in our discretion, to meet the requirements of this magazine. Editorial material is selected on the basis of general interest to the radio-control enthusiast, and the publisher assumes no responsibility for accuracy of content. The opinions stated in published material are those of the individual author and do not necessarily reflect those of the publisher. R/C Modeler Corporation assumes no responsibility for loss or damage of editorial contributions. Upon acceptance, payment will be made within 30 days of publication, at our existing current rate, which covers all authors' rights, title to, and interest in, the material mailed including, but not limited to, photos, drawings, and art work, which shall be considered as text. Submission of the manuscript to R/C Modeler Magazine expresses a warranty, by the author, that the material is in no way an infringement upon the rights of others."

A number of magazines offer to send brochures or folders spelling out editorial requirements. *The Mother Earth News* sends out 14 legal-size pages of information for would-be writers, much of it going beyond mere requirements for that magazine. Some excerpts: "It's amazing how many 'how to' articles we get from people who don't know 'how to.' " ". . . remember that you're communicating directly to *ONE* single individual who is exactly as intelligent as you are." "*Every paragraph of every article should be treated as a little story all its own.*"

Here's an article opening *The Mother Earth News* liked:

> If you're a passably-fair guitar player looking for a way to make some extra bread, look no further . . . because I'm going to tell you exactly how I use *my* guitar to clear better than $40 almost anytime I feel like conducting a pleasant, four-hour-long workshop.

"This is a tough lead paragraph to ignore," the magazine explains, "(especially if you're looking for a way to pick up a few extra dollars, and who isn't these days?) . . . and, once read, it all but grabs the reader by the scruff of the neck and *throws* him or her into the paragraphs that follow."

Signature's two pages of "Editorial Requirements" describe its typical reader as "a Diners Club member, a businessman, urban, affluent, well traveled and young (average age, 39)." The mailing points out that the magazine uses "upbeat" travel pieces (example: a sportsman travels to New Zealand in quest of the ultimate trout experience), personality sketches, articles dealing with current issues (example: the fight against noise pollution), articles on business (example: corporate head-hunting), articles on eating and drinking, articles on sports, articles on entertainment, and humor pieces (example: a spoof on the wood–metal tennis-racket controversy). ". . . We pay a base rate of $400 for a 1,500-word piece. We rarely ask a writer to handle the photography also, though if he has photos of the subject we will consider them for use. Picture stories of support are usually assigned to photographers we have worked with in the past. Queries from writers should be in the form of outlines which state fairly concisely the story concept and premise."

Boys' Life used to send out an "Information for Contributors" booklet that reproduced some "Article Leads We Liked" as well as "These Leads Made Us Shudder." One of the good leads:

He was a wiry, spade-bearded young adventurer, as skilled with the sword as he was with the saw. Partly because of his sword, but mostly because of proficiency with carpenter's tools, Spain conquered the New World when she did — yet, today, the name of this man who had so much to do with the success of the conquest is hardly known. [James Norman, "The Navy that Crossed Mountains."]

And some of the bad ones:

Say, Fellas. . . .

* * * * *

It was the day the Boy Scouts of the four towns of Leeds County were to meet at the four corners. . . .

* * * * *

Alarmists who are upset over teenagers and think of them only as juvenile delinquents. . . .

The mailer suggested that *Boys' Life* seldom buys manuscripts that come with cover letters that go like this:

I read this to the boys in my class . . . and they all thought it should be published.

• CATEGORIES OF MAGAZINES

Any bound publication that comes out regularly fits the definition of a magazine, and there are tens of thousands of them. No one of the several directories lists them all, although *Ulrich's International Periodicals Directory*, with its 60,000 entries, comes close. A few hundred magazines find space on the newsstands. Most go to subscribers by mail.

• General-Interest Magazines

The demise of magazines like the original *Saturday Evening Post*, the original *Liberty, Collier's, Woman's Home Companion, American Magazine, Look*, and others (we won't count *Life* because it was largely staff-written) signals that the era of the general-interest magazine is over. Freelancers turn more and more to the multiplying specialized magazines as places to sell to.

The remaining general-interest magazines themselves tend to narrow their focus. Some of them could almost be classified as specialized magazines. Conversely, the specialized magazines tend to branch out. *Christopher Street*, a monthly for homosexuals, was in 1976 calling itself "The Gay Magazine for the Whole Family."

Thus a writer with an idea for a magazine article may find that the old categories of "general-interest magazines" and "specialized magazines" no longer hold. But what if you come up with an idea that seems more appropriate for a general-interest than a specialized audience? Must you accept the premise that the general-interest market is moribund? No!

The Saturday Evening Post, for instance, lives on as a monthly rather than a weekly, in the Midwest rather than in the East, with an emphasis on the old values rather than the new. *Reader's Digest* lives on, as strong as ever. Only *TV Guide* outcirculates it nationally. (*Reader's Digest* still has the largest world-wide circulation.) *Pageant* continues to buy material that falls in the general-interest category.

• Quality or Class Magazines

While some of the general-interest magazines offer articles that match the quality of articles published anywhere else, it is helpful to set up a separate category for magazines of general interest that appeal mainly to persons of above-average intelligence and income levels. The first magazine that comes to mind is *The New Yorker*. But its level of sophistication, its insistence on accuracy, its penchant for fine, if sometimes casual, writing make it the least likely newsstand magazine for beginners to crack.

Two other quality magazines, *Harper's* and *The Atlantic* (monthlies, where *The New Yorker* is a weekly), are more likely markets for beginners, although the standards are demanding there, too. Once *The Atlantic*, published in Boston, seemed more literary than *Harper's*, published in New York, and *Harper's* seemed more devoted to the social sciences, but these distinctions probably no longer hold. And no longer do these magazines give so much space to fiction. *The New Yorker*, on the other hand, continues to run a high ratio of fiction to nonfiction.

The weekly *Saturday Review*, once almost solely a magazine of book reviews, now runs a high percentage of articles, most of them on cultural subjects.

Magazines like *Psychology Today, Scientific American*, and the venerable *National Geographic*, also quality magazines, move closer to the specialized-magazines category, although they tailor their articles to be understood by the lay reader as much as by the reader with special training or background.

• In-flight Magazines

Magazines given out to airlines passengers provide another market for general-interest articles. A single organization, East/West Network, Inc., with editorial offices in New York (488 Madison Ave.) and Los Angeles (5900 Wilshire Blvd.), publishes nine of them (for United, Eastern, Delta, Hughes Airwest, Continental, Pacific Southwest [PSA], Alleghany, Ozark, and Pan Am), plus two motel magazines, all of which use freelance material. East/West buys an estimated 500 articles a year. Webb Publishing Co., St. Paul, also edits in-flight magazines.

Richard Cramer in *Writer's Digest* (March 1975) reports that, when he was editor of United Air Lines's *Mainliner*, he received queries from writers offering to write articles on skyjackings, plane crashes, and unhappy experiences with travel accommodations. "Nothing turns editors [of in-flight magazines] off more than getting queries about death, unhappy vacations, or chaos. That's not to say this audience doesn't care about such topics; but not when they're at 30,000 feet and they've just hit an air pocket."

Because business people account for 70 percent of airlines passengers, the magazines have tailored their content away from straight travel pieces toward business/entertainment features, Cramer reports. Of course, some travel material is still run, but it always involves cities served by the airlines.

This example may give you a better idea of in-flight magazine content. The January 1977 issue of *Sundancer*, the Hughes Airwest magazine, carries Charles Hillinger's article, "The Mormon Files," which discusses the interest in geneology fostered by the Church of Jesus Christ of Latter-day Saints. A short note at the end of the article mentions that the airline serves Salt Lake City.

• News Magazines

Time, Newsweek, and *U.S. News & World Report* do not provide much of a market for freelancers, but the upstart *New Times* does. It is not really a news magazine. It is a left-leaning bi-weekly that advertises itself as "The mouse that roars." One of its most talked-about articles was "The Ten Dumbest Congressmen," an article that named them.

Publisher George A. Hirsch said that he wanted the magazine to be "one that would combine the timeliness of a traditional news magazine with the in-depth coverage and the personalized writing of the feature monthlies, a magazine that could speak to today's audience — the people who came of age in the sixties — with the liveliness of the best of the old underground papers and the professionalism of the established media."

In many respects, *The National Observer*, which died in 1977, was a news magazine, even though it came in a newspaper rather than a magazine format. A weekly, like *Time, Newsweek*, and *U.S. News & World Report, The National Observer* took a feature approach to the news. It did not attempt to cover all the news.

• Newspaper Magazine Sections

Parade, Family Weekly, and *Weekend Magazine* (Canada), appearing as magazine sections in newspapers, serve as national markets in that they are published outside the newspapers and then syndicated to them. But many of the larger newspapers — and some of the smaller ones, too — publish their own magazine sections in addition to or in place of the syndicated supplements. These are for writers with purely local stories to tell.

The typical locally edited magazine section contains personality sketches of local residents, travel and historical pieces, think pieces, and articles on recreational facilities, cultural events, gardening, and business ventures — all with local angles. Some branch out into general-interest areas.

The most prestigious of the locally edited magazine sections with a national base is *The New York Times Magazine*, which provides background material for national news. With a pay scale of between $850 and $1,000, *The New York Times Magazine* ranks as one of the nation's best markets for freelancers, provided they have the experience and skill to write for the magazine's highly educated audience.

Freelancers look upon national newspapers like *The Christian Science* *Monitor, The National Observer, National Enquirer, National Star,* and *Grit* as magazines, too, because they run more feature material than straight news stories.

• City Magazines

Philadelphia, Boston, Washingtonian, Cleveland, San Francisco, Los Angeles, and other city magazines blossomed with the death of general-circulation magazines. All of them, even those that pride themselves on exposés, offer "survival" articles for high-income readers threatened by big-city problems. Entertainment articles are also a staple. The most noticed, although not the earliest, of the magazines is *New York*, a "new journalism" publication, arising from the ashes of the New York *Herald Tribune*, where it was a magazine section.

When Australian press lord Rupert Murdoch bought *New York* in 1977, a number of upper staff members resigned, but Murdoch, who had been associated with newspapers dealing in sensation, assured staffers, readers, and advertisers that the magazine would undergo no radical changes. It would, however, cut back on its emphasis on national affairs and return to more emphasis on New York City matters. "We'll get back to what *New York* was intended to be by Mr. [Clay] Felker," Murdoch said.

Although it already had a respectable circulation outside New York

City, *New York* took its lively editorial philosophy to Los Angeles in 1976 to establish a sister publication, *New West*. Dealing with San Francisco as well as Los Angeles (cities that already had city magazines), *New West* was more a regional than a city magazine. The idea of regional magazines seemed to be catching on.[4] In another part of the country, *Texas Monthly Magazine*, established three years earlier, was already widely respected for its in-depth articles. It was directed to an upper middle-class audience numbering 100,000. The magazine said it was for Texans "in and out of the state."

The growth of city and regional magazines is welcomed by writers interested in producing local material not likely to command the attention of people outside their areas.

• Religious Magazines

Leola Archer in *Reader's Digest* told of a writer's being rejected by a religious publication. Thinking the rejection came as a result of using the word "darn" in the conversation of one of her characters, the writer rewrote her story and resubmitted it. "I have cut the 'darn' out . . . I hope you can use it now." The editor wrote back: "We do not wish to appear irreverent, but if you cut the hell out of this story we still could not use it." The writer had underestimated the sophistication of the market she had chosen.

Religious magazines, like any group of specialized magazines, vary widely as to what they will accept for publication. And even when you subdivide them, you can't assume a sameness. Protestant religious magazines, for instance, range from "fundamentalist" to social-activist. And even when you stay at one end of the spectrum, there are some deep differences, as among those that promote the charismatic movement in Protestantism (*Logos Journal*) and those that are more traditionally evangelistic (*Decision Magazine*).

Some religious magazines are not much more than fraternal magazines for the sponsoring denominations. Others, like *The Christian Century*, or its Catholic counterpart, *Commonweal*, deal with religious as well as secular controversy and exert influence far beyond their modest circulations.

[4]Michael Putney, "Dead Aim at the New West," *The National Observer*, July 24, 1976, p. 6.

Within a single denomination, as within the Roman Catholic Church, you will find magazines widely separated in their beliefs and interests.

The *Adventist Yearbook* of the Seventh-day Adventist Church lists more than eighty English language publications and hundreds published in foreign countries. "A number of these magazines pay fairly well for freelance pieces," says Dave Schwantes, instructor at Walla Walla College, who writes for them.

The *Catholic Press Directory* lists more than 500 Catholic newspapers, magazines, and book publishers.

One of the biggest denominational magazines is *A.D.* a merging (in 1972) of *United Church Herald*, which was published by the United Church of Christ, and *Presbyterian Life*. *A.D.* delves more deeply into social matters than, say, *The Pentecostal Evangel*. *A. D.* comes in two editions: one for Congregationalists, one for Presbyterians. Some of the content of the two editions overlaps.

One of the biggest religious magazines cutting across denominational lines is *The Christian Herald*. A more scholarly magazine of this type is *Christianity Today*. Both would be considered conservative from a theological as well as a social standpoint.

The following names will give you some idea of the variety of magazines falling under the "Religious Magazines" heading: *The Christian Athlete, Evangelizing Today's Child, Lutheran Women, Moody Monthly* (the name comes from the name of a bible college, not from a state of mind), *Today's Christian Mother*, and *The War Cry* (published by the Salvation Army).

So active a market do these magazines make that book publishers bring out how-to-do-its and several organizations sponsor writers' conferences just for Christian writers.

• Men's Magazines

Can't you just see *Playboy*'s top editors in the 1970s coming solemnly to their decision to enter the pubic-hair age? Meanwhile, imitators like *Penthouse* were springing up everywhere, doing their damnedest to outshow the original. *Playboy* itself had to launch a more raunchy competitor called *Oui*, a magazine appealing to a younger age group than *Playboy*'s.

Hustler Magazine, a late entry into the market, made a prurient appeal to dirty-T-shirt/beer-drinking types. It said in 1976 that it wanted "hard-hitting, exposé type articles . . . all submissions should be in a simple, straightforward style that is easily read and not overly academic. The tone should be irreverent and amusing."

Playboy managed to grab headlines when, during the 1976 Presidential campaign, it published an interview with candidate Jimmy Carter, who confessed to lusting after women and when, after the election, it published an interview with UN ambassador Andrew Young, who called Presidents Ford and Nixon, among others, "racists."

The men's magazines (skin-magazine division) like to point to the thoughtful articles they carry on topics of significance. "What Magazine Had the Nerve to Publish These News-Making Articles?" *Penthouse* asked in an ad headline in a 1975 issue of [*More*]. There followed a brief summary of 11 articles, including Harrison Salisbury's "Failure of the Press" and David Brower's "The Last Days on Earth," a warning of ecological disaster. Who could deny that *Penthouse*, *Playboy*, and the others run worthwhile articles? But who would argue that these articles are what give these magazines their wide appeal? Still the skin magazines do represent a good market — possibly the most lucrative market — for controversy and articles of the essay type.

In addition to the skin magazines, the men's magazine group in-

"Your last issue was thoughtful, relevant, penetrating, courageous, and worthwhile. Bingle, you're fired!"

cludes a number of adventure and hunting and fishing magazines.

Probably the most respected man's magazine is *Esquire*, but *Esquire* is more than that. With its emphasis on social, political, and literary matters, it probably belongs in the quality-magazine group and appeals almost as much to women as to men. It was not always so. It took many years before *Esquire* was finally included among those magazines indexed in *Readers' Guide to Periodical Literature*.

• Women's Magazines

Women's magazines range from those that do little more than give kitchen advice to those at the farthest edges of liberation. Some don't use the mails at all, counting on women going out to the grocery stores to pick them up. Some devote themselves almost exclusively to glamour; and some do that but with only teenagers in mind. Several took their cue from *Playboy: Cosmopolitan*, and later *Viva* and *Playgirl Magazine*. Two of the big ones, *McCall's* and *Ladies' Home Journal*, pride themselves that some of their material deals with intellectual matters. So, for that matter, does some of the material in *Redbook, Good Housekeeping, Family Circle*, and *Woman's Day*.

In volume alone, *Good Housekeeping* looks like an excellent market for writers. As the magazine says in its trade advertising, it offers "Hundreds more editorial pages each year than any other woman's magazine."

Mademoiselle and *Glamour* appeal to career-oriented young women, with *Mademoiselle* taking the more sophisticated approach.

Ms., the most vibrant and controversial of the important women's magazines, has mellowed somewhat since its 1972 launching. Like many magazines based on a cause, this one has broadened its appeal. It likes articles observing new lifestyles for women and chronicling women's changing roles.

In 1977 *Ms.* enjoyed a circulation of more than 500,000, but, according to *Newsweek*, Gloria Steinem, president, at a birthday party for the magazine, said that she felt "an odd mixture of elation and celebration that we have survived and prospered and grown for five years — and seriousness sometimes bordering on despair of how far we have to go."

• Shelter Magazines

If you have an interest in houses, landscaping, gardening, interior decorating, gracious living, and home-centered activities, your market may be a shelter magazine like *Better Homes and Gardens* or *House Beautiful*. *Better Homes and Gardens* tends to cover how-to aspects, while *House Beautiful* tends to merely inspire. Like most shelter magazines, *Better Homes and Gardens* does not mind moving out into the areas of travel, health, finance, and even entertainment.

One of the most successful of the shelter magazines is a regional — *Sunset*, but it is mostly staff-written.

• Confession Magazines

Jean Jackson in *The Writer* (May, 1975) reported, after 20 years of writing for them, that the confession magazines were in "a state of confusion." They were not as good a market as in the past. She traces the problem to the "conglomerates who have bought out many of the confession magazines."

The standard "sin, suffer, and repent" formula seems to be giving way to a formula that allows greater flexibility in the story line. This market also buys service pieces similar to those in the women's magazines. But you should remember that your readers here belong to the lower to lower-middle classes.

• Farm Magazines

You can get some idea of the variety of farm magazines from a *New Yorker* cartoon by Jack Ziegler. He shows a newsstand set in a farming community. The dealer stands behind his magazines, pipe in hand, dressed as a farmer. Among the many magazines on display are these: *True Cow Stories, Spinach Review, Tractor 'Toons, Eggtime, Squash Jokes, Today's Hay, This Week in Broccoli, National Review of Wheat*, and *Goats in the News*. If you look through a listing of farm publications you will find that Ziegler's list is not too far afield.

In addition to general farm magazines like *Farm Journal, The American Farmer, The Progressive Farmer*, and *Successful Farming*, all markets for freelancers who really understand farming, you will find specialized farm magazines covering specific crops, dairy farms, livestock, poultry, and other areas. In addition there are many local farm publications you can contribute to.

• Sports Magazines

Sports Illustrated, established by the Time/Life organization only in 1954, enjoys the distinction of being the most important sports magazine in the country. A weekly, it is almost as much a news magazine as a sports-features magazine. When it started it emphasized participant sports, but gradually shifted to spectator sports. It welcomes contributions for regional editions as well as for the entire issue.

WomenSports, started in 1974 by tennis star Billie Jean King and her husband Larry, covers the sports women participate in or watch. Magazines dealing with tennis cropped up everywhere in the 1970s to accompany the broadening interest in that sport. Other magazines deal exclusively with every one of the other sports, as well as hunting and fishing and other outdoor activities. *Writer's Market* lists some 140 magazines under its "Sport and Outdoor" category.

• Trade Journals

Here is a place in American journalism where the old criticism of advertiser dominance or intimidation of the editorial side still has some validity. It is not unheard of, even today, for a trade magazine to notify a potential advertiser that an article mentioning him is scheduled. Wouldn't he want to consider advertising in that issue? And some trade journals encourage writers to work into their articles the names of equipment manufactured by the magazine's advertisers. These magazines often are read as much for their advertising as for their editorial content. Some do not charge subscription rates; called "controlled circulation" magazines, they go out to "subscribers" free, provided those subscribers belong to the trade or profession covered.

But you would be wrong to assume that all — or even most — trade magazines exist only to sell space to advertisers. Many of them maintain the same high standards we associate with other segments of the

"But *Southern Stationer and Office Outfitter* bought my article. Do I still get a 'C'?"

magazine industry. Not a few prod the industries they serve to raise standards, to modernize, to operate more ethically. One of the strengths of *Advertising Age*, for instance, is its willingness to editorialize against unethical advertising practices and ridicule shoddy advertising campaigns.

Ron Lovell, who for a number of years worked as a writer for several McGraw-Hill trade journals and who now teaches at Oregon State University, tells of the time he stumbled onto a story about faulty electrical connectors made, it happened, by an advertiser in his journal. His magazine, *Electronics*, broke the story anyway and — for a time — lost the advertiser. Another of the McGraw-Hill magazines, *Electrical World*, came down hard on price fixing in the industry, and enough advertisers withdrew that the magazine almost died. Fortunately, McGraw-Hill thought enough of the magazine to keep it alive through some lean years; it has since come back to full and profitable size. A magazine with less backing might not be expected to stand up so firmly to real or implied advertiser pressure.

One of the most outspoken of the trade journals — *Time* calls it a "muckraking journal" — is *Overdrive*, "The Voice of the American Trucker." It documents corruption in the trucking industry, like abuses of the International Brotherhood of Teamsters' pension fund. "In a racket-infested, violent industry, maverick *Overdrive* (circ. 56,000) speaks with high-tonnage authority," *Time* noted in 1975.

Journalists who work for general publications watch the trade journals. What appears there may provide the basis for an article appealing to readers removed from the trade. *Aviation Week & Space Technology* among others often finds itself quoted in newspapers and general-circulation magazines.

Several large chains dominate the trade-magazine industry, including Cahners Publishing Company, Chilton Company, Dun-Donnelley Publishing Corp., Harcourt Brace Jovanovich, Inc., Penton-IPC, McGraw-Hill, Inc., and, in Canada, Maclean Hunter Ltd., and Southam Business Publications Limited. But magazines that belong to a chain have their own editors and, usually, their own editorial policies.

Not all trade magazines look at freelance submissions. Their editors may feel that the field covered is too technical for an outsider to deal with. But most do buy from outside, and some are eager enough to hear from freelancers that they advertise in the writer's magazines for contributions, or send letters out to teachers of article writing asking for student-written articles and even offering to make assignments.

You'll find the most current listing of trade journals in *Business Publication Rates & Data* (Standard Rate and Data Service, Inc. publishers), a regularly-issued publication available in big libraries and major advertising agencies and agencies specializing in industrial advertising. The information in this directory is chiefly of interest to advertising people, but one paragraph under each entry, "Publisher's editorial statement," will help you assess the magazine as a market for your writing. The "Market Classification" section in the back of the directory carries the names of all the magazines in any business category you may be interested in. Additional editorial information about a number of the magazines will be found in *Writer's Market*.

To cite a few of the trade-magazine markets: *Fuel Oil News*, which goes to retail fuel-oil dealers, uses interview articles involving dealers and articles describing unusual installations; *American Drycleaner*, for professional drycleaners, uses articles on, among other things, sales programs, diversification, customer relations, and dry-cleaning methods; *Nation's Restaurant News*, which circulates to executives of big and chain-owned restaurants, uses articles about new kinds of restaurants, personality sketches, even humor, provided it relates to food service.

You are most likely to find trade magazines in the offices of companies belonging to the trades represented by the magazines. Libraries carry some of them. You won't find them on newsstands.

You may have to send away for sample copies. Some editors are willing to send samples to writers requesting them. Increasingly, these magazines — and magazines in all other categories — expect writers to pay for the samples. Send the single-copy price to the circulation department.

• Company Magazines

A likely place for freelancers to make their first sales is to the magazines published by the companies they work for or the colleges they attended. Company magazines that serve an outside rather than purely an inside audience — magazines like *Ford Times*, *Small World* (Volkswagen), *Industrial Progress* (Goodyear), and *The Furrow* (John Deere & Co.) — buy from freelancers not necessarily connected with the sponsoring company. That company magazines exist to do a public relations job for their sponsors affects the approach the articles should take.

Gebbie House Magazine Directory, published every few years, lists and describes some 4,000 publications, many of them markets for freelance writers. *The Journal of Organizational Communication* and *IABC News*, both published by the International Association of Business Communicators, provide insight into the problems of running company publications.

• Fraternal Magazines

When your article involves members or projects of fraternal organizations, you have a potential market in magazines that serve these organizations — magazines like *The Rotarian*, *The Elks Magazine*, *The Kiwanis Magazine*, *The Lion*, and *The American Legion Magazine*. Such magazines are also interested in subjects that go beyond members and activities of the organization.

• Magazines for Blacks

Some 20 magazines in the United States direct themselves primarily to black audiences, and many of them owe a debt to John H. Johnson, the founder (in 1945) of *Ebony*, a general-interest magazine patterned after the then 10-year-old *Life*. *Ebony* was a pioneer in catering to the pride and aspirations of black readers. The magazine today appeals mainly to middle-class readers. *Essence*, a recent entry, appealed at first to fashion-conscious black women, but broadened its base to include "black awareness" and the interests all women have.

About 300 newspapers in the United States direct themselves to primarily black audiences. Included are the Amsterdam *News*, a weekly published in Harlem; the Chicago *Defender*, a daily; the Atlanta *World*, also a daily; the Baltimore *Afro-American*, a semiweekly with several regional editions outside Baltimore; and the San Francisco *Sun-Reporter*, a weekly.

• Opinion Magazines

Most of the opinion magazines of any consequence cluster at the left of the political spectrum. Two of the best-known are *The New Republic*, now on slick paper, and *The Nation*, after all these years still struggling to survive on newsprint. *The Nation*, published in New York, is less forgiving of the establishment than *The New Republic*, published in Washington, D.C.

These and similar markets do not pay much, but writers like to appear in them because of the prestige they can earn among an elite of similar thinkers. That the general-interest magazines have taken up many of the causes of the left-leaning opinion magazines (*The New Yorker*'s "Talk of the Town" section some weeks could just as well be the editorials opening up *The New Republic*) removes part of their reason for being and makes their struggle for subscribers all the more frustrating.

Easily the most readable of the opinion magazines, because it gives space to writers who delight in style as much as dogma, is William F. Buckley's slick-paper *National Review*. It is far over on the right, pretty much by itself.

Occasionally one of these magazines runs an article with a stand that, for its readership, is unpopular, as when *National Review* ran an article by Steve Allen. But mostly the opinion magazines are predictable. None of them is likely to adopt the policy of *Monocle*, the defunct satirical magazine: "The views of our contributors, no matter how conflicting and contradictory, are the views of the editors."

They are surprisingly receptive to student work. It is not true that you have to have academic credentials to appear in *National Review*, *The New Republic*, *The Nation*, *The Progressive*, or other opinion magazines.

Commentary, the highbrow opinion magazine published by the American Jewish Committee, prides itself on uncovering new talent. Essay articles on political and social matters especially interest the editors here. *Commentary* is not doctrinaire.

Commentary and another magazine to which it has been compared, *The Public Interest*, are said to be "neo-conservative." Irving Kristol, co-editor of *The Public Interest*, defines neo-conservatism as a political philosophy that is sympathetic to social reform but wary of bureaucracy. It welcomes change, provided the change is gradual.[5]

• Alternative Publications

The "underground press," after an explosive start in the 1960s, makes less of an impact today, but some of its philosophy lives on in the many small- to medium-circulation magazines that serve as alternatives to the traditional slick-paper publications. And the magazines of this genre that started off with narrow interests and modest formats have themselves turned slick and catholic. Look at what has happened to *Rolling Stone* and those two publications devoted to press criticism: *More* and *Columbia Journalism Review*.

Students find *The Mother Earth News* with its 160,000 circulation a likely market among the alternative publications (it buys up to 200

[5] For a more thorough definition, see Irving Kristol, "What Is a 'Neo-Conservative'?" *Newsweek*, Jan. 19, 1975, p. 17.

manuscripts a year, but writers find it is slow to report its decisions). "We're the only publication that recognizes that a New Age of decentralized, grow-your-own, work-for-yourself, build-your-own-home living is upon us," editor John Shuttleworth told the editors of *Writer's Market*. He offers this advice to writers: The magazine "Does not want to see anything trite in the 'I grew an organic garden successfully' vein, or anything preachy. Our readers want to know how to do things themselves, not how someone else takes an ego trip."

• Other Specialized Magazines

The list goes on and on. There are magazines specifically directed to people interested in art, astrology, automobiles, airplanes, business, children and youth, conservation, crime, drama, eating and drinking, education, fiction, films, health and medicine, history, hobbies, humor, the media, the military, music, photography, poetry, politics, retirement, science, social science, and unions. There are even magazines for dope smokers.

No writer should attempt to write for any of these specialized magazines unless he knows the specialty at least as well as the average reader. The editor can quickly spot a phony.

• PICKING YOUR LEVEL

Teachers often advise their students to start with small magazines and work their way up. But Hayes B. Jacobs, who writes the "New York Market Letter" column for *Writer's Digest*, says, "I don't recommend that anyone *start* with minor markets. . . . Working steadily for the less demanding minor publications is, of course, the only thing for those with limited abilities and energies. For others, years of work in the minor leagues affords only a limited chance to test yourself, to see how really good you can be. Suppose Edison had tried only to make a better candle!"

He adds: ". . . *Listen to me! Listen*: If your work has made the rounds of all the top markets, and nobody has taken an interest, *then* try the minor markets."[6]

[6]Hayes B. Jacobs, "Freelance at Work," *Writer's Market '76*, Writer's Digest, Cincinnati, 1975, p. 13.

• The Filler Market

A way to start selling to the major magazines — and smaller magazines, too — is to do fillers or short pieces for regular departments. *Essence* likes to see pieces from beginners for its "Essence Women" or "Bring It Down Front" sections. When these show promise, the magazine encourages writers to try full-scale acticles. *Commentary* likes new writers to try book reviews. A number of magazines invite short personal-experience articles from their readers. *McCall's*, for instance, offers $50 for each 150-word "Survival in the Suburbs" item.

Reader's Digest remains the best-known true-anecdote market, but there are many others. *Catholic Digest*, like *Reader's Digest*, has several filler categories, paying up to $50 per item. *American Legion Magazine*, *Changing Times*, *Good Housekeeping*, *Parent's Magazine*, and *Woman's Day* all buy anecdotal or helpful-hints fillers. *The New Yorker* pays a token fee ($5) for amusing mistakes or peculiar phrasing spotted by readers in other publications. If the reader supplies a tag line, the fee is more.

• A Magazine's Several Editions

To better serve their advertisers, many magazines run several editions of each issue.[7] The editions may be designed to allow advertisers to buy circulation only in areas where their ads will draw the most response or among groups who would be most interested. Either way, the shuffling of ads results sometimes in blank editorial pages, which must be filled with short articles and features. This means that articles of only regional interest could have a chance with national magazine editors.

• Spreading Across the Markets

With the research done, the article written and sold or at least on its way to the editor, the writer looks over a mountain of material, much of it not used in the final draft, and decides it must not go to waste. Ken Metzler, upon completing research on the port of Coos Bay on the Oregon Coast, put five articles together, each with a different slant, and sold all five. One on shipping went to *Ships & the Sea* (no

[7]An issue includes all the copies printed for a given date; an edition includes only some of the copies, which are directed to one segment of the total audience.

longer published); one about a man who lived in a converted mine-sweeper, which also served as a salesroom and shop for outboard motors, to *Family Weekly*; one about a tour of the port and the surrounding country, to *Sunset*; one about a fisherman who ràn a miniature steam train around his yard, to *Family Weekly*; and one about an interesting old steamer captain, to a newspaper's locally produced Sunday magazine section.

The professional writer will not only milk an idea for all it can produce but also keep articles on a variety of subjects circulating to various markets. Keeping accurate records of where manuscripts go and when they return is part of the business. A professional in a given month may find publication in several magazines. The late Richard Gehman once counted 30 of his articles in magazines then on the newsstands. A Canadian writer, Paul Brock, sells some 200 articles a year, mostly to minor or secondary markets. Brock keeps about 300 manuscripts in the mails at all times. "I have submitted an article to as many as thirty different publications before finally placing it."[8]

• The Writer as Specialist

Concentrating on a few markets, you tend to develop a specialty. The more articles you write on a subject, the more expert you become. Soon editors begin thinking of you when they need articles on that subject. They call you.

In the legend at the foot of your published articles you are identified as a writer on environmental subjects, on child care, on problems of the aged, or whatever. A specialty leads eventually to articles for encyclopedias, a book, even assignments from PR organizations. It can also lead to an editing position.

• THE CHANGING MAGAZINE

Where would you expect to find this kind of title-blurb?

Federal regulatory agencies, created as watchdogs in the public interest, often in fact protect the industries they are supposed to regulate — and reforms have been aimed at the wrong target.

[8]Curtis. W. Casewit, *Freelance Writing: Advice from the Pros*, Macmillan Publishing Co., Inc., New York, 1974, pp. 67, 105.

"Sorry. Your article doesn't quite make it here. . . ."

Not in the conservative *Reader's Digest*, surely, which once was described as suffering from "hardening of the articles." But there it was, in the July 1975 issue, over an article by James Nathan Miller, who in his article asked that the first efforts at correcting the problem be directed to the Congress — "the regulators' masters."

Pigeonholing magazines is dangerous business. They often are more complex than simple study can bring out

And they change. They change as times change. They change with changes in ownership. They change as one editor leaves and another takes his place. Writers have sold articles to magazines that said *No, thanks* a few months earlier. *Esquire* grew up when *Playboy* came along to take over the girl watchers.

Take the *National Enquirer*. (Please!) The *National Enquirer* "used to be a weirdo's delight," *Newsweek* observed in 1975. "But now . . . the *Enquirer* is peddling a moral uplift so blameless it could be handed out in Sunday schools." With a circulation close to 4,000,000, the weekly magazine with a newspaper format no longer features "Mom Uses Son's Face for an Ashtray" headlines.

• ANALYZING THE MAGAZINE

Rather than develop your opinion haphazardly, you might want to make a formal analysis of each magazine you intend to write for. Your analysis could cover these points:

1. *Full name of editor* (or articles editor, if there is one, or managing editor), *exact name of magazine* (Is a "The" included? Is it "Reader's," "Readers'," or "Readers"?), and *address of editorial offices*.

2. *Editorial formula*. What is the "editorial mix" of the magazine? What kinds of articles — personality sketches, essays, narratives, etc. — does it carry? Does it seem to prefer one kind of article to the others? And what seems to be the preferred length?

3. *Editorial philosophy*. Do the articles seem to add up to a particular point of view? On the political spectrum, does the magazine belong on the left or on the right or somewhere near the middle? Can you come up with a sentence or paragraph that describes the magazine's character or personality?

4. *Format*. You won't be concerned with the design of the magazine or the printing process used; you will be interested in the kind and number of illustrations. Will you have to submit photographs with your article in order to sell it? Or does the magazine assign its own photographers or dig out its own art?

   Some magazines carry magazines-within-magazines that make especially good markets for freelancers. For instance, *Ladies' Home Journal*, for 1,000,000 of its press run in the mid-1970s, included "Prime Showcase," an insert of ads for high-priced merchandise and short articles that were more sophisticated than its general run of articles. *Harper's* for its entire press run had its "wraparound" section.

5. *Nature of audience*. Do the letters to the editor, the ads in the magazine, the ads placed by the magazines, the listings in directories, or the editorial-requirements sheets tell you anything about the education and income level of the readers and their other characteristics?

   Writing for a magazine that circulates mostly from newsstands, you can assume that in most cases you are writing for a young audience.

Advertisers support those magazines because they assume that they have a low percentage of middle-aged or older readers who are more careful of products they buy and who buy less frequently than the young. One of Peterson Publishing Company's main reasons for unloading *True* on another publisher was that, according to *Advertising Age* (Aug. 25, 1975), the average age of *True's* readers had "climbed above what advertisers consider their best prospects."

6. *Percentage of freelance material.* If there are no bylines, or if most of the bylines repeat names listed in the masthead, forget it. The magazine is mostly staff-written, a poor market for freelancers.

   What are stated rates for freelance material? Does the magazine pay on acceptance or on publication?

7. *Writing style.* Formal or informal? Concise or rambling? Simple or complex? Objective or subjective?

   Do the article openings fall into a pattern? For instance, do most of the articles start out as stories?

   And how do the articles end? With a fillip? Or do they just trail off?

   How important are statistics? And do the authors "humanize" them?

   What about the use of direct quotations? Are sources cited in the text?

   Do anecdotes, dialogue, or figures of speech play an important role in the articles?

   Is narrative used?

   How much description do you find?

8. *Themes used for some of the articles.* Do they fall into a pattern?

9. *Comparison of recent issues with past issues.* Does the magazine seem to be heading in a new direction?

10. *Ideas for three articles you might write for the magazine.* See if you can come up with titles, too — titles that approximate those used on other articles in the magazines.

• WRITING THE QUERY

Many editors will not look at a manuscript — or at least they *say* they won't — unless you write a query first explaining the article idea and telling how you intend to develop it. Impressed by a query, an editor may react in one of two ways: by telling you to go ahead and write the article — but on speculation; or by telling you to write the article and submit it, period. Inviting you to submit an article on speculation leaves the editor free to reject it when it comes. Perhaps, the editor finally decides, the promise of the query did not carry over to the article itself. But at least you knew, when you wrote the article, that you had a chance of selling it. You did not submit a totally unsolicited manuscript.

The second reaction, rarer when untried writers are involved, at least to some extent commits the editor. Should the editor reject, finally, an article written in response to that kind of reaction, the writer can probably count on at least some reimbursement for the work.

Even when you write for a magazine that does not insist on a query first, you may find writing one worth the effort. The response you get may tell you you'd be wasting your time on an article you thought ideal for the market you picked, or it may advise you to change your course slightly in order to increase your chances to sell to that market.

To write a query that brings encouragement from an editor, you must have your idea firmly in mind and your research started. If you find it difficult to contain your enthusiasm for the project, so much the better. You have to be something of a salesman, in order to write a successful query. And the quality of the writing in the query ought to match the quality of the writing in the article itself. Put a query together carelessly and your editor will conclude that your article will come out the same way. Under those circumstances, an editor would not want to encourage you to go ahead with the project.

So what should a query do? It should:

1. state precisely the writer's idea and theme,
2. estimate reader interest in the subject,
3. tell how the story line will run,
4. offer a sample anecdote,
5. mention research sources,
6. describe the writer's qualifications to write the article,
7. suggest length and delivery time,
8. discuss art possibilities, and
9. ask for reaction from the editor.

Not every query will cover all these matters, but at least the writer will consider them before sitting down to write to the editor.

Even though it is a business letter you write, you do not have to lapse into the formalities and jargon of the business executive. Try to picture your editor facing the morning's mail, letters from writers everywhere asking for attention. The editor is anxious to get through this stack of correspondence and be free to process manuscripts already on hand. Your job is to capture attention and fire the editor's imagination. One way of doing this is to open your query with the same paragraph or paragraphs you would use to open your article. If you do start with something dramatic, make sure somewhere in your letter you say it is an article idea you are proposing.

Perhaps reader interest in the subject will be evident enough that you will not have mention it. At any rate, don't make the mistake of telling the editor what audience the magazine serves. "Because your magazine appeals to young women preparing for careers in nursing. . . ." does little more than tell the editor that you went hunting through the pages of *Writer's Market*.

Not only should you spell out your idea in precise terms, but you should also indicate what your theme and your conclusion will be. The editor may want an approach a little different from what you have in mind, and the time for you to learn this is before you start your writing.

A sample anecdote or two will tell the editor something about your writing style.

Let the editor know whether your research will be from primary or secondary sources and how extensive it will be.

Don't dwell on yourself in the query. That you served as editor of your high-school or even your college paper will score few points. *Everybody* is an ex-school editor, one editor has observed. If you have no previous professional writing credits to point to and if you are not really an authority, a single sentence about yourself expressing your enthusiasm for the subject will suffice. Mentioning that you are a student doing the article for a class will do little for your cause.

In discussing length and delivery date, assure the editor that you remain flexible.

If the market runs photographs or art, give the editor some idea of picture possibilities and tell whether you would take the pictures yourself or arrange to have them taken. Be sure to specify whether you have black-and-white or color photographs in mind.

The call for action at the end can take such forms as: "I will be looking forward to your reaction," "Say the word, and I'll get right to work on the article," "Does this idea interest you?", "Let me know whether this is the kind of article your readers would like to see," and "I'll be happy to produce this article for you within the next month and submit it for your consideration. Does my suggested length sound about right?" You might also mention your willingness to do the article on speculation.

Including a self-addressed, stamped envelope with your query (as you would do with the finished manuscript) is a thoughtful move, especially when you deal with a shoestring operation. Even the bigger magazines like to see S.A.S.E.s. "If an S.A.S.E. is supplied with queries," said Gene Balliett when he was editor of *Physician's Management*, "I will usually answer it the same day it arrives. If not, it could be sometime after two weeks."

Make sure you are ready to do the article when you write your query. It is not unusual for a student to write a sparkling, convincing query only to freeze when the editor's invitation to proceed comes back. You should be able to produce the finished article within a month of getting the editor's favorable response. If you encounter an unexpected delay, let the editor know. Consider your letter a progress report.

• When to Query

Your principal reason for writing a query is to save yourself work on a project that is not right for the market you've chosen. If you already have your article written, you lose time writing a query. Go ahead and send the manuscript in, unless you know the editor won't consider unsolicited completed manuscripts. You might also want to *avoid* a query when:

1. the nature of the article can be appreciated only in the final writing;

"I have in mind an article of 2,237 words."

2. the finished article — maybe it will be a filler — won't be much longer than the query; or
3. the article is based on fast-breaking news and the market is a weekly.

You *would* write a query when:

1. you want to avoid research and writing on something that won't sell;
2. you want to comply with the editor's requirements, as stated in a market guide; or
3. you feel genuinely torn between two (or among several) angles to develop in your story, and you need advice from the editor.

It doesn't always make sense for students to write queries, especially in a term-long rather than a semester-long course, because students cannot afford to wait for "Yes" answers before beginning their writing. Anyway, their initial "sale" is the instructor's acceptance of the manuscript at the end of the term.

A system that works for some students is to pick out two similar markets. They begin writing their articles for one of the markets on pure speculation; meanwhile they send queries off to the second market. If the second market expresses interest, that market gets the contribution when it is finished. A "No" does not demoralize the students; they still have their first-choice markets to try.

• The Length of the Query

Knowing that the editor is a busy person, you would try to confine your query to a page or two. When your query runs longer than two pages, your editor may think "What's left to write?" Richard Dunlop reports feeling "quite chastened the day that an editor wrote and said there would be no need for me to write an article. He simply planned to publish my query."

Still, it is better to give the editor too much information than too little. It took this author a full two pages, single-spaced, to sell *The Christian Century* on an article about an attempt to keep a communist leader from speaking at the University of Oregon. Looking back to that time in the early 1960s, it seems incredible that people could have been so aroused by what today would be regarded as a routine and insignificant event. This is the way the query read, following an opening paragraph which said that the writer had an article idea he wanted the editor to consider:

> Yesterday afternoon Gus Hall, former general secretary of the Communist Party, spoke to 11,000 persons in Hayward Field in Eugene. The meeting was first scheduled for one hall, then a larger one; then it was moved at the last minute to the football field (because of the swelling crowd, University officials said, but frankly also because of two bomb threats). What gave him his largest audience since a 1948 address to a Madison Square Garden audience was an almost hysterical campaign against his appearance at the University, a campaign organized by the American Legion, the Elks Club, and Christian anti-Communist groups in Portland and Eugene. One local minister took out a full-page ad in a local morning tabloid to drum up protest against the meeting. Just before the meeting a caravan of citizens headed for Salem to ask Governor Mark Hatfield, who had said Hall shouldn't be allowed to speak at any of the state's public-supported colleges, to get the University to call off the meeting or to fire the University presi-

dent. The State of Washington earlier had closed its colleges to Hall appearances.

The man singled out for the bitterest attack was Arthur S. Flemming, former secretary of Health, Education and Welfare [and then president of the University of Oregon]. . . .

Followup paragraphs offered anecdotes and assessments.

The article seemed a natural for *The Christian Century* because of its concern about civil rights matters and its interest in Flemming, who was active in the National Council of Churches, an organization the *Century* strongly supported. And it came to pass that the managing editor, Kyle Haselden, to whom the query was addressed, wrote back that he liked the idea and would like to see a 2,500-word article. He advised including in the article a chronicle of events similar to that contained in the query and emphasizing the fact that the extreme right wing was not so much interested in destroying Communists as people like Arthur Flemming. Haselden warned of possible harassment to the author if the article were published.

Because the *Century* is a weekly and because the story had some news aspects, it had to be written quickly. In about a week it was on its way to Haselden. It went out with a cover letter, which opened with this:

> The big job was deciding what to leave out. I have gone through the state's newspapers, the University files, the hate literature (sample enclosed); I have talked to University administrators, faculty members and students, but my article has not been "cleared." Nor would Flemming want that. Two colleagues have read the manuscript and are satisfied it tells the story accurately. So here it is, slightly longer than the 2,500 words you suggested. I hope it meets with your approval. . . .

The next three paragraphs straightened out a couple of inconsistencies in the query and briefly discussed the title. Enough happened after the article was accepted that, as the article was being processed, another letter had to go to the editor to suggest changes.

The above represents a typical exchange between author and editor, the correspondence adding two or three hours, perhaps, to the time spent researching and writing the article. If writers were to add correspondence time to research and writing time and divide the total into the amount earned from article sales, especially sales to specialized magazines, they would no doubt conclude that there are more lucrative ways to earn a living. There have to be other rewards in freelance writing. In this case it turned out that becoming a martyr was not one of those other rewards; if the right wing threatened any retaliation over the *Century* article, word of it never got back to the author.

Another case involving a query is instructive. While she was a graduate student, before she joined the faculty (first at Southern Illinois University and then at Linfield College), Lauren Kessler sold an editor on an idea by thoroughly describing it, using the same graceful prose she uses in any of her writing done for publication. The complete query follows:

Sybil C. Harp, Editor
Creative Crafts Magazine
P.O. Drawer C
31 Arch Street
Ramsey, New Jersey 07446

Dear Ms. Harp:

Craftsmen are starving all over the country, but in Eugene, Oregon, they are supporting themselves selling their wares at the Saturday Market — this city's permanent crafts fair.

Saturday Market is a profusion of colors and textures, of sounds and smells. Here, every Saturday from May to December, area craftsmen gather, set up booths that reflect their individual style and sell to the people of Eugene. It is a happening in which the entire city joyfully participates. As an older woman who operates a food booth confided in me, "We have all types rubbing elbows in front of a bean sprout sandwich."

Each week, hundreds of people visit, meander through and participate in the fun of the Market. They buy handcrafted goods that range from pottery, leatherwork, and jewelry to wooden toys, quilts, stained glass and carved flutes — all sold personally by the craftsmen who have created them.

I would like to do a 2,000- to 3,000-word article entitled, "The End to the Starving Craftsman," [later changed to "The Potter, the Baker, the Candlestick Maker: The Story of Saturday Market"] on this unique and exciting phenomenon. I envision it as being a highly descriptive piece that will bring the color and life of the Market to the pages of your magazine. But more importantly, it will supply your craft-minded readers with concrete information about this "alternative to starvation." For those readers who have developed craft skills at home and are looking for an outlet for their work, it would provide the data necessary to get a Saturday Market started in their own community.

I mean to tell the story of the Market through its people. I have researched its humble beginnings, its structure and internal operation, its successes and failures along the way — and the story is an intriguing one. I have conducted lengthy interviews with Lotte Streisinger, the woman who first conceived of the Saturday Market idea four years ago, and Lou Elliot, the manager and general trouble-shooter. By roaming around the Market every Saturday for the past three months, I have gotten a strong feeling for what it is all about and the vital part it plays in the lives of the craftsmen and the character of the community. Also, I have spoken in depth to various craftsmen and have notes on these lively conversations: what the Saturday Market has done for them and the commitment they feel toward it.

I can supply you with black and white photos that would complement the descriptive passages of the piece and feature unusual craft items. The article could emphasize one craft in particular — there are so many in evidence at the Market — depending on the current needs of your magazine.

The Eugene Saturday Market has received enormous local press coverage and two other towns in Oregon, Corvallis and Albany, have already picked up on the idea and are operating Markets of their own. I think this may be the beginning of an exciting, new trend in the crafts field: an idea that would inspire craftsmen in other communities around the country.

My interest in the Saturday Market is far from a casual one. I have attempted to support myself by selling my handicrafts in New York, Chicago, and San Francisco. I have covered the fine arts beat for the Medill News Service, Evanston, Illinois and worked as a newspaper reporter in Burlingame, California.

I hope to hear soon that you would be interested in a piece on the Saturday Market.

Sincerely,

Lauren Jeanne Kessler

In a letter of response an assistant editor thought the suggested article would be "a fascinating piece" and told how and when the magazine planned to feature it. The letter even discussed payment. All this, and only a query to go on.

But usually, an editor okays a query with less commitment. There is always the possibility that the finished article will not live up to its billing. It may have to be rejected. In the Kessler case, though, the finished article was just what the editors wanted, and the author made her sale.

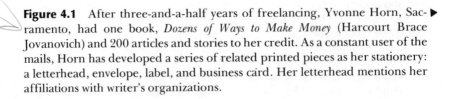

Figure 4.1 After three-and-a-half years of freelancing, Yvonne Horn, Sacramento, had one book, *Dozens of Ways to Make Money* (Harcourt Brace Jovanovich) and 200 articles and stories to her credit. As a constant user of the mails, Horn has developed a series of related printed pieces as her stationery: a letterhead, envelope, label, and business card. Her letterhead mentions her affiliations with writer's organizations.

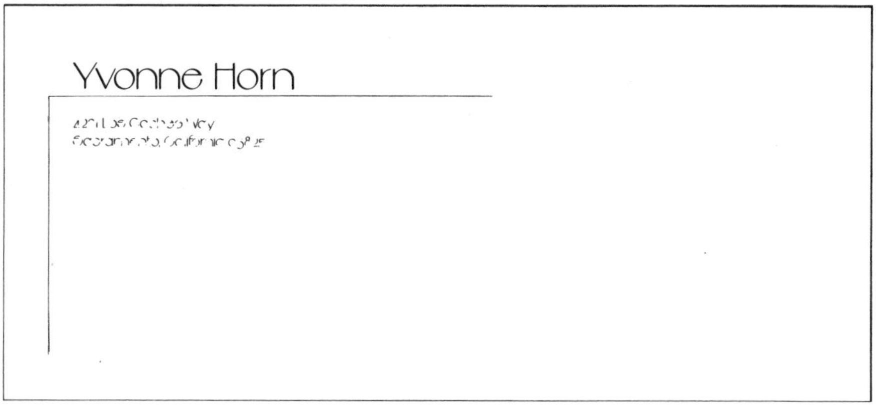
Yvonne Horn

Yvonne Horn
writer
Yvonne Horn
writer
Yvonne Horn
Postmaster: □ Manuscript □ Photos □ Return postage guaranteed
MEMBER
OUTDOOR WRITERS ASSOCIATION OF AMERICA
Member Society of Magazine Writers, Inc

• Letterheads

Some writers think that a printed letterhead impresses editors, and maybe it does. Certainly it suggests to the editor that the writer means business. If you don't have your own letterhead and if your article involves an area covered by your job, perhaps you could use company stationery to approach the editor.

If you develop your own stationery, let it show that you are a writer and have it include your phone number as well as your address. If you are moving around a lot, it being early in your writing career, you can do as Randy Shilts, a young San Francisco writer, has done. His business stationery carries only his name, tastefully arranged at the top; he types in the address each time near where he types the date.

• The Telephone Query

Increasingly, writers, especially established ones, use the telephone rather than the mails to get go-aheads on articles. "I seldom, if ever, use written queries," says Steve Neal, a reporter who freelances. "When I feel like doing an article, I call up the editor of *The Nation* or whatever publication I have in mind. If they give me the green light, I proceed. The postal service is so unreliable and journalists, myself included, such poor correspondents, that I find the written query almost useless. By contrast, the phone is very efficient."[9]

• SUBMITTING THE MANUSCRIPT

If once you served as the mistress to a President and now you choose to edify us all with an article about your experiences, your handwritten manuscript might get past the first readers and on up to the editor of the magazine, but in other cases you are not likely to get serious consideration unless you follow the accepted rules of manuscript preparation. This means double-spaced typed copy (triple-spaced for some newspapers) on 8½ x 11 sheets, the script running only on one side of each page.

[9]Letter to the author from Steve Neal, Nov. 10, 1976.

At the top-left of the first page goes your name and address, at the top-right the number of words. To figure the number of words, count the average number per line and multiply by the number of lines. Your count can be rough. You'll get anywhere from 275 to 350 words per page, depending upon whether you use an elite or pica typewriter.

Under the number of words you can type in the name of the intended market (if you don't mind retyping the first page when the manuscript comes back) and below that the rights offered, if that is important to you. A magazine may buy "all rights," which means it can use and reuse and even resell the article without further payment to the author; or "first serial rights" or "first North American serial rights," which means the author can resell the article to some other publication after it is published; or "second serial rights," which means the magazine buys the article knowing it has already run somewhere else; or "simultaneous rights," which means that the author is selling the same article to several publications at once.

Your title and subtitle (blurb) fall about a third of the way down on the page, centered, and your byline (it may be different from the name of record in the top left corner), also centered, goes below that. Then, skipping three or four lines, you are ready to start.

Leave a reasonable margin (about an inch and a half) all around. Indent your paragraphs. Avoid hyphenation at the ends of lines. Number each succeeding page, and at the top of each put a slug line: your last name or the title of the article.

Use a 16- or 20-pound bond paper, preferably not one of the slick-finish erasable bonds. Editors don't like erasable paper because the typing smears and the stock does not readily take pencil or pen marks. And editors abhore fancy typewriter faces, especially scripts.

Students who use pica typewriters to impress their instructors with long term papers are likely to switch to elite-type typewriters when they freelance, because typing in a smaller face not only saves paper; it also saves postage.

As a writer you can take advantage of a special fourth-class manuscript rate, but if you can afford first-class postage you'll get your work to the editor much sooner and probably with less sign of wear. You would use a manila envelope large enough to carry your unbound 8½ x 11 pages unfolded. Photographs should be protected with a piece of chipboard or corrugated cardboard. If you have no photos to send, and if your manuscript runs for only two or three pages, you can fold it to fit a regular No. 10 business envelope. Always include a stamped, self-addressed envelope of the size of the outside envelope, folded so it will fit inside. Some writers, feeling quite sure their manuscripts will be purchased, paper-clip rather than fasten the stamps to the return envelope. Maybe they will get the stamps back if the manuscript is purchased, they reason; and with the price of first-class postage being what it is, that could represent a windfall.

• The Cover Letter

If you think it necessary, include a cover letter. A cover letter is useful if the editor should know your special qualifications or be aware of the extent and nature of your research. If the letter is just to say that you are submitting a manuscript for the editor's consideration, forget it. The setup on the first page of your manuscript has already told the editor that the manuscript is for sale.

Marsha McCormick of Baton Rouge attached a cover letter to her article on belly dancing when she sent it to *The National Observer*.[10]

> This is the article I expected Diane Shah to write, but she never did.
> For a while I even thought Douglas Looney would get around to it, but no such luck.
> It's the kind of article I expect to find in *The Observer*, and I've watched for it week after week.
> Finally I sat down and wrote it myself. Enjoy.

While the letter perhaps had little to do with selling the article — her first and in the words of editor Henry Gemmill "the most illuminating report on belly-dancing education I've ever read" — it did at least reveal to the editors that she knew something about her market. She had been an avid reader of *The National Observer* for three years.

You *would* need to include a cover letter if you previously received encouragement from a query. In the letter you would remind the editor of your previous exchange of correspondence. Having dealt with many authors and conducted much business since responding to your earlier letter, the editor needs to be reminded.

---

[10] "Post Script from the Editor," *The National Observer*, Nov. 16, 1975, p. 28.

• Timing Your Submission

When you send your manuscript can make a difference. A magazine reported as "overstocked" in the writers' magazines won't buy even if it likes your manuscript.

An article with a news angle is perishable in that, after a first rejection, enough time may have elapsed to make it passé.

Seasonal articles must get to the editor in time to work into the magazine's plans, which are often months ahead of the cover date. *Mediamatic Calendar of Special Editorial Issues* (423 W. 55th St., New York, N.Y. 10019), which comes out three times a year, lists editorial and special-issue plans of about 500 publications, mostly trade journals. But it is probably too expensive for the average freelancer.

• Multiple Submissions

Some writers engage in multiple submissions of finished manuscripts, sending copies out to several markets at once. Some magazines don't seem to mind. Some encourage the practice. Of course, the magazines should be notified that others are also considering the manuscript. But unless you have a hot, timely topic, you had better stick to one-at-a-time submissions and make sure that your editors get original typed manuscripts to look at rather than office-machine copies.

One student didn't get the word. Both pleased and troubled, he came to his instructor with the information that within one day he had been notified by two opinion magazines that they wanted to buy his article. Neither knew that the other was considering the article. He had to call one magazine to say that the article had sold to the other. No doubt the student-writer's stock went down with the magazine that lost out.

Safer than multiple submissions of manuscripts is multiple submission of queries. In the unlikely event you find two editors wanting to look at your manuscript, you can say "Sorry" to one knowing that you have not cost the magazine a lot of valuable reading time.

• Milking the Article

If you see further sales possibilities for your article, try to retain second rights in your dealing with the editor. Then you can resell the article to a noncompeting market. But even if you sell all rights, you are free to reuse your research material — and to use material you couldn't squeeze into the original article — for a second article, which would take a different slant for another audience.

You may one day do a book incorporating material from your articles. Then second rights will be important to you. If you don't have them you can often get them by requesting them from the magazine editors you sold to.

• Persistence

Some writers can't take "No" for an answer. Greg Marton of Weed, California, tells of sending a query to a young people's magazine and getting a form rejection. "I decided to send the manuscript anyway. When the editors saw the manuscript, they decided they *were* in the market for my material after all . . . They sent me a . . . $400 check." A number of other writers report selling articles to magazines that previously had rejected either queries or finished manuscripts. Triumphs like these can be explained by changes in editors' moods, changes in society, and successions of editors. A new editor on a publication may mean a complete change in editorial policy. People, not magazines, buy manuscripts.

CHAPTER 5

Research: Working with Primary Sources

When a woman in his home state lost her entire family in an auto accident, and when the drunk driver of the other car got off with a token fine and a suspended sentence, Booton Herndon, disturbed by what he read of the trial, decided to do an article — an as-told-to article — with the woman telling the story. It would carry a strong plea for mandatory punishment for "drunk-driving murderers on the highway." He fired off a query to *Better Homes and Gardens*, a large-circulation magazine interested in more than house-painting and tree-planting hints. Would the magazine be interested in such an article?

Well, yes and no. The editors liked the idea of an article on the general subject of drunk driving and its dangers to families, but this story as Herndon outlined it, sounded incredible. And there was danger of libel. The article, for *Better Homes and Gardens*, would be better with a broader base.

A suggested change of approach was all right by Herndon. "Between you and me, frankly, I would much rather do a carefully researched, nationwide study of the frightening problem of the drunken driver than go through the harrowing experience of drawing . . . [the woman's] story out of her," Herndon wrote the editor. Herndon's revised idea was to use this accident as one of several to illustrate his thesis that laws on drunken driving are "much too lax, and our enforcement of those laws is even laxer."

A certain amount of research had already gone into Herndon's article. His original query not only showed the approach he had meant to take but also cited a few facts. After the idea was modified and finally okayed by the magazine, the real research phase began.

It is not enough, *BH & G* editors have told writers, to "artistically report a meager supply of facts." Herndon, of course, knew this; nor would he want to put his name on an article that was not thoroughly researched. Here's the lineup of sources he tapped: (1) the woman survivor whose story prompted the article; (2) a doctor friend; (3) the dean of the University of Virginia law school; (4) the chairman of the American Medical Association Committee on Traffic Crash Deaths and Injuries; (5) state police inspectors; (6) the director of Northwestern University's Traffic Institute. Then, after the rough draft was in, the editorial staff of the magazine called on the following sources for additional information and checking: (7) the National Safety Council; (8) a professor of psychology at Iowa State University; (9) the magazine's legal adviser (to check matters of libel); (10) the dean of the College of Law of the State University of Iowa (a statement from him was carried in the magazine as a sidebar to the article); (11) the head of the driver training laboratory at Iowa State University.

What was uncovered in the magazine's research was forwarded to Herndon to be worked into a new draft of the article as he saw fit — a service reserved for regular contributors, it should be pointed out.

These 11 persons and organizations were contacted face-to-face, by mail, by phone. This research was in addition to what reading Herndon did in magazines, books, and newspapers. What went on here is in no way unusual. Although this case cannot be considered typical — every magazine article requires a different research procedure — it does illustrate that an article designed for a major magazine, if it treats a serious subject, is not written off the top of the head. Nor does it result from a single interview or a single reading.

The article, "Drunk Drivers Are Getting Away with Murder," was only one of several appearing in a single issue of *Better Homes and Gardens*.[1] The case history of every other article in that issue of the magazine would show similar work on the part of the writer and editorial staff members.

Every form of writing — even fiction writing — demands, or at least benefits from, a preliminary period of searching, questioning, read-

---

[1]The article became something of a classic because Meredith Publishing Co., Des Moines, Iowa, included information and memos on it in a kit made available in 1957 to journalism schools and departments.

ing, noting. Even the novelist has facts to check. William Golding showed a lack of familiarity with optics when he allowed the children in *Lord of the Flies* to use Piggy's glasses to start a fire. Piggy was nearsighted. Glasses used to correct nearsightedness have concave — not convex — lenses, and concave lenses have no focal or "fire" point. You can't use them to start a fire. A literal-minded reader pointed this out in a letter to the editor of *The New York Times Book Review*.

A later case involved Gore Vidal who, in the first edition of *Burr*, had people using postage stamps. Postage stamps were not in use in Aaron Burr's time.

All writers, whether they produce fiction or nonfiction, face the problem of digging out facts and checking their accuracy. All writers learn to engage in research.

As an exercise, try reading articles or features not to discover writing tricks or organization patterns but to see if you can figure out what research sources the writer tapped. Take Ken McKenna's "Goofing Off: A Not-So-Fine Art" feature in the New York *Daily News* (June 30, 1976, p. 45). Whom did he talk to, what did he read to come to his conclusion that people who goof off on the job — and too many do — are not very happy about it? Going down the paragraphs we can count a psychologist (not named), a business professor, a telephone company executive, Barbara Garson's *All the Livelong Day*, a management consultant, and Studs Terkel's *Working*. McKenna brings back the business professor at the end to nail down the article's thesis with a direct quote. To get the several anecdotes about workers calling in sick or failing to do anything more than what was expected of them, McKenna also may have talked to some workers.

For most articles, writers work from both primary and secondary sources. Primary research comes from the writers' own experiences or observations or from working directly with persons whose stories the writers want to tell or whose ideas they want to spread. Studying personal papers, correspondence, diaries, etc., also qualifies as primary research. Some of this material is available through the library's archivist or curator of special collections. Primary research, because it is closest to the source, is the preferred kind of research.

Secondary research involves working from already published sources. It will be the subject of the next chapter. This chapter will deal with primary research.

• PERSONAL EXPERIENCE

If you really want to sell an article, have yourself a brain operation, get yourself committed to a prison or asylum, agree to act as umpire for Little League baseball games, hop aboard an ocean liner and without funds travel to the Orient, tack onto your house an additional three-room unit of your own design. Do something. Then put the details down on paper as you remember them.

Not all of us can afford the luxury of these experiences, but it's still true that the best research comes through personal experiences. It's best to get information first hand. The most rewarding writers are those who have felt, tasted, heard, seen, smelled their subjects.

Personal experience need not be spectacular in order to interest others. Sometimes an everyday happening — a trip, a party, a discovery, completion of a project of some kind — presented in a humorous, helpful, or interesting manner is article material. Sometimes mere comment on human foibles is worth recording. Certainly in the life of every writer there is one experience or set of ideas on a topical or controversial subject that can be developed into a useful article.

As a writer working on an article, you will go out of your way to get experience upon which you can draw. If it's an article on restaurant workers, you'll roll up your sleeves and scrape and dunk dirty dishes or don an apron and take customers' orders; if it's an article on the work of private detectives, you'll accompany a typical one on his calls, or spend a day, in the background, watching the detective at work at his office; if it's an article on cranberry growing, you'll slosh around in the bogs, or wherever, for whatever time is needed to get the feel of the activity. This in addition to time spent questioning authorities and taking notes.

• OBSERVATION

One of the advertising textbooks quoted *The Design of Advertising* as saying that the typical advertisement consists of a piece of art, a headline, some copy, and a logotype (or signature). The author was quoted correctly. But he had written that only as an aside as he discussed the procedure for laying out an ad. It was an observation anybody could make, an observation too obvious to merit crediting.

Too many writers fail to utilize their own powers of observation. They lack confidence in themselves. They seem to feel that unless someone else has seen it first, then reported it, it isn't worth working into what they are writing.

In *Zen and the Art of Motorcycle Maintenance*, Robert M. Pirsig tells of a girl in a rhetoric class who found it difficult getting started on a 500-word essay on Bozeman, Montana. The instructor told her, then, to "Narrow it down to the *main street* of Bozeman." Still, she couldn't get started.

The instructor lost his temper. He told her she wasn't looking. "Narrow it down to the *front* of one building on the main street of Bozeman. The Opera House. Start with the upper lefthand brick."

Soon she came back with a 5,000-word essay, explaining that "I sat in the hamburger stand across the street and started writing about the first brick, and the second brick, and then by the third brick it all started to come and I couldn't stop."

The instructor didn't at first understand how the system he advocated worked, but then he figured it out.

> She was blocked because she was trying to repeat, in her writing, things she had already heard. . . . She couldn't think of anything to write about Bozeman because she couldn't recall anything she had heard worth repeating. She was strangely unaware that she could look and see freshly for herself, as she wrote, without primary regard for what had been said before. The narrowing down to one brick destroyed the blockage because it was so obvious she *had* to do some original and direct seeing.[2]

Neil Simon draws this picture of the writer as observer: "A look, the sound of a voice, a stranger passing on the street — and in an instant the transformation takes place. The mildmannered Human Being suddenly dashes for cover behind his protective cloak called skin and peers out, unseen, through two tiny keyholes called eyes. He stands there undetected, unnoticed, a gleeful, malicious smirk on his face watching, penetrating, probing the movements, manners, and absurd gestures of those ridiculous creatures performing their inane daily functions."[3]

---

[2] Robert M. Pirsig, *Zen and the Art of Motorcycle Maintenance*, William Morrow and Company, Inc., New York, 1974, p. 186.
[3] Quoted by John Lawing, "Neil Simon Knows Love Still Exists," *National Courier*, April 2, 1976, p. 27.

"A journalist must have an artist's eye for *significant* detail," says freelancer Louise Melton. That you observe that a man is bald and record it does not necessarily add to the reader's understanding of him. But the fact that he touches his collarbone whenever he uses the word "I" does set him apart somewhat and may be worth mentioning in your sketch, she adds.

Here is how one professional writer capitalizes on his powers of observation. We come upon Caskie Stinnett working on a piece for *The Atlantic*:

> A few days ago in Central Park I saw a man leaning on a litter can drinking a carton of orange juice, and when he finished he tossed the container not in the receptacle but on the ground.

It was an incident, observed rather than dug out, that did more than statistics could do to describe the indifference of New Yorkers to the filth around them. "I don't understand why the city has no soul, no detectable heartbeat, why the chief element in the city's emotional economy is indifference," Stinnett went on to say.

To illustrate the fact that New York suffers from "a lack of caring, a sickness of the soul, that I find difficult to accept and impossible to forget," Stinnett recalls "the New Year's Eve when,

> after a dinner party, a friend of mine went down to the street to get a taxicab and the cab veered too quickly and hit him. His wife and I took him in the cab to Lenox Hill Hospital, and while we were trying to get emergency treatment for him the cabdriver was screaming at us for his fare.[4]

Training yourself to observe what goes on around you is valuable only insofar as you train yourself also to file it away in a corner of your mind to be brought out later when you write an article touching on the subject.

• THE INTERVIEW

For the reporter as well as the feature writer and article writer, no research tool gets more of a workout than the interview. And yet, for writers, the interview came along late in the game. James Gordon

---

[4]Caskie Stinnett, "Farewell, My Unlovely," *The Atlantic*, August 1976, p. 23.

Bennett I, founder of the New York *Herald* and one of the founders of the Associated Press, introduced the interview to American journalism in 1836 when he asked questions of madam Rosina Townsend, in whose "fancy house" a murder had been committed, and relayed answers to his sensation-hungry readers.[5] Probably the first journalistic interview to make use of direct quotations — the story took a question-and-answer form — ran August 20, 1859 in Horace Greeley's New York *Tribune*. Greeley produced the piece after a two-hour meeting with Brigham Young in Salt Lake City. But the technique was denounced as "the most perfect contrivance yet devised to make journalism an offense, a thing of ill savor in all decent nostrils."[6] An excerpt from that published interview:

H.G.: How general is polygamy among you?

B.Y.: I could not say. Some of those present [heads of the Church] have each but one wife; others have more; each determines what is his individual duty.

H.G.: What is the largest number of wives belonging to any one man?

B.Y.: I have fifteen [he is said to have had 27 in all before he died]; *I know no one who has more;* but some of those sealed to me are old ladies who I regard rather as mothers than wives, but whom I have taken to cherish and support.[7]

Greeley ended the question-and-answer part of his story with criticism of the way women were treated. "Taking his stand on the side of woman's rights," Louis L. Snyder and Richard B. Morris write, "Greeley had fired the opening gun in his campaign against the Mormon marriage system. Three years later Congress prohibited polygamy for the future in the territories, and ultimately the Mormons bowed to the sentiment of the country."[8]

Writers today interview people at random for "typical" answers and reactions to trivial or important problems or events; they interview celebrities or unusual characters whose life stories have entertainment or inspiration value; they interview recognized experts who have in-

---

[5]Mitchell V. Charnley, *Reporting*, Henry Holt and Company, Inc., New York, 1959, pp. 12 and 206.

[6]Reported by Louis L. Snyder and Richard B. Morris in *A Treasury of Great Reporting*, Simon and Schuster, New York, 1949, p. 106.

[7]*Ibid.*, p. 108.

[8]*Ibid.*, p. 109.

formation or ideas that might carry weight with readers. The approach and the handling differ in each case; the type of question depends upon the kind of article to be written and the market to which it is to be sold.

One of the contributions the "New Journalism" made to interviewing was to pay as much attention to what the average person says and thinks as to the elected official. John Kenneth Galbraith helps explain what's wrong with relying solely on what officials tell us: "Nearly all of our political comment originates in Washington. Washington politicians, after talking things over with each other, relay misinformation to Washington journalists, who, after further intramural discussion, print it where it is thoughtfully read by the same politicians. It is the only completely successful closed system for recycling of garbage yet devised."[9]

While it is best to deal with the interviewee face to face, it is possible to interview by telephone and even by mail. Either of these last two methods would be used only to bring out answers to a few specific questions.

To interview by mail you would construct some sort of questionnaire, holding your questions to two or three pages, and formulating them in such a way as to allow the respondent to fully explain the answers.

When you must reach several persons, you would print or photocopy the questionnaire, sending each with a covering letter and a stamped, self-addressed envelope. You could not hope to draw up a truly representative sample of opinion. But you would select your respondents to create a sort of mosaic of opinion.

You might be lucky enough to stumble onto a built-in audience. For his Elvis Presley biography, Jerry Hopkins got Elvis fan clubs to distribute 3,000 copies of a questionnaire asking such questions as "How were you first attracted to Elvis?" and "What do you have in your Elvis collection?" He used the information to write one of the book's chapters, which later became a cover story for *Popular Music and Society*.

For his cross section of opinion about the taste of Coors Beer for his Dec. 7, 1974 *National Observer* article, Edwin A. Roberts, Jr., contacted just a few persons from around the country (not necessarily by ques-

[9] Quoted in *Reader's Digest*, January 1976, p. 65.

tionnaire) and quoted them. For such a "sample," a writer tries to let his reader hear from each class of person and from every major geographic area.

It is also possible to conduct an interview in association with other writers or reporters, in a press-conference setting. You don't even have to participate. You could sit back and take notes while others ask the questions. You might produce a passable news story this way but not much of a feature or article.

Barry Farrell in a *Harper's* article, "George in the Afternoon" (August 1975), shows how inexact a science interviewing — at least group interviewing — can be. As an exercise for his 26-member nonfiction writing class at the University of California at Santa Barbara, he brought up actor George Segal from Los Angeles. The *Harper's* article carried conflicting excerpts from the student-written papers. The students' "disharmonious impressions of what George looked like, what he said, what he stood for, and what he was doing there in the first place struck me as highly amusing at first, leading me to take a sentence or two from each paper and arrange them into the composite interview that follows," Farrell writes in an introduction. "But in defense of my students, and in the art of interviewing generally, I submit that our . . . Segal dossier rivals in accuracy most government profiles, newsmagazine features, and other literary enterprises involving the work of many hands."

• What's in it for the Interviewee?

"Anyone who has ever done interviews knows how easy it is to make an interview subject sound foolish by quoting his casual conversation with a waiter, or by asking him asinine questions," observes Nora Ephron.[10] Art Buchwald says he doesn't like being interviewed because "you start thinking about things you haven't thought about and then you get depressed. . . ."[11] So why do people agree to let themselves be interviewed?

For any of several reasons: They like the attention, they think it their duty, they welcome the chance to advance their pet theories,

---

[10]Nora Ephron, "Barney Collier, Rotten to the Corps," *Esquire*, January 1975, p. 48.

[11]Quoted by Lael Scott, "Focus on Art Buchwald," *Harper's Bazaar*, September 1973, p. 176.

they feel sorry for the writer, they like to talk, they can't say "No," they don't realize the consequences of subjecting themselves to a writer's questions. Interviewees earn no pay, but sometimes the writer rewards them in other ways. Thomas Griffith in *Time* (Aug. 16, 1976) suggests that "a college thesis could be written about how Woodward and Bernstein, or Theodore H. White, reveal their most useful sources by the praise they bestow upon them in passing."

What the interviewee stands to gain from the interview should influence the amount of time the writer takes to ask questions and get answers. A public servant can be expected to grant more time than a business executive, especially if that executive has very little to gain from the resultant publicity. Whether the ordinary citizen should give away a great chunk of his time would depend upon how enjoyable the experience is.

Some interviewees love the attention. "It's irresistible," Alice Roosevelt Longworth at 90 told Sally Quinn. "The delight of pouring out yourself to someone who listens with rapt attention and takes down every precious word."

Ken Metzler says, "Our need to communicate comes because we tend to live in watertight compartments. Our major contact with the world is little more than shadowy figures on television. It's an unsatisfactory substitute for human contact. So when an opportunity comes to be *listened to*, our urge is to spill everything in a kind of catharsis."[12]

The session should be pleasant for interviewer and interviewee alike. "If you can't make people laugh or cry, sing or despair, love or hate — or if you can't share those emotions — you've got no business writing in the first place," says Bob Donath, senior editor of *Advertising Age*.[13]

If you have the personality or training for it, you can conduct your interview as a psychiatrist or psychologist conducts an interview with a patient. There is no reason why the interviewee should not be left with a good feeling about the session. When this author did a book of interviews with 30 magazine art directors, he apologized at the beginning of each session for interfering with the busy schedule of the art director. But in nearly every case, a promised "no more than an hour of your time" spilled over into a whole morning or afternoon. It was

[12] Ken Metzler, *Interviewing Handbook*, privately published, 1975, p. 34.
[13] Quoted in "The Art of the Interview," *Folio*, February 1976, p. 63.

the art director's doing, not the author's. He often got the feeling that nobody else — nobody else even on the magazine — had ever evidenced such interest in Times Roman and Caslon Swashes and other appurtenances of the art director's compartmentalized profession.

Ideally, the interviewee gets something out of the interview other than a name in print. Bob and Ray illustrate. We come in on one of their admirable routines involving correspondent Wally Ballou, working out of Times Square. He has stopped cranberry grower Ward Smith:

Ballou: . . . After you harvest . . . [your cranberries], Mr. Smith, do you have your own processing plant?

Smith: Processing plant? What do you mean by that, Mr. Ballou?

Ballou: By that, I mean, do you have your own factory for squeezing the juice out of the cranberries?

Smith: Squeezing the juice out of cranberries? I never heard of —

Ballou: Yes . . . to make cranberry juice.

Smith: Juice? Out of cranberries?

Ballou: Yes, for your cranberry juice cocktails.

Smith: Cranberry juice cocktails?

Ballou: Or perhaps you make cranberry sauce out of them?

Smith: What would that be for? A dessert?

Ballou: No, you serve it as a side dish . . . with turkey or meats.

Smith: Well, I never! You know, you've triggered something here.

Ballou: Then you can make sherbet out of them. That's especially good after a big meal. Very refreshing.

Smith: Say, have you got a pencil? I want to write all this down.[14]

• Lining up the Interviewee

With a go-ahead from an editor in response to a query, you are on safer ground asking for time from an interviewee. But working strictly on speculation, with no contact as yet with a market, you can still ask for the appointment. You tell the interviewee, simply, that you

---

[14]Bob Elliott and Ray Goulding, *Write If You Get Work*, Random House, New York, 1975, p. 6.

are working on an article you hope to sell to (name of magazine). If you have a record of sales, you bring this up to suggest that the interviewee's time is not being wasted.

You can't very well barge in unannounced. And even if you call ahead, you may have trouble getting through. When the secretary asks that insulting question, "May I tell him who's calling?" you might be tempted to answer, "Yes — if you know" or, simply, "No," but you probably will give your name and say you're a magazine writer who wants to get Mr. Blank's reactions . . . or that you need the person's help.

Unfortunately, some writers ruin it for others by resorting to subterfuge. Mike Edelhart, who calls himself a "phonojournalist," advises readers of *Writer's Digest* to sound authoritative and confident if they want to get past the secretary. All right. We can accept that. But then he says: "Tell his secretary that your receptionist took a call from his town while you were out, but didn't get the message. You've had some pending business with him and are certain it was he who called. What was it that he wanted, please?" And good luck when you do get through.

You may find that you not only have to go through a secretary but also a PR person. Sometimes the PR person can be helpful. But seeing the real authority often is important to your article's credibility. There is no denying that, to be successful as a writer, you must be sales-oriented. You must sell what you write to markets. That is obvious enough. But you must also sell yourself to research sources as a person capable of handling material accurately and deserving of the interviewee's time.

One session may not be enough. Not only will you want to get back to your interviewee for a second or third time; you will also want to get to other persons. If you do, ask some of the same questions. See if you get the same answers.

• Sizing up the Interviewee

Let's say that, for a personality sketch, you're interviewing a woman just elevated to a high government post. You will find that watching the interviewee may be as important as listening to her. What she wears, where she lives, how she lives, what mannerisms she has — these help form the total picture.

Even if the article deals mainly with her opinions rather than her personality, sizing her up can be important. She may be a person who telegraphs her punches. Her movements while talking may help you decide what's important, what's not. You will listen for inconsistencies in what she says and for discrepancies between what she says and what others say.

The interviewee may not want to reveal herself, at least at first. What she says may not coincide with what she thinks. More often than not she will try to impress you.

"Hear . . . [the interviewee] out, listening . . . for the broken rhythm that proclaims a lie," Roger Kahn advises. "Listen for the defiant cadence of truth."

When an answer is vague or confusing, ask for clarification. When the answer is clearly wrong, politely challenge it.

It is important to follow up an answer with additional questions. There is no telling where this might lead you.

• The Cold-Feet Interviewee

Sometimes the interviewee, deep into the interview — or afterwards — gets cold feet. Perhaps she has been too candid. She asks that what she has said be withheld from the article or at least that it not be credited to her.

This puts you in an awkward position, especially if you can get the material in question from another source. The material may even already be in print. You should think out the consequences before making any promises to delete material you think essential to the story.

Sometimes the interviewee is not so much concerned about what comes out of the interview as that it will be credited to her. If you suspect that this will be a problem, you should work out an understanding with the interviewee ahead of time. The two possibilities are these: an "off the record" interview, meant to broaden the interviewer's understanding but not to be reported; or a "background only" interview, meant to be reported but not credited to the source. A "background only" interview results in attributions like this: "A top official in the agency said . . ." or "An official who preferred to remain anonymous pointed out . . ."

• The Interviewer's Approach

Do you approach your interviewee quietly, shyly, letting her take control or at least think she's taking control? Or do you overwhelm her with your outgoing personality, perhaps even intimidating her with your questions? Obviously what would work well on one interviewee might not work well on another.

More to the point: The approach you use should be the one that is natural to you. Successful interviewers don't fit any particular personality category, although a basic curiosity and understanding are probably essential. One of the world's celebrated journalists happens to bully her interviewees. She is Oriana Fallaci, the Italian who got Secretary of State Henry Kissinger to describe himself as a lone gunslinger on a horse. She uses what *Time* calls "the clawing interview." A highly opinionated woman, she does not refrain from shouting at her subject when she feels like it. Interviewing Portuguese Communist leader Alvaro Cunhal, she yelled: "Aren't you ashamed of what you are saying? For Christ's sake, don't you blush?"

"When I make an interview" she told a *Time* writer, " it's a parliamentary debate."[15] Here's an opening question Oriana Fallaci threw at former CIA Director William Colby at his home in Washington:

> The names, Mr. Colby. The names of those bastards who took CIA money in my country. Italy isn't some banana republic of the United Fruit Company, Mr. Colby, and it isn't right that the shadow of suspicion covers a whole political class. Don't you think that Mr. Pertini, the president of the Italian Parliament, should have those names?[16]

Not the kind of approach, surely, for the interviewer freshly graduated from Northwest Nazarene College, Caldwell, Idaho. And not the approach to use when someone like John Glenn is the interviewee.

[15] "An Interview Is a Love Story," *Time*, Oct. 20, 1975, pp. 69–73.
[16] "The CIA's Mr. Colby," *The New Republic*, March 13, 1976, p. 13.

Perhaps for most interviewers the best way to proceed is to first engage the interviewee in a friendly exchange, not necessarily on the topic at hand, and then move gradually onto the subject, leading gently, prodding some of the time to keep things on course. The interviewer should resist the urge to do most of the talking.

• Preparing for the Interview

You would not go to an expert or a celebrity to conduct an interview without first reading about the person. At least you would check biographical data in *Who's Who in America* or some similar volume; and using *Readers' Guide to Periodical Literature*, you would trace articles back at least a half a dozen years. You would not, then, ask your respondent "Where were you born?" but "What was it like growing up in a small town?" or "Do you ever get back to Ellendale?" Of course, after skirmishes like these the questions would take on more significance.

Your preparation takes place on two levels. One is biographical. The other involves the subject area your interviewee is interested in: Indian affairs, auto mechanics, veterinary sciences, whatever. You do as much reading on the subject or talking to other authorities as possible before conducting the interview.

"You're really in trouble if you go in to someone who's experienced in dealing with the press without knowing at least as much as he knows about the areas you're most interested in," Richard Reeves, political writer for *New York*, said in a panel discussion at the fourth A. J. Liebling Counter Convention in 1975. "And it's a very old saying but it's very true that you should not ask a question unless you know the answer to it." Reeves added that, in dealing with a politician, an interviewer should read what the politician said earlier and then re-ask the questions that elicited those responses to see whether the story changes.[17]

In preparing for the interview you should consider the possibility of writing articles for several magazines. Going to the interviewee with your markets in mind, you ask questions leading to information of interest to different groups of readers.

[17]Quoted in "The Art of the Interview," [*More*], July 1975, p. 12.

Figure 5.1 To illustrate an interview article with board chairman R. Hal Dean, the editor of a Ralston Purina Company *Special Report to Employees* publication ran this photograph as a full-page bleed. It shows the chairman in a relaxed pose, away from his desk, responding to a writer's questions. The appearance of the writer, silhouetted in the foreground, helps convey to readers that an interview is going on without detracting from the principal figure in the photograph. The copy of *Forbes* on the table, and, in the background, the briefcase and desk, help put the setting in context. (*Photo courtesy Ralston Purina Company.*)

• Conducting the Interview

Richard Reeves believes that journalists have a lot to learn from lawyers in establishing interview techniques. "We think that we are very clever because we have a good question. But if you watch good courtroom attorneys work, their questions are often in a long series. The answer to the first five questions may do nothing but box the person in, or they may even be meaningless. I think all reporters could be much more sophisticated about questioning techniques."[18]

David Halberstam uses a technique he calls "bracketing." He likens it to a military maneuver. "You lob a shell over here, then one closer to the other side. Then you narrow in."[19]

Question your interviewee as much as possible for "why" answers rather than "what" answers. The "what" answers often can be obtained readily from printed sources. Besides, interviewees are notoriously wrong about "what" answers.

Some years ago, this author worked on a story about the construction and use of a portable indoor track for runners. Many persons were involved, and all had to be interviewed. There was the sponsor of both the building of the track and the staging of the track meet; there was the track-meet promoter; the track-meet director; the architect who designed the indoor track; the firm that built the track. These persons offered various answers to questions on the seating capacity of the coliseum where the track was to be used for the first time, on the price paid for the track, on the type and amount of surfacing used for the track, on the uniqueness of the track, on the use to be made of money from track rentals and earnings from the track meet (the sponsor was a nonprofit organization), on the exact name of the firm that built the track.

The interviewee often is "pretty sure" of his facts. Especially the spelling of proper names. You're interviewing a subject, and the name of the late columnist Walter Lippmann comes up. "Is that L–I–P–M–A–N?" you ask.

"No. It's got two 'P's'."

Yes, and two N's, but your respondent does not tell you this. He doesn't know it or remember it. Names always need rechecking.

---

[18]*Loc. cit.*
[19]"David and Goliath," *Time*, Dec. 22, 1975, p. 44.

At the end of the interview, Norm Schreiber, who writes for *Playboy*, *Saturday Review*, and other magazines, usually asks: "Is there anything I haven't asked that I should have?" It seldom yields anything of value

Figure 5.2 "Come on, now, there must be more to the story than that," student Jan Brown seems to be saying to her interviewee as she gathers information. Some gentle prodding often is necessary in an interview session. (*Photographed by the author in natural light using Tri-X film in a miniature full-frame Olympus 35 RC with automatic exposure.*)

that hasn't already emerged, Schreiber reports, but it reassures the interviewee that the writer is conscientious. And it gives the interviewee a chance to say all that he wants to say.[20]

Ken Metzler writes: "Experienced interviewers will tell you that some of the best, most quotable material comes as a kind of afterthought as you are standing at the doorway saying goodbye. Here the respondent, relaxing after the 'ordeal,' offers interesting anecdotes or interesting observations. The interviewer will listen carefully (pulling out a notebook or turning on the recording would destroy the mood), and write down the material as soon as possible after he's left."[21]

That famous interview in *Playboy* of Jimmy Carter, in which, as the questioning at Plains came to a close, the candidate made his offhand remarks about lust, bears Metzler out.

• Phrasing the Questions

You can learn a lot about phrasing questions by reading the question-and-answer pieces in magazines like *Playboy*, *Psychology Today*, and *U.S. News & World Report*. Not that you would be able necessarily to duplicate the showing of erudition of the interviewers represented there. They no doubt have enjoyed some self-editing prior to appearing in print. But you will see that many of the provocative quotations from the subjects were triggered by provocative and informed questioning.

You must avoid phrasing questions that force the respondent into expected answers. Allow yourself the luxury of some surprises. Ask open-end questions that give the interviewee room to elaborate.

When the conversation bogs down throw in some move-along questions, like "Why is that?" and "Would you describe it for me?" and "Can you think of any reasons?" Occasionally use an exclamation, like "You're kidding!"

Your questions don't have to be phrased as questions. You can make a statement that will cause the subject to react.

Colin Campbell [in *Psychology Today* (February 1976, p. 95)]: "You seem to have taken an intellectual turn or two over the years. Once you were a lib-

---

[20]Quoted in "The Art of the Interview," *Folio*, February 1976, p. 65.

[21]Ken Metzler, *Creative Interviewing*, Prentice-Hall, Inc., Englewood Cliffs, N.J., 1977, p. 21.

eral. Now you're classed as a kind of a modern Malthus, a pessimist, one of those 'prophets of doom' politicians are always complaining about."

Robert Heilbroner: "You're right about a change of heart, but I object to the word pessimist. My latest book, *The Human Prospect*, is a grave book and it speaks of real dangers, but it isn't doomsday. It's a picture of some unpleasant things that seem likely to happen."

And then interviewer Campbell comes back with a question that doesn't need a question mark:

For instance.

In interviewing, it may be the best two-word question of all.

• The Value of Silence

Sometimes complete silence becomes the interviewer's tool. A. J. Liebling's technique was to sit quietly in front of his subject and make no move to get the interview started. The subject would begin to fidget, and then, somewhat unnerved, began volunteering information.

Mike Wallace told writer Dan Foley that "Silence during the course of an interview is often as important as talking. Ask a question, get the answer, and then just let it hang there. The subject will often try to help you out. . . . "

Another technique Wallace mentioned: ". . . reveal an intimate detail about yourself, thus indicating to your subject you expect the same."[22] You get the interviewee into a sort of "Can You Top This?" session. But ". . . No techniques, no tricks, no ploys will substitute for the impression you make as a person," writes Hugh C. Sherwood. "Despite the thrill that some people feel at the prospect of being interviewed by a journalist, despite the suspicion, even hostility, that others exhibit, they will ultimately respond to you not as a journalist but as another human being. Make a good impression and, if the person whom you are interviewing is intelligent and informed about the subject at hand, you should get a good interview. Make a poor impression and you will fail — or at least come away with less than you might have."[23]

[22]Quoted in "The Writing Life," *Writer's Digest*, March 1976, p. 5.
[23]Hugh C. Sherwood, *The Journalistic Interview*, Harper & Row, Publishers, New York, 1969, p. 5.

• Writing Questions in Advance

The beginning interviewer may feel it necessary to write out questions in advance. This could be a help, provided the list contains only a few questions to get things started, or questions whose answers are vital to the article. The list should not dictate the exact course of the questioning. It is the give and take between interviewer and interviewee that produces the material of which readable articles are built. Ken Metzler's definition of the journalistic interview is worth noting: "A conversation designed to *exchange* information so as to produce intelligence for publication neither participant could produce alone." Metzler suggests that the journalist "bears much responsibility for bringing information to the conversation. It's not a one-sided affair. The sum total of the interchange is greater than that of both persons operating independently."[24]

As one of the college textbooks on reporting points out, if the interviewer "succeeds in getting his subject to volunteer facts, and not merely give minimum answers to . . . questions, he is on his way to a much better . . . story than he might otherwise obtain."[25]

• Inept Questions

Charlayne Hunter, then a college sophomore, now a *New York Times* reporter, was escorted from the University of Georgia in 1961, suspended "for her own protection" after a riot broke out under her dormitory window. Hunter and one other student, both blacks, had just been admitted to the University, which for 175 years had been segregated. The change was too much for a segment of the students and, riled over a basketball defeat that night anyway and urged on by members of the Ku Klux Klan, they began throwing literal and verbal garbage at the young coed who stood in her room. After she left, the victim of unbelievable abuse, an NBC reporter stuck a mike in her face and asked: "Charlayne, why did you cry when you left the school?"

[24]Ken Metzler, *Magazine Article Writing I*, correspondence course manual issued by The Office of Independent Study, Oregon State System of Higher Education, Portland, 1974.

[25]Phillip H. Ault and Edwin Emery, *Reporting the News*, Dodd, Mead & Company, New York, 1959, p. 123.

Nora Ephron's favorite TV interviewer's question, possibly apoc-
ryphal, delivered to a victim being removed on a stretcher from a
burning building, is: "How do you feel about the fact that your legs
were just blown off, sir?" The trouble with TV interviewers is that
they are after the *feel* of the event, not the substance, Michael J. Arlen
points out in a *New Yorker* article.[26] They ask questions often only as
an excuse to put their subjects on camera or before the microphone.
You can see them there sometimes paying no attention to the answers
they get, trying only to figure out a next question in order to fill up
the time segment assigned them.

"When a reporter jams a microphone into the face of the President
of the United States, after he has fallen harmlessly on the ski slope,
and asks if the fall makes him look like an accident-prone bumbler
and will it hurt him in the coming elections, it seems like a new low in
inanity," *Editor & Publisher* editorializes.[27]

But interview ineptness is not confined to the electronics media. It
is just easier to point out there because the instances can be witnessed
or heard by everyone.

More interviewees should adopt the style of a response used by Dr.
Michael E. DeBakey, the heart-transplant specialist, who was interviewed following his marriage. The question was: why had he wanted
to get married? "Just from looking at you," the surgeon said evenly to
the reporter, "I can't believe you're that stupid."

• Taking Notes During the Interview

Many interviewees are bothered by notetaking. As soon as they see
their remarks going down on paper, they become a little too careful.
The spontaneity goes. That is why you should engage in small talk at
first, putting down a note only occasionally, and quickly, as the respondent warms to you or the subject being discussed. You might
even ask, when you make that transition, "Do you mind if I take that
down?"

H. Allen Smith, in *How to Write Without Knowing Nothing*, told of a
writer who solved the note-taking problem by carrying a stub of a

[26]Michael J. Arlen, "The Interview," *The New Yorker*, Nov. 10, 1975, pp. 141–150.
[27]"President Ford's Skiing," *Editor & Publisher*, Jan. 10, 1976, p. 6.

pencil in his coat pocket, and a tiny scratchpad. While the interviewee talked, the writer sneaked his hand into his pocket and scribbled.

In doing his extensive interviewing for *In Cold Blood*, Truman Capote took no notes. "People who don't understand the literary process are put off by notebooks, and tape recorders are worse – they completely ruin the quality of the thing being felt or talked about," he said. "If you write down or tape what people say, it makes them feel inhibited and self-conscious. It makes them say what they think you *expect* them to say."[28] Of course, Capote trained himself to retain what he hears. Even so, while working on *In Cold Blood* he did not allow more than three hours to elapse between listening and writing down what he had heard.

On the other hand some interviewers may be insulted if the writer doesn't take notes — or worried that the writer won't get his facts straight. You will have to size up your interviewee and then, taking into account your own strengths, decide which procedure to follow.

In most interviews, you will use your pencil and notebook only occasionally, putting down a few impressions, a few direct quotations. Often, during the interviewing, a beginning for the article will occur to you, or a title will leap out at you; you'll mark these down, too, before they get away from you.

You will be on the watch always for anecdotes. Some interviewees have to be prodded for these. But "Can you think of any good anecdotes I can use?" is not the way to do it. In the first place, "anecdote" is a writer's word, not an interviewee's or even a reader's word. The interviewee might not even know what you mean by "anecdote." In the second place, the interviewer, not the interviewee, should be the one to decide what makes a good anecdote.

Questions like "What happened then?" or "Have you ever felt threatened?" can be used to flush out anecdotes. An even more productive way to get them is to engage in a story-swapping session. You tell about something that has happened to you, and he counters with something that has happened to him.

Maurice Zolotow, who produces personality pieces, allows the conversation to ramble during a first interview, then gets down to substantive questions in subsequent interviews. Zolotow likes to move in

---

[28] Quoted by Jane Howard, "How the 'Smart Rascal' Brought It Off," *Life*, Jan. 7, 1966, p. 71.

with his subjects, often well-known people, and spend several days observing and questioning. Then he looks up friends and enemies of the subject, searching out anecdotal material. The interviewing completed, he immerses himself in the subject, living with his notes, rereading them, "gradually formulating them into an article pattern." He says, "When a lead begins to take shape in my mind, I know I am ready to prepare a reasonably coherent outline, which I follow, more or less, as it gives me unity and provides sensible transitions from one topic to another."[29]

There is much to be said for letting an interview wander off course. The story that emerges could be better than the story the writer originally envisioned. But sometimes it becomes obvious that such wandering is going nowhere.

André Fontaine suggests ways to bring an interview back under control. "If he wanders too far from the subject you can often call him back simply by leaning back in your chair and looking out the window in obvious boredom. You can exert many degrees of influence by the way you take notes. Normally the man watches what you write down and what you don't. This serves as a guide to him; he wants to say things that will make you take notes and once he sees what you write down and what you ignore, he'll try to feed you more of the significant material. You can use this: when he wanders, simply stop taking notes. He'll get the message. If he doesn't I've sometimes gone so far as to close my notebook and toss it disdainfully on the desk. That jars him."[30]

It is a good idea to save the more controversial questions for last. Take a leaf from the rule book of the professional public-opinion pollsters. These people always wait until after they have the bulk of their questions answered before suggesting that the respondent "Check the figure on the card that most closely approximates your annual salary" or before blurting out, "May I ask what your annual salary is?" If the pollster then finds himself being ushered out by an irate respondent, it is not a serious matter. The bulk of the information has already been gathered.

[29]Maurice Zolotow, "Style, Personality and the Magazine Article," *The Writer's Handbook*, The Writer, Inc., Boston, 1958, pp. 338, 339.

[30]André Fontaine, *The Art of Writing Nonfiction*, Thomas Y. Crowell Co., New York, 1974, pp. 50, 51.

Fortunately, most interviewing done by magazine article writers does not involve embarrassing questions. The interviewing experience is usually a pleasant one.

• Using the Tape Recorder

Tape recorders have become so portable, so inconspicuous, that their use in interviewing has become almost expected. Writers use them in two ways. One way is to turn the recorder on right at the beginning and let the first few minutes of the interview go along awkwardly while the respondent gets used to the idea of being on tape. Soon he forgets about the recorder, and the conversation proceeds smoothly and informally. The other way is to talk with the respondent infor-

"If you don't mind, I'd like to record our conversation. . . ."

mally at first, to loosen him up, and then, when the conversation is nicely underway, to reach over inconspicuously and press the button. Of course the respondent has been told previously that the material will be recorded.

Using a tape recorder is advised for those articles that are controversial or where the respondent is likely to come back later to disclaim what he has said. The tapes in such cases are kept on file.

The user of a tape recorder must watch for the tape's ending and switch it over to the other side to catch the remainder of the respondent's remarks. Many a recorded interview has ended abruptly on one side of a cassette tape because the interviewer did not remain alert. For some writers a system with a built-in buzzer system is worth the extra money. Ninety- or 120-minute tapes minimize stopping and turning problems.

Tad Szulc, who writes mainly on foreign affairs, interviews with a tape recorder only when he thinks the interviewee can take it or when the subject matter demands it. When he gets home, even though he has taken handwritten notes, he dictates impressions into a recorder and sends the cassettes to a typist.[31]

Some writers use tape recorders not just to record their notes but to actually write their articles. But many writers, distrustful of all machinery (their whole life flashes before them when they put a plug into an electric outlet), or steeped in habits that have worked well enough over the years to merit continuing, scoff at the use of tape recorders. Nora Ephron seldom uses one. "I find there are few people worth listening to twice."

Patricia O'Brien, then a feature writer for the Chicago *Sun-Times*, encountered a switch on the use of tape recorders. When she interviewed Phyllis Schlafly, the anti-ERA activist, she found the *respondent* turning on a tape recorder. From O'Brien's published feature:

> "I get misquoted all the time," she explained cheerfully. "You've no objections, have you?"

• Checking Back with the Interviewee

The interviewee may ask to see the manuscript — or at least a portion of it — before it is published. The interviewer agrees to the condition

[31]Frank S. Joseph, "The Last Entrepreneurs," *Chicago Journalism Review*, September 1975, p. 21.

if that is the only way to get the interview and the interview is vital to the story, or if the material is complicated enough to require the checking. In some cases the writer initiates the request to check back, as this author did for a personality sketch of Charles Schulz. It was clear that Schulz was not one to split hairs. What he did offer were two or three corrections to factual errors. But giving an interviewee a crack at your manuscript can be dangerous. The interviewee may quarrel with you at every or any turn. "You can write the most wonderful piece in the world about someone," Nora Ephron observes, "and the only word they'll see is 'plump.'"

The bigger magazines like *Esquire* and *New York* do not want their writers to give their interviewees access to the unpublished manuscript. The trade journals, on the other hand, generally approve such arrangements. Sometimes a sale there is helped along with a letter from the interviewee attesting to the accuracy of the information and quotes.

What many magazines — big ones and little ones — encourage their writers to do is to check only the direct quotations with the interviewees. It is the rare writer who is able to reproduce quotes with complete fidelity. Besides, the interviewee might want to clean up the quotes a bit. The edited versions might be closer to what the interviewee really wants to say. Some interviewees who have been stung in the past by inaccurate quotes like to type out their answers to tough questions rather than respond orally and quickly.

• Quoting Out of Context

The quotation from your interviewee may not be wrong, exactly; it just starts and stops without adequate introduction or explanation. Not knowing what preceded the quotation or what followed it, the reader leaps to a wrong conclusion. And the interviewee is embarrassed and angered.

The writer of a nonfiction book tells an interviewer: "It's research that separates the successful from the unsuccessful writer. What makes nonfiction writing less attractive to students than fiction writing is the specter of research. Long hours in a musty library, tedious correspondence, or trips to unfamiliar offices for backgrounding. And facts. Dull, cold, unyielding figures . . ." But the book writer also tells the interviewer that "Fact-finding is not just for the writer of nonfiction. Fiction writers also must spend hours — years, maybe — getting background information before proceeding to tell a story." Unfortunately the interviewer is too busy getting down "What makes nonfiction writing less attractive to students than fiction writing is the specter of research" to listen carefully, and so misses the "Fiction writers also must spend hours . . ." line. The book writer is about to be quoted out of context.

To avoid quoting out of context you must listen for ideas and themes as much as for words. You should offer introductory and summary material to your reader as well as quotation. To keep the material in context, you may even find it necessary to indicate the kinds of questions that prompted the answers you got.[32]

• Phony Quotes

An out-of-context quote shows up in an article, usually, because the writer is not sharp enough to sense it. Or maybe he is just lazy. A made-up quotation, on the other hand, is deliberate. The writer chooses to be in error.

"The extensive space given . . . [the] interview with me is certainly flattering," writes a political party official to a campus newspaper. But "the use of the question and answer format is not justified as the answers are not completely mine. In an approximation of my answers, . . . [the reporter] has put together many random comments, some direct quotes, and a large amount of published information into paragraphs surrounded by quotation marks. While most of the statements are correct as to content, the language, clarity (or lack of it), and style are not mine."

A surprisingly restrained complaint, considering the enormity of the offense. Is such contempt for fairness and accuracy confined to the college press? Not at all. Frank Graham, Jr., who wrote "The Story of a College Football Fix" for *The Saturday Evening Post*, which cost the magazine a libel judgment in 1963, said that re-creating quotes is "a common practice in journalism."[33]

[32] Paul F. Boller in *Quotemanship: The Use and Abuse of Quotations for Polemical and Other Purposes* (Southern Methodist University Press, 1967) shows how speakers and writers unfairly use quotations. The problem involves the use of secondary as well as primary sources.

[33] *Time*, Aug. 23, 1963, p. 34.

If you have ever been interviewed for publication yourself, you no doubt have read direct-quote paragraphs that couldn't possibly have come from you. You just don't talk that way. Probably you don't even agree with the content of the paragraphs. The reporter completely missed your nuances.

And yet reporters and writers justify the practice of "re-creating" quotes — or creating them — because "that is what he meant to say" or "that is about what he said." Why these journalists can't settle for *indirect* quotations in such cases is a mystery, unless for typographic reasons they feel that direct quotes provide a nice change of pace.

Readers assume, and rightly, that when direct quotes go around a sentence or paragraph, that is exactly what the person said. A writer should avoid using quote marks, then, except in those places where his notetaking has been stenographic.

There may be occasions when a piece of conversation, enclosed in quotation marks, is fictional, as in an historical piece. The writer could not possibly have been there to hear the exchange between his characters. But the reader understands this.

If a direct quote has a spelling or grammatical error, you may be right to correct it. An editor does as much for a reporter, and in handling a quote you are acting as a sort of editor. But sometimes leaving the errors untouched helps establish the character of the quotation. In a magazine article, in contrast to a book or thesis, you would avoid using "[*sic*]" to show that you know you are perpetuating an error. A "[*sic*]" in the magazines has a smart-alecky ring. Maybe the best solution is to change the direct quote to an indirect quote, and improve the language in the process.

• Direct vs. Indirect Quotes

In case you have forgotten the difference between a direct quote and an indirect quote, consider these two sentences. The first carries a direct quote, the second an indirect quote.

> J. Frank Dobie said, "The average Ph.D. thesis is nothing but a transference of bones from one graveyard to another."

* * * * *

> J. Frank Dobie said that the average Ph.D. thesis is nothing but a transference of bones from one graveyard to another.

An indirect quote can be rewritten (this one wasn't) to improve the grammar, to shorten it, to make it clearer. A *direct quote*, on the other hand, must be left alone, except to shorten it. It is seldom a good idea in a magazine article to run a direct quotation of more than a couple of sentences. Sometimes the whole sentence is not needed — only a part of it. In this case, you take that part you need and put quotation marks around it, placing your paraphrasing in front of it or behind it, or both.

If you want two parts of a sentence or paragraph, but they are separated, you can keep the entire excerpt within the same quotation marks if you indicate with an ellipsis (three periods) those words you left out. If you remove the tail end of a sentence, leave in its period. This will sometimes mean you'll have four periods rather than three. If you want to insert a short comment of your own within the direct quotation, enclose that comment in brackets, not parentheses. Parentheses indicate that the comment is the parenthetical thought of the original writer.

Magazine editors themselves are vague on some of these rules, and they may change your handling of periods, brackets and parentheses; this should not discourage you from sticking to correct style.

The thing to remember about a direct quote is that whatever you put between the quotation marks *must be exactly what that person said or wrote*. Even more important, the direct quote (and the indirect quote, too) *should agree with the theme of the section from which it is taken*.

• Words of Attribution

The best word to attach to your source name is "said" (or "says"). It is a word that, because it is not important, can be used over and over again. In that respect, it is like "the." You do not need a synonym for it.

If the person quoted suddenly steps up his tempo, shows emotion, or does something else to give force to an utterance, or to tone it down, you can then reach for the appropriate synonym: "sputtered," "cried," "shouted," "whispered," or whatever. Or you can add an adjective, like "cheerfully" or "warily." But ordinarily, "said" by itself is good enough, relieved only occasionally by terms like "pointed out," "emphasized," "added," "admitted," or "agreed." You do not want to detract from what is inside the quotes. Your purpose is not to dazzle your reader with your arsenal of words that can stand in for "said."

If you must use a synonym for "said," make sure it is a word that carries with it the notion of words coming from someone's mouth. Be reminded that a person cannot "smile" or "grin" a sentence.

Finally, make sure the synonym fits the occasion. Ring Lardner taught us that with his "'Shut up,' he explained.'"

The attribution chosen can help you let the reader know what you think of the quotation. "To hear *The Nation* tell it . . . ," writes M. J. Sobran, Jr. — and you know right away that he does not share the ideology of that publication.

In presenting bits of conversation, you don't always need an attribution. The attribution is understood. The context covers it. From a George Leonard article on running in *New West*:

> "Can he outrun you?"
> "No."
> "How does he feel about that?"
> She laughed. "Everybody asks him. Actually, it's no big deal."

Note that she does not laugh the sentence. She laughs first. Then she speaks.

The interviewer's question can be included in the article as an indirect rather than a direct quote, and without an "asked." See how Sally Quinn does it in a feature about Alice Roosevelt Longworth:

> What kind of people does she like, who amuses her, interests her?
> "Oh, just the people in this very room, my dear," she coos.[34]

• YOUR VOLUNTEER STAFF

Any number of persons out there, in business and government or even unaffiliated, stand ready to help you gather your facts. Chamber of Commerce and trade association officials, as well as directors of public relations for companies and nonprofit organizations, do this kind of work routinely as part of their jobs. At the government level — federal, state, county, and city — you have public information officers ready to serve you. Often, dealing with these people, you can get what you need without going to persons higher up in the executive ranks.

---

[34]Sally Quinn, "Alice Roosevelt Longworth at 90," *Writing in Style* (Laura Longley Babb, Editor), Houghton Mifflin, Boston, 1975, p. 165.

Whatever you get from such sources, however, public as well as private, you would check carefully for evidence of bias. Whenever possible, you would search out sources with opposing philosophies.

You should use members of your volunteer staff not only for the information they can supply but also for the help they can give you in getting information from some other source. Let's say you have some questions about the issuance of driving licenses in the various states. Of course, you can send off letters to the 50 Divisions of Motor Vehicles, or whatever they may be called. But that would not only be time-consuming; it would also be expensive. The information you seek may already have been gathered and possibly published. If so, someone in your own state Division would know about it.

College campuses provide a wide range of research sources. Pennsylvania State University has gone so far as to issue to writers a directory of its faculty members who are experts on various subjects. *Press Contacts* is available from the director of public information.

Don't overlook the possibility of help from private citizens. To gain some additional facts and anecdotes for a ship-disaster story he was writing for *Argosy*, Joseph E. Brown in San Diego, near where the disaster occurred, put an ad in the "personals" column of the *Union* inviting survivors to get in touch with him. "My telephone jangled for weeks," he reports.

Some writers, especially book authors, ask magazines to run notices asking for information about biographees. You have seen such notices — published letters — in *The New York Times Book Review*.

If you need professional help in a city too far away to travel to, considering the pay you will be getting for the article, you may be able to get inexpensive help from a freelancer in the area. The annual *Literary Market Place* lists research-oriented persons under "Freelance Editorial Work."

• THE VALUE OF PRIMARY RESEARCH

Conscientiously pursued, primary sources yield the information and ideas that form the core of most of the articles and features appearing in magazines and newspapers. Some articles stop with primary research. But others rely on another form of research as well. That research — digging into secondary sources — will be described in the next chapter.

CHAPTER 6

RESEARCH: WORKING FROM SECONDARY SOURCES

A case history: An author lets a file folder accumulate newspaper stories and features and magazine articles on cigarette smoking and health. He has nothing in mind, particularly. No theme. No market. He's just interested. The file folder soon bulges, and another takes the overflow. One afternoon he takes out the folders and, scanning the material, comes up with an idea: an informative article for nonsmokers, telling about the risks, and costs, even to people who don't smoke. Without any further research, not even a scanning of the listings in a guide to periodical literature, he constructs an article, "What the Nonsmoker Should Know About Smoking," and sends it to a family religious magazine likely to have a high percentage of nonsmokers among its readers. The article sells.

Was this enough of a service for a journalist to perform? Probably; because he shifted and sorted and picked out tidbits his readers otherwise would have missed, put them into context, added some observations of his own, and organized the package. That, too, is article writing.

But ordinarily you would want to supplement your haphazard collection of materials with more formal inquiry into secondary sources as well as material gathered from primary sources.

In working from secondary sources you deal with material that theoretically has already been seen by people. This somewhat devaluates the material; you have lost your scoop. And there is another disadvantage in secondary material: it has been run through a filter, in the form of another writer, an editor, a proofreader, a typesetter, or maybe even a person engaged in abridgment. The reproduction can never be as faithful as the original — in art, in photography, in

"I'm doing an article for a journalism class. Where do I do research?"

music, in the source material for research. It may be more polished, freer of error, easier to get at. But people have stepped between you and the true source, and they have made some decisions, decisions you might not have made.

Obviously, from a research standpoint, secondary sources are not as good as primary sources. But they are often good enough.

The closer the secondary source is to the primary source, the better it is likely to be. Better to take statistics from *Statistical Abstract of the United States* than from a book that took them from *Statistical Abstract of the United States*, but better to take them from that book than to take them from a magazine article that got them from the book, but better to take them from the magazine article than from a digest of the magazine article, but better to take them from the digest of the article than from a press release or news story based on the digested article.

You do some of your digging into secondary sources in your own home, as when you consult a dictionary, encyclopedia, atlas, or almanac, and when you take notes from trade books and textbooks you have purchased and magazines and newspapers you subscribe to. Mostly you work at a good library. Familiarizing yourself with secondary sources is largely a matter of familiarizing yourself with the library. Perhaps the place to start, if you are new at secondary research, is with a recent book on the use of the library like Jean K. Gates's *Guide to the Use of Books and Libraries* (McGraw-Hill).

• THE LIBRARY

The writer living in the Washington, D.C., area has access to the ideal library: the Library of Congress with its 72,000,000 items (1975 count), including 17,000,000 books and pamphlets. The collection also includes microfilms of some 1,200 daily newspapers and every doctoral dissertation written since the 1950s. But big-city and big-university libraries serve the writer well enough in most cases.

A library, so far as the article writer is concerned, has two main departments: the call department and the reference department.

• The Call Department

The call department, including the circulation desk, includes periodicals and all regularly circulated books, along with the card index that lists them. Libraries file their call cards under one of two systems: the Dewey Decimal system or the Library of Congress system. The former system is used by most public libraries, the latter by most research libraries, because it carries more detailed categories. Librarians can expand the Library of Congress system indefinitely.

In either case, cards are filed in small file drawers, and for each book in the library there are three cards: one is filed by author, one by title, one by subject. On the cards will be some description that will help you decide whether the book is worth asking for, and a call number, which shows you (if the library operates on the open-stack principle) or the librarian where the book is located. If a book you're after is not indexed, this means the library doesn't have it. If you have sufficient information about the book from some other source (name of book, author, publisher, date of publication), your library can get it for you under its interlibrary loan system.

• The Reference Department

The other department is the reference department. Here you'll find listings of countless writings and compilations that may have a direct bearing on the article you are working on. In the department, too, you will find many of the sources themselves. These sources are to be used on the premises. They do not circulate. Other sources you uncover in the reference department can be traced down in the call department and checked out for home use.

If you feel lost in the reference department, go for help, first to the reference librarian, then to Constance M. Winchell's *Guide to Reference Books* and its three supplements compiled by Eugene P. Sheehy. With each entry annotated, you can familiarize yourself with some 7,500 different reference works. If that does not satisfy you, you can turn to similar guides: A. J. Walford's *Guide to Reference Materials*, Frances Neel Cheney's *Fundamental Reference Sources*, William A. Katz's *Introduction to Reference Work*, the *American Reference Books Annual*, and Sarah L. Prakken's *The Reader's Adviser*. The last-named work, in three volumes, had reached a 12th edition by 1974. With its annotated entries covering both books and periodicals, it is as much for browsing as for research.

When you go to one of the reference books described in any of these guides, study its organization, style, and promise before settling in on the pages that seem to serve you in your current quest. You may be surprised at the book's scope. You may also find there are tricks to using the book. You may find, for instance, a different kind of alphabetizing than you're used to. For instance, where telephone directories carry names like David McKay Company in the "D"s, directories like *Literary Market Place* alphabetize them by last name. David McKay appears in the "M"s.

What seems useless as a reference work to one writer may seem invaluable to another. When Tom Wolfe was in graduate school he roomed with some medical students, and he picked up many of their terms. Anatomical references turn up often in his writing. To keep himself abreast, he refers often to *Gray's Anatomy*. "I think it is one of the things a writer should have around."[1]

• NEWSPAPERS AS RESEARCH SOURCES

Because reporters and editors work against such tight deadlines, newspapers contain more errors — certainly more typographical er-

[1] "Tom Wolfe on Writing," Pennsylvania *Gazette*, March 1976, p. 35.

rors — than other research sources. Even so, newspapers provide much that a researcher needs. Even the historians have come to regard newspapers, with all their imperfections, as indispensable.

Taking material from newspapers, you should distinguish between reportage, which usually is objective, and editorial writing, which carries opinion.

When you quote from a news story, paraphrase a section of the story, or simply borrow a fact or two, you should note whether the story was staff-produced or supplied by the Associated Press, United Press International, or one of the smaller associations or syndicates. If the story carries a byline, you should mark down the writer's name. Whether or not you later credit the source in your article, you still should work into your notes these bits of information.

When you quote from a signed, syndicated column of opinion on the page — from conservative James J. Kilpatrick, for instance, or, at the other extreme, Anthony Lewis — the quote does not necessarily represent the thinking of the newspaper in which the column appears. If you quote from an editorial on the same page (usually found in the lefthand column), you are right in suggesting to your readers that what is quoted represents the opinion of the paper.

It helps the article writer doing research to know the editorial philosophy of the newspaper quoted. A quote seeming to support a conservative political or economic idea from the editorial columns of the Washington *Post*, for instance, would be more significant than a similar quote from the conservative Indianapolis *Star* or Phoenix *Republic* or *Gazette*.

You have three systematic ways to hunt out information from this source. One way involves the use of the card file system of the library's call department. In a large library, there will be a card index available covering the stories in one or more important local or regional papers. A university library might even have a card index covering stories in the university paper.

A second way involves the use of bound indexes to newspaper stories, found in the reference department. Several newspapers publish indexes. In 1977 it became possible to easily track down the syndicated columns appearing in newspapers. The Microfilming Corporation of America, Glen Rock, New Jersey, began publishing *Viewpoint*, a monthly magazine carrying all the columns, indexed, written by 100 writers with "the widest possible ideological balance." Facts on File,

New York, publishes a semi-monthly, *Editorials on File,* covering 140 United States and Canadian newspapers.

A third way is through the use of a newspaper's own library or morgue. A good newspaper maintains for its staff members a rather comprehensive file of past stories — folders full of clippings — sometimes open to outside writers. "I've found that it's wise to write the newspaper library instead of the newspaper city desk," reports Jerry Hopkins (*Writer's Digest,* June 1975), who has had some luck getting past city-room barriers. "Perhaps that's because librarians, like the researcher, are interested in facts in a more historical sense than are most reporters, who are too busy reporting the day's news to have the same perspective, or the time."

• MAGAZINES AS RESEARCH SOURCES

As research sources, the most useful of the magazines are those edited for elite or specialized audiences. Such magazines present material not available to the average reader and often in a stilted form that begs for popularization. But the more general magazines are useful, too.

If you go back several years for an article, you may find one that differs in philosophy from what the magazine now runs. Magazines change as times change. The editorial philosophy of *The New Yorker,* for instance, seen in "The Talk of the Town" section, differs considerably from what it was, say, ten years ago. The *Newsweek* of the mid-1960s and later is a very different magazine from the *Newsweek* of the 1950s. You can't even say that *National Review* fully resembles the *National Review* William F. Buckley, Jr., launched in the 1950s upon his graduation from Yale. Close readers of *The New Republic* saw subtle changes in that magazine's focus as a new owner took over in the 1970s.

It is possible to know enough about magazines to assume some differences among them but not enough to realize that magazines sometimes surprise researchers with out-of-character articles.

In crediting your source it is not enough to say *"Harper's* says . . ." or *"The New Republic* argues . . ." if the article you quote contains a byline. The name of the writer is more important than the name of the publication. The opinion expressed is the writer's, not the magazine's.

Of course, if it is an unsigned editorial you are quoting (some magazines run editorials) or something out of a magazine like *Sunset* that does not identify writers, you would then credit only the magazine. This holds true, generally, for the news magazines, although they are moving away from the "group journalism" that was for so long their benchmark.

• BOOKS AS RESEARCH SOURCES

Before giving your attention to a book, you'll want to find out what you can about the author. You will also pay some attention to the publisher imprint. Is it the kind of publisher who can be counted on to produce books worth quoting from?

A study of catalogs in *The Publishers' Trade List Annual* will teach you much about the preferences and peculiarities of given book publishers. Regular reading of *Publishers Weekly* will, after a while, make you something of an expert in book publishing.

In evaluating a book, it is important to note the recency of publication. It is also important to study the table of contents, the foreword, and the introduction. And you'll come to appreciate the author who has been thoughtful enough to include an index (speeding up your search for specific information) and some footnotes (giving you new ideas for further research).

• Reference Works

The following sections call your attention to some of the reference works useful to conducting research for articles.[2]

• **Dictionaries.**   Writer James M. Dunn uses this sentence to begin "Lobbying Isn't a Dirty Word," an article in *Eternity* (July 1975):

> Webster's dictionary says that lobbying is simply attempting to influence legislation.

---

[2] To keep the listings manageable, this chapter will omit publishers' — and authors', editors', and compilers' — names. Among the most active publishers of reference works are R. R. Bowker Co., H. W. Wilson Co., and Gale Research Co. You might want to study their catalogs in *The Publishers' Trade List Annual*.

Two problems: Was "simply" part of the definition? Or was it a word added by the author, here using an indirect quote? The reader can't be sure. The second problem: which "Webster's" dictionary is Dunn quoting from?

G. & C. Merriam Company holds the original claim to the "Webster" title by virtue of its buying the unsold copies of Noah Webster's dictionary at his death in 1843 and promoting and revising it. But Webster's book is now long out of copyright, and many companies have affixed the Webster name to their dictionaries. "Webster's name was a fertile source of litigation for decades, producing, in some years, more suits than Brooks Brothers," Felicia Lamport wrote in *Harper's* (September 1959).

Looking at them from the standpoint of number of words covered, dictionaries, Webster or not, fall into three categories: unabridged, abridged, and school or college. A school or college dictionary differs from an abridged dictionary in that it is often separately compiled and contains fewer words — no more than about 160,000.

An *unabridged* dictionary is an exhaustive compendium, sometimes spreading out over several volumes. The *Oxford English Dictionary on Historical Principles* in 12 volumes is easily the most impressive of all dictionaries in the English language. Published in Great Britain, it offers, in addition to the definitions, information on the origins of words, giving examples of their first uses in literature. The *O.E.D.*, as it is known, also comes in an abridged, two-volume edition and in an unabridged two-volume edition with a magnifying glass to read the tiny type.

The most famous unabridged dictionary published in America is G. & C. Merriam Company's *Webster's New International Dictionary of the English Language*. And the most honored edition of that dictionary was the second, published in the early 1930s. Like dictionaries before it, it distinguished between right and wrong usage. The third edition, coming out in the late 1950s, did not discriminate. Commenting on this philosophy, cartoonist Alan Dunn showed a secretary at G. & C. Merriam Company talking to a visitor. "Sorry. Dr. Grove ain't in." The New York *Times* ran an item with this lead: "A passel of double-domes at the G. & C. Merriam Company joint in Springfield, Mass., have been confabbing and yakking for twenty-seven years — which is not intended to infer that they have not been doing plenty work —

and now they have finalized Webster's Third New International Dictionary, Unabridged, a new edition of that swell and esteemed word book."

A number of purist editors refused to accept the new edition, guarding their Seconds as though they were part of the incunabula.[3]

Dictionaries can also be specialized. For instance, if you are interested in slang, you might want to consult Eric Partridge's *Dictionary of Slang and Unconventional Language* or Harold Wentworth's and Stuart Berg Flexner's *Dictionary of American Slang*.

Many professions and businesses have their own dictionaries, called "glossaries" if they are confined to the back pages of a book. Poets have their rhyming dictionaries. There are also dictionaries of synonyms and antonyms, the most famous of which is Roget's *International Thesaurus*. It groups words that are similar but not strictly synonymous. It classifies words by categories. One version classifies words alphabetically, as a regular dictionary would do.

Terry Tucker Francis, who specializes in articles on legend and lore, uses a thesaurus to get more out of the card catalog. If she is looking for works on magic, for instance, she looks up the word in her thesaurus and finds additional headings to explore: "conjury," "sorcery," "enchantment," "wizardry," "incantations," "occultism," and "supernaturalism" — headings she might not think of on her own.[4]

Other dictionaries of synonyns include *Allen's Synonyms and Antonyms, Funk & Wagnall's Standard Handbook of English Synonyms, Antonyms and Prepositions, Funk & Wagnall's Modern Guide to Synonyms and Related Words, New Webster's Dictionary of Synonyms,* and *The Writer's Book of Synonyms and Antonyms*.

Theodore M. Bernstein, author of several books on grammar and usage, in 1975 brought out *Bernstein's Reverse Dictionary*, published by Quadrangle. It is designed for the writer who has a meaning in mind but can't think of the word it fits. The meanings — 13,390 of them — are listed alphabetically. The purpose of the book, Bernstein says, is to help users of English and particularly serious writers avoid settling for a second-best word.

[3]James H. Sledd and Wilma R. Ebbit in 1962 brought out an anthology of articles on dictionaries, especially the controversial Webster's Third: *Dictionaries and That Dictionary* (Scott, Foresman).

[4]Terry Tucker Francis, "Writing About Legend and Lore," *The Writer*, August 1975, p. 24.

- **Encyclopedias.** An encyclopedia starts the writer off in his research, giving him background information and pointing him to more thorough and perhaps controversial sources.

A good encyclopedia is as important to a writer as a good dictionary, consulted almost as often. It is something you should have where you do your writing. You shouldn't have to run to the library each time you need to consult it, although you will, on occasion, want to search through the various encyclopedias only a library would have.

But a good encyclopedia runs to several volumes — and costs several hundred dollars. An alternative to one of these sets is *The New Columbia Encyclopedia*, a single-volume work that came out in a fourth edition in 1975. Its 50,000 articles spread out over 3,052 pages that weigh well over 10 pounds. *The Random House Encyclopedia* came out in 1977 to compete with the *Columbia* volume. It is more family-oriented.

Do not settle for one of those cheap grocery-store or discount-drugstore sets that are little more than clip and paste jobs. They are not only inadequate; they contain misleading or outdated information.

The more ambitious the title of the encyclopedia, the more suspicious you can afford to be. Publishers of the lesser encyclopedias also like to incorporate words in their titles to make them sound like the more established encyclopedias. Korvettes in New York in 1975 was offering a 15-volume *Illustrated World Encyclopedia* for $29.99 and, although it may have been worth the price, it was hardly in a class with *World Book Encyclopedia*, a monumental work that some buyers may have had vaguely in mind as they purchased the cheaper item.

Writers familiar with the editorial process at *World Book* can appreciate its value as a quick source of information even though it is edited for young readers. Each article, no matter how short, goes to the editors with a filled-in form citing sources used. Of course, whatever is submitted funnels into an editorial meatgrinder, and what comes out to the author for final checking is without much juice, but the facts are there, simple, objective, informative. When the editors add material, it coincides with what the author knows about the subject. Like any good multivolume encyclopedia, *World Book* presents each of its articles with a byline.

How different is this procedure from that used by the publisher of one of the off-brand sets. That publisher used to send photocopied materials from other publications, including other reference books, to freelancers and ask them to pick out what facts they could and construct pieces to given measurements, all standardized. That meant setting the typewriter for so many characters per line and typing an assigned number of lines each time. Authors would send in batches of biographies each week, and that's the last they ever saw of them.

Of course all these compendiums are fallible — even the *Encyclopaedia Britannica*. The 14th edition carried some articles on Russia provided by Novosti, the Soviet press agency. The articles were "about what one might expect from that source," Paul Greenberg said in his syndicated column (late November 1975). "In these articles, there is no mention that the Communist Party is the only one allowed in Soviet republics; it's just described as the 'leading' or 'guiding' party. As if there were others." Greenberg catalogues several other faults, and then explains: "The quality of such articles was perfectly foreseeable once the editors had commissioned party hacks and then disdained editing their work."

Following complaints from a number of critics, the publisher promised changes in later printings.

Sometimes the errors are merely typographical, but typographical errors can thwart the researcher, too. Even the Bible, in its various translations, has proved fallible. "The King James Bible stands as the great monument of English prose," Ben D. Zevin, head of a Bible publishing house, tells us. But "almost 150 years were to pass before this fine Biblical translation appeared without an excess of printer's errors." Among the various printings of the King James version was the "Wicked Bible," in which the Seventh Commandment mistakenly was printed to read: "Thou shalt commit adultery." There was also a "Wife-Hater's Bible" in which "wife" mistakenly was substituted for "life" in Luke 14:26.[5]

The *Britannica* changed things around for its fifteenth edition, calling it *Britannica 3* because of a three-part organization too complicated to go into here. Professor William L. Rivers of Stanford in his *Finding Facts* (Prentice-Hall, 1975) thought "The result is a readable and highly innovative encyclopedia that might change encyclo-

---

[5]Ben D. Zevin, "The Bible Through the Ages," chapter in *Bouillabaisse for Bibliophiles* (edited by William Targ), The World Publishing Company, Cleveland, 1955, p. 142.

pedia-making." Other big and important multivolume encyclopedias published in America include *Collier's Encyclopedia* and *Encyclopedia Americana.*[6]

The term "encyclopedia" is elastic enough to include specialized reference books, like *Encyclopedia of Associations, The Encyclopedia of Jazz,* and *Encyclopedia of Psychology.*

• **Biographical Guides.** For biographical information, you can turn to the various *Who's Who* books, starting with the prestigious *Who's Who in America* and moving down to the regional and specialized *Who's Who* books such as *Who's Who in the West, Who's Who in American Art, Who's Who in Commerce and Industry,* and *Who's Who of American Women.* Many of the lesser *Who's Who* books are vanity books, existing mainly to allow the publishers to sell copies to persons listed. But whether vanity or not, any of these can be useful if they contain entries for persons you are writing about. *Who's Who* books almost always contain material supplied directly by the person listed.

The British *Who's Who,* appearing first in 1849, served as the prototype for *Who's Who in America.* Unlike the American publication, *Who's Who* allows a little humor to slip into the material supplied by its biographees.

To find information about persons no longer living, you can turn to *Who Was Who in America.*

Other sources of biographical information include *Current Biography, Dictionary of American Biography, Dictionary of Canadian Biography, National Cyclopedia of American Biography, Webster's Biographical Dictionary,* and *Dictionary of National Biography* (Great Britain).

Congressional Directory provides biographical material on members of Congress. *Congressional Staff Directory* covers staff members.

If you are looking for information about an author, and you can't find an entry in a *Who's Who* you might turn to *Contemporary Authors* or *Twentieth Century Authors.*

For information on college professors, you can consult *Directory of American Scholars, American Men and Women of Science, The Physical and Biological Sciences,* or *The Social and Behavioral Sciences.*

There are many, many other biographical guides. One of the most useful to writers dealing with business subjects is *Poor's Register of Cor-*

[6]To learn about the differences among the various encyclopedias, consult the most recent edition of *General Encyclopedias in Print: A Comparative Analysis.*

porations, Directors and Executives, an annual that lists corporations and their officers and directors, gives biographical information about many of the executives, and names industrial products sold.

There is also a *Biography Index*, a quarterly that lists biographical material appearing in books as well as biographical articles appearing in magazines.

- **Guides to Magazine and Newspaper Material.** Any writer interested in what the magazines have run on a subject automatically turns to *Readers' Guide to Periodical Literature*. You can use this annual index with its periodic current-year updates for two purposes:

1. to see if an article on your subject has appeared during the past couple of years (if it has, and it sounds as though its angle is pretty close to yours, you may have to put yours off for a while); or
2. to note articles similar to yours and trace them down to see what they have to say.

You should remember that *Readers' Guide* covers only about 160 periodicals, voted in by librarians. If it covered many more, its size would be unmanageable. (There is an abridged *Readers' Guide* for small libraries.) Not all the magazines covered are general-interest. For instance, using *Readers' Guide*, you could trace down articles in *American Artist, BioScience, Car and Driver, Foreign Affairs, The Negro History Bulletin, The Writer, Writer's Digest, Seventeen*, and *Esquire* (but not *Playboy*). Most of the opinion magazines are covered.

Two recently established periodical guides cover magazines not covered in *Readers' Guide*. They are *Access: The Supplemental Index to Periodicals* (*Modern Bride, Pageant, People Weekly, Playboy*, and *Oui*, among others) and *Popular Periodical Index* (*Playboy, Human Events, Prevention*, among others).

To really measure what has been done with your subject, you can, after first exploring the guides to popular magazines, turn to one of the specialized indexes: *Social Sciences Index, Humanities Index, Art Index, The Music Index, Biological and Agricultural Index, Index Medicus* (covering medical and health journals), *Applied Science and Technology Index, Engineering Index, Bibliography and Index of Geology, Business Periodicals Index, Accountants' Index, Current Index to Journals in Education, Education Index, Index to Legal Periodicals, Biography Index* (mentioned earlier), *Psychological Abstracts*, and *Sociological Abstracts*. Appearing in *Journalism Quarterly* each issue is an index of articles about mass communications that have appeared in various magazines and journals.

There is even a *Fiction Catalog* (listings with annotations), *Short Story Index, Essay and General Literature Index, Play Index, Granger's Index to Poetry*, an index to songs, another to illustrations, one to mystery books, and many others.

For material appearing in magazines prior to 1907, you would turn to *Poole's Index to Periodical Literature*, defunct but still available in big libraries.

Most of these indexes list material by name of author, title of article, and subject matter covered.

A number of magazines run their own indexes each year to articles they have run. The New York *Times, The Times* of London, *The Wall Street Journal,* and *The Christian Science Monitor* publish indexes to the news items they publish. In addition, the New York *Times* publishes an index to its obituaries.

• **Book Listings.** A library's call cards list only the books in stock. With some 40,000 new books coming out each year, a library cannot hope to stock more than a fraction.

Several printed directories help you determine what is available if you can go outside. *Cumulative Book Index* lists all books that have been published in the English language. *Library of Congress Catalog* lists books on file at the Library of Congress, which means most books. *Books in Print* covers books you can still order from publishers. *The Publishers' Trade List Annual* carries catalogs of close to 1,400 publishers.

To find what reviewers said about books when they were published, consult *Book Review Digest*. For *listings only* of reviews, see *Book Review Index*, which covers more periodicals than *Book Review Digest* covers.

Every discipline has its scholars who put together specialized bibliographies. These often are annotated, helping you decide whether you really want to go after a book whose title sounds promising. In the field of journalism, for instance, the late Warren C. Price brought out *The Literature of Journalism*, to be followed by his and Calder M. Pickett's *Annotated Journalism Bibliography* and Eleanor Blum's *Basic Books in the Mass Media*. A field like journalism also has its specialized bibliographies, like one on public relations books or, narrower, one on *armed forces* public relations books.

• **Guides to Theses and Dissertations.** College libraries hold an advantage over public libraries in the theses and dissertations they stock. These bound but seldom-read manuscripts contain all varieties of statistics and quotations, all carefully footnoted (if abominably strung together).

Dwight Macdonald in *Against the American Grain* warns that sifting through this material in its raw form can be a disheartening activity. "The amount of verbal pomposity, elaboration of the obvious, repetition, trivia, low-grade statistics, tedious factification, drudging recapitulations of the half comprehended, and generally inane and laborious junk that one encounters suggests that the thinkers of earlier ages had one decisive advantage over those of today: they could draw on very little research."

The card catalog will help you trace down these and dissertations housed in your own library. *Comprehensive Dissertation Index 1861–1972*, *Dissertation Abstracts International*, and *Masters Abstracts* will help you trace down others.

• **Books of Quotations.** The 12th edition of *The Reader's Adviser* lists and describes 28 books of quotations. The best-known is *Bartlett's Familiar Quotations*. But Burton E. Stevenson's *Home Book of Quotations* and Bergen Evans's *Dictionary of Quotations* deserve your attention, too.

• **Books of Facts and Statistics.** *World Almanac and Book of Facts, Information Please Almanac*, and *Reader's Digest Almanac & Yearbook*, government and industry yearbooks, and books like *Famous First Facts, What Happened When*, and *The Guinness Book of World Records* offer you dates, times, sizes, and, especially, superlatives often useful for adding interest and credibility to your article.

Statistical Abstract of the United States digests data collected by government and nongovernment agencies. *Statistics Sources* leads you to the right books and sources for numbers.

Statesman's Yearbook offers information on countries all over the world.

Facts on File Yearbook puts together the issues of *Facts on File Weekly News Reference Service*, useful in that the researcher can trace events by person, subject, organization, or country.

- **Directories.** To help you find editors or their publications, the annual *Ayer Directory of Publications* covers most daily and weekly newspapers and just about every magazine in the United States and Canada and a few other places. *Ulrich's International Periodicals Directory* lists 55,000 existing publications from around the world, plus a number that have died. *Editor & Publisher International Year Book* concentrates on United States and Canadian newspapers, but it carries other information as well. And there are other directories in journalism, already alluded to in this book.

And hundreds of directories in other fields. Like *Women's Organizations & Leaders Directory, Academy Players Directory* (listing agents' names), *Official Museum Directory, The Research Centers Directory*, and *Directory of Special Libraries and Information Centers*.

- **Other Guides and Collections.** A part of a chapter can't do justice to the wealth of material available in a good reference department. But a few more passes at the various guides and collections, not easily classified, might be useful.

Vertical File Index lists all kinds of pamphlets and booklets published by both private and public organizations.

Monthly Catalog of United States Government Publications gives you the longest list of materials published by federal agencies.

Dee Stuart once almost gave up writing an article about gourds when she could find nothing in already published sources that could help her with her research. *Readers' Guide to Periodical Literature* contained no listing that showed any promise. Then someone told her about "Uncle Sam's Bookstore," the U.S. Government Printing Office, Washington, D.C. It had two modestly priced booklets on the subject.

"I promptly sent for them," Mrs. Stuart reports. "A few weeks later I had more information about gourds than I could ever use."

As a result, she sold two articles: "Gourds — Pretty and Practical" to *Popular Gardening* and "Gourds Are for the Birds" to *Flower Grower*.[7]

Public Affairs Information Service Bulletin indexes public affairs articles and other materials from a variety of sources.

Television News Index and Abstracts provides you with a guide to videotapes of network news broadcasts and documentaries available

---

[7]Dee Stuart, "Research at Uncle Sam's Bookstore," *The Writer's Handbook* (A. S. Burack, editor), The Writer, Boston, 1975, p. 565.

for rental at Vanderbilt University. *TV Season* records everything produced and broadcast by the television industry.

General World Atlases in Print: A Comparative Analysis helps you decide which atlas or gazetteer will be most useful to you.

Thomas' Register of American Manufacturers names products, trade names, and manufacturers. *The Trade Names Directory* tells you who makes what.

Acronyms and Initialisms Dictionary spells out the full name or names of any set of initials you uncover (the fourth edition, for instance, listed nine different organizations with the initials NCP).

The only way you can really appreciate these or other guides and collections is to sit down with those that seem promising to you in your writing specialties and see what they offer and how they are organized.

• COMPUTERIZED ABSTRACTING SERVICES

A number of government and private agencies have set up computerized abstracting services that will retrieve information useful to writers. For example, the National Clearinghouse for Mental Health Information, maintained by the National Institute of Mental Health, Rockville, Maryland, could give a writer a digested report about legislation on alcoholism or drug abuse. Probably the best-known of these services is ERIC at Stanford University, which is tied into most university libraries. The services, either free or provided at a minimum cost, give writers short summaries of articles, reports, papers delivered at scholarly and professional meetings, and other materials not otherwise available.

• NOTETAKING

With an article idea in mind, you would set up a file folder, or folders, into which would go relevant newspaper or magazine clippings (identified by name of publication, date, and page numbers), photocopies of book pages (also fully identified), folders and other direct-mail pieces, correspondence, and notes made from reading and interviewing. A major article develops slowly, over a period of weeks, months, even years. As a professional writer you would have a number of articles going at the same time, each with its own folder or folders.

The materials come to you more or less haphazardly. After they have had a chance to incubate, you can devote serious and full attention to the article. By now, perhaps, you have a favorable response to a query sent to an editor. Your research becomes more formal. You search out sources you know will be useful to you in rounding out the story.

At this stage you may set up two sets of notes or cards. One for bibliography, one for subject matter.

Keeping the bibliographical information on separate cards, you can refer to sources easily, without having to dig into cluttered notes. Keeping the notes on separate sheets, you can shuffle them into a logical order.

The bibliography consists typically of small cards (3 x 5) — one card per book or article. For books, each card carries (1) the name of the author, (2) name of the book, (3) name of publisher, (4) place of publication, (5) date of publication. On the back goes information about the book or author that you think may be important. For articles, each card carries (1) the name of the author (if there is a byline), (2) title or headline of the article, (3) name of the periodical in which it appears, (4) date of the issue, (5) pages on which the article is found. It is important to get all details down the first time around. Having to make a special trip to the library to dig out a name or page number can cost you hours.

The subject-matter cards or sheets can be larger than the bib cards. A handy size is 8½ x 5½ — typewriter paper half-sheets. At the top of each sheet goes, at the left, the quoted author's name (for later reference to the bib card) and, on the right, indication of the subject matter of the particular note. Use separate sheets for each item of interest, even when the items are from the same article. After any important notation put the page number in parentheses.

In taking notes, it's best to quickly scan the source material, to get an idea of the author's theme and reliability. You may decide the material is not worth borrowing from. If it *will* help the article, go back to the beginning to read it more carefully. Part of the time you can outline as you read, part of the time you can paraphrase large blocks, part of the time you can quote word for word.

Always look for signs of inaccuracies or bias. Wherever possible, check what you find against other sources. Retain a healthy skepticism throughout the research phase.

Some authors develop a special shorthand or set of abbreviations to speed up copying chores. This is fine, but it can bring later problems. Will you be able to tell later, for instance, whether the "comm." you put down is "committee" or "commission"? Does the "pub." mean "publisher" or "publication" or maybe "publicity" or "public"?

It may be that, having taken voluminous notes during the research phase, you may not actually refer to them, at least not while doing your first draft. That you have written down your facts and observations is enough to fix them in your mind. Not having written a fact down may well mean that a short time after noticing it you will have forgotten it.

Even though you do not cite all your sources in the article or use all the information you record, you will feel confident that, should the published article be challenged, you will be able to defend it.

• THE HANDLING OF STATISTICS

Benjamin Disraeli said "There are three kinds of lies: lies, damned lies, and statistics." You can "prove" almost anything with statistics. A given set can satisfy the needs of writers on both sides of an issue. Darrell Huff wrote an entertaining book showing you *How to Lie with Statistics*.

But people are impressed by statistics. A writer, to be convincing, must use them. Writer Wina Sturgeon says that "Statistics, properly applied, make anything more believable." And there is no denying that statistics, properly used, can tell the story as accurately as it can be told.

Reader infatuation with statistics does not mean an understanding of numbers. Big numbers become meaningless to most readers. As a writer, then, you try to reduce the numbers to manageable units. "One out of three Americans" is easier for readers to comprehend than "70,000,000 Americans."

Much of your work with secondary sources will involve digging out statistics. Some of the books you work with may be nothing more than tables of statistics. If the books are published by the agencies that gathered the statistics, you are, in effect, working with primary-source material. But many of the books of statistics will be re-presentations of statistics gathered by others. Other books — and periodicals — you work with will carry statistics only incidentally.

You should make sure that the statistics you choose lose nothing in their translation from table to prose. At the same time you want to put some flesh on them.

Make sure you fully explain your statistics. Wina Sturgeon tells of attending a governmental hearing on the canning-lid shortage in 1975. There she encountered a printed statement that the average number of jars used by America's home canners was 100. But there was no indication of what time period was covered. Was that 100 per month, per year, per lifetime — or what? she rightly asked.

In writing their articles, most writers hold back the statistics they have uncovered until they have hooked their readers with a narrative opening. That opening dramatizes a typical case. What follows, then, is a paragraph or two ticking off total numbers involved. But it is possible to present statistics right away, in a rat-a-tat-tat way, overwhelming the reader with the enormity of the problem.

It is necessary, in some articles, to scatter statistics throughout. Ralph Blumenthal, in a feature in the New York *Times* with a Salt Lake City dateline, relies mainly on figures to paint his picture of mass transit systems in various parts of the country. His feature (Aug. 31, 1975) was occasioned by an announced subway fare increase in Manhattan.

> Eat your heart out, New York City, home of the 50-cent transit fare.

is Blumenthal's single-sentence lead paragraph.
Then:

> The fare here is 15 cents, lowest in the nation, along with Atlanta's. Students, children, the aged and handicapped ride for 10 cents and all transfers are free. In Atlanta, the elderly and handicapped pay only 7 cents in off-peak hours.

Subsequent paragraphs take up the low fares in Seattle, St. Louis, and Cleveland. Then Blumenthal throws in some paragraphs explaining how these cities do it. (By taxes levied to supplement the fares.) Accompanying his article is a box listing a sampling of 30 cities with their transit fares. American Public Transit Association supplied the figures.

To relieve the monotony of all the figures in his text, Blumenthal presents a number of direct quotes from transit users and officials.

• CREDITING YOUR SOURCE

You do not want to slow the pace of your article with too much crediting of sources, but when what you lift is information that is controversial or unique, or when it consists of an idea that is original, you owe it to your source to supply the name. Furthermore, adequate crediting adds to your own credibility. The reader gets the idea that you have done your homework.

That publication names vary so much poses a problem on what to use inside an article. Some magazines are "The" magazines, others are not. It is *The New Republic* but *National Review*. If an apostrophe is involved, it is as likely to fall before the "s" as after it. *Publishers Weekly* in the 1970s dropped its apostrophe, which had stood there for years after the "s." Some magazines run a "Weekly" or "Monthly" on the nameplate on the cover but drop it inside when the name is mentioned in the masthead.

A magazine that runs its name in all caps on the cover does it for typographic reasons; that should not influence the writer's reference to the magazine in the usual caps-and-lowercase style. Hence: *Time*, not *TIME*.

Newspapers are even more troublesome. Is the name of the city part of the official name? Should it be *The New York Times* or just the New York *Times*? That depends on your market's style specifications, which the occasional contributor may not know. It probably is best to use the official name, all in italics, and let the editor change it to conform to some consistent style the magazine follows.

Then there is the market that does not use italics — any italics — for names of publications. In that case, treat the names as you would any other proper names. No underlining. Hence: The New York Times. You still have the problem of deciding whether "The" is capitalized. (No wonder comic-strip artists print everything in all caps!)

When you name the writer you are quoting, use the name exactly as it appears in the byline. If the writer is a three-namer, or a first-initial-middle-namer, honor his affectation.

One universally welcome change that has come out of the women's movement is the dropping of sex and marriage distinctions placed on subsequent mentions of names. Now, as a writer, you no longer have to worry over whether Kirk Polking of *Writer's Digest,* for example, is a he or a she; you can simply refer to her as Polking.

What do you do when the person or publication you are quoting is himself — or itself — quoting a person or publication? Do you credit both, or just the one you have stumbled onto, or just the original? The answer is: Go back to the original if you can, read him — or it — yourself, and confine your credit there, inwardly thanking the source that called the original to your attention. If you can't get to the original, go ahead and credit only your handy source; or, if you can do it without bogging down your article, credit everyone who deserves the credit. That's not much of an answer, admittedly; but article writing is that flexible.

• FACING THE FACT CHECKERS

Digging out additional material and forwarding it to a writer for inclusion in the final draft, as *Better Homes and Gardens* did for Booton Herndon, would be a service reserved for regular or known contributors, but checking a writer's facts is commonplace enough on magazines. *The New Yorker*, with its staff of seven checkers, goes over every single fact in all articles accepted. *Playboy*, impressed by *The New Yorker*'s reputation for accuracy, has established a similar department. *Harper's, Esquire*, and *Rolling Stone* also have checkers. With no formal checking department, a magazine at least engages in some spot checking. It may be nothing more than a simple phone call to the subject of a personality sketch. One writer reports that when a magazine accepted an article he did about a museum, the editor sent the museum director a questionnaire with 46 yes-or-no questions based on statements made in the article.[8]

• THE WRITER AND THE LAW

As a writer you lean heavily on the First Amendment to the Constitution guaranteeing you the right to say what you want; but other rights sometimes intervene. For instance (1) other writers' rights to earn profits from what they produce and (2) people's rights to a good reputation. While this book cannot do justice to the subjects of copyright

[8] Allan W. Eckert, "Checklist for Unsalable Articles," *Writer's Digest*, March 1962, p. 25.

and libel — or even treat the related subjects of the right of privacy, pretrial publicity, contempt, shield laws, obscenity, and censorship — it can at least bring up some of the problems.

• How Much the Writer Can Copy — Safely

The material a researcher works with is either "in the public domain" or it is protected by copyright. Anything in the public domain — where much of our cultural effects lie — can be copied word for word, page after page. Why writers would want to do that is not clear — they would be like artists backing their models against pieces of paper to trace them — but they can engage in so pedestrian a task if they want to.

What falls into the public domain, now that the 1976 copyright revision law is in effect, is not easy to determine. Up until Jan. 1, 1978, writers held copyright protection on their words for 28 years, plus another 28 if they applied for copyright renewal; for material produced now, writers get protection for life plus 50 years. After that their material falls into the public domain.

What about material still under copyright? How much copying can you do there?

You might just as well ask "What percentage of its time must a television station devote to public service programming in order to satisfy FCC regulations?" or "How long is a piece of string?" There is no clearcut answer.

The federal law of copyright, passed in 1790 and revised a number of times since, was designed to give writers a sort of monopoly over what they produced, guaranteeing them the right to whatever profits their works might bring. Other writers could not appropriate "substantial portions" of the copyrighted material and peddle it as their own.

Such protection, however, must not interfere with the free flow of information and opinion, necessary if the democracy is to flourish. So what is protected cannot be the facts or ideas but the way they are expressed and presented. This means, essentially, that even working with copyrighted material, researchers may copy lavishly, provided they copy — or is "borrow" a better term? — only what is said, not the language in which it is said.

But the way a writer says it might be important to you in making a point in your article. The writer may be an authority, and you're afraid that, in the paraphrasing, what was said will lose something in the translation. Or the writer is something of a character, and the color of the original remark will make your article more readable. Take it, then. Put quotation marks around it, and use it, by all means. But (1) credit the source and (2) keep the quote to a phrase or, at most, a sentence or two.

Some authorities suggest you can take up to 50 words, but the courts have never settled on an exact number. What's more important is the percentage of the whole that has been lifted. Using all of a six-line poem without permission of the copyright owner, for instance, puts you in more danger of a suit for copyright infringement than taking several paragraphs out of a book-length work.

You are apparently safer borrowing from scholarly than from popular works. If you criticize or praise what you borrow, so much the better. You are playing a critic's role. Adding some primary research helps, too. So does spreading out your borrowing. Wilson Mizner, who wrote plays early in the century, concluded that "When you take stuff from one writer it's plagiarism; but when you take it from many writers, it's research."

If what you want to quote directly is likely to exceed what the courts or the copyright holder would consider as "fair use," you still have a chance of using it. You can request permission of the copyright holder, but you may have to pay a fee.

The beginning writer usually is disappointed in what books such as this have to say on the subject of copyrighted material. He looks for firm rules. Unfortunately there are none. The advice boils down to this: use your good judgment. Take what you need. Put most of what you take in your own words. If you quote directly, and your quote runs more than a few lines, write to the copyright owner for permission. It will almost certainly be granted. Wherever possible, give credit in your article to the source, but don't think that acknowledgment in your article is an automatic safeguard against copyright infringement. "If you poach on private property, you can't purge yourself of trespass by tipping your hat to the property owner," Alexander Lindey has pointed out.[9] Use more than one source. Add material to your article based on your own experience or on information gathered from primary sources.

[9]Alexander Lindey, *Plagiarism and Originality*, Harper & Brothers Publishers, New York, 1952, p. 11.

You can get a copy of the new copyright law, Public Law 94-553, from the Copyright Office, Library of Congress, Washington, D.C. 20559.

The law of copyright is violated constantly by writers who are either ignorant of the law or who know they won't be prosecuted. A copyright holder is not likely to haul into court a small-time writer, with no money, working for third-class publications, also with no money. Not many suits are pressed. In order to really stick, a suit will have to prove that a substantial part of the original was borrowed by the offending writer and that the original writer suffered through a lessening in value of the original work. The possibility that a magazine article can accomplish this is remote. But why ask for trouble?

More than that, why give up the real satisfaction you have of watching your *own* work take shape and move out to influence people's minds? When you copy the work of another, without acknowledging the debt, without adding anything of your own, without at least improving the presentation, you cheat your readers, true, but you cheat yourself, too. You perform uncommonly routine duties and, considered on an hourly basis, probably not very profitably.

• Avoiding Libel

The first draft of an article Booton Herndon wrote for *Better Homes and Gardens* caused concern among editors because in it the author said (1) the man who wiped out all but one member of a family in an automobile accident was "drunk beyond the shadow of a scientific doubt," (2) an agency suppressed a report of a police inspector, and (3) a state legislator bottled up drunken driving laws because his law firm was profiting from the laws the way they stood. Each of these items, the editors believed, could if published touch off a libel suit.

Too timid, these editors? Not at all.

Consider the charge that a driver was "drunk beyond the shadow of a scientific doubt." It's true the driver *was* convicted of a charge of drunk driving, and it's true Herndon did not name him in the article. But it's also true that the editors didn't have the court record of exactly what had been decided, and in the article Herndon had named the family hit by the drunk driver's car and the state in which it occurred. The driver could argue that readers in that state would know it was he who was "drunk beyond the shadow of a scientific doubt." He might even be able to convince a jury that Herndon, angered by the light sentence meted the driver, acted with malicious intent to discredit him.

All three items were modified in the second draft. Such is the nature of libel.

"Libel is a nasty subject," Prof. Warren C. Price, a late colleague, told his Law of the Press class each year. And he shuddered as he said it. Nasty because it involves malice of one human being for another but nasty, too, because it's such an evasive subject, much more so than copyright. Unlike copyright, libel is a state matter rather than a federal one. The law varies from state to state.

What is libel? It's any written statement that tends to harm a person's reputation. Libelous words are those that suggest that a person is guilty of a crime or of immorality, or that he is suffering from a loathsome, infectious disease. They're words that may hold a person up to ridicule, hate, contempt, or ostracism, or that may hurt his chances of making a living.

That an accusation was previously published and is merely perpetuated by a new writer, who cites the source, would get only minor consideration by a jury in a libel case.

It's possible to libel a corporation or a nonincorporated organization as well as a person. It's even possible to libel a dead person.

The editor and legal counsel are primarily responsible for weeding out libel, but occasionally it slips by them. A manuscript that carries some libel may be worth editing to get it out, but rather than work to get the libel out, an editor is likely to give up and ship it back to the writer with regrets. There are too many other manuscripts to consider that involve no risk and little editing.

Both the writer and the editor can be sued. So libel is a matter to be considered with some seriousness by the researcher. The chances of committing libel are probably strongest when the writer is working from personal experience and observation and other primary sources.

Does this mean that attacking another person's reputation is out as far as article writing is concerned? No. You are free to say what needs to be said under these circumstances:

1. When what is said is "fair comment." This applies to statements made about politicians, public servants, entertainers, writers, artists, athletes — anyone who seeks public favor. In a democracy,

such persons are "asking" for it. They're subject to criticism as well as praise, provided comments are directed toward their performance or achievements, not toward their private lives. It is safe for a writer to say that Singer A can't carry a tune but it is not safe to say he beats his wife. If he was convicted by a court of wife-beating, that is another matter.

2. When what is said is "privileged." Decisions of courts, statements made during congressional or legislative debate, statements made on a police blotter or in public documents are not libelous. It's safe for a writer to say that the police arrested Citizen A on a charge of contributing to the dependency of a child (by the way, don't get it mixed up with "contributing to the *delinquency* of a child") but not that Citizen A in fact contributed to the dependency of a child.

    Whether material is fair comment or privileged, still (1) it must be true and (2) the author must not bear a personal grudge or have an evil intent as he reports it.

The defense of fair comment "has undergone considerable change in recent years," the authors of *New Strategies for Public Affairs Reporting* observe. It used to be that writers could say whatever needed to be said about public officials provided the writers didn't say it with malice. But the courts had difficulty determining malice. The 1964 *New York Times v. Sullivan* case before the Supreme Court seemed to narrow in on a definition, and the concept of fair comment later broadened to allow writers fair-comment privileges with people merely caught up in the news. Some observers felt that the fair-comment idea had gotten out of hand. In 1974 the Supreme Court in *Gertz v. Welch* "pulled back from its liberal standard," giving the private citizen more protection from libelous press coverage. "What the *Gertz* case indicates is the dynamic nature of law and particularly the law of libel."[10]

Sometimes a plaintiff files a suit for its nuisance value. The way to avoid becoming embroiled in a libel suit is to insist on the facts as you conduct your research. Look for evidence. Take facts down accurately

[10]Hage, George S., Everette E. Dennis, Arnold H. Ismach, and Stephen Hartgen, *New Strategies for Public Affairs Reporting*, Prentice-Hall, Inc., Englewood Cliffs, N.J., 1976, p. 131, 132.

(a wrong name, address, or charge can lead to a libel charge). Tell both sides of the story. And, if it seems borderline, don't use the item.[11]

• BRINGING THE READER INTO IT

It is a good idea, in the text of an article, to give the reader some indication of the extent of the research engaged in by the writer. Trevor Armbrister does this nicely in "Time to Clean Up the Food-Stamp Mess," an article published in — where else? — *Reader's Digest* (July 1975 issue). His assurance-of-authenticity paragraph doesn't show up until the article is well underway.

> To assess the implications of this dramatic growth [of the food-stamp program], I recently visited food-stamp offices across the country, talking with caseworkers and receptionists alike, interviewing USDA officials. From these discussions emerged a troubling picture of a program that has literally run amok — and which, according to USDA's own figures, wastes at least 740 million taxpayer dollars a year. Consider these major problems: [The major problems, as Armbrister listed them in followup paragraphs, were needless complexity, loose eligibility standards, and recipient and caseworker fraud.]

Mildred Ladner, writing on low-back pain in *The National Observer*, reassured the reader this way:

> But [Dr. Paul C.] Williams says those who wish to keep limber can at least get an idea of the exercises from the following sample — and he personally approved this wording:

Sometimes the writer feels obligated to let the reader know the amount of time spent with the subject. In a UPI interview with actress Elizabeth Ashley in 1975, the writer said:

> Here [in Washington] for the Kennedy Center's month-long revival of the Thornton Wilder classic, "The Skin Of Our Teeth," in which she plays Sabrina, the maid, Ms. Ashley had some scathing observations about government bureaucrats during a lively 70-minute interview in her dressing room.

Increasingly, writers are leveling with readers, taking them into their confidence. With so much attention to the media these days,

---

[11] Two book-length guides that can help you: Paul P. Ashley, *Say It Safely*, University of Washington Press, Seattle, 1976 (Fifth Edition) and Robert M. Cavallo and Stuart Kahan, *Photography: What's the Law?* Crown Publishers, New York, 1976.

there is a feeling among writers that readers want to know how the story is obtained. Perhaps the reader wants to be there with the writer during the fact gathering.

Sally Quinn, in interviewing Alice Roosevelt Longworth for the Washington *Post*, brought the reader right along into the Longworth home.

> Her maid, Janie McLaughlin, answers the door and leads the way through the darkened foyer, up the stairs, past the rattiest looking animal skin that you ever saw, hanging on the wall. The Siberian tiger skin belonged to her big-game hunting father, Teddy Roosevelt.[12]

Note that writer Quinn presents this paragraph — in fact she presents most of the feature — in present tense. This helps create the illusion that the reader is there.

Don Bishoff, in a Eugene (Oreg.) *Register-Guard* feature, brings the reader into the interviewing process through use of a one-word transitional paragraph. (To understand this excerpt, you should know that Roger Senders and Bill Gartner are promoters of a "beauty" pageant featuring men as well as women.)

> Senders added: "And we're now emphasizing the ability with which someone dresses themselves in relation to the appearance with which it fits their body."
> Huh?
> "That means someone with knobby knees should wear a slack suit." Gartner said. "Or," said Senders, recovering control of his syntax, "a person who is of a larger build, rather than wearing a swim suit, might wear a mumu."

Bishoff could have merely summarized what these men said here, but letting the exchange occur with the reader there made the feature move along more pleasantly.

• WORKING FROM AN ABUNDANCE

All this — and only one lifetime to go. Researchers fight hard to keep from being overwhelmed by the mass of material they stumble onto. The experienced researcher decides it is better to take on selected ma-

---

[12]Sally Quinn, "Alice Roosevelt Longworth at 90," *Writing in Style* (Laura Longley Babb, Editor), Houghton Mifflin, Boston, 1975, p. 159.

terials and give them careful study than to push recklessly through it all. A knowledge of both authors and publications helps in the selection.

A minimum amount of research for the typical article written for a middle-quality market would involve these steps:

1. Going first to a good encyclopedia for a broad picture, resolving to track down one or two of the books cited at the end of the encyclopedia article.
2. Consulting whatever indexes are available, covering newspapers, magazines, books, and other publications, and noting at least half a dozen articles that sound particularly valuable.
3. Scanning each article or book picked out, spending time on those that prove most useful, taking down both fact and opinion, watching all the while for anecdotal material.
4. Seeing and interviewing at least one authority in person or, if that's not possible, reaching him through a phone call or questionnaire.

This minimum program of research would hold even for an article written as a personality sketch. The primary research would involve persons friendly or even unfriendly to the subject of the sketch. The secondary research would delve into his field of interest, to give you background material to work into your article and to prepare yourself to ask intelligent questions of those you interview.

Research conscientiously conducted is likely to change your mind somewhat. If you go into the subject clearly committed to one side, you may come away seeing some merit in the opposite side.

"The important thing I learned professionally," reporter Webb Miller declared, "was that the truth about anything is difficult to obtain; that the more I studied the various aspects of any particular subject, the more qualified, the less definite and clearcut my opinions became."[13]

---

[13]Webb Miller, *I Found No Peace*, Simon and Schuster, New York, 1936, p. 317.

CHAPTER 7

WRITING: GETTING IT TOGETHER

The time has come when, having seen all the people you need to see and read all the articles and books you can find on your subject, you face the challenge of writing. Perhaps you've done some of it along the way: you've rewritten hastily scribbled notes before they could cool on you, and as a result you've created some excerpts that can fit into the manuscript. Your job becomes, now, a job of getting your material together, of picking and discarding and arranging and re-arranging — of bringing order to a chaos of information and ideas.

Some writers at this stage look over the accumulation of notes, push them to one side, think about them for a while, and begin writing, ignoring them until a rough draft emerges. Perfect recall is not vital, because where memory falters, stand-in figures and names take over. Searching through notes can interrupt the flow. These writers then check their rough drafts against their notes and make corrections and additions.

Other writers move back and forth from notes to typewriter, checking all the while.

Another way of dealing with the notes is to begin writing immediately after completing research into a first source. With each additional research period, you rewrite the draft, adding the new information, making the necessary changes. Each draft gets longer and more complete. Still another system is to work up a section of the article after each period of research, polishing the writing as though it were a complete unit. After all the research is concluded, writing consists primarily of organizing sections and working out transitions.

"Thank you for reading your article out loud, Ms. Lee. My first impression is that it needs a little more focus. . . ."

Harold Ross told of Ring Lardner's procedure. "I asked Lardner the other day how he writes his short stories, and he said he wrote a few widely separated words or phrases on a piece of paper and then went back and filled in the spaces." No doubt Lardner was kidding. But what makes writing so intriguing as an activity is that there are so many ways to do it.

• OUTLINING

Some writers start off not knowing, really, where their inspiration and facts will lead to. Art Buchwald is like that. Often he doesn't know, when he begins, how his 600- to 650-word column will end. A column can contain a surprise for Buchwald. He has been known to laugh out loud at what he has just written.[1]

[1] Alice Hornbaker (Interviewer), "I Could Have Been a Gangster" tape interview with Art Buchwald, *The Writer's Voice*, Writer's Digest, Cincinnati, n.d.

```
Your Name                          Approximately 0,000 words
Address
City, State, and Zip Code




                    THE TITLE OF THE ARTICLE

              The blurb.  It can run for several sentences.  It
              elaborates on the title.  You can single-space it
              and type it narrower than the body of the article
              to make it stand out.  You don't want the editor
              to think that it is the first paragraph for your
              article.

                         _____

                    By Your Professional Name


         Skipping a few spaces, you begin your article, typing it in a width

    that leaves about an inch margin—maybe a little more—at the sides and at

    the bottom.  You double space between lines to give the editor a chance to

    copyedit the manuscript.  Some newspapers prefer that you triple space.

         Each paragraph takes an indentation.

         Do not hyphenate words at ends of lines.  If the word looks as if it

    will be too long to fit, save it for the next line.  Then the typesetter

    doesn't have to guess whether the word is a term that should be hyphenated

    or whether it is a word you had to break because you didn't have enough

    space.

         At the top of the next page, type your last name or the title of the

    article and the page number, skip an extra space, and begin typing more of

    the manuscript.

                              (MORE)
```

Figure 7.1 No rules dictate what form to use in typing your manuscript, but this setup works as well as any.

Longer pieces for most writers require outlining. Writers can outline formally, on paper — or merely in their heads. Some writers develop an outline even before they begin their research, which, as a result, is more deliberate than research conducted by writers who let whatever they stumble onto dictate story lines.

Your outline does not have to be one of those 1-2-3, a-b-c things you might do for a term paper. It may be just a listing of main points you want to make, in the order you want to make them.

Chapter 5 suggested that you study some current articles in magazines to figure out what research sources the authors used. This chapter suggests that you study articles to figure out the author's outlines. If you were to do this, say, to Sonny Kleinfield's "Dwarfs" article in *The Atlantic* (September 1975), you might come up with something like this:

Plight of a representative dwarf (who is named)
Place of dwarfs in history (one paragraph)
Formation of The Little People organization
Push for legislation to benefit dwarfs
Dwarfs and midgets who were "movers and shakers"
    Attila the Hun, Charles III, Ladislas I, Richebourg, Sir Jeffrey Hudson, Coppernin, Nicholas Ferry, Tom Thumb (and his relationship to P.T. Barnum)
The smallest dwarfs
    Including John Louis Roventini who called for "Phil-lip Mor-rees!"
More information about dwarfs
    Late spurt in growth, short life span (according to legend)
Special problems dwarfs face
    Getting jobs, family relationships, finding mates, social life, admitting dwarfism
Difference between dwarfs and midgets
    Medical explanation, numbers
Research into causes and treatment of dwarfism

Such an outline, put together after the fact, cannot reflect the character of the writing or what is actually said, but it does show what the writer attempted to cover and his order of presentation. Looking at such a listing, you might conclude that the material could have been rearranged and that some other aspect of the subject could have been covered.

An outline can be designed to present your material in either a chronological or a psychological order.

• Chronological Order

In telling a story chronologically (first this happened, then that), you move almost effortlessly from one item to the next. Time provides your transitions. This works well enough for adventure and historical pieces, but it does not work for most of the other kinds of articles. And even when you tell your story chronologically, you may want to interrupt the flow occasionally, as when, to prepare the reader for some event, you suddenly move ahead in time, or, to put your facts into better perspective, you fall back for a few paragraphs, giving the reader a "flashback."

You may find it difficult, in chronological telling, to avoid the obvious. Moving the subject of your story from point A to point B, you may tell readers more than they need to know.

> Getting up from the chair, Jenkins walked to the door, grabbed the handle, pulled upon the door, and walked out onto the porch.

Hardly worth all the telling, unless you are being paid by the word. "Outside on the porch, . . ." does the job (such as it is) just as well.

• Psychological Order

A chronological order will not work for most articles because passage of time isn't a factor. And even if it is, the beginning of the story may not be compelling enough to make it a good article opener. More important, a chronological order of presentation may not serve the reader's needs.

Newspapers long ago found that a chronological order for news stories not only took too much space but also put off readers who were in a hurry to find out what's going on. So newspapers came up with the inverted pyramid, a form of writing that places the most important of exciting elements of a story first, to be followed by lesser facts in a descending order of importance. The form also made possible the cutting of stories at the ends to make them fit layouts.

Inverted pyramid

The preceding chart, familiar enough to journalism majors, illustrates the form. Each of the bars represents a fact or unit in the story. (There could be many more bars than the chart indicates.) The width of each bar represents the importance of the fact or the extent of interest the fact holds for the readers.

Obviously, this is no way to write an article. Its organization is more complicated because it makes use of a greater variety of literary devices. In an article, for instance, you may find it necessary to move from narrative to description to theory to statistics to quotation — and back to narrative. The diagrams that follow suggest some of the forms your article may take.

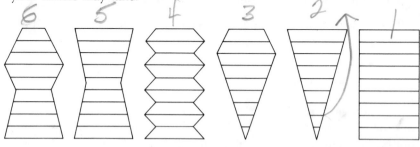

The first diagram illustrates a psychological approach in writing that says to the reader, "All the items I have to present are so important or interesting I can't arrange them in any particular order." Perhaps you offer only a string of anecdotes. You don't have any particular point to make. You just want to inform or entertain.

The second diagram represents a reaction against the inverted pyramid. You start with something trivial (as you would in a conversation when you ask, "How's the weather?") and then build up to something important.

The third diagram is a more useful version of the second. You build up to a climax, then ease out of the article, perhaps on a light note.

The fourth diagram suggest a two-level collection of material: important and unimportant units arranged alternately. Something factual or profound is followed by something light or anecdotal, which is followed by something factual or profound . . . . Or: A fact is followed each time by a verbal illustration.

The fifth diagram suggests starting and ending with important or exciting material, using the middle of the article for lesser material.

The sixth diagram in most cases is the diagram to follow. It starts out with some excitement, then narrows in on less exciting but still important aspects, then builds to a climax of some kind, and finally — and rather quickly — winds down to a good ending.

• WRITING HABITS

In his biography of his father, Gerard Willem van Loon tells us that Hendrik Willem van Loon, the journalist/historian who illustrated his material with charming, almost childish line drawings, planned his books "while first drawing the pictures." Whether used or not, they served as checkpoints — and as checks. Writing without them permitted him to ramble, discoursing at ever greater length on the subject which never ceased to fascinate him: himself."[2]

The younger van Loon contrasts his father's methods with that of Thomas Mann, Nobel prize winner and acquaintance of the elder van Loon.

"Hendrik could write or draw with furious concentration, dressed or undressed, shaven or unshaven, before breakfast or after dinner, in fits and starts or for hours at a stretch, off and on around the clock. Not so Dr. Thomas Mann. Upon his arrival [at the van Loon home for a visit], he let it be known that every morning he wished to have a card table placed on an open veranda on the shady side of the house. At the stroke of ten the foremost man of German letters would appear, impeccably groomed, sit at the table, remove the fountain pen from his pocket, and, in incredibly small, neat handwriting, write steadily until noon."[3]

By contrast, a reporter-turned-freelancer no doubt would compose mostly at the typewriter, and on an old Underwood No. 5 at that — the kind that gives a satisfying clink each time a key moves its long distance to the platen. Perhaps this writer would move occasionally from the old cast-iron typewriter to an electric one, as the mood of the article changes, and to a yellow pad and pencil when phrasing becomes especially difficult.

[2]Gerard Willem van Loon, *The Story of Hendrik Willem van Loon*, J. B. Lippincott Company, Philadephia, 1972, p. 214.

[3]*Ibid*, p. 306.

For some writers, typewritten copy comes out so badly marred by crossovers and arrows that it has to go through the typewriter again before outside typists can follow it. And then, when these writers see the final typing, they see many places where the writing can be improved. Their manuscripts, even when professionally typed, go out to editors with enough copyediting marks to qualify as "dirty copy."

Then there are writers like Prof. John L. Hulteng, a man who handles weighty topics with a finely crafted, inviting style. The first draft comes out of his typewriter, pounded with only two fingers, rapidly and virtually flawless, with no crossovers and little need for copyediting. Those first drafts could go directly to editors.

A writer at the typewriter who makes a lot of false starts might want to consider half-sheets rather than 8½ x 11 sheets for first drafts. With half sheets, a writer can do more shuffling of paragraphs. Some writers move in an opposite direction, choosing legal-size (8½ x 14) sheets to allow better grouping of their paragraphs.

It is said that the late P. G. Wodehouse wrote his novels by feeding a roll of paper, rather than sheets, into his typewriter at the beginning of his work day. At the end of the day he would chop the roll of paper into 8½ x 11 segments, pin them in a row to the wall, and read for the first time what he had written. If a page didn't satisfy him, he would lower it on the wall for one kind of revising, hang it crooked for another. When he had finally gotten all the pages lined up, the manuscript was ready to go to the editor.

Mike Price reports in *Writer's Digest* that he types his first drafts on teletype paper, which he purchases by the roll from the business supply department of his phone company. He says the paper is cheaper than typing paper and he likes the idea of not having to stop at the end of an 8½ x 11 sheet, remove it, and insert another.

Some writers may more or less limit the amount of time each day they spend writing, but they go on until they come to a logical stopping point. That way they can look back to a tidy package put together during a single work session. Other writers, finding it hard to get started at the beginning of a new day, purposely close shop in the middle of a sentence. The act of completing the sentence the next day releases any creative logjam.

Other writers put off writing until they feel they are really ready and then go into a marathon session that lasts deep into the night. They may write almost continuously for several days, with only a few hours off each night to sink into an exhausted sleep. But "My experience is that no man can write continuously for more than three hours — in fact, it is seldom that he can go beyond two hours," H. L. Mencken said. "After that, though he may keep on writing, he will not produce anything fit to print."[4]

Many writers like to set a specific goal for themselves for each day: say 1,000 words. That amounts to about four pages of double-spaced copy. Some writers, especially those trained in newspaper work, can produce considerably more than that. Some cannot produce as much. The subject matter would make a big difference in the rate of production.

To turn out a readable 1,000 words in a single day, you probably would have already done your research. If you are typical, you probably can turn out the 1,000 words in one sustained creative spurt. You may do your writing only in the early morning hours, using the remainder of the day to recover your energies, to read, or to work at some task that pays better wages.

A few freelancers work all day, maybe even at a writing job, and then devote themselves to freelance writing at night, presumably at some expense to their health. The writer who combines physical — or at least nonwriting — work with freelancing is probably better off than the writer who combines a staff-writing job with freelancing.

The talking with people, the observation and reading, the contact with editors — all this can be fun. But the writing itself: that can be drudgery, especially for the extrovert. Somewhere along the line writers must isolate themselves. Writing can be a lonely activity. J. D. Ratcliff quotes a writer friend: "No one likes *writing*. But everyone likes *having written*." It may be more nearly true to say that no one likes *writing* or even *having written*. But everyone likes thinking about being a writer.

• WRITING FOR THE READER

That you should write for the reader seems like advice too obvious. Yet some students enter Articles and Features classes to, uh, express themselves.

Novelist Charles Johnson (*Faith and the Good Thing*) says, "The point of writing isn't self-therapy. You have what amounts to a contract with the reader, and the reader has the right to quit at any time."

[4]H. L. Mencken, "Newspapers, Women, and Beer," *Harper's*, September 1976, p. 53.

Readers are not interested in Writer A and her search for identity; they are interested in what she knows that they can benefit from.

"As a general rule, I advise . . ." wrote a student in a how-to article. That is a roundabout way of getting there. The reader doesn't want to know that the writer *advises*; the reader only wants to know *what* that advice is. This is true especially if the writer is unknown.

Not only should you put yourself in the place of the reader, anticipating needs and serving them, but you should also think of the reader as singular. Your article appears in a mass medium, that is true; but your writing is for the individual. You should think of yourself as more a letter-writer than a lecturer up on a platform.

• YOUR CAST OF CHARACTERS

Your job as a writer is to present all the facts and mention all the important names. But you don't want to overwhelm your reader. You assume that your reader can take away from your article only a single thought or idea and keep track of only a few people. So you keep your cast of characters small. If you find you must bring in a lot of people, to describe or to quote, you keep many of them anonymous. You concentrate only on those characters vital to your story.

• YOUR POINT OF VIEW

If you write for the general market you should be able to guide readers through your story without their ever being conscious of your gender, age, race, or even political leanings.

You can't assume that your background is their background.

"By virtue of education and income," says Susan Jacoby, a freelance writer, "most journalists (especially those who write for influential publications in New York and Washington) belong to a relatively privileged segment of the upper middle class. Most Americans are *not* members of this class. The class barrier influences reporters' attitudes not only toward the poorest members of society but towards the working-class men and women who make up the bulk of the American population."

Your religious background — or lack of it — no doubt affects the facts presented to your readers. When *The Total Woman* came out in the 1970s to a chorus of boos from liberated women and some church officials, one reviewer, noting its surprising sales record, said it bore the imprint of "an obscure New Jersey publisher." It may have been obscure to the reviewer, but to anyone who had any background at all in evangelical Protestantism or who knew anything about book publishing, the publisher, Fleming H. Revell of Old Tappan, N.J., was something of a household word, having published works by such show-business, sports, and religious figures as Pat Boone, Anita Bryant, Johnny Cash, Billy Graham, Jerome Hines, Kathryn Kuhlman, Catherine Marshall, Norman Vincent Peale, Oral Roberts, Dale Evans Rogers, Bob Richards, and Bobby Richardson.

You cover a funeral in a Baptist church. You are there because the deceased was a well-known politician. If, in your story or feature, you mention that the audience said an "Our Father," your Catholic background would be showing. Although their prayer starts out with an "Our Father," Baptists don't refer to it as an "Our Father." They call it "The Lord's Prayer."

Social or economic status affects point of view. So does commitment to a cause. ". . . I am a writer and I am a feminist, and the two seem to be constantly in conflict," writes Nora Ephron. "The problem, I'm afraid, is that, as a writer, my commitment is to something that, God help me, I think of as The Truth, and as a feminist my commitment is to the women's movement. And ever since I became loosely involved with it, it has seemed to me one of the recurring ironies of this movement that there is no way to tell the truth about it without, in some small way, seeming to hurt it."[5]

• PERSONALITY AND THE WRITER

Responding to *Crazy Salad*, Anatole Broyard describes the author, Nora Ephron, as "attractively feminine, in the obsolete sense of that battered word and a regular fellow at the same time. I would even say 'one of the boys' if I were not afraid of being misunderstood. She is tender and tough, sentimental and cynical, old-fashioned and modern in just about the right proportions."

Provided your article is not destined for a trade magazine or a magazine designed only to offer readers practical advice, your personality

---

[5]Nora Ephron, *Crazy Salad*, Alfred A. Knopf, New York, 1975, pp. 105, 106.

should come through. A reader who knows the writer should be able to read a piece and exclaim: "That sounds just like her!"

If it is your nature to be ebullient, do not rely on exclamation marks to broadcast your enthusiasms. Make your *phrasing* do the job. And do not get into the habit of underlining words to give them emphasis (unless you're writing a textbook). Get your emphasis by word choice and placement in the sentence.

If the word you chose is not exactly the right word, don't cover up by putting quotation marks around the word. Quotation marks do not purify slang; and they cannot dignify a cliché.

• DEVELOPING A STYLE

If what you have to say is interesting or worthwhile, and if you write it clearly, you can probably find a market, somewhere, for what you write. For some writers, that is not enough. They want in their writing a distinct quality that sets it apart from the writing of others. Let's call it "style."

Style "is not something to be adopted," writes Mary Wallace. "It develops from the writer's own personality, from every thought and feeling he has ever had, from his whole attitude toward the world about him, and, to some extent, from everything absorbed from years of reading. In short, *it is the writer*."[6]

Without a well developed style, Annie Dillard would produce just another nature-study book instead of the lyrical *Pilgrim at Tinker Creek*, which so beautifully celebrates the wonders of nature.

"What we loosely call 'good writing' has three main ingredients — sense, sensibility, and style, in the correct proportions, so that none of them overwhelms the others," says Sydney J. Harris, the syndicated columnist.

Harris's candidate for the writer who best brings this off is Milton Mayer, a writer who appears frequently in *The Progressive*. Milton Mayer "happens to be the most famous obscure writer in the United States, who is sometimes confused with Martin Mayer, the most obscure famous writer in the United States."

". . . what is most singular about this man is his unique gift for dealing with 'cosmic' issues in a manner wholly delightful, ironical, and

[6]Mary Wallace, "Style and the Fiction Writer," *The Writer*, February 1976, p. 18.

paradoxical. He does not know how to be dull, and he is probably the most comic writer in America, in the classic sense of high comedy. There are trivial writers who are funny, and profound writers who are trenchant, but none I know of who combine dead seriousness of purpose with good-humored mockery that makes us laugh out loud."[7]

As a journalist intent on developing a style, you should read authors of good fiction as well as admired journalists. Even the writers of light prose have something to teach. P. G. Wodehouse, for instance. ". . . When we come to Wodehouse, we are in the presence of one of the minor masters of the English language," observes L. J. Davis in *The National Observer*. "His eye was splendidly exact, his ear perfectly tuned. One can read him for his rich gift of phrase alone, his charming metaphors, and the casual precision of his imagery."

A danger is that you will let style obscure accuracy. This was the criticism Dwight Macdonald brought against the writing of new journalist Tom Wolfe, following Wolfe's New York *Herald Tribune* attack on *New Yorker* editor William Shawn in 1965. Macdonald, in the *New York Review of Books*, said that Wolfe's errors, though trivial, produce "a rhetoric that builds up, with so many little 'knowing' factual touches, a general impression which only those with some acquaintance with the subject can detect as . . . unfactual."

• The Art of Paragraphing

Think of each paragraph as a unit, with its own beginning, middle, and end. Think of each paragraph as a sort of article within an article.

The first sentence of the paragraph, typically, states a premise. The followup sentences elaborate. The final sentence summarizes or brings the discussion to a climax, readying the reader for the following paragraph. If possible, you will make the last sentence the most important in the paragraph. It is the last read; therefore it has the best chance of being remembered.

Occasionally you will want to slip in a single-sentence paragraph, to provide a change of pace.

Or maybe even a sentence-fragment paragraph.

[7] Sydney J. Harris, "Milton Mayer: A Jewish Christian Quaker Thomist," *The Progressive*, August 1975, p. 41. Harris was reviewing a collection of essays by Mayer: *The Nature of the Beast*, University of Massachusetts Press, 1975.

You will also want to give readers an occasional long, almost rambling paragraph, in an effort to keep them alert. You don't want to mesmerize them with even-sized, predictable paragraph units. You want to surprise them when you can. More important, you want the paragraph to do justice to its assigned topic. Some paragraph topics are more complicated than others. They just naturally take up more space.

No wonder many teachers of Articles and Features courses start their students off writing fillers. Fillers, like paragraphs, are articles in miniature. Often a single paragraph is enough.

- **"On the Other Hand" Paragraphs.** "On the other hand" paragraphs play an important role in most articles. The author makes a point, then counters it with a paragraph of opposition. Back and forth the article goes, until finally the author comes to a conclusion that favors one side over the other.

Ken Metzler illustrates: The paragraphs that follow are from deep inside one of his features in the Honolulu *Star-Bulletin & Advertiser*. They deal with a rise in the educational level of policemen.

> [It is] A laudable trend, says one high-ranking officer, Maj. Norman Osthoff of Research and Development. "It takes officers of increasing educational levels to cope with the complexities of society today."
>
> But the change is not applauded in all quarters, particularly among older men whose lack of education blunts their promotion potential. Says one veteran cynically:
>
> "Just try waving your college certificate in front of the belligerent drunk you're struggling to subdue. See how far that gets you."
>
> Even the degree holder is not so naive as to suggest that college grads are necessarily quicker on the draw or straighter shots.
>
> "If I'm in a tight spot," says one sergeant, a college graduate, "degrees don't matter. I'd prefer help from a long-time veteran than from some young guy fresh out of college."

Then back to Metzler's main point:

> But there's more to police work than gunplay. . . .

You can give a paragraph to one side, then one to the other, then another paragraph to the first side again, then one to the other side — and so on for several paragraphs. Or you can build the one side with several paragraphs in a row, then give several paragraphs to the other side. It may turn out that each case is so convincing you refrain from giving the nod to either side. You leave it to the reader to decide.

• Show — Don't Tell

Whenever you have the space for it, allow your interviewee to voice one of her witticisms. Don't just say that she has a good sense of humor. Don't talk about the pretty landscape; describe the trees, the rolling hills, the stream, the buildings. If you have an unknown candidate for office, show how unknown he really is. Christopher Lydon in the New York *Times* nicely dramatized the obscurity of a Democratic presidential candidate in the 1976 elections when he began a feature like this:

> Stanley Arnold — or was it Arnold Stanley? — opened his Presidential campaign at a Waldorf Astoria news conference in New York last week. . . .

• The Subtle Approach

When you have a feature with humorous or suggestive implications, try to let the story write itself. Resist the urge to guffaw and point.

Jerry Uhrhammer showed marvelous restraint when, for the Eugene (Oreg.) *Register-Guard*, he covered a legislative hearing on the future of a cemetery bordering the University of Oregon campus. The University wanted to buy the land for expansion, but the association that owned the cemetery objected. (The Flegel mentioned at the end was a state senator and member of the legislative committee.)

> While the trustees were saving most of their opposition to the acquisition bill until Tuesday's hearings, they did let the legislators know they want the cemetery to be saved.
>
> Mrs. Holmes said, "We even have students tell us they find this a very restful spot."
>
> Another trustee, Mrs. Louis Koppe, said the daughter of one member of the cemetery association had expressed much disappointment over proposed plans to move the cemetery. "She became engaged here," Mrs. Koppe said.
>
> "I can believe that," said Flegel.

It was a note Uhrhammer found good enough to end on.

Build the reader's self-image by assuming — or pretending to assume — that he already knows something you are going to tell him. Notice how Gerald W. Johnson does this in the following excerpt from *The Man Who Feels Left Behind*:

> Three of the four great mysteries that puzzled Solomon have been almost completely illuminated by knowledge acquired since his day. Aero-

dynamics, hydrodynamics, and the coefficient of friction have revealed much about the way of an eagle in the air, the way of a ship in the sea, and the way of a serpent on a rock; but as regards the fourth and darkest mystery of them all, the way of a man with a maid, remarkably little of real significance has been learned since Adam delved and Eve span.

He doesn't just list the four mysteries, as an academician would; he works them gracefully into a paragraph that tells something about them.

You don't have to shriek, even when you are angry. One of J. A. Spender's rules was "to make my language most moderate when my views were most extreme. Follow this and you may earn a reputation for sobriety and moderation while steadily expounding the most subversive views. The reputation which the Westminster *Gazette* had for moderation was serviceable, and enabled it to advocate left-wing radicalism as if it were the normal creed of the sensible and moderate people who read it."

One of the best examples of a subtle dig — this one against advertising — comes in the Author's Note to Dorothy L. Sayer's *Murder Must Advertise*.

> I do not suppose that there is a more harmless and law-abiding set of people in the world than the Advertising Experts of Great Britain. The idea that any crime could possibly be perpetrated on advertising premises is one that could only occur to the ill-regulated fancy of a detective novelist, trained to fasten the guilt upon the Most Unlikely Person. If, in the course of this fantasy, I have unintentionally used a name or slogan suggestive of any existing person, firm or commodity, it is by sheer accident, and is not intended to cast the slightest reflection upon any actual commodity, firm or person.

As a public speaker suddenly lowers his voice to make his listener strain to hear, the writer can partially describe his subject, forcing the reader to supply the missing words. Instead of saying that TV programs were imitating each other, Jeff Greenfield in *New York* said:

> In the midst of a fall TV season devoted to the sincerest form of flattery, NBC is buying something different.

How far you can go in making readers participate depends upon their levels of sophistication. This is something you determine from a study of your market.

• The Use of Paradox

People you write about won't be all one thing or another. They will be a combination of things, and often the combination will be paradoxical. That people are paradoxical gives them dimension. It makes them believable. More than that, it makes them interesting.

Louise Melton, in a personality sketch of "Frank Perdue: The Tough Man Behind the Tender Chicken," written for *Buffalo Spree Magazine*, demonstrates in her writing how conflicting qualities come together in one man:

> He reads voluminously and has attended workshops at the Harvard Business School. He utilizes the modern techniques of computerized market research as well as personally grubbing about in butcher shops and grocery stores from Williamsville to Washington to talk chicken with meat buyers and startled housewives. He spent $100,000 developing a means of getting about eight hairs off chicken wings but is known by associates to be "as frugal as any small-time clod kicker on the Shore." He's gone lusting after better processing methods in Italy and spends a million dollars a year on xanthophyll, the yellowing agent in those famous marigold petals [which he feeds in a mixture to his chickens]. But he still says *tars* when he means *tires* and *crick* when he means *creek* and is in demand on talk shows where he's media-wise enough to lay it on a little thick for the folks.

• The Elongated-Yellow-Fruit School of Writing

The late Charles W. Morton, who contributed regularly to *The Atlantic*, placed writers who overused synonyms into what he called the elongated-yellow-fruit school of writing. The inspiration for the name came from a news story he saw about the capture of some fugitive monkeys. Police used bananas as bait. The reporter used "bananas" early in the story, but as it unfolded he felt the need for a synonym. He chose "elongated yellow fruit."

Morton's school exists because writers seem impelled to appear clever and resourceful to their editors and readers. It is applauded by scattered, well-meaning English and journalism teachers.

In *A Slight Sense of Outrage*, Morton runs a list of elongated-yellow-fruit words and phrases, like "aperture for visual observation" for "sheet of glass," "hen-fruit safari" for "Easter-egg hunt," and "that green folding stuff that hubby brings home every week" (reportedly used by Dr. George Gallup) for "money."[8]

[8]Charles W. Morton, *A Slight Sense of Outrage*, J. B. Lippincott Company, Philadelphia, 1955, pp. 100-102.

Prof. Walter Steigleman in *Editor & Publisher* called the problem "Synonymnitis, an affliction growing out of the reluctance of a reporter to repeat a name. And it also is caused by the attempt to diffuse background material . . . The silliness of such a style is brought home if it is converted to ordinary conversation such as this dialogue between two college men."

"Did you hear that the dean has placed Bill on probation?"

"No, what is the trouble with the serious-minded commerce student?"

"The former all-state football star cut too many classes. . . ."

And so on for several paragraphs of stilted conversation.

• First-, Second-, and Third-Person Writing

Whether you write in first, second, or third person depends upon the nature of your material and the policy of the medium you write for.

Start out with the thought of writing in third person. Writing in third person helps you avoid preachiness. And the reader will have less reason to suspect that you are on an ego trip.

But sometimes first or second person works better. After an opening paragraph, Lou Kotler Levine's New York *Times* feature on a famous bakery moves along like this:

I was about to join 47 other Sara Lee devotees on a free tour of the company's bakery in Deerfield, Ill., not far from Chicago. After years of gorging on brownies and overdosing on cheesecakes, I was to visit THE SOURCE.

A telephone call the previous day had gotten me an appointment for the 10:15 A.M. tour. . . .

When you feel that you should bring yourself into the story, do it with a first-person "I" or "me" and not a third-person "this writer" or "this observer" or, God forbid, "yours truly." You should start your first-person writing early in the article. A sudden turn to first person late in the article, after columns of third person, comes as too jarring a change.

Do not try to minimize your participation in the story by resorting to first-person plural. A "we" or an "us," unless used with a double byline or to include a companion, can only be interpreted as false modesty. Mark Twain had the right idea: "Only presidents, editors, and people with tapeworms have the right to use the editorial 'we.'"

Writing an article offering instruction, you are likely to turn to second-person writing. But try to remember that the "you" your article serves is an individual. Do not use such second-person constructions as "you people" or "you students." Try to imagine one individual sitting there, paying close attention to your advice.

Second-person writing is useful, too, for involving the reader in a "you are there" situation.

> You pull up to the Chevron station and a sign on the pump catches your eye. . . .

If you can, stick to one-person writing throughout. At least write *mainly* in one of the three persons. And make your switches gracefully and infrequently.

• Writing in Present Tense

While the traditional news story appears in past tense (after all, the news has already happened), and so does the typical article and feature, occasionally a writer turns to present tense to make the reader feel he is there, while things are happening. Louise Melton demonstrates this in her Frank Perdue piece. Writing in first person, she is now, deep in the article, inside the chicken-processing plant with Perdue:

> The "Walk, Don't Run." signs don't apply as I scurry under dripping disassembly lines of naked chicken carcasses to keep up with him. He dodges water hoses and lunges into abrupt conversations with men in hard hats and women in transparent plastic aprons. A pretty girl, her hair covered by a bright scarf, is the only thing that slows him down but not for long. A black foreman shouts over the din of machinery, "Fine, Frank! Ain't seen you in a while!" Women on break loiter for a moment of ribaldry outside a ladies' room marked "Pullets."

Most often you would turn to present tense in essays and how-to-do-it pieces, but any kind of article, including an adventure piece, can profit from its use. Used too much, though, present tense can become self-conscious and tiresome. Past tense remains the most useful tense for article writers to use.

• UNITY

Your article should read as though one person wrote it, perhaps at one sitting, maintaining the same mood throughout. If you want some humor in it, for instance, don't wait until a midway point. Start out right away with a show of wit, a hint of laughter to come.

If you engage in a collaboration, both writers could conduct the research, both could write parts of the rough draft, but only one would write the final draft. A single style should prevail.

At the same time, you want a little variety in the piece. You want some change of pace. You want one part of the article to stand out. The combining of the principles of unity and contrast make article-writing the art it is.

One way of achieving unity in an article is to set up an event or introduce some people and then, after wandering off with another idea, come back to that setup. The reader will recognize it if not too much else has intervened.

Andrew Tobias in a *New York* excerpt from his biography of Charles Revson says of his subject that he was a perfectionist.

> You could even say he was a fanatic in the same way Bobby Fischer is or J. Edgar Hoover was. Each lived for his own particular "business," and each knew his business better than anybody else.

Later in the article, Tobias brings up the trio again.

> Charles would not joke about the business any more than Hoover would joke about the Bureau or Fischer would joke about a chess match. The enemy, whether Communists, as in the case of Hoover (and Fischer), or competition, as in the case of Charles, was anathema.[9]

An unlikely combination — an FBI director, a chess champion, and a business tycoon — but Tobias puts it together in order to better describe his subject. That he brings it up early in the article and then later returns to it helps tie the article together.

But the real key to unity lies with the transitions worked out between sentences and between paragraphs.

• Transitions

Having information on cannons — information he was anxious to share — and not sensing a break in the conversation at a dinner, Her-

---

[9]Andrew Tobias, "Charles Revson — A Remembrance of Fire and Ice," *New York*, Sept. 8, 1975, p. 42.

bert Bayard Swope, the newspaperman, made his own transition when suddenly he butted in with: "Boom! Boom! Speaking of cannons . . ." Some written transitions are like that, especially in the newspapers. In the magazines, writers and editors tend to develop smoother transitions, if for no other reason than that they have the space. And the time.

Your transition can come *mechanically* from a word or phrase designed to serve as a transition or *thematically* from the content of the sentence.

Perhaps the most commonly used word of transition is "but" and its uptown cousin "however." Of the two, "but" does the best job, especially at the start of a sentence, because it does the least damage to the rhythm of the sentence. Unlike "however," it needs no comma afterwards. "However," when it is used as a "but" transition, works best inside a sentence, set off by commas.

J. A. Spender believed that writers overuse "but" and "however." "One may train on indefinitely . . . , with 'buts' and 'howevers' balancing and qualifying, until the reader is muddled and the point fogged, if there ever was a point." By avoiding the two words, Spender said, "I not only helped say what I wanted to say at first intention, but braced and tightened the whole structure of an article."

• Words of Transition

Maybe the following categories with their incomplete listings will help you think about words and phrases of transition:

• **Addition:**   and, in addition, furthermore, moreover, more than that, besides, not only that, add to that, best of all, most of all, above all, what's more

• **Agreement:**   yes, of course, naturally, to be sure, certainly, indeed, granted, no doubt, doubtless, I confess

• **Amplification:**   again, to repeat, to explain, once more, as he pointed out, that is, in other words, obviously

- **Argument:** no, hardly, never, yet, still, nevertheless, on the other hand, on the contrary, even so, the fact is, after all, otherwise, only, in contrast, more important, besides, except that, in the first place, unfortunately (and of course "but" and "however")

- **Cause:** because, the reason is, why?, this can be explained by, so, therefore, consequently, hence, as a result, the result is, for this reason, since, if

- **Citation:** first, in the first place, for instance, for example, to illustrate, a case in point, another case, namely, as follows

- **Conclusion:** in short, to sum up, on the whole, to conclude, finally, in all

- **Demonstration:** here, here again, in this case, in all this, in this connection, on such occasions, under these circumstances, in the same way, just as

- **Interruption:** by the way, anyway, at any rate, parenthetically, to continue, to return, seriously, actually, I exaggerate, but I digress

- **Time:** now, now that, then, at the same time, by that time, formerly, previously, meanwhile, in the meantime, at last, already, next

Understand, you don't need words like these, necessarily, to form your transitions. And when you use one you don't have to *start* the sentence with it. A transitional word or phrase can be buried in the sentence.

- **Other Transition Devices**

Max Gunther speaks of the "echo" transition — the transition that simply repeats a word or phrase used in the previous sentence or paragraph.

It was hard for him. It was hard work because he didn't have the training for it. . . .

Good luck with it in these days of paper shortages.

Because it refers to a noun or name previously or subsequently mentioned, a pronoun in one sentence can serve as the transition from the previous sentence. You can also achieve a transition by asking a question in the one sentence and answering it in the next.

In a column in *Esquire* on a columnist who rates restaurants, Nora Ephron ends one paragraph with: "But I'm getting ahead of my story." Later she begins a paragraph this way: "At this point, we must pause to introduce a new character in this drama. . . ."

See how Robert Mayer dramatizes his point in this excerpt from "The Quiet Hour," a "My Turn" guest column for *Newsweek*:

> I propose that, for 60 to 90 minutes each evening, right after the early-evening news, *all television broadcasting in the United States be prohibited by law.*
>
> Let us pause for a moment while the howls of anguish subside.
>
> Now let us take a serious, reasonable look at what the results might be if such a proposal were adopted.

• Subheads

Textbook writers enjoy an advantage over article writers in that they can resort to subheads at breaks in the copy flow. The subheads act not only as guides to content but also as transitions of sorts. So the breaks between sections of a chapter can be rather abrupt. Although an article can be as long as a chapter, it does not, customarily, carry subheads. And if it does, the subheads come later. Editors, in cooperation with their art directors, write them as part of the process of laying out pages. Subheads are there for design reasons.

Unless you know that your editor wants them, do not write subheads for your article. Certainly you should not rely on them for your transitions. If you do want a serious, dramatic break, consider leaving some extra space. The editor can decide whether or not to show the extra space. Perhaps the editor will help you indicate a break by arranging for the setting of a large initial letter or by using some other graphic device.

• RHYTHM

Some years ago, before United Press swallowed International News Service and became United Press International, there served as chief of the Salt Lake City bureau one Murray Moler (now associate editor of the Ogden *Standard-Examiner*). He may not have been aware of the impact he was making on his reporters, but those young hirelings, coming in from outside the area to be schooled for further assignments with UP, looked over in awe as Moler, in one corner of the room, typed furiously on a story in an attempt to get it out in time to make the trunk wire. You could almost see smoke rising from the keys. More vivid yet was the sight of Moler tapping his feet as he typed. He did that, one likes to think, because of the rhythm of what he wrote.

Good writing needs rhythm. As a writer, you should be able, almost, to rearrange your lines to make a page of blank verse. Each word in each sentence should do its job to carry the reader effortlessly along the several lines until the article ends.

Sometimes when you write/ try to pick your words/ not for what they say/ but for how they sound. Don't do that on assignment; only as an exercise. But do develop a feel for words that permits your using them for flow as well as meaning. Sometimes, for example, you will want to substitute a two-syllable word for a three-syllable one, just to help the rhythm.

Although it may be a column he would look back upon with some uneasiness, in view of the fact that the subject of the column later lost his life, William F. Buckley, Jr., used rhythm nicely when he wrote:

Bobby, Bobby, everywhere. It drives a man to drink.

The column went on to discuss the fact that Bobby Kennedy was in those days (1966) overly busy ("a marvel of industry"), and:

No one, so far, dares say him nay. . . .

You feel the rhythm in the two short sentences Penelope Gilliatt uses in a *New Yorker* review to summarize a paragraph of her feelings about the movie *Jaws*:

The shark is plastic. The film is punk.

The rhythm does not have to come in short, choppy sentences. Here's Brendan Gill in *Here at the New Yorker*, closing a paragraph about A. J. Liebling:

> He was sensual and vain and talented and extremely hard-working and he was just beginning to enjoy the fame he had counted on and long waited for when, in 1963, he died.

Gill underscores the suddenness of Liebling's death with a suddenness of sentence ending.

Russell Lynes is less successful as a rhythm-maker in this excerpt from *Harper's* (he is talking about "internal symbols"):

> I recently, however, came upon with some surprise one that will, I trust, explain what I mean.

With the easy access now of office copying machines on campus, classes in Articles and Features encourage students to make inexpensive extra copies of their manuscripts and circulate them for outside reading and later classroom discussion. This has the advantage of reserving valuable and limited class time for discussion and argument. But the older system of having students read their manuscripts aloud in class and then stand up to criticism (and praise) has much to be said for it. Not the least of its value comes from dramatizing the rhythm of the writing. Faltering or monotonous rhythmic patterns quickly emerge as the prose is exposed to the voice. When out-loud reading cannot be a part of the classroom experience, you might want to try it on a long-suffering friend or roommate.

All of these considerations can lead to an article that moves along logically and smoothly from beginning to end. There are other writing considerations, too, of a more specific nature. The next chapter will elaborate.

CHAPTER 8

WRITING:
PUTTING IT ACROSS

Organizing the material into a sequence easy for the reader to follow and presenting it with enthusiasm and flair make writing a highly creative activity, but there is more to writing than that. To put the material across, writers follow some rules, rules that bring consistency to the printed page.

Some writers consider the rules an unnecessary burden. "They stifle my creativity," a writer might argue. Or "I leave grammar and usage matters to my editor." A few writers with that attitude get away with it; but they are important enough, or what they have to say is interesting enough, that editors willingly provide the necessary services to make the material publishable. Most writers must familiarize themselves with the rules and then write under the restrictions they impose.

The rules vary enough to make absolute mastery of them virtually impossible. Not even the experts agree all the time on what's right and what's wrong. Certainly editors don't. There is enough universality about the rules, though, to make a chapter touching on them appropriate for inclusion in this book. What follows does not attempt to spell out the rules (that would be too momentous a task); it merely draws some generalizations from them. The discussion centers on matters that give the most trouble to writers of articles and features.

"What are you trying to tell me, Rodney?"

• CLARITY

If one quality in writing should stand out above all others, that quality is clarity. No matter how solid the research or graceful the writing, if what you say isn't presented clearly, you don't really communicate with your reader. Robertson Davies in an article in *The Saturday Evening Post* wrote, "Not straining forward to completion, but the pleasure of every page as it comes, is the secret of reading." Not bad, but an advertising copywriter said essentially the same thing for a luxury liner — clearer, and in fewer words: "Getting there is half the fun." A Washington, D.C., taxi driver, so the story goes, was asked by his fare the meaning of an inscription (Shakespeare's) on a building: "What's Past Is Prologue." The driver had an easy answer: "You ain't seen nothing yet!" A janitor, also in Washington, wrote a note on the back of an envelope and Scotch-taped it to the door of an apartment complex he watched over: "The gas that you smell, I, Andy, the janitor, is merely trying to kill a few bugs in the basement." The tenants would have no trouble deciphering the message.

One key to clarity is simplicity: short words, short sentences, short paragraphs. But along with simplicity, at least in longer pieces in the magazines, must go a little variety: longer words, occasionally, a sentence here and there that borders on the complex, a paragraph that covers more space than usual in prose coming from journalists.

Another key is precision. Precision in writing means not only picking the right word but also picking the word having just the right intensity. It means, for instance, not settling for the weaker "apparently" when the stronger "obviously" is what you have in mind. When you have a choice between two similar words, pick the word with the narrowest meaning. Don't use "book" when you can use "autobiography." If your editor is above worrying about who may benefit — or suffer — from mention in the publication, say "Porsche 914" instead of "sports car" or "Pepsi" instead of "soft drink." This can be overdone, of course; but sometimes brand-name preferences tell your readers something additional about your subject.

That the dictionary, in a second meaning, bears you out in your use of a word does not excuse your failure to communicate clearly. "Discursive" may mean in philosophy "going logically from premises to conclusions," but to the lay reader — and one with a good vocabulary at that — it means "skimming over many apparently unconnected subjects."

What is the reader to assume when you say "government"? Do you mean federal government, state government, or local government? Are you referring to the executive branch, the legislative branch, or the judicial branch? And are you being precise enough when you use the term "last year" or "this year" in your article? How do you know when it will be published? Won't you be safer using numbers for the year and letting the editor transcribe them to "last year" or "this year" if that is the magazine's style?

James J. Kilpatrick shows a lack of precision when he says of George Wallace that he is "half-paralyzed by the bullet of an attempted assassin. . . ." Is being "half-paralyzed" the same thing as being totally paralyzed from the waist down, which is Wallace's true condition?

• OBSTACLES TO CLARITY

Writing to put your material across to readers consists essentially of overcoming the obstacles to clarity. The obstacles begin with the necessity of confining what you have to say to a word limit as stringent as 1,500 words and seldom any more generous than 3,500 words.

• The Limitations of Space

Having spent long hours writing and rewriting paragraphs to get them into shape, a writer, understandably, does not like to eliminate any of them. By the final draft, the paragraphs have become old friends, and if they have flaws, the writer is numb to them. It takes someone from outside, often — an editor — to trim a finished article. It's a job that may have to be done just because space is limited. Sometimes the cutting improves the article by tightening its construction.

Working on an early draft, you can keep the article from going beyond the desired maximum length by avoiding phrases like these:

- **it seems that.**   If what follows such a phrase is only speculation, the phrase, or a variation of it, serves a purpose, but if what follows *did* occur, the phrase should not be used.

- **needless to say.**   If what you say is needless, don't say it.

- **may or may not.**   Obviously.

- **only time will tell.**   Obviously.

Among words, "that" often gets the axe in copy, and deservedly. Some sentences, though, lose clarity when a "that" goes. When you've taken a "that" out, you should read your sentence again to make sure it says what you want it to say. "Conclude the report" is quite different from "conclude that the report."

Clarity often suffers when the writer mistakenly assumes that the reader will supply some of the words. One of the most common student writing errors goes like this:

As far as his art classes, he did much better.

The writer means to say:

As far as his art classes are concerned, he did much better.

When the Boston *Globe* ended an editorial thought with "Politics and mental health don't mix," it meant to say that "Politics and *setting up or running* mental health programs don't mix." Or did it?

"She likes working better than her husband" means something quite different from a slightly longer version: "She likes working better than her husband does."

From an AP story about Mamie Eisenhower's illness at 79:

> "All her vital signs are in pretty good shape."

It is a doctor speaking. What he means to say, of course, is that all her vital signs *indicate* she is in pretty good shape.

• Ambiguity

Ambiguity serves the editor who writes "I shall lose no time in reading your manuscript" and the professor who says of a student seeking a job, "I can't recommend him too highly," but it has no place in an article, where meaning must be singular.

What is the reader to make of a sentence like this (from a student paper analyzing a magazine)?

> But these characterizations relate to full-page advertising which is at best indeterminate in its prevalence at any one time.

Unfortunately an ambiguity problem typically does not confine itself to a single sentence. It spreads over the entire article. And the person who has the problem may not realize it. If you suspect you have the problem — maybe a teacher marks "Vague" in the margins of what you write — you might try talking out the article to some willing listener before writing it. You may be one of those persons who express themselves better orally than at the typewriter.

Another solution is to start over again, using, in your first draft, anyway, only simple subject-predicate sentences.

> I am talking about advertisements in magazines. Some of them occupy a full page. . . .

For the student who has solved the problems of sentence and paragraph ambiguity, there is still the matter of word ambiguity. "Unemployed" is one of those words that is hard to pin down. One set of statistics on the unemployed may include seasonal workers temporarily out of a job and workers out on strike; another set may not include these people. Be sure to explain to your readers, then, what "unemployed" means. Even "stop" has its ambiguity. One of the standard jokes in the college humor magazines of a more innocent age had it that "The Dean of Women and the Dean of Men have decided to stop necking on campus." And "looks." Bernie Allen, the comedian, told of a doctor called to the bedside of an ailing man. "Madam," the doctor whispered after the exam, "I don't like the looks of your husband at all." The wife replied "I know, I know. But really, he's very good to the children."

• Wrong Combinations

Terms like "the cold war" work well enough by themselves, but in combination they can confuse the reader. What happens when a cold war "thaws"? Does that mean it's getting closer to being a hot war? Confusion can also result from the combination of up words or thoughts with down words: This from "TRB" in *The New Republic*:

> How outrageous it is that the world's richest country lags behind others in infant mortality!

The *New Yorker*, reprinting this sentence as part of one of its back-of-the-book fillers, commented: "Come, now, don't be downcast!"
Another example:

> He has found a way to reduce his income tax payments up to $500 a year.

The "reduce" and "up to" tend to cancel each other.
From *Time* in 1975:

> But last week it became evident that Trans World Airlines is in bad trouble. TWA announced that its losses have gone up, up and away. . . .

Didn't TWA *wish* its losses had gone away!
A major problem in writing involves wrong placement of phrases within sentences. Related words or phrases get separated, and the reader sees unintended combinations, as in this sentence:

> You can learn basic methods of protecting yourself from an experienced instructor.

Certain words used together can cancel each other out. For instance:

> Soybeans are our second biggest crop after corn.

What is the *first* biggest crop after corn?
An unfortunate combination of terms is often a problem.

> . . . an organization dying to put senior citizens to work.

• Double-Meaning Words

When you use a double-meaning word — and the dictionary is full of them — be sure your reader doesn't pick out a meaning you don't intend. Put the word in proper context.

> Robert Frazier, associate editor of the Eugene *Register-Guard*, will discuss the appeal of Annette Buchanan, managing editor of the Emerald.

This from a campus newspaper story announcing a Sigma Delta Chi meeting. No, Frazier was not likely to assess the charm and looks of Miss Buchanan; he was to talk about her judicial appeal from a lower court conviction for refusing to reveal a news source.

Columbia Journalism Review in its "The Lower Case" column reprinted with amusement this excerpt from the Arlington *Citizen Journal*:

> Police officer Bill Avery relied on intuitive judgment when he exposed himself to an armed suspect who had abducted two children. The gamble paid off when the man surrendered.

The Gunning Formula of Readability, named by Robert Gunning, author of *The Technique of Clear Writing*, states as one of its ten principles, "Write as you talk." While the advice will be clear enough to most readers, isn't it possible that someone will see that "as" as synonymous with "while," making the advice somewhat peculiar?

• Saying the Opposite of What You Mean

Some of the words and phrases beginning writers use mean the opposite of what they want them to mean. For instance:

> I could care less.

The writers more than likely mean "I couldn't care less." That they *could* care less means that they *do* care.

> He laughed all the way to the bank.

That *could* be what the writer meant, but chances are he meant "He cried all the way to the bank." The subject of the sentence has endured criticism for his unorthodox ways, and that makes him sad. Still, he makes a lot of money, so he has mixed feelings. The *Christian Century*, in an editorial written shortly before Barry Goldwater won his party's Presidential nomination in 1964, shows how "all the way to the bank" *should* be used:

Although Senator Goldwater has received in no state primary the kind of popular support he has expected, he is crying all the way to his party's nominating convention in San Francisco with his pockets full of pledged delegates.

• Lookalike Words

"Don't tell me you're nauseous (because you certainly *are*) . . . when you mean, nauseated,'" says John Shuttlesworth, editor of *The Mother Earth News*. "Nauseous" and "nauseated" are just two of scores of lookalike words or terms that writers have trouble with. The sets that follow are some of the others.

colored picture/color picture	infinite/infinitesimal
defrock/disrobe	issue/edition
disinterested/uninterested	madding/maddening
fatalities/casualties	oral/verbal
formula/format	publish/print
infer/imply	selfish/self-centered

Your dictionary will show you the differences. But perhaps the first set on the list needs explanation here. "Colored picture" suggests after-the-fact coloring, as when you tint a black-and-white print with oil colors. "Color picture" suggests the color is there to begin with. The photographer has used color film in the camera.

• Euphemisms

Euphemisms are words used to make something unpleasant sound pleasant or at least acceptable. Or they are words meant to add dignity or prestige to words that sound only ordinary. Advertisers, public relations people, trade organizations, and pressure groups are among the most faithful users of euphemisms. So are educators.

A used car becomes a "pre-owned car" or "a car with previous service." A house in the hands of a real estate agent becomes a "home." Nobody sells paints or fabrics in ordinary colors; these things come in "decorator colors." Pornographic movies are movies with "adult themes." The TV networks don't show you re-runs; they show you "encore performances." Auberon Waugh, in a *National Review* piece, tells about angering BBC executives because he said "loonybin" on the air. Pretending that his BBC critics were reading the article he was writing, he referred to mental institutions as "our — ah — clinics for the cerebrally indisposed."

The people in education are given to using "depends on others to do his work" for "cheats," "can do more when he tries" for "lazy," and "exceptional child" for "retarded child." A library becomes a "learning resources center."

Euphemisms have taken over most job descriptions. "Engineers" is a favored word. Janitors are "maintenance engineers," crane operators are "hoisting engineers," plumbers are "sanitary engineers."

Professor Sharu S. Rangnekar of Long Island University, amused by the euphemisms business people use, drew up "A Communicator's Glossary," from which the following samples are taken:

> *Expedite:* to confound confusion with commotion.
> *For your approval:* I am passing the buck.
> *For your comments:* I haven't the foggiest.
> *For your file:* I seem to have an extra copy.
> *Under consideration:* Never heard of it.
> *Under active consideration:* We're looking in the file for it.[1]

The swim suit and bra makers give special attention not to fat or bosomy women but to women with "full figures." The new journalists don't give you propaganda; they give you "advocacy journalism." The grass-seed growers in the valley don't burn their fields at the end of the season anymore, causing smoke to engulf the city; they engage in "field sanitizing," but the smoke unfortunately bothers city residents just as much. Politicians backing down from previous statements call press conferences to "clarify" what they said.

The elderly become "senior citizens." And when they die they "pass away." Their "loved ones" put themselves in the hands of "grief therapists." Birth control becomes "planned parenthood." And a woman doesn't have an abortion; she has an "interruption of pregnancy."

The word "rape" is now generally accepted in the mass media, but once it was "criminal assault," causing one paper to report once (or so it is said) that a woman ran down the street yelling, "Help! Help! I've

---

[1] Sharu S. Rangnekar, "A Communicator's Glossary," *Service for Company Publications*, December 1971, p. 2. Reprinted from *Uniroyal Management*.

been criminally assaulted!" and leading to sentences in newspapers like this: "She was beaten severely about the face and knocked unconscious, but she was not criminally assaulted."

This from the New York *Times*:

> The child was found dead at 10:30 A.M. Friday in the half-filled bathtub of the apartment. The Medical Examiner's staff found after an autopsy that the death had been due to homicidal strangulation and submersion. The police refused to say whether she had been molested.

The need to euphemize extends to entertainers, who, perhaps rightly, feel (or felt) that "Jack Benny," "George Burns," "Roy Rogers," and "Kirk Douglas" looked better on marquees than "Benjamin Kubelsky," "Nathan Birnbaum," "Leonard Slye," and "Issur Danielovitch."

While journalists rightly accept any proper-name change, they do not — should not — buy terminology changes dreamed up by pressure groups unless it is obvious that the previous terminology was wrong or unfair. What happens, though, is that over the years the euphemisms, used over and over again by the perpetrators, finally become more familiar than the words they were intended to replace, and journalists then have no choice but to accept the changes. Soon the new words take on coloration some groups may not like, and programs start up to substitute still newer words.

• Jargon

"I live in terror of not being misunderstood," said Oscar Wilde. And from the way some of the people in academia write, you would conclude they live in terror, too. One of Edwin Newman's targets for ridicule in *Strictly Speaking* was "the academic world . . . in which somebody talking to somebody else is considered to be engaged in information transfer." Charles Kuralt, the CBS-TV newsman, said: "I think one of the reasons for our national malaise is the language of advertising — cars that are 'accessorized' with radios and heaters; soaps which give you a lot of clean; pills which prevent 'gasid' indigestion." He added "And the language of youth, uptight, groovy, full of hangups and copouts. And the language of politics, at this point in time, stonewalling, taking the hangout road. And the language of

---

[4]You'll find Riley's table reproduced on page 55 of the October 1975 issue of *Journalism Educator*.

business and education with input and feedback, opting for lifestyles, studying in depth."[2]

As an assignment for her students at San Jose State, where she tried being a visiting professor, Jessica Mitford asked each of her students to take any paragraph from a sociology textbook and rewrite it into clear English.

Theodore M. Bernstein of the New York *Times* heard a speaker urge more emphasis on vocational guidance, placement, and "attitudinal reconditioning, particularly in terms of value structures relating to nonprofessional job opportunities." "If one might essay a translation into plain English," Bernstein wrote, "what he seemed to be saying was, 'Get them not to look down on blue-collar jobs.'" Bernstein added: "Everyone's trying to be a social scientist these days — or to sound like one. A little more windyfoggery like that and human beings won't be able to communicate with one another."

James P. Degnan, who teaches writing at the University of Santa Clara, worries about what academic jargon is doing to the best students, students he calls "straight-A illiterates." The "ordinary illiterates who overpopulate our schools" concern him, of course, but the straight-A illiterates represent more of a problem because they are more influential. He offers this writing example from a senior who had just won a fellowship to a "prestigious graduate school":

> The choice of exogenous variables in relation to multi-colinearity is contingent upon the derivations of certain multiple correlation coefficients.

What the student meant to say, Degnan felt sure, was:

> Supply determines demand.

The villains, Degnan thinks, are the textbooks and professional journals college students have to read. He cites "barbarous jargon" like "ego-integrative action orientation" and "orientation toward improvement of the gratificational–deprivation balance of the actor." The journals never use "alike" when they can use "homologous" or "isomorphic." Degnan notes that things aren't "different," they are "allotropic"; people don't "divide" things, they "dichotomize" or "bifurcate" them.[3]

Closely rivaling the academicians in the use of jargon are the

[2]Charles Kuralt, in a September 1975 speech to a meeting of radio and television news directors, Dallas, Texas.

[3]James P. Degnan, "Masters of Babble," *Harper's*, September 1976, pp. 37, 38.

bureaucrats and politicians. The Washington *Star* saw so many choice examples from its advantaged location that in 1975 it launched a regular "Gobbledygook" column to record them.

In the late 1960s there circulated a word table pretending to help people construct phrases in keeping with what bureaucrats were writing. The origins of the table were vague — *Time* said it may have come from someone in the Royal Canadian Air Force — but Philip Broughton of the U.S. Public Health Service first circulated it in the United States. The table, reproduced in the Sept. 13, 1968 issue of *Time*, consisted of three colomns of ten words each. The first column offered words like "integrated," "total," and "systematized"; the second, "management," "organizational," and "monitored"; the third, "options," "flexibility," and "capability." Each word was numbered, so you could pick a three-digit number at random, and applying one digit to each column come up with a combination like "Compatible Incremental Time-Phase."

More recently, Professor Sam G. Riley, then of Temple University, in a malevolent mood, put together a similar table — five different columns, actually — of words and phrases taken from "a leading mass communications journal." He explained, "Journalism or communications students, most of whom realize that in confusion there is profit, might find this specialized digest of jargon handy in the preparation of term papers, theses, or dissertations. The results could be underwhelming."

Illustrating use of the tables, Riley comes up with this sentence: "Normative multidimensional perceptual states relate directly to nonpolitical modernity." It "doesn't mean much," he admits, "but [it] has a decided learned ring when spoken with conviction."[4]

Don Aitken, for the *National Times* of Sydney, once did a column on jargon used by academic people in convention, where false civility takes over. He listed some commonly heard statements made by speakers in debate, and then offered "free translations" in parentheses. Three samples:

> . . . I don't seem to have explained myself very well. (You are a very dull fellow.)

> There may be something in what you say. (If there is, I haven't been able to discover it.)

I think this is mostly a question of emphasis. (I seem to have missed the point completely.)

The use of jargon, a practice to be shunned, should not be confused with the journalist's occasional playful reaching for what James J. Kilpatrick calls the "butterfly noun" or what Westbrook Pegler called an "out-of-town word." When William F. Buckley, Jr., referred to Nelson Rockefeller's "opsimathy," Kilpatrick, a fellow columnist, called the word, which means "the ability to learn late in life," "a perfectly splendid specimen." "Almost all writers fall unconsciously into the habit of working certain words to death, and nearly all would be the better if occasionally they spent an hour or two with a dictionary to discover what quite serviceable words they are neglecting," J. A. Spender said in *Life, Journalism and Politics*.

While clarity should be your main concern, reaching for an occasional uncommon word can add zest to your writing and help build your own vocabulary and that of your reader. Neil Hickey drops three or four of them in "Daydreams *Can* Come True," an article about Dolly Parton in *TV Guide* (Jan. 22, 1977). "Sometimes she speaks like that, without elisions." And: "Only scoundrels, scamps and scapegraces would take aim at the splendent, clinquant image. . . ."

An uncommon word does not have to slow down the reader; its context can help explain it. Here is a starter set of words with delicious sounds. How many could you use correctly?

angst	paradigm
autarky	perfervid
contretemps	perfidious
evanescent	smarmy
gelid	succubus
lachrymose	shibboleth
lugubrious	tautology

• Redundancy

Hilaire Belloc, an English author, had this idea about writing: "First I tell them what I am going to tell them; then I tell them; then I tell them what I told them." The Belloc approach, even for today's articles, is not unreasonable. There is merit, certainly, in revealing your theme in the opening paragraphs, developing it in succeeding paragraphs, and summarizing in the last paragraph or paragraphs. Even within a paragraph, even within a sentence, you can contribute to your reader's understanding by repeating a phrase or by using the same word several times in succession.

But most of the time you can improve your writing by cutting much of the phrasing that creeps into your article's first run through the typewriter. Someone observed that Dickens used "briny denizens of the deep" instead of "fish" because he was being paid by the word. Too many articles today read as though the authors know too well that they are being paid by the word. They write as the ballad writer of old, who gave us:

> The conductor could not answer,
> He could not make reply. . . .

This from a student-written review:

> However, you will have to wade through a lot of extraneous, unnecessary, and wordy copy to find the facts you are seeking.

Working on an article on electronic news-processing systems, another student wrote:

> As the American Revolution Bicentennial celebration swings into full motion, another "revolution," of a different sort, is taking place in newsrooms throughout the country.

Putting the second "revolution" in quotation marks, the student already had indicated it is " of a different sort," so he didn't need that phrase.

"Upcoming" is a word to be avoided because of a built-in redundancy. Along with "unknow" it was a word invented by teletype operators to save money. When you paid by the word, "upcoming" cost half as much as "coming up." Reporters, then other writers picked up "upcoming" and began using it for "coming" as in "the upcoming game." When the late Bernard Kilgore, publisher of *The Wall Street Journal*, saw an "upcoming" in his paper he sent this message to his staff: "If I see another upcoming in the paper, I'll be downcoming and somebody will be outgoing."

"Etc." is a word that, used with phrases like "such as," becomes redundant.

> She worked with such organizations as Georgia Pacific, Weyerhaeuser, Crown Zellerbach, etc.

"Such organizations" *says* that the list that follows is not complete, eliminating the need for "etc." The "etc." would be needed only if the sentence were phrased this way:

She worked for Georgia Pacific, Weyerhaeuser, Crown Zellerbach, etc.

A discussion of her affiliation with forest-products industries would probably precede such a sentence.

Examination graders know that students use "etc." to suggest that they know more than they have time to write down. In some respects, "etc." is a snow-job word.

"The reason is because" is redundant because "reason" has "because" built into it. You should use, instead, "The reason is that." Or drop the "reason" and go with just the "because."

Sometimes a writer with two different words that have essentially the same meaning can't bear to part with one of them. Hence: "necessary and essential" and "totally and completely." The redundancy may be unconscious, as when the writer uses: "9 A.M. Tuesday morning."

Sometimes you can have fun with redundancy, as Garry Maddox, centerfielder for the Phillies, did when he was asked to describe his first grand-slam homer. "As I remember, the bases were loaded." But as a bumper sticker clearly put it, let's "Help stamp out and abolish redundancy" in article writing.

• Redundant Combinations

Here are commonly used redundant word combinations. In every case, a single word (italicized so you can pick it out) would do the job.

true *facts*	general *rule*
first *commence*	necessary *essentials*
repeat again	necessary *requirements*
few in number	basic *fundamentals*
hidden *secrets*	different *alternatives*
final *conclusion*	viable *alternatives*
fatal *slaying*	revised *second edition*
completely *surround*	*consensus* of opinion
Easter Sunday	different *variations*
future *prospects*	surprising *upset*
successful *triumph*	*many* in number
fellow *colleague*	same *identical*

"Repeat again" would be redundant unless it refers to a third occurrence.

Many times you can substitute a single word for a combination of words. For instance, you can use:

for	for	*for the purpose of*
for	for	*in the amount of*
believe	for	*am of the opinion that*
most	for	*the majority of*
now	for	*at the present time*
suddenly	for	*all of a sudden*
named	for	*by the name of*
about	for	*in the neighborhood of*
I think	for	*to my way of thinking*
on	for	*on the occasion of*
if	for	*in the event that*
as or *since*	for	*in view of the fact that*
supports	for	*is supportive of*
to	for	*with a view to*
though	for	*despite the fact that*
need	for	*have need for*
consider	for	*give consideration to*
encourage	for	*give encouragement to*
instruct	for	*give instruction to*
adjust	for	*make an adjustment in*
use	for	*make use of*
conflicts	for	*comes into conflict*

But don't get the idea that these redundancies should never be used. Sometimes redundancy helps clarify the thought. "Write," "write down" (used in this chapter), and "write up" all have slightly different meanings. Even "very" can be defended on the grounds that it increases the intensity of feeling or thought. A "very good man" does convey the fact that a person is a shade better than a "good man."

• Lack of Logic

Writers can write themselves into boxes, as Robert Markus did in 1971 in *Chicago Tribune Magazine* when he said of Muhammad Ali:

When he enters the ring tomorrow night he will wear a mien of utter confidence. He will strut a bit and he will glare at Frazier and chances are he will say something to him. And no one will ever know that underneath, where no one can see it, where no one has EVER seen it, Muhammad Ali will be afraid.

But after Markus told several million Chicago *Tribune* readers, surely *some one* will know it.

In an article he wrote for *The Saturday Evening Post*, Norman Rockwell told about attending one of President Eisenhower's stag dinners.

After leaving the President, as we were standing on the steps of the White House, we sounded like a bunch of kids discussing the high-school football hero. A secretary had told us that our evening had lasted one-half hour longer than any of the President's other informal evenings. We were delighted and flattered, which shows how President Eisenhower affects people. You just can't help liking him.

This is the kind of logic that often creeps into a magazine article. Can Rockwell rightly conclude that because the President gave him and his party more time than he had given similar groups "you just can't help liking him." What about those persons who attended earlier stag parties? That Rockwell's group had the President's attention "one-half hour longer" than usual hardly would make a favorable impression upon *them*. If the President *usually* stretched a stag dinner past the stated closing time, this would support Rockwell's contention that Eisenhower favorably impressed people — that they just couldn't help liking him. But that he was so gracious to *one* group negated the use of the all-inclusive "you" and called, instead, for the use of the first person "I."

Just a slight miscalculation in word choice can damage the logic of a sentence.

Her interests centered around her children.

How is it possible to "center around"? What the writer means to say is "centered on." If he wants the "around," he should combine it with "revolved," not "centered."

An innocent switch from a plural to a singular reference also can hurt your sentence. Reader Dan Harrison spotted one of these switches in *New York* and wrote: ". . . the statement that, in the accident in Queens last month, '30 people were carried out on a stretcher,' puzzles me. It must have been quite a big stretcher." What the writer of the original piece meant to say was that thirty persons (plural) were carried out on *stretchers* (plural).

One of the arguments against first-person plural centers on logic problems the writer can get into. "As a fan of rock music, we took in a concert. . . ."

When you say that "The average person is one and one-half inches taller than he was 50 years ago," you hope that the reader knows you are comparing an average person now with an average person then, but it is possible the reader will think you are talking about *one* average person who has, in 50 years, grown slightly taller.

You have to wonder what Peer J. Oppenheimer's idea of non-extravagant living is when in *Family Weekly* he writes of Cary Grant: "Except for driving a Rolls-Royce and possessing an expensive wardrobe and a lovely home, Cary never has been extravagant with money. . . ."

When a student wrote about something being "at the opposite end of the fence," he probably meant it was "on the opposite side. . . ." When another student observed that "Both autos landed in a ditch on top of each other," he probably meant that one was on top of the other.

Sign makers run into similar logic problems. The AP reported a sign at the door of a factory in Johannesburg, South Africa: "Staff are reminded that the signing-on book is intended to provide an accurate record of their times of arrival and departure. Under no circumstances should staff sign the book before they actually arrive or after they have actually left." And how about the people who write our laws? Shortly after the turn of the century a town in the Midwest passed an ordinance that read: "When two cars approach a grade crossing at the same time, both shall come to a complete stop and neither shall move until the other has passed by." A couple of cars, no doubt, are still there.

Even college catalogs can provide examples. One catalog promoted an "Earth Awareness" course. "We must be sensitive to . . . [the earth] and its needs so that we . . . can survive. . . ." Then at the end of the description: "consent of instructor necessary. . . . 12 student limit."

Problems in logic extend to the article's byline. In 1962 William P. Lear, Sr., millionaire aircraft-instrument manufacturer, revealed in *Reader's Digest* six ways to become a millionaire. The first was: "Learn to Communicate." The article byline carried these words after Lear's name: "as told to Charles Sopkin."

When a press release out of Washington, D.C., announced an interstate highway system on which "motorists will be able to drive from the Atlantic Coast to the Pacific Coast and from the Mexican border to the Canadian border without stopping for anything," the Eugene (Oreg.) *Register-Guard* commented in an editorial: "The author must be a believer in perpetual motion machines, a man of slim appetite, and certainly not the father of any small children."

In *The Christian Century*, Clair M. Cook, reviewing *Working Men*, noted: "The text is illustrated by a dozen full-page and eight small charcoal drawings from the pen of David Collier." That he could produce charcoal drawings with his *pen* must have come as a surprise to David Collier.

Louis Nizer, as quoted in *Grit*, said that "When a man points a finger at someone else he should remember that four of his fingers are pointing at himself." Presumably Nizer was thinking of someone with five fingers plus a thumb on his pointing hand.

• The Non Sequitur

Ring Lardner, in one of his stories, said of a baseball player: "Although he is a bad fielder he is also a poor hitter." It was no mistake. The *non sequitur* was one of Lardner's favorite devices. Stephen Leacock used it, too. "Although defended by some of the most skilled lawyers of Aucherlocherty, he had been acquitted." The *non sequitur* can provide a different kind of light touch. Just so the reader understands. Too often the *non sequitur* appears accidentally. What the writer puts into one sentence or phrase does not follow logically what appears in the previous sentence or phrase. Often an "although" or a "but" causes the problem. "It gets poor mileage in the city, but it doesn't get good mileage on the highway." Changing "but" to "and" would rescue the sentence.

• Wrong Placement

The wrong placement of a phrase in a sentence can create a peculiar picture in the reader's mind. When the Arlington (Va.) *Northern Virginia Sun* said in a news story that "He has sent cuttings of this plant which have been grafted to Mrs. Holden," *The New Yorker*, reprinting it, commented: "Known locally as Mrs. Holden the Uncomfortable."

Who could blame the reader for seeing in the following sentence the birth of a full-grown man: "A Baptist minister who has preached in every state in the nation, the Rev. Mr. Foster was born in. . . ."

First things first. A fraternity executive, speaking at an interfraternity conference, forgot that, when he said: "Not only does high scholarship provide excellent publicity; but it is of practical advantage to the individual."

• Misusing Familiar Expressions

The phrase "everything from soup to nuts," though trite, makes sense because it confines itself to an area narrow enough to be measured. Used either literally or figuratively, it refers to a complete meal, one that starts with soup and ends with something to munch on. The reader can visualize any number of main courses in between. But when you use the same idea to cover, say, ways people make their livings, it doesn't work so well.

> She has done everything from working in a cannery to being an assistant curator of an art museum.

And what are those intermediate jobs? The reader can't possibly know.

One of the most remarkable misuses of an old expression came from Sen. Joseph McCarthy of Wisconsin when he said: "That's the most unheard of thing I ever heard of." While a Congressman, Gerald Ford was quoted by *Newsweek* as saying: "If Abraham Lincoln were living today, he would turn over in his grave." For a column written for *IABC News*, this author gave that expression a slightly different twist — on purpose. Referring to a fellow columnist: "No doubt Phil Douglis, if he were dead, would spin in his grave on hearing that. . . ."

The context of the contorted expression makes a difference. If, for instance, a reviewer ends a generally favorable review with "fills a much-needed void," she probably does not mean what she says. But if the review damns the book as well as the field the book covers, "fills a much-needed void" makes sense.

• Doing Violence to Science

A good vocabulary or a willingness to use the dictionary would prevent your saying that a speaker stood *on* the lectern or *behind* the podium.

A knowledge of forestry or tree growing would prevent your accepting the "fact" from an interviewee that the initials he carved on a tree trunk years ago are now several feet higher up.

When Donald Grey Barnhouse said in an article in *Eternity*, "Man has a body, is a soul, and has a spirit. . . .If any one of the parts is deficient, man wobbles like a three-legged stool with one leg short." George Mounce of Portland, Oreg. wrote in to the magazine to point out: "Dr. Barnhouse seems to have forgotten his solid geometry which postulates, 'A plane is determined by three noncollinear points.' Any three-legged stool will rest without wobble on the uneven surface of the ground, regardless of whether the legs are of equal or unequal lengths."

When *The Times* of London quoted someone as saying that people are disturbed because about half the children in the country are below average in reading ability, a reader wrote in to point out: "This is only one of many similarly disturbing facts. About half the church steeples in the country are below average height, about half our coal scuttles below average capacity, and about half our babies below average weight." He added: "The only remedy would seem to be to repeal the law of averages."

Numbers of any kind mystify many writers and editors. *Parade* in its "Intelligence Report" estimated that "there are only 200,000 lions left in the world, a 100 percent decrease from the lion population of 25 years ago." That a 100-percent decrease could still leave 200,000 amused Thomas Williams, who made "A Faint Fanfare . . ." item out of it for *The National Observer*.

When Sid Bernstein in a column in *Advertising Age* said that a roll of toilet paper with 1,000 sheets has a "normally expected" 50 percent advantage over a roll with 500 sheets, reader Robert B. Sackheim wrote in to say that when he went to school he learned that "something twice as big as another was 100% larger, not 50%."

In a booklet about its pianos, Sohmer talks about "over 3,696 adjustments" being made in one part of the manufacturing process, "over 2,024 adjustments" in another. But you cannot use "over" in so precise a context. Either you have *exactly* 3,696 adjustments and *exactly* 2,024 adjustments or you don't. If you don't, round off the figures to 3,600 (or 3,690) and 2,000, and *then* use "over" or (better) "more than."

Sometimes the logic is inescapable. "As a group, tavern patrons were more favorably disposed toward taverns than nonpatrons," Julian Roebuck and Wolfgang Frese tell us in *The Rendezvous: A Case Study of an After-Hours Club*.

• FRESHNESS

The professor warns his class: "There are two words I will not tolerate in your articles. One is 'lousy,' and the other is 'swell.' " A pause. Then from the back of the class this question: "Well, professor, what are the two words?"

The following section will attempt to discourage your settling for tired, inadequate phrasing and encourage your bringing freshness to your writing.

• Built-in Color

You may be lucky enough to pick for interviewing someone whose colorful language brings your article the freshness it needs. To illustrate his point of view that "Coyotes are as notorious for their sly adaptability as for their penchant for mutton," Mike Tharp, in a *Wall Street Journal* feature on a program to keep coyotes from killing sheep, quotes a "veteran trapper" as saying: "If you put a coyote on a tennis court with nothing else in there, he could hide behind the ball."

Dick Mills, a Bible teacher, tells about a man living along the San Andreas Fault. The man isn't particularly concerned. "Why should I worry? If the California coast falls into the Pacific I'll have beach front property."

As a writer you constantly search for the quotation that will add life and spirit to your article. In interviewing, you try to bring out the colorful expression from your respondent. But mostly you create your own freshness through your thought process and the way you fashion your sentences. See how M. J. Sobran, Jr., does it in a *National Review* article about what in most hands would be a dull subject: another opinion magazine, *Commonweal*, which, unlike *National Review*, leans somewhat to the left.

> Though traditionally Roman Catholic, it seems to have been taken over by Irish Unitarians, politically progressive types who think of Christianity as an interesting possibility.

• Description

Perhaps the best test of the writer's skill comes in descriptive passages. There a literary touch is needed. There a freshness counts most. Description involving that which can't be seen represents a special challenge. The following excerpt shows what can be done with the elusive subject of music. It is from Chris Chase's article on "The Country Girl" in *The New York Times Magazine*. Chase is discussing Dolly Parton.

> In "Love Is Like a Butterfly," Dolly's work is itself as sheer and delicate as a butterfly's wings; she skitters over the surface of the words, barely touching them, while in "Travelin' Man," she hoots and hollers and drives and mocks. Sometimes she hits a high note and it breaks into pieces, and a little shower of crystally sounds comes down. . . .

This from someone who says in her article "I'm no authority on country singers."

"Skitters" is a good example of a lively word to use in description. John Lawing uses it in *National Courier* describing the writing of Neil Simon. "Mr. Simon's funny fast-paced dialogue skitters along like a stone skipping across water."

Some other examples of description: P. G. Wodehouse described his own frivolous but beautifully written, similarly plotted novels as "musical comedies without music." (He had written close to 100 books by the time he died at 93.) Arthur "Bugs" Baer described a ballplayer who had trouble stealing bases: "He had larceny in his heart, but his feet were honest."

Few writers can resist using a pun. "Portland Trail Blazer Bill Walton has done more dribbling at the mouth than on the court lately," said pun-obsessed *Time* when the basketball star was spending much of his time on the bench with injuries.

Sara Davidson in *The Atlantic* talks about "the Carpenters, a brother and sister team with personalities so bland they make Tricia Nixon Cox seem mysterious. . . ." Thomas Griffith in *The Atlantic* refers to the "wide crockery smile" of John F. Kennedy. Nathanael West describes one of his characters in *The Day of the Locust* as "a very complicated young man with a whole set of personalities, one inside the other like a nest of Chinese boxes." Finis Farr in *Fair Enough*, a biography of Westbrook Pegler, makes side comments about Henry Wallace, among others: "It was hard to describe Henry Wallace, for he lacked crispness of outline, though he seemed to be a decent sort of man, with a strain of mysticism that perhaps qualified him for the definition of harmless crank." Of Westbrook Pegler, novelest Homer Croy says, in a magazine article: "His sense of humor runs through him like a wick through a candle."

An unsigned review in *The New Yorker* says that in *A Touch of Class* Glenda Jackson played a dress designer "with a wit that flickers like an anteater's tongue." Whitney Balliett in the same magazine describes an "unprepossessing middlebrow writer whose prose was knotty pine at best."

Wilfred Sheed in *A Middle Class Education* describes a woman as "placid and well to the left of plain." An intriguing association. What would she look like were she to the *right* of plain?

Someone described Heywood Broun as "looking like an unmade bed." Bob Hope said of Howard Cosell: "The one man Will Rogers never met." Richard Reeves in *New York* moved in on then President Ford with some fine-line description. "Gerald Ford is good-humored without having a particularly good sense of humor. He laughs a lot, but usually a split second too late."

When you are spending some time with a single character in your story, you do not have to bunch all your descriptive terms into a paragraph or two. It is probably best to bunch *some* of the description, but there is no reason why you can't build a picture as the story progresses. You can combine some description with the action, as Aaron Latham does in *New York* when in the first paragraph of an article about William Loeb, the New Hampshire publisher, he writes: "He calls the paper from his home and dictates off the top of his balding bullethead."

Make sure that the descriptive segment you work into a paragraph belongs there. In the following middle-of-the-story paragraph, written by an AP reporter in 1970 upon the election of Salvador Allende as President of Chile, the description of the country's shape is almost a *non sequitur*.

Even though Allende is a long-time Marxist who has praised Fidel Castro and Mao Tse-tung, the 62-year-old senator is not expected to convert his stringbean-shaped country overnight into a Communist state.

• Creating Pictures

See if you can draw a picture with words. Someone did it when he described the Edsel as "an Oldsmobile sucking a lemon." *The New Yorker*'s "Talk of the Town" section did it when it referred to ". . . one of those squat modern office buildings that make Washington look as if it had been emptied out of an ice-cube tray." Roger Angell, writing in *The New Yorker* of the sudden decline of Pirate's pitcher Steve Blass, did it with: ". . . and then the pitch, delivered with a swastika-like scattering of arms and legs and a final lurch to the left. . . ."

Daniel Yergin, writing from Rome to *The New Republic*, creates a "photograph" of Sergio Segre, the Foreign Minister of the Italian Communist Party, saying he "looks a good deal like that photograph of Paul Samuelson that runs in *Newsweek*." Most readers of the photo-free *New Republic* would be familiar with the picture that heads Samuelson's *Newsweek* column.

• Figures of Speech

Work some similes and metaphors into your writing. C. S. Lewis uses a simile in *Surprised by Joy* when he writes ". . . they had a talent for happiness in a high degree — went straight for it as experienced travelers go for the best seat in a train." He uses a metaphor when he writes, in the same book, "I could never have gone far in any science because on the path of every science the lion Mathematics lies in wait for you."

When you start a figure of speech, follow it through logically to the end. Art Seidenbaum does it well in *West*. "The public school is our political playground in which liberals do knee-jerk exercises on freedom and conservatives play capture-the-flag."

Be careful that your figure of speech fits the subject. When in 1971 a study showed that black children (then called "Negro children") did not tolerate milk well, an AP story quoted a nutritionist as saying that the report "has to be taken with a grain of salt." It was an unpleasant association of words.

Avoid mixing two metaphors in one sentence, either directly or by implication, as in "The hopes for a settlement in the Middle East, kindled in recent weeks, evaporated today. . . ." Of an editorial writer, someone in the *Columbia Journalism Review* said: "He aims more at the spleen than at the brain, and he hits his target right between the eyes." Perhaps the *CJR* writer was inspired by a line from a country and western song: "My heart has a mind of its own."

Sometimes the writer reaches too far, and his analogy becomes forced, as when the New York *Times*'s Vincent Canby wrote:

> In any compilation of the modern world's 10 most unrewarding stunts, the casting of Barbra Streisand in a straight comedy, especially one as flimsily fabricated as "The Owl and the Pussycat," must rank close to Charles A. Stephens's 1920 attempt to ride over Niagara Falls in a barrel, which turned out to be fatal.

When you have to explain the event you bring in for comparison, you sidetrack the reader.

• Contrast

Contrast can bring freshness to your article. It can be contrast in pictures drawn as well as in words chosen. S. I. Hayakawa has differentiated between the Republican and Democratic parties in this way: If a person is drowning 50 feet from shore, the Republican will throw him 25 feet of rope and tell him to swim the other 25 feet because it is good for his character. The Democrat will throw him 100 feet of rope and walk away looking for other good deeds to do.

Burt Prelutsky in the Los Angeles *Times* sets up some word contrast inside a sentence when he tells of a pet shop "located on South Central Avenue, in the midst of a neighborhood otherwise devoted to light industry and heavy drinking."

• Surprise Context

You can bring freshness to your writing by occasionally using words in an unexpected context. "Spectacularly" ordinarily has a positive connotation. But see how L. E. Sissman uses it in a *New Yorker* review of a biography of Evelyn Waugh: ". . . Waugh then proved himself one of the most spectacularly unsuitable officers in the British Army." Another example comes from someone outside *The Wall Street Journal* who tried unsuccessfully to fix a story going into that estimable organ. He said the paper was "rotten with integrity from top to bottom."

Sometimes an inappropriate word or term is just what you need to register disapproval. See what one writer does with "Dutch treat." Commenting on *Playboy*'s alleged identification with parts of the women's movement, M. J. Sobran, Jr., in *National Review* says, ". . . *Playboy*'s notion of sexual equality probably means no more than going Dutch treat on the abortion."

If someone is well known for some personality trait or habit, you can use his name generically. *New York* invoked the name of a writer known for his extravagant expense-account living when it published this line: "It is also rumored that the [*National*] *Enquirer* pays [Jack] Martin's expenses — which sometimes run to a Hunter Thompsonish $3,000 per column. . . ." *Time* used the same device, only with a fictional character (James Thurber's), when it covered the conviction of Ferdinand Demara, "The Great Impostor." The magazine said that the judge suspended the sentence "because of Mittygating circumstances."

Don't be afraid to use a not-so-familiar synonym once in a while. When historian Arthur Schlesinger, Jr., wrote a piece for *Playboy* in 1971, Smith Hempstone, the newspaper columnist, noted: "And there he is. . . , nestled amidst the mammae."

• In-Character Writing

Try to use language appropriate to the subject. An unnamed writer in "Book Ends," *The New York Times Book Review,* says: "A new book by Billy Graham has its publisher, Doubleday, crying hallelujah. The book is called 'Angels' and the publisher is claiming sales as of Oct. 8 of 220,000 copies. . . ." After more data on sales prospects for the book, the item (it isn't really a review) concludes with: "Add to that the book's low $4.95 cover price — almost unfair competition these days — and Mr. Graham's optimistic, as well as other-worldly message in 'Angels' and you have the makings of some heavenly sales figures."

Sometimes the person you are writing about has some characteristics that can be worked into the writing itself. Anybody who has heard a Paul Harvey broadcast would understand what is going on in the following excerpt from a feature written by Paul Hendrickson for *The National Observer*. After describing and quoting the man in a first paragraph, Hendrickson interrupts himself with this second paragraph:

Hello, Americans. That was Paul Harvey. Now stand by for page 2.

When Frank Sullivan died in 1976, *Time* in an obit used this phrasing to call attention to his humorous writings on cliches:

It now becomes our sad duty to report that Frank Sullivan, who at 83 was not as young as he used to be and had been under the weather for months, passed away last week. What's that, Mr. Arbuthnot? But of course — old cliché experts never die or even pass away; they cash in their chips, give up the ghost, and cross the Great Divide. We stand corrected.

• Avoiding Clichés

A charming — and pathetic — character in modern literature is Ditto Boland in Edwin O'Connor's *The Last Hurrah*. On his deathbed, the hero of the story, politician Frank Skeffington, spends a last few moments with each of his cronies. When Ditto steps up to shake the chief's hand, the chief says: "Thanks for a million laughs." Ditto never really quite understood what Skeffington meant. What had amused Skeffington about Ditto all those years was Ditto's tendency to load every conversation with the trite expressions or clichés, often doubled up in improbable combinations.

Presented by O'Connor through Ditto, the cliché is uproarious, as it is in the hands of author Frank Sullivan, who did a celebrated piece for *The New Yorker* called "The Cliché Expert Takes the Stand" (*q*. Then where do you live? *a*. Any old place I hang my hat is home sweet home to me.). But used by magazine article writers, the cliché — or the trite expression — is ruinous.

Trite words and expressions got that way through overuse. Once they were novel. Everyone then wanted to use them. With extended use the novelty wore off. Now only lazy or unimaginative writers reach for them.

The following list, by no means exhaustive, presents some of the most common clichés — some of the most tiresome words and expressions you could choose for your article.

a pretty penny
add insult to injury
after all is said and done
agree to disagree
all things being equal
all work and no play
almighty dollar
apple of his eye
as luck would have it
beat a hasty retreat
better late than never
better left unsaid
bitter end
blushing bride
bright and shining faces
bright-eyed and bushy-tailed
burn the midnight oil
busy as a bee
by leaps and bounds
call a spade a spade
cold as ice
cool as a cucumber
conspicuous by his absence
cut down in his prime
Dame Fortune
diamond in the rough
each and every
easier said than done
errand of mercy
face it
fair sex
festive occasion
few and far between
flat as a pancake
food for thought
for all intents and purposes
foregone conclusion
gala occasion
goes without saying
good as gold

green with envy
Grim Reaper
hale and hearty
heated argument
hectic weekend
high on the hog
hungry as a bear
last but not least
let's face it
method in his madness
miraculous escape
Mother Nature
needless to say
nipped in the bud
none the worse for wear
order out of chaos
on the ball
on the beam
other things being equal
quick as a flash
ripe old age
see the light of day
skeleton in the closet
slow but sure
straight from the shoulder
superhuman effort
supreme sacrifice
sweat of his brow
this day and age
through thick and thin
throw caution to the winds
tired but happy
too funny for words
untimely death
untiring efforts
weaker sex
wee small hours
without rhyme or reason
white as a sheet
words cannot express

While "new cliché" may sound like a contradiction and "old cliché" may sound redundant, it is true that some words and expressions, now badly worn, only lately entered the language mainstream. Among them are these from hippie, hip, bubblegum-chewing, and Watergate sources:

at this point in time	meaningful relationship
bag	nitty gritty
bread	no way
bummer	not all that [different, etc.]
busted	out of sight
dig	rap
do his own thing	right on
do your own thing ·	split
far out	the bottom line
for openers	the name of the game
fun idea	the whole bit
get it all together	turn on
get it on	uptight
has this thing	who's counting?
into [meditating, etc.]	would you believe?
is he for real?	you better believe it
let it all hang out	you've got to be kidding

Writing for most markets you will want to avoid these tiresome and even embarrassing words and phrases and look for fresh ways to express yourself. You will not be able to avoid them altogether. In some cases you will find no other phrasing that explains things better. *Time* in 1963 put a couple of clichés together at the end of a paragraph (about a Richard Burton/Elizabeth Taylor/Eddie Fisher entanglement over the making of *Cleopatra*) with interesting results:

> And where does this leave Richard Burton? Well, for his work in the same picture, he made $250,000. And if that seems grim enough, there is something even grimmer. In a burst of generosity some years ago, Liz gave her husband a 50% cut of her proceeds from the picture. So Eddie Fisher, who is still her husband, will make perhaps 14 times as much from *Cleopatra* as Richard Burton. He'll be rolling in money, but that ain't hay.

• Adapting Well-Known Expressions

It is sometimes useful, though, to take a well-known expression or slogan and give it a twist to fit your thought. The twist makes it new enough. In a column on the unnecessary gabbiness of sports announcers, John Leonard in the New York *Times* commented: "Nobody ever told them that a closed mouth gathers no feet." Richard Schickel in a *Time* piece on inferior TV programs said that viewers are "loyal through thin and thin." Feeling sorry for visitors to New York who leave with a stereotype of the city, Jim Hoffman in the defunct *Lithopinion* said: "New York is a great place to live, but I wouldn't want to visit here." Stanley Kauffmann in *The New Republic* said that Ali McGraw in *Love Story* proves that "without talent, a pretty girl is like a malady." William Safire, in his newspaper column, noted after Watergate that "public boredom will help stabilize the ship of state by proving once again that it is always darkest before the yawn."

"His body took a bad hop," Joe Garagiola said of Pete Rose in the 1975 All-Star game, as Rose, in left field, doubled over, bounced, and finally came up with the ball. Referring to an aging actress, *Newsweek* said she was "pushing 50 if she isn't pulling it."

Mary Leimach in the defunct Washington *Daily News* applied after-hours terminology to the politicians' tendancy to avoid answering embarrassing questions. ". . . Washington's most popular dance, the side-step. . . ."

You may remember Senator Edmund Muskie's decline as a candidate for the Democratic nomination for President in 1972 because, some say, he broke down and cried after a newspaper made critical remarks about his wife. Afterwards, Lee Byrd began his AP analysis of the campaign with "Whatever happened to Ed Muskie, for crying out loud?"

• Making up Names

At times, you are better off inventing names to make your point rather than using real ones, especially if your points are general and if you worry about libel. Just so the reader understands. Russell Kirk's *National Review* readers know well enough there is no "Behemoth State University," and they also know what big midwestern University the columnist really has in mind when he uses the term.

National Review did its thinking out loud as it tried to come up with a
name for a credit card after the announcement in 1975 that some
churches will accept credit-card contributions in their collection
plates. "Master Tithe? BankAmiracle?" A. Robert Smith shows a
touch of irony, even sarcasm, as he coins the term "participatory parenthood" in a column dealing with parents making an effort to
understand their children. Bill McGlashen in *Catholic Digest* comes up
with "rerun-of-the-mill" TV shows. Reed Whittemore in *The New Republic* calls TV cops-and-robbers shows "Wheelies" or "Detroit Ballet"
because so much of the show-time is given to cars cruising or sometimes racing, people getting in and out of cars, and car doors slam-
ming.

> In Detroit Ballet the car shots are of elephantine late models and give us no
> society and no flesh and blood, give us only the purgatory of cop following
> robber down the years as the vehicles house them and pace their vacant
> ritual.

Allison Lurie in the novel *The War Between the Tates* uses the phrase
"stamp-album countries" to list countries most of us never heard of.
(That novel also provides a good example of an author's giving life to
an object. ". . . the engine, as usual, roars once boastfully and dies.")

• Name-Calling

Some writers like to play Don Rickles' role, slashing out at people
without worrying much about their feelings. Bo Burlingham wrote
such an article — a personality sketch — for *Esquire* in 1975, saying
that calling his subject "arrogant and abrasive" did not do justice to
the man's "power to offend." Later in the article, Burlingham reported that his subject had been referred to, mistakenly, as an Italian
journalist with a hangover, an observation that "constitutes a slur
against Italians, journalists, and people with hangovers. . . ."[5] James J.
Kilpatrick engaged in name-calling of a sarcastic nature when he
applauded Senator Eugene McCarthy's refusal to accept a set of campaign standards introduced by executives of Common Cause. It was
1976 and McCarthy was running for President again. In his column
Kilpatrick referred to the executives as "these two eminences," "their
supremacies," "the two exalted ones," "their nobilities," "the royal
highnesses of Common Cause," "King John," and "El Supremo."

[5]*Esquire* later ran a retraction and made an out-of-court cash settlement to the subject.

When you want to tear someone down, engaging in name-calling is an inviting prospect, but it is a dangerous one, too. You stand the chance both of bringing on a libel suit and of moving the reader over to the other side in sympathy. You fare a little better, perhaps, when you taken on a group, although the possibility of libel is not completely eliminated. Malcolm Muggeridge engaged in some sweeping — and effective — name-calling in a review in *Esquire* praising Edwin Newman's *Strictly Speaking*. Newman, Muggeridge wrote, "gives a whole series of splendid examples [of the appalling pollution of the English language] from newspapers, network offerings, politicians' speeches, and other linguistic cesspools." Gore Vidal also took in a lot of territory when, by implication, he gave a name to the Radical Right: "Well, sir, the Radical Right really hit the fan."

• GRAMMAR AND USAGE

Frank Versagi, a writer and editor, has said,"If you need consciously to concern yourself with sentence structure, punctuation, the choice of words, let's be honest; you're in the wrong business." But a few paragraphs might be useful here to remind you of things you may have forgotten from your high-school Language Arts classes and your college English Composition classes. If you missed out on grammar and usage lessons altogether, this section can alert you to a deficiency.

Several book-length guides can help. William Strunk, Jr.'s and E. B. White's *The Elements of Style* (Macmillan), out in a new edition in 1972, remains a favorite. A more complete guide is Henry W. Fowler's *A Dictionary of Modern English Usage* (Oxford). The 1965 revision (by Sir Henry Gower) maintains the flavor of the original. ". . . impeccably British, and in many of its longer entries deliciously opinionated," observes *The Reader's Adviser*. Margaret Nicholson in 1957 finished an Americanization of Fowler in *A Dictionary of American-English Usage* (New American Library). A more permissive guide, but yet authoritative, is Bergen and Cornelia Evans's *A Dictionary of Contemporary American Usage* (Random House, 1957). Another worthwhile guide is Eric Partridge's *Concise Usage and Abusage* (Greenwood, 1965).

Harper & Row in 1975 brought out *Harper Dictionary of Contemporary Usage*, compiled by William Morris and Mary Morris, calling it "the first dictionary of current usage in years." A total of 136 writers and editors contributed to the volume. The same house, the same year, published Jacques Barzun's *Simple & Direct: A Rhetoric for Writers*.

Roy H. Copperud, author of *A Dictionary of Usage and Style*, in 1970 put out a book, *American Usage: The Consensus* (Van Nostrand Reinhold) that compared the advice and directives of several of the books on grammar and usage then in print. *American Usage* dramatizes the complexity of the problem of figuring out which words to use — and how.

A 1961 controversy over a newspaper headline illustrates the uncertainties of grammar.

> Hardin One of Coaches
> Who Revere Mr. Stagg

Maybe you will understand the controversy better with some flesh put into the headline: "Mr. Hardin is one of the coaches who revere Mr. Stagg." The argument centered on the word "revere." Shouldn't it be "reveres"? Does the pronoun "who" refer to a singular or a plural subject?

As reported in *Editor & Publisher*, an instructor and a professor said "reveres." Members of a sports staff, a high-school principal, and a department head said "revere." Finally, the Encyclopaedia Britannica Library Research Service settled the matter, saying "revere" was right and diagramming a sentence to prove it.

Just your logic should tell you "revere." Look at it this way: You are dealing with "coaches who revere Mr. Stagg." Mr. Hardin is one of them.

• Some Confusing Pairs

Having learned to distinguish between the words in each of the following pairs, you would be a step up on the way to correct usage.

• **affect** and **effect.** In ordinary use, "affect" is only a verb. "Effect" is both a verb and a noun. As verbs, the two words are not synonymous. "Affect" means *to move, touch, or produce an effect on.* "Effect" means *to accomplish, cause, or bring about.* You *affect* two people when you *effect* a reconciliation. The *effect* (noun) of the reconciliation would be that the two people will live together again.

• **all right** and **alright.** This should be easy. There is no such as word as "alright."

• **be sure to** and **be sure and.**   It almost always would be "be sure to." "Be sure and" suggests two *different* actions. Also, use "try to do" instead of "try and do."

• **between** and **among.**   It's "between" two persons but "among" several.

• **different from** and **different than.**   Although "It . . . has been used by many good writers, . . . ['different than'] is not recommended" by Margaret Nicholson.

• **infer** and **imply.**   "Infer" means *to deduce*; "imply" means *to suggest*. The student infers (believes) that, after reading a book like this and following its advice, he can produce articles suitable for publication. The writer of the book implies (suggests) that the reader can do it.

• **less** and **fewer.**   It would be "less food" (bulk) but "fewer potatoes" (items).

• **provided that** and **providing that.**   "Provided that" is preferred.

• **verbal** and **oral.**   "Verbal" is a broader word than "oral." It means having to do with words — all words. "Oral" has to do with spoken words only. "Oral" has to do with the mouth. Words need not be involved.

A lot of writers have trouble with double-word combinations that also come in single-word versions, like "take off" and "takeoff"; "lay out" and "layout"; "every day" and "everyday." It may help to remember that the two-word form is a verb or verb form; the one-word form is a noun or adjective. Hence: "The plane will take off" but "The takeoff was smooth"; "You can lay out the page" but "The layout is ready"; "She does it every day" but "It is an everyday activity."

• **Parallel Structure**

Writers who learn how to use parallel structure make things clear for their readers and bring rhythm to their sentences. Parallel structure involves an even presentation of coordinate elements (two or more words, phrases, clauses, or sentences that occur one right after the other). The most obvious place to use parallel structure would be in a list. If you want to show a relationship among items on the list, each item should have the same grammatical construction. For instance, if it is a list of phrases, each phrase would begin with the same part of speech: a verb, a noun, a preposition, or whatever.

To illustrate: "learning how to get along with others, to trust your own judgment, and to manage your own affairs" is better than "learning how to get along with others, to trust your own judgment, and managing your own affairs." To illustrate again: "This is true not only of young readers but also of older ones" is better than "This is not only true of young readers but also of older ones." The same grammatical constructions should follow "Not only" and "but also."

Consider this lead from an AP story out of Portland some years ago:

> For many years Oregon had one of the lowest infant death rates in the country, but now there are only 20 states with a higher infant mortality rate.

It is not a clear lead because it changes from low to high, it changes from active to passive voice, and it brings in an unnecessary synonym. Here is a way to improve the lead through parallel structure:

> For many years Oregon had one of the lowest infant death rates in the country, but now 29 states have lower rates than Oregon's.

Patrick Anderson in this excerpt from an article on "The Real Nashville" in *The New York Times Magazine* uses parallel structure to compare two kinds of fans. See how it works:

> . . . both groups sees [sic] themselves as a persecuted minority. The country fan thinks that pointy-headed bureaucrats want to bus his children, tax his wages to support loafers, and ultimately destroy his way of life. The rock fan knows for a certainty that there are cops outside the concert hall who want to hassle him for his life-style and bust him for the weed in his pocket. And if the rock fan's danger is more immediate, the country fan's is more poignant, for time is not on his side and, in the long run, bureaucrats are always more dangerous than cops.

"... The country fan thinks ... The rock fan knows ..." "... bus his children, tax his wages. . . , and . . . destroy his way of life." ". . . the rock fan's danger is more immediate, the country fan's is more poignant ..." "... time is ... bureaucrats are . . ." Anderson's structure is no accident.

• Dangling Construction

The following excerpt represents probably the most persistent construction error in student-written papers.

Instead of reading captions, he wants people to look at his drawings.

A clear case of "dangling construction." The reader associates "he" with "reading captions." To get rid of the dangling construction:

He wants people to look at his drawings rather than read captions.

• The Case Against "Hopefully"

The battle against "hopefully" goes on, but hopelessly. Now, not only students but also their professors — their *journalism* professors — use the word blatantly. Here's Prof. Daniel R. Williamson in the preface of his *Feature Writing for Newspapers* (Hastings House, Publishers, New York, 1975): "Hopefully, this technique . . ." The *technique* hopes?

The trouble with "hopefully" as it is now used is that it often just floats there, usually at the beginning of a sentence, accountable to nobody. It could be — and usually is — that the *writer* is hopeful, but it could be, too, that *society in general* is hopeful or that the *subject of the sentence* is hopeful. The reader cannot be sure.

"I *told* you not to use the word 'hopefully' in your feature. . . ."

A writer uses "hopefully," usually, because false modesty precludes use of the more direct "I hope." But if use of the first person is a problem, the writer can always turn to third person ("one hopes") or passive voice ("it is to be hoped"). Or (better) the writer can restructure the sentence. The word itself has its legitimate uses, as in the excerpt from Anthony Amaral's article, "Quest for Arabian Horses," in *Smithsonian Magazine*:

> [Homer] Davenport flopped on the sand under the sun . . . and waited, hopefully, for another coach.

It is clear that it is the subject of the sentence, Davenport, who has the hope that eventually he will get out of the desert.

Another correct use of the word comes from Agatha Christie's *Elephants Can Remember*:

> "You could find out things," said Mrs. Oliver hopefully, "and then tell me."

• -wise Words

Another writing practice now widely accepted, unfortunately, involves inventing words by putting "wise" at the ends of established words. "Injurywise, the team. . . ." "Let's finalize the report. . . ." "Weatherwise, the weather. . . ." The ultimate insult to the purist can be read from an Al Ross cartoon in *The New Yorker*. One man is talking to another at a bar. The first is angry. He says: "'Hopefullywise'! Did I understand you to say 'hopefullywise'?"

• "Hopefully" Makes One Feel Badly

Another misused word is "badly." To many writers it sounds better, somehow, than "bad," so they write that someone feels badly (which really means that the person has no feeling in his finger tips as he touches) or that he wants to play football badly (which means that he wants to throw the game). "Do you feel bad when you hear the broadcaster say he feels badly?" asks Prof. Warren J. Brier of the University of Montana. "Just remember that all men are created equally."

• Spelling Problems

Angry by the misspellings he counted in a job-application letter from a recent college graduate, an editor at the Peterborough (N.H.) *Ledger* wrote a for-publication letter to the editor of *Editor & Publisher*. "We will not consider anyone for editorial work who, to start with, can't spell, and equally worse, can't edit his own copy." Equally worse? Whitney R. Mundt, who teaches reporting at Louisiana State University (not the university in question), wondered: "Could it be that . . . [the editor's] emphasis on correct spelling is misplaced? That some of his emphasis could be shifted profitably to grammatical habits of those closer to Peterborough . . . ?"

While spelling problems are less important than grammatical problems, they are more out of control. In this age of devotion to the electronic media, where spelling is not a factor, few in the schools seem willing to work on such mundane matters as whether it's "ent" or "ant" or whether to use one "t" or two. A single letter can make a big — and embarrassing — difference. This from one newspaper's story about women's anger over a doctor's report on emotional stability during menstrual periods and menopause:

> WASHINGTON (UPI) — By his own count Dr. Edgar Berman has treated thousands of women over the years and developed strong views about what ails them. Now he knows first hand about a woman's furry.

In the print media, *somebody* has to bother. Editors resent the fact that all the correcting falls to them. So, to write as a staffer or freelancer, you had better learn to spell. That correct spelling does not come naturally to you should not prove an insurmountable hurdle. You have dictionaries at your disposal, even a "reverse dictionary"; you have several "word books" that present words without definitions to speed the looking-up process; you have books designed specifically to teach you how to spell.

An editor might rightly conclude that if you are too lazy to look up words, you are too lazy to check facts. Don't spoil your chances of placing a good article by failing to spell its words correctly.

• Punctuation Problems

The use of punctuation — all punctuation — is more a matter of judgment and feel than a matter of rules. It is also a matter of consistency. If you decide, for instance, not to use a comma after the next-to-last word in a series, you will handle the next series in the article the same way.

Often a writer will start off a phrase with a comma but fail to put it in at the end of the phrase, as in "James Shea, Vice-President of Temple University will speak. . . ." Or the writer will put a comma where it is not needed, as in "Vice-President, James Shea, will speak. . . ."

Neither comma is needed in the second example. But if you say "The Vice-President of Temple University, James Shea, will speak. . . ." you do need the commas, because the name is an interruption.

Do not use a comma to join two sentences. End the first with a period. Begin the second with a capital letter.

Nearly every publication now, to save confusion, asks that you put all commas and periods at the ends of quotations *inside* the quote marks. Using any other punctuation mark at the end of a quotation, you must make a conscious decision as to whether it goes inside or outside the quote marks.

Magazines like *The New Yorker* expect a lot of commas, probably because the magazines welcome sentences more complicated than normal. H. Allen Smith tells of an editor somewhere so comma happy that his writers gave him last names first, just to work in extra commas. Other editors (seriously now) feel that commas slow the reader down.

The test is: does the use of the comma make the sentence clearer? A comma can make a lot of difference. See what happens in this sentence when you put a comma before "because":

Not a merchant was complaining, because sales were down.

The comma makes the sentence say the opposite from what the writer wanted it to say. (Even without the comma the sentence is not as clear as it could be.)

Peter DeVries has some fun with the comma in *The Blood of the Lamb*:

The cocktail guests were an ill, assorted group.

* * * * *

My long, suffering father. . . .

* * * * *

This is a swash, buckling story. . . .

The semicolon is an overgrown comma whose use requires a little more sophistication. The late Al Englehard, columnist for the Park Forest *Star* outside Chicago, wrote a tribute to the semicolon. "Vulgar indeed are those moderns who insist that the semicolon, being a little more than a comma and a little less than a period, is limited in application and complicated in usage. The subtleties of this most delicate and delightful of all punctuation marks is entirely lost on them. This indicates to me a total disregard of graciousness in rhetoric in favor of simplicity, the functional line replacing the aesthetic curve, the exquisite giving way to the expeditious."

The comma, he said, is useful, but "it has no class." It is used to indicate any pause in thought or, increasingly, whenever a sentence becomes too long.

The period only signifies the end of a sentence (". . . it has very little imagination about it") while "The colon is also a technician without charm. It says there is an enumeration to follow. The exclamation point a swashbuckler, a braggart, an exhibitionist. . . . The interrogation point [question mark] with its ceaseless bewilderment, is definitely neurotic. . . ."

Englehard explained that the semicolon helps a sentence's rhythm, something "tragically neglected in much of modern prose." "It is a tempo mark, a means of separating and connecting at the same time by means of a beat; like the lines of a poem which effect continuity and discontinuity at once, the semicolon cuts and binds." But mainly, Englehard argued for the semicolon because it makes writing civilized.

The main function of the dash is to interrupt a thought. It should not be used as substitute for a colon. Use the dash sparingly. If your typewriter does not have a dash key, make it by typing *two* hyphens side by side, and butt the word on the left and the word on the right against your dash, without any spacing. Or type *one* hyphen and leave one space on either side of it.

Hyphens are necessary when you want to modify a modifier, as in "cream-colored Dodge" or "like-minded people" as well as in longer coinages: "holier-than-thou attitude" and "six-year-old boy." When you have two or more related coinages needing hyphens, you include them each time even though some of the words are missing, as in "19- and 24-inch sheets."

Correctly used, the hyphen can clarify meaning. "Fifty odd teachers" are something quite different from "fifty-odd teachers." "Hot type face" could be something quite different from "hot-type face." Sometimes its use is vital. "Re-cover" for instance, means something quite different from "recover."

Perhaps the least understood — or remembered — punctuation mark is the apostrophe. Students even at the college level still use "mens wear," and retailers in their signs never seem to get it right. Neither do stores use the apostrophe in their names, even though the names are possessives. In mentioning these store names, you should use the name as the store uses it. Hence, "Gimbels," even though the store was named for Mr. Gimbel. (And you put an "Ole" rather than an "Ol'" in "Grand Ole Opry," because that's the way the organization spells it.) If the aberration is merely for design reasons, as in the "JCPenny" signature in the store's ads, you should use traditional punctuation. Hence, "J. C. Penny."

If a person's name ends in "s" and you want a possessive, put your apostrophe down after the "s" and, if you wish, add another "s." Hence, "Jones's car."

You would use the full "and" in "ham and eggs," but if you ever give in to the temptation to use the shortened version of "and," make the phrase "ham 'n' eggs," not "ham 'n eggs." It's "rock 'n' roll," not "rock 'n roll."

Some students cannot get straight the difference between " its" and "it's." In their confusion, a few settle for a mythical "its'." One way of solving that problem is to vow never to use the contraction; then you can always use "its."

Finally, quote marks. Always, for American publications, use *double* quote marks, no matter how short the quote. Use single quote marks only for quotations within quotations.

Wrong placement of quote marks can confuse the thought.

Under the "cult" of objectivity. . . .

The writer of this line finds fault with objectivity as a goal in journalism. That's why he uses the word "cult." But by putting quotation marks around the word, he is suggesting it *isn't* a cult, just as, when you put quotation marks around "lawyer" or "teacher," you suggest they are not good at their jobs. If the writer must use quotation marks in the sentence above, he should use them around "objectivity."

Some writers cover up their insecurity about punctuation by using sets of three or four periods between phrases. Don't. You should use sets of periods only to indicate material left out of direct quotes or, infrequently, to allow one of your own paragraphs to trail off. . . .

Getting it organized, writing it clearly, looking for fresh ways of saying things, and avoiding grammatical, spelling, and punctuation problems, you readily get your message across to readers. What more could an editor ask of you? Just one more thing, sometimes: a light touch running through it all. That will serve as the topic for discussion in the next chapter.

CHAPTER 9

THE LIGHT TOUCH

In "Bird's Don't Carry Hospitalization Insurance," an article in *Exxon USA* about the Suncoast Seabird Sanctuary near St. Petersburg, Fla., Downs Matthews, who happens to be editor of the magazine, does not so much write as talk to his reader, as though the reader is there with him. This is his start:

> The place resembles the aviary at your local zoo. Birds everywhere — standing, stalking, squawking. But look closer. See the difference?
> That heron there. It has a splinted leg. The egret in that cage? It's nursing a broken wing. The pelican that sits so quietly? It's blind. There are others. Hundreds of them.

Later in the article, Matthews explains that the birds, when fixed or cured, are released.

> Back in the wilds, birds resume their normal life styles. But they don't forget the sanctuary. Many drop in once in a while for a free meal, and some even bring their friends. Significantly, [Ralph] Heath [,founder of the sanctuary,] reports a number of occasions when birds treated and released at the sanctuary subsequently returned for help when they needed it. A pelican Heath released several years ago recently came back to have a fisherman's lure removed from its neck. A heron, whose illness Heath cured, returned months later and tapped on the heron compound door. When Heath opened the gate, the bird staggered in and collapsed, sick again.[1]

[1]What's an article on a bird sanctuary doing in a magazine put out by an oil company? One answer is that many of the external company magazines these days deal in general-interest material. Another is that there was a tie to Exxon, mentioned in passing: the firm had given $5,000 to the sanctuary, which operates mostly on donations. Still another answer is that the article has an ecology angle, which a company like Exxon is interested in. You can read the entire article in the Third Quarter 1975 issue of the magazine, which is published by the Exxon Company, U.S.A., Houston.

Matthews is applying the light touch. He is dealing with the reader on a person-to-person basis, using a conversational tone, showing enthusiasm for his subject, appearing to enjoy telling his story. His article moves along effortlessly.

While the light touch is appropriate for good-news subjects, it can also be used effectively for more weighty ones. The line between comedy and tragedy, as you know, runs thin and indistinct. Peter DeVries beautifully demonstrates this in his wildly funny yet poignant novel, *The Blood of the Lamb.* Not that the light touch necessarily involves humor. It may mean, simply, a relaxed writing style. The trick is to use the light touch without hating yourself in the morning. The light touch can easily turn into the cute touch. One safeguard to take is to put a lightly-styled manuscript away for a few days and review it carefully once it has cooled.

A proven way of achieving a light touch — safe enough for anyone to try — is to pepper the manuscript with anecdotes.

• ANECDOTES

A frequent complaint the beginning writer hears from a editor, if the writer is lucky enough to get a letter rather than a rejection slip, is that the article carries no anecdotes. The writer offers only bald facts, failing to come up with stories to illustrate the facts.

"It's one thing to describe a millionaire as frugal, but the description takes on much more meaning when you follow it with an incident in which he drove back home from his office because he had forgotten his brown-bag lunch," says M. L. Stein, chairman of the journalism department at California State University, Long Beach.[2]

In *Backstage at the Strips*, Mort Walker uses an anecdote about the late George McManus (*Bringing Up Father*) to show how comic-strip artists fight deadlines. McManus lived in California and airmailed his work to New York. Any plane crash that occurred would give him an excuse to wire his syndicate that a week's work was on the plane and request that earlier material be reused, considering the emergency.

[2]M. L. Stein, "Take Five: The Most Common Mistakes Among Beginning Freelancers," *Writer's Digest*, February 1976, p. 43.

The syndicate had no choice but to comply, running the somewhat phony "rerun by popular request" line at the bottoms of the strips during the week in question.

> Like many good schemes, [writes Walker] it was used once too often. Another plane went down and McManus sent another telegram. The syndicate's reply shot back, "DEAR GEORGE, NO WONDER YOUR WORK IS ALWAYS LATE. THAT PLANE WAS TRAVELING WEST. YOU'VE BEEN SENDING THEM THE WRONG WAY."

Robert Lusty in *Bound to Be Read* tells of a publisher's putting off another publisher who liked to make precise appointments many months ahead: "I am very sorry but I have to go to a funeral on that day."

An anecdote can be described as a short — very short — story, usually no more than a paragraph or two in length, told to prove a point or breathe life into a generalization. It may have a plot, but it can do a job without it. Some anecdotes merely lay out a scene. Others merely present snatches of conversation.

Anecdotes can precede or follow a generalization. Sometimes the writer uses a series of them to make a point all the more convincing or sprinkles them throughout the manuscript, using them as oases for readers making their way through the more prosaic prose.

You need to look for anecdotes at the time you interview people and when you read secondary sources for facts. Finding a good anecdote should excite you as much as stumbling onto a little known fact. Looking for them can become an obsession. Ray Stark, producer of *Funny Girl* and *Funny Lady*, so appreciated his mother-in-law, Fanny Brice, whose life provided the basis for the movies, that whenever his wife threatened to leave to go home to her mother, he urged: "Bring back anecdotes."[3]

Where do you find them if your sources don't appear to yield any? One way is to pick out key words, facts, or ideas in your manuscripts and look up what's been written on them in the *New York Times Index* or *Readers' Guide to Periodical Literature*. But if in the ordinary course of your research you don't find any, you probably haven't been alert enough. Or it may be that your article idea is not worth developing after all.

---

[3] Told originally by Frank Farrell in the *New York World-Telegram and Sun* and quoted much later by *Reader's Digest*.

• The Made-up Anecdote

Failing to find anecdotes, writers sometimes make them up. "But when you do create them, be sure they sound true and can be true," Dona Z. Meilach, a Chicago writer (*Better Homes and Gardens, Suburbia Today, Today's Health*) some years ago told readers of *Writer's Digest*.

More recently in answer to the question, "Do all illustrative examples and anecdotes cited in articles have to be true?" Rebecca Greer, articles editor of *Woman's Day*, said, "Not necessarily. Anything involving real names should be accurate, of course, but it's more important for anecdotes to be *believable* than to be true. Sometimes a made-up example sounds more plausible than one that actually happened. In that case, no editor is apt to ask you if it's true. But if your material *sounds* fake, you're in trouble."[4]

This is dangerous advice. The reader might well ask: "If the writer will make up his anecdotes, isn't it possible he will make up his facts, too?"

Fortunately, enough opposition exists to at least make life uncomfortable for the anecdote fakers and inventors. In *The Sex Kick*, Tristram Coffin describes "an episode that took place in an upper-middle-class suburb of Washington." It involved parents who discovered their daughter in bed with a boy. They lectured her on the danger of pregnancy. The daughter reassured the parents that she had been taking her mother's birth control pills. The mother said that couldn't be. She had been counting her pills. The daughter answered: "Oh, I can explain that. Whenever I take one, I put a saccharin tablet in its place." Robert J. Levin, an editor at *Redbook*, was unimpressed.

"The joke is at least eight years old; this reviewer has heard it many times, and no one ever was foolish enough to offer it as an actual happening, if only because a person would have to be astonishingly ignorant not to realize that a saccharin tablet bears no resemblance to any birth control pill," Levin wrote in *Saturday Review*. "Mr. Coffin, however, reports the story as fact, and to buttress it he pretends to locate it geographically in such a way, of course, that it can never be checked."[5]

[4]Rebecca Greer, "Any More Questions?" *Writer's Digest*, July 1974, p. 13.

[5]Robert J. Levin, "In Defense of Modern Romance," *Saturday Review*, Nov. 26, 1966, p. 36.

The least the writer can do is let the reader know when an anecdote is made up. The writer can use an introductory line like: "This is the way it might have happened:" Or "The conversation might go like this:" Here's how Hans Fantel handled a made-up anecdote in a New York *Times* feature on the "distressingly high" percentage of records sold with surface defects:

> "You don't like it?" asked the clerk. "What do you want to exchange it for?"
>
> "The same thing. Just give me a better copy."
>
> This exchange is often heard in record shops as dismayed customers turn in brand-new records. . . .

This exchange is better, certainly, than the made-up single-instance anecdote presented as fact, but flawed, nevertheless, because "This exchange," obviously, is not "often heard" but rather "Exchanges like this are often heard. . . ."

Here is a made-up anecdote (from an AP story in 1976) no one could object to:

> The way things are going these days, it may not be long before a television camera zooms in on some starlet to see her pull a card from an envelope and announce:
>
> > "And the award for the best award show goes to . . ."
> >
> > Television is in the grips of award show mania. Already this year . . . .

Marsha McCormick, in a 1974 *National Observer* feature about a belly dancing class, demonstrated how "unbelievable" the teacher's "pectoral development" was by having her walk through a dining room, with this result:

> It is whispered that one of the men was rushed to the Baton Rouge General Hospital with a fork in his ear.

As readers, we suspect it never happened, but we are not unhappy with the writer, because she has protected herself with the "It is whispered" line. No doubt someone told her the story, she didn't believe it, but she liked it well enough to pass it along.

Nels F. S. Ferré in *God's New Age* offers the anecdote — you could call it a parable — to explain some not-easy-to-understand terms:

> Three baseball umpires were arguing.
>
> > "I call balls and strikes exactly the way they come," said the first. He was an objectivist.
> >
> > "I can't do that," replied the second. "I call them balls and strikes just the

way I see them." He was a subjectivist.

But the third had an idea all his own.

"They are neither balls nor strikes," he declared, "until I call them." He was an existentialist.[6]

Have you ever read a clearer explanation of what an existentialist is?

Of course the anecdote is made up. But the reader understands that Ferré did not happen onto three real-life umpires engaged in so convenient a conversation.

• Segregated Anecdotes

For an occasional article, a writer may not want to integrate the anecdote but may want to run them instead as little islands set off typographically from the article's regular flow. Perhaps they will appear as boldface insets, or in italics, or even in colored ink. The editor or art director decides on the typographic handling, of course; but the writer, in typing the manuscript, makes an effort to show that these anecdotes are set apart, typing them at the end and indicating, through keying, where they should go. Or the writer types them within the manuscript, setting them apart by indenting them or by including a row of stars above and below or by underlining. Like the remainder of the copy, the anecdotes would be double-spaced.

Jim Shahin, a University of Michigan student, used this technique for his article, "Students Under the Domineering Shadow of the Sixties," which appeared in Dow Chemical's *Elements*. You would read along for awhile, picking up generalizations about the campus scene of the seventies, and then you would come upon a three- or four-paragraph section in colored ink that started out like this:

> Steve sits hunched over his desk, scribbling strange mathematical doodles till after midnight. He surfaces occasionally to walk the crease out of his legs, then settles again at the desk. . . .

And later another:

> Shelley returns from school after six, usually. She drops into bed for a short nap, takes a shower, then prepares for about three more hours of study. . . .

And there were two more. Each humanized the generalizations made by the writer in the main part of the text.

You can use the technique, too, to draw contrasts. Handled right,

---

[6]Nels F. S. Ferré, *God's New Age*, Harper and Brothers, New York, 1962, p. 34.

your anecdote could present material that brings out irony or paradox in the text.

• The Joke

A joke differs from an anecdote in that it makes no pretense that it actually happened. A joke can serve the article writer, too. In his article on saltpeter, reprinted in his book, *The Haircurl Papers and Other Searches for the Lost Individual* (Harper & Row, 1964), William K. Zinsser uses this joke to make a point about lingering fears among men that, back in school or the Army, the cook put saltpeter in the food.

> So closely is . . . [the fear of saltpeter] threaded into the American folklore that it even figures in our jokes. Only the other day I heard of a boy entering the army who was worried about his threatened maleness, so he asked his father if the food was saltpetered in *his* army days in World War I.
> "Of course," said the father.
> "Did it work?" asked the boy.
> "You know," the father replied, "it's just beginning to work."

Maybe you remember what one woman is supposed to have said after the *Titanic* ran into an iceberg: "I ordered ice, but this is ridiculous!" Jerry Izenberg remembered, and used this lead on his Newhouse News Service feature story on Canada's problems with the 1976 Olympics:

> The suspicion grows that if Prime Minister Pierre Trudeau of Canada were the pilot on the Titanic, his last official act would been to telephone room service for more ice. . . .

Izenberg used sarcasm throughout to argue with the logic of Trudeau's stated position in the controversy.

> . . . If you understand what follows as Mr. Trudeau's explanation, then you should be well-advised to contact the Hebrew University in Jerusalem where they would appreciate it if you would drop by and translate a little item that is puzzling them called the Dead Sea Scrolls.

A Ring Lardner-like touch there.

• HUMOR

Abraham Lincoln said, "I have found in the course of a large experience that common people . . . are more easily informed through the

medium of a broad and humorous illustration than in any other way."
George Bernard Shaw said, "When a thing is funny, search it for a
hidden truth." And John F. Kennedy had this epigraph engraved on
a silver mug he gave a friend: "There are three things which are real:
God, human folly and laughter. The first two are beyond our com-
prehension. So we must do what we can with the third."

There is a place, certainly, for humor in magazines and newspapers. Editors ask for humor in nonfiction as well as fiction. They want
all-humor pieces; they also like to see some humor in pieces that treat
serious subjects.

Philip Nobile manages a humorous touch of sorts in a deadly serious article on "King Cancer" in *Esquire*. Comparing the amount of
breast, lung, and colon cancer in the United States to the amount of
stomach cancer in Japan, he decides that diet probably is a factor.

> Which food is better for your health — American or Japanese? That de-
> pends on whether you prefer cancer in your colon or your stomach.

Even a how-to-do-it can benefit from a humorous touch. In the
book, *How to Raise a Dog in the City*, James R. Kinney (with Ann Honeycutt) first tells how dogs originally were bred to do certain jobs, then
says:

> Today only a handful of dogs ply a trade of any kind or even attempt to
> justify their existence on any grounds other than that of being "man's best
> friend." A dachshund, for instance, would think you had lost your mind if
> you asked him to go out and dig up a badger; a collie would yawn if you
> asked him to herd a sheep or two, and if you asked a bulldog to pull himself
> together and go out and bait a bull he would look at you with a cold eye and
> remind you that bullbaiting was abolished by law before your grandfather
> was born. . . .[7]

Later he tells how to keep a dog from scratching his eye:

> . . . put a Queen Elizabeth collar on him. A Queen Elizabeth collar . . . is
> made of heavy cardboard or very lightweight wood. Cut a hole in the mid-
> dle of it just big enough to fit around the dog's neck. Slit it down one side.
> Put it on the dog and then fasten the slit with adhesive tape. This will keep
> the dog from scratching his head. It will also make him unhappy. Dogs
> don't like to wear these collars, as a rule — not for reasons of discomfort
> particularly, but for reasons of pride. They think they will look silly in
> them.[8]

[7]James R. Kinney with Ann Honeycutt, *How to Raise a Dog in the City*, Simon and
Schuster, New York, 1966, p. 16.
[8]*Ibid.*, p. 157.

You even have *The New Republic* — yes, *The New Republic* — running an item by Woody Allen, who, with his *New Yorker* pieces, is establishing himself as a writer of humor as much as public performer. In "Nefarious Times We Live In" (*The New Republic*, Nov. 22, 1975), Allen, writing in first person, has one Willard Pogrebin confessing to an assassination attempt on the President. Pogrebin, it appears, before being apprehended, had been "forced to undergo total sensory deprivation for three weeks. Following that I was tickled by experts and two men sang country and western music to me until I agreed to do anything they wanted."

Even *The New York Times Magazine*, which nobody is likely to mistake for, say, *The National Lampoon*, applies humor where it can, including, of all places, the author's legend that goes at the bottom of one of the columns. Here's how the magazine in 1975 described the author of an article entitled "On True Identity": "Arthur Miller is, well, Arthur Miller."

When in your writing you deal with someone known for humor, humor in your writing becomes almost mandatory. Not that you try to upstage your subject, but you do make good use of the humor he created, and you do it in a style appropriate to the subject. The beauty of Robert Lewis Taylor's biography of W. C. Fields is that, though adulatory, it is written with irreverence and understatement much in keeping with Fields's own manner. For instance, here's Taylor on Fields's reliance on whisky as a tuberculosis cure: it was, according to Taylor, a "specific that probably would not withstand medical scrutiny." And here he is on Fields's lack of interest in gambling (in real life if not on the screen): "He felt that there was an ugly element of chance in gambling which made it possible for somebody other than himself to win."[9]

• Unintentional Humor

Sometimes the humor in nonfiction is unintentional, as when "Holy" Hubert Lindsey, writing of his preaching to the unwashed of Berkeley, said in *Bless Your Dirty Heart*:

> On another occasion a girl stripped to her waistline and made sensual passes at me. . . . Later this young girl came and apologized, admitting she merely wanted to poke fun at me.

[9]*W. C. Fields: His Follies and Fortunes*, Doubleday & Company, Inc., Garden City, N.Y., 1949.

In a news story, AP reported that Rep. Bella S. Abzug, chief sponsor of a bill in 1975 to strengthen rights of homosexuals, said that it was needed "to guarantee that all individuals, regardless of differences, are entitled to share in the fruits of our society."

It is hard to know, sometimes, whether the humor is intentional or unintentional. What are we to make of an author who says of the subject that "his limitations knew no boundaries"? Is the author underlining the versatility of the subject or telling us, cleverly, that the subject has his problems?

• Humor: Who Should Write It?

Most writers find it easy enough to weave into their articles the anecdotes they uncover, but few writers appear to be comfortable with humor.

In *The Writer's Handbook* Sylvia Dee singles out the person who should try his hand at humor:

"Do you wake up in the morning with a feeling that doomsday is rapidly approaching?

"Are you a morbid, morose, introverted, easily depressed, gloomy sad sack of an individual?

"If so, and you can write, I'd say you're well on your way to becoming a top-notch writer of humor."[10]

Well, maybe not a *top-notch* writer of humor, but possibly a person who could write saleable humor. At least you have the disposition for it. The clown is always crying on the inside, is he not?

The biographies of our humorists suggest that they are not the best-adjusted of persons. Burton Bernstein's *Thurber* (Dodd, Mead & Co., New York, 1973) is especially instructive. The sterotype seems to fit the lover of humor as well as the producer of it. One of the best of the humorists, Stephen Leacock, known for his slapstick and *non sequiturs*, said: "If a man has a genuine sense of humor he is apt to take a somewhat melancholy, or at least a disillusioned view of life. Humor and disillusionment are twin sisters."

Elton Trueblood in *The Humor of Christ* adds another dimension. "It is not possible to have genuine humor or true wit without an extremely sound mind, which is always a mind capable of high seriousness and a sense of the tragic."

[10]Sylvia Dee, "Have You Tried Your Hand at Humor?" *The Writer's Handbook*, (Edited by A. S. Burack), The Writer, Inc., Publishers, Boston, 1964, p. 262.

• Humor: What it Is

The deep thinkers centuries ago peddled the idea that the human body was made up largely of four liquids (or *humours*, in Latin): blood, phlegm (mucus), yellow bile (fluid secreted by the liver), and black bile (whatever that was). Whenever an imbalance occurred in those *humours*, the person took on abnormal characteristics. He became an oddball.

An overproportion of blood, it was said, made him more optimistic than his fellow citizens. Too much phlegm made him sluggish. Too much yellow bile made him short tempered. Too much black bile made him melancholy.

Gradually the term "humour" or "humor" covered anything odd; and the person who could provoke laughter by pointing up the oddities of life became a "humorist."

We associate humor today with criticism. Even graphic humor does more than merely entertain. Al Capp, creator of *Li'l Abner*, said in a *Playboy* interview: "You can't write or draw *anything* without making some comment on society. No cartoonist, no matter how talentless or obscure, has ever drawn a dog without making a comment on the state of dogs. He's never drawn an outhouse without making some incidental comment about rustic life in America."

One of the loftiest definitions of humor comes from Romain Gary in *Promise at Dawn*: "Humor is an affirmation of dignity, a declaration of man's superiority to all that befalls him." Max Eastman in *Enjoyment of Laughter* sees humor as something a little less than that: "a kind of disappointment." Ralph Waldo Emerson said, "The essence of all jokes, of all comedy, seems to be an honest or well-intentioned halfness. . . . The balking of the intellect, the frustrated expectation, the break of continuity in the intellect, is comedy. . . .".

Another view has it that a feeling of superiority is involved. Someone slips on a banana peel and we laugh at his misfortune or clumsiness. We laugh nervously if we think it could happen to us. But humor involves combinations. "Self-confidence is not comical, stumbling is not comical; they are comical only when seen together," writes novelist and playwriter Max Frisch. H. L. Mencken defined humor as the capacity to discover hidden and surprising relations between apparently disparate things."

Obviously, to define humor adequately is not possible. "Perhaps laughter is a simple gift of the gods," concludes Steve Allen, wrestling with the problem in his *The Funny Men*, "a potentiality of the mind that, because it varies from individual to individual, will never be completely understood." "When we think we have found the explanation, laughter ceases," says Joseph Wood Krutch in an essay. "If that is all there is to it, what seemed gloriously funny isn't funny anymore."

• Subject-Matter Humor

So far as the writer is concerned, humor divides itself into (1) subject-matter humor (funny of itself) and (2) literary humor (funny in the phrasing).

It is easier to produce subject-matter humor than literary humor. But you need the ability to recognize the humorous event when it occurs. And then you need to report it clearly, without clutter.

The subject doesn't have to be an event. It can be an object. But what to look for? "An egg is funny," said Fred Allen, "an orange is not."

Richard Armour finds humor in the human body. He has become something of a specialist. "A Short Dissertation on Lips" for *Playboy* concentrated on the lower lip. "I may write an article on the upper lip, once I have done enough research on the subject." What intrigued him in "Looking Over the Overlooked Elbow" for *Playboy* was that "the elbow and the knee are joints that bend in opposite directions. I speculated at some length on what would happen if the two were reversed, the knee bending forward and the elbow bending back."[11]

One form of subject-matter humor is gentle, reassuring, predictable. It celebrates ordinary events and everyday frustrations. It puts the writer in exactly the position of the reader. The reader responds: "Isn't it the truth!" It is the kind of humor that brings a smile — maybe a smile of recognition; it does not evoke a hearty laugh. The success of this kind of humor rests with genuineness of feeling and clarity of telling.

A variation of life-is-like-that humor is in-character humor, in which someone plays his familiar role *out of context*. He takes what is known as a busman's holiday. The opposite of in-character humor is out-of-character humor, in which someone plays a role completely different from what you would expect. An old lady uses hip language; a child talks like a grownup.

[11]Richard Armour, "What Can You Be Funny About?" *The Writer*, December 1970, p. 21.

Writers of subject-matter humor often write about themselves. They become the butt of the jokes. It is always safer making fun of yourself than making fun of others. "I never made *Who's Who*," said Phyllis Diller, "but I'm featured in *What's That?*" And "I had to give up exercising — I can't stand the noise."

Hypocrisy is often an ingredient in this kind of humor. You make the case against some human weakness, perhaps with some disdain, but reveal yourself at the end as one who has the weakness, too.

From a Peter DeVries character:

"I can't stand name-dropping, as I once told Bea Lillie."

• Literary Humor

The humor in nonfiction may lie not in the subject itself but in the way it is described. The order of description — what comes first — can make the difference.

To many, humor is largely a matter of surprise, promising the reader one thing early in a sentence or paragraph and then delivering something quite different, as when Milton Berle says, "I had a wonderful compartment on the train on the way down. But the conductor kept locking me in at every station" and when Woody Allen says, "My wife was an immature woman. I'd be in the bathroom taking a bath and she would walk right in and sink my boats." "Have a nice weekend, unless, of course, you have other plans," says the radio announcer. Earl Wilson quotes Rodney Dangerfield as saying this about his marriage: "We sleep in separate rooms, we have dinner apart, we take separate vacations — we're doing everything we can to keep our marriage together." Reggie Jackson, then of the Oakland Athletics, said of teammate Joe Rudi: "He's a misfit. He gets along with everyone on the club."

Sometimes the surprise is better when it comes a little late or when the reader has to solve a sort of puzzle. In *My Life in Court*, Louis Nizer tells of being approached by a front group that has been indicted by the federal government for subversion. Would he defend them? The group would pay $100,000. Nizer said: "I will accept your retainer on the following condition: You will deposit $100,000 in a bank; if I lose the case, the fee will instantly be turned over to me; if I win, I will receive nothing!"

The writer serves a function by merely gathering the witticisms of others and presenting them to the reader in a convenient form. A favorite article of this kind, among editors of college newspapers and magazines, is the one that surveys the markings on desks ("Due to lack of interest, tomorrow will be canceled") and in restrooms ("Smile, you're on Candid Camera"). For off-campus publications, a similar article can be put together from bumper-sticker slogans ("Don't honk, I'm pedaling as fast as I can") and even T-shirts ("Make me an offer"). The special-order letter combinations on license plates in many states are also a possibility.

• VARIETIES OF HUMOR

Possibly to its detriment, humor over the years has drawn the serious attention of scholars, who have attempted to analyze and categorize it. (The categories generally accepted do not necessarily distinguish between subject-matter and literary humor.) A study of the categories cannot make a humorous writer out of one who is deadly serious, but it can remind the writer with an inclination to humor of the several approaches possible.

You may want to try working out an article or part of an article to fit into one of the categories. You may find that what you write does not fit wholly into one category or another. "The best jokes and wittiest replies seem to combine several of . . . [the categories]," Joseph Wood Krutch observes.

If you suspect that the humor you attempt does not quite come off, you will be much better off sticking to clear, straight writing. Do not put much store in the encouraging words you get from friends or relatives; try your humor on someone willing to give you an unbiased reaction.

• Irony

The late Reinhold Niebuhr in *The Irony of American History* brought out the difficulty of distinguishing pathos and tragedy from irony. Pathos, he said, elicits pity; There is no reason for the condition depicted, and no guilt. Tragedy, because it involves a choice of evil for the sake of good, elicits pity *and* admiration. Using the threat of atomic destruction as an instrument for preserving peace was, in Niebuhr's view, a tragedy.

Irony, in contrast to pathos and tragedy, elicits laughter and understanding. When you use irony, your words mean one thing to the uninitiated, something quite different to the person in the know. You create an intimacy between you and your more intelligent or sophisticated readers. Early writers used irony to get dangerous doctrine past the censors.

Sheridan Baker in *The Practical Stylist* said that irony "gives the truth an emphasis beyond that of bald statement. Alongside irony, plain statement seems uncouth."

Robert Pear uses irony in writing his lead for an AP story on an impending move of the National Rifle Association.

> WASHINGTON — The National Rifle Assn. is considering moving its headquarters out of Washington, partly because of gun-related crimes against employees here.

Walter Goodman provides another example with a letter to the editor of *Esquire* following the publication of an article by William F. Buckley, Jr., asking Americans to stand up and complain more.

> I know just how William Buckley feels. The other day a shoeshine boy did a slap-dash job on my black-and-whites, and had the gall to demand his fifteen cents anyway. I didn't pay him, needless to say, but sheer, weak-minded, bleeding heart conformity prevented me from kicking the kid's teeth in.

The writer looks for irony sometimes when none is there. "The lungs that pushed the swinging notes of Julian 'Cannonball' Adderley's jazz through his saxophone were themselves being pushed mechanically today as he lingered near death," wrote an anonymous reporter in 1975, following Adderley's stroke.

Pretending to praise a person when, in reality, you condemn him, is a form of irony. Listen to Sen. William Fulbright (D-Ark) "praise" a speech by Sen. Barry Goldwater before the Arizona senator won the Republican nomination in 1964.

> It is indeed a remarkable speech. At no point does it burden the reader with the complexities of current foreign and domestic problems.
> The Senator has a rare gift of clarity. So lucid is his discourse that he makes us wonder what all the fuss has been over nuclear weapons and international tensions and unemployment and all the other stubborn problems that perplex the American people.

Senator Fulbright here is using one of the lower forms of irony: sarcasm. It isn't so much another meaning he means to convey as the *opposite* meaning.

You see — and hear — many examples, as in the sentence: "The school did a great job of getting him ready for a career." You can't know that it is sarcasm you are reading until you get deeper into the article and read all the troubles the subject had on the job; only then do you realize that "great" means "terrible." James Thurber in his *The Years with Ross* tells about a Rip Orr whose job it was to answer much of the mail to *The New Yorker*. A testy male subscriber, an army colonel, once wrote: "Every time I pick up your magazine I fall asleep trying to read it." Orr's answer: "Dear Colonel ———: Pleasant dreams."

In one of its forms, irony involves a circumstance that is the opposite of what should be expected or one that is highly inappropriate: an oddity of fate. An American Cancer Society executive dies of — lung cancer. A doctor saves a patient's life, and — gets sued for malpractice. A fire breaks out at — the fire station. A student studies harder than ever before, and, for the first time — flunks an exam. A woman waits in line so long to pay a traffic fine that when she gets back to her car she find that — the meter has run out and she has another ticket.

• Satire

Satire makes use of irony, including sarcasm, to expose foolishness, cupidity, and pretension. It also makes use of exaggeration and incongruity.

Perhaps the most celebrated satirist in the English language was Jonathan Swift. His *Gulliver's Travels* (not to be confused with Ring Lardner's "Gullible's Travels") so smoothly and subtly satirized the politics and science of his day that it became an accepted book for children.

The satirist may write to right a wrong or simply to hold something up to ridicule. When the humor becomes so bitter that it offers no hope, it becomes known as "black humor." (The term does not refer to the humor of any race or ethnic group.)

In a satire on holding world championship matches in obscure, far away countries, Gordon Cotler in *The New Yorker* writes about an airline with the slogan "The World's Most Experienced Airplanes."

With all the "God is Dead" talk in the mid-1960s, Anthony Towne used the language of newspapers (particularly that of the New York *Times*) to do the obit, which ran in *Motive* and other publications.

> ATLANTA, GA., Nov. 9 — God, creator of the universe, principal deity of the world's Jews, ultimate reality of Christians, and most eminent of all divinities, died late yesterday during major surgery undertaken to correct a massive diminishing influence. His exact age is not known, but close friends estimate that it greatly exceeded that of all other extant beings. While he did not, in recent years, maintain any fixed abode, his house was said to consist of many mansions.

That was the lead to a many-paragraphed story. It carried an Atlanta dateline because the "surgeon," Dr. Thomas J. J. Altizer (actually one of the "Death of God" theologians), was there.

At one point in the news story, the Pope is quoted as saying, "We are deeply distressed for we have suffered an incalculable loss. The contribution of God to the Church cannot be measured . . . " Former President Harry S Truman was quoted as saying, "I'm always sorry to hear somebody is dead. It's a damn shame."

Satirizing the trivialities of scholarship, Marshall Brickman in *The New Yorker*, builds a story around a "Dr. Kentish, Winkle Professor of Clinical Psychology at Tony's College, [who] won a Nobel Prize in 1948 for his work in isolating and defining the common nap as 'any rest episode up to twenty minutes' duration involving unconsciousness but not pajamas.' " Satirizing the preoccupation of the media with psychic phenomena, F. P. Tullius, also in *The New Yorker*, creates the "Unpsychic Man of the Year," whose "only hobby seems to be collecting pictures and data of what he calls IFO (Identified Flying Objects) sightings. He showed me some of the voluminous files he keeps on the subject, and I examined a number of blurry snapshots of sparrows, pigeons, pop flies, airliners, acrobats, windblown newspapers, and so forth. Sigafoos believes almost fanatically that the skies above us are full of flying objects, all of which can be traced as coming from the planet Earth."

Woody Allen, in *The New Yorker*, satirizes inspirational biography with his tribute to the Earl of Sandwich, inventor of the sandwich. We take a slice out of the middle:

> 1745: After four years of frenzied labor, he is convinced he is on the threshold of success. He exhibits before his peers two slices of turkey with a slice of bread in the middle. His work is rejected by all but David Hume, who senses the imminence of something great and encourages him. . . .

Using satire, you always risk some reader misunderstanding. Readers may take you literally. When Gerald Nachman, one of the nation's new syndicated humor columnists, wrote a column on "Ye Olde Nostalgia Shoppe," an imaginary store whose stock was running so low it resorted to selling back issues of *People* magazine, a number of nostalgia buffs wrote to Nachman for the shop's address.

• Parody

No one is likely to mistake the parodist as a comic genius. The parodist mimics rather then invents. Even so, parody can be high art.

Wolcott Gibbs provided many good parodies for *The New Yorker*, including a memorable article on "Time. . . Fortune. . . Life. . . Luce" written in what was then *Time* style. The two most widely quoted lines from the piece are "Backward ran sentences until reeled the mind" and "Where it all will end; knows God!"[12]

Some of the happiest moments in jouralism come when one magazine parodies the style of another. *Mad*, the *Harvard Lampoon*, and the *National Lampoon* have devoted articles and whole issues to the affectations and peculiarities of the *Reader's Digest*, *Playboy*, *Cosmopolitan*, the newsmagazines, and others. *Newsweek* itself in 1975 began a "Newsmakers" item on William Shawn this way:

> When our copy of The New Yorker arrived last week, there on the cover was the annual drawing of dear, foppish old Eustace Tilley, reminding us that our well-esteemed fellow magazine and midtown-Manhattan neighbor had reached another anniversary — the golden 50th, at that. We dropped everything and hurried over to West 43rd Street to congratulate . . . .

Any regular reader of *The New Yorker* would recognize "The Talk of the Town" style.

Dwight Eisenhower was not known for his precision of speech. *Monocle*, a defunct magazine of satire and parody, tried to imagine what the Gettysburg Address would sound like had Eisenhower delivered it.

> I haven't checked these figures, but 87 years ago, I think it was, a number of individuals organized a governmental setup here in this country. I don't like to appear to take sides . . . .

An unnamed AP writer, on the announcement in 1975 that How-

[12]See the piece in its entirety in Wolcott Gibb's *More in Sorrow*, Henry Holt and Company, New York, 1958.

ard Cosell was to host an ABC variety show, came up with an imaginary interview with the ebullient sportscaster. A sample question:

> It is well known that from a humble Brooklyn beginning you have achieved a state of salubrious success as a caster of sports with a pronounced propensity for telling it like it is, as it were.
> Why then, one must ask, are you entering this new area as a common hawker of stars, song, and the dance?

When the Museum of Modern Art in New York underwent some renovations, *The New Yorker* in "The Talk of the Town" pretended to see aspects of art there and described what it saw in the language of the art critic:

> A shifting display of modern art, by anonymous artists, is on view these days in front of the Museum of Modern Art, whose interior is closed for renovations. The show as a whole is marked by the slashing style, inflated scale, and promiscuous receptiveness to accident characteristic of Abstract Expressionism, but the ironic precision of pop art and even some neo-naturalistic undertones are present as well. The show has been mounted in a deliberately jumbled manner, so that some of the most provocative works are virtually eclipsed, and the complete lack of titles will probably addle museum-goers accustomed to such helpful labels as "Painting No. 4" and "Form No. 5."[13]

The secret of good parody is to make it as interesting — or nearly as interesting — to persons who may not be familiar with the work being parodied as to persons who are. Take the radio skits of Bob and Ray. It wasn't necessary to have been among the followers of *Mary Noble, Backstage Wife* to appreciate today the triviality of the Bob and Ray version: *Mary Backstage, Noble Wife*.

• Understatement

Robert Benchley writes about a stuffed animal, the work of a taxidermist, that was in "a moderate state of preservation." Arthur Schlesinger, Jr., says ". . . my enthusiasm for Mr. Nixon has always been well under control. . . ." Bob and Ray, in one of their skits, refer to the United States mint as "one of the nation's leading producers of authentic new money." James Branch Cabell describes a woman like this: "She was not unbeautiful."

[13]For the complete "review," see "Modern Art," *The New Yorker*, April 11, 1964. pp. 31, 32.

These are examples of understatement, a delightful, subtle variety of humor often associated with the British. A disaster of some kind becomes "a bit of a nuisance." In understatement, the information never quite measures up to the gravity of the subject. "It got so cold that winter in Alaska," somebody says, "that I had to button up my shirt."

Using understatement you have to be careful that your reader understands you are holding back. As in other forms of humor, context is important.

• Exaggeration

The opposite of understatement is exaggeration, a form of humor not likely to be misunderstood, provided the exaggeration is extreme. A story comes to mind about a man shouting a greeting to a friend across the Volga River. It was so cold that before the words could get across they froze. They were not heard until the next spring, when the thaw released them. An expression from out of the South has it that a man tells so many lies that he needs someone else to call his dog.

Nobody objects to a little fictionalizing or exaggeration provided it is obvious what the writer is doing. In "There's No Place Like Home," an article in *TV Guide* telling about turning over her house to TV commercial makers, Terry Martin Hekker discusses how the weather can be manipulated.

> Once, during a snowstorm, they taped laurel leaves onto my windows and aimed great yellow lights through them. The effect was so springlike that my sinuses started to close up.

Although he wrote *The Story of the Bible*, a popular book of the 1920s, Hendrik Willem van Loon was not a religious man. But late in life he joined the Unitarian Church. "I like the Unitarian Church," his son, Gerard Willem van Loon, reports him as saying, "because the only time the name Jesus Christ is uttered is when the janitor falls downstairs."[14]

Quentin Reynolds in *By Quentin Reynolds* wrote: "Unlike so many writers, Dorothy [Parker] is an intensely practical person. She can even change the ribbon on her typewriter in a matter of an hour or two with virtually no outside help." T.R.B. in *The New Republic* wrote:

[14]Gerard Willem van Loon, *The Story of Hendrik Willem van Loon*, J. B. Lippincott Company, Philadelphia, 1972, p. 11.

"If the military left Hawaii it would probably rise three feet out of the water." Comedian Mark Russell said Washington, D.C., is so dull in August that young people sit around getting high listening to recordings of the speeches of Sen. Henry "Scoop" Jackson.

• Puns

That potential political appointee over there. The one with long hair. He is to replace a bald headed incumbent. When you refer to him as the "hair apparent" you manufacture a pun. Likely you get groans rather than laughs for your trouble. Oscar Levant observed: "A pun is the lowest form of humor — when you don't think of it first." "I never knew an enemy to puns who was not an ill-natured man," said Charles Lamb. And: "May my last breath be drawn through a pipe and exhaled in a pun."

A pun is a play upon words that sound the same — or nearly the same. Its occasional use in an article or feature can be excused if not applauded. Like alliteration, a little punning goes a long way.

"Why can't the captain of a vessel keep a memorandum of the weight of his anchor, instead of weighing it every time he leaves port?" asked George D. Prentice, a nineteenth-century journalist.

Sir Walter Scott is said to have written this note in an attempt to get back a borrowed book: "Please return this book: I find that though many of my friends are poor arithmeticians, they are nearly all good bookkeepers."

Edwin Newman dreams up this exchange for inclusion in *Strictly Speaking*:

"I am glad we're out of Vietnam."
"So am I. It was time to let Saigon be Saigon's."

People Weekly, like Mother *Time*, is given to using the pun. In a short for the "Chatter" column for March 17, 1975, the magazine said: "As scenarist of the movie blockbuster *Love Story*, Erich Segal, 37, has long been America's most eligible bachelor of the arts (not to mention Ph.D.)." We must assume that *People* was stretching a point for the pun. The magazine continued: "But, as a marathon runner, he has been an elusive catch until now. Apparently the jog is up." The item went on to describe his new fiancee, then ended on this note: "So much for the loneliness of the long-distance runner."

In an article about the loss of tenure among professors, Fred M. Hechinger in *Saturday Review* noted that "the debate over tenure has become anything but an academic question." A *New York* blurb pointing to an article surveying various chairs and ranking them for comfort said this: "The results may not sit well with some of our highly touted furniture designers, who may find their products bringing up the rear." Christopher Morley, novelist, offered this: "The plural of spouse is spice."

• **Tom Swifties.** Perhaps you will want to try using a verb or adverb that relates itself through punning to a chunk of conversation. Such a device is called a Tom Swifty, from the mannerism used by the writer of the *Tom Swift* books. Bert Rosenfield offered one in a letter to *Time*:

"I dropped my toothpaste," said Tom, Crestfallen.

The *Saturday Review*'s "Trade Winds" column offered some, among them:

"That makes 144," he said grossly.

* * * * *

"I drove from Maine to California," he stated.

* * * * *

"Give it to me on the level," he said flatly.

• **The Double-Entendre.** Closely related to the pun is the double-entendre, a term with two meanings, one of them risqué. What little humor there is comes from the feeling of superiority in figuring out the risqué meaning. In a more innocent age, song writers thought they were being daring when they ended a line with ". . . to make you" and waited until the next line to add a "mine." *Playboy* still likes to use the double-entendre.

• **Manufactured Words.** You can also achieve a humor of sorts by manufacturing words. A too familiar example is "couth," coming from the elimination of "un." A fresher example comes from John Simon in his review of *The Return of the Pink Panther*. After a barrage of gags, he says, the viewer becomes "totally slap-unhappy."

• The Malapropism

Richard Brinsley Sheridan's 1775 play, *The Rivals*, brought to life a delightful character named Mrs. Malaprop, a woman given to hilarious misuse of words, producing grotesque effects. Her misuse came about because of a lack of appreciation of word meanings and a confusion in sounds. Edwin O'Connor's Ditto in *The Last Hurrah* was cut from the same cloth. So is Archie Bunker on TV.

Usually the users of malaprops — or malapropisms — don't realize they're being funny. A woman rushed up to Rep. William S. Morehead (D-Pa.) in the early sixties, so the Congressman reported, to exclaim: "Why, Congressman, your speech was superfluous, just superfluous." The Congressman thanked her, and said: "I'm thinking of having it published posthumously." "Oh, wonderful," the woman said, "and the sooner the better."

It made a good filler for AP to move over its wires.

You'll find a good selection of malaprops in Bel Kaufman's pungent *Up the Down Staircase*. College students have supplied a few, like "the up and coming election," "his severe of influence," "he was a conscious objector in World War II," and "they awarded it to him posthumorously." A radio announcer in one town said, "He requested a court-appointed attorney because he was indignant." One of those car dealers who do their own commercials on TV said of a sale that it was coming "at the end of our physical year." One writer wrote of somebody doing something "in a half hazard way." Bubba on *Sanford and Son* said, "He played hunchback for Notre Dame," causing Fred Sanford to respond: "Bubba, when you talk I don't want you to open your mouth." Peter DeVries in *Reuben, Reuben* had a character say ". . . cutting off your nose despite your face" and ". . . food sprayed with various and Sunday poisons."

H. Allen Smith in *How to Write Without Knowing Nothing* came up with "an expensive black dress all covered with Seagrams," "they were A.F. of L. from the army," and "Woe and behold!"

"Pullet Surprise" is a term coined by the late Ansel Greene to describe the malaprops of her students. It was inspired by a high-school boy who wrote in a paper: "In 1957, Eugene O'Neill won a Pullet Surprise." Greene, who admired more than she ridiculed many of the misuse of words by her students (". . . student errors are often marvels of ingenuity and logic"), considered the following examples, among others, as worthy of "Pullet Surprises":

We found it hard to understand his Scottish derelict.

* * * * *

The doctor said to take some milk of amnesia.

* * * * *

The Rocky Mountain road was the most cynic of our trip.

Jack Smith, a Los Angeles *Times* writer who did a column, "A Study in Engine Newity," on a recently published book, was grateful for all he learned: that space flying may be affected by comic rays, that Moses went up to Mt. Cyanide to get the Ten Commandments, that in the Sarah Desert they travel by Camelot, that a monetary is where monks live, that an antithesis is something given before surgery, and that a paradox is a lovely place to go when you die.

Presumably the article writer, using a malaprop, would keep it in a quotation coming from someone else.

• The Spoonerism

Closely related to the malaprop is the spoonerism, named for the Rev. William A. Spooner, warden at New College, Oxford, who is supposed to have said "The Lord is a shoving leopard." And trying to say "half-formed wish," he said "half-warmed fish." A spoonersim is an unintentional interchange of the initial sounds in words. *Webster's New World Dictionary* gives an example: "It is kistomary to cuss the bride." H. Allen Smith lists a number of spoonerisms in his book, too, among them this gem: "a jar of odorarm deunderant." And "Does your husband wake up mornings dill and lustless?"

Because spoonerisms are more a speech than a writing problem, they don't play much of a role in articles, unless you want to count the transpositions that sometimes show up in typing.

• The Practical Joke

Reporting practical jokes perpetrated by characters in your story is another way of adding humor. If anyone ever writes an article about Wm. McHolick, a bone specialist in Eugene, Oregon, he would have to tell about what the doctor did to a fellow doctor who was dieting and telling everyone about it. From time to time when the dieting doctor changed clothes to go into the operating room, the first doctor rushed the man's pants to a tailor just up the street to take them in, ever so slightly. This greatly frustrated the dieting doctor. But when he found out, finally, what had happened, he found it amusing enough, until the tailor, at the first doctor's instigation, sent the dieter a bill for the alterations. The episode bore some resemblance to something that happened in one of Peter DeVries's novels and eventually found its way to the screen: a father and son, under cover of night, adding gas to the VW belonging to a neighbor who bragged about the mileage he was getting, and then reversing the process and siphoning gas out of the neighbor's tank.

H. Allen Smith devoted a whole book to *The Compleat Practical Joker*, cataloguing the exploits of real people like William Horace De Vere Cole, who inconvenienced London by hiring some men to dig up a main street, and Hugh Troy, who brought a park bench and got himself arrested many times for moving it around New York's Central Park. The book evolved from a series of articles Smith wrote for the New York *World-Telegram*. One memorable Hugh Troy exploit, reported by Smith, involves Troy's buying a stack of tabloids in 1933 with the banner: ROOSEVELT ELECTED. Three years later, on New Year's Eve, Troy called in some friends, and, together, they rode a subway train, each reading a copy of the paper, ". . . and great was the bewilderment of other passengers. . . ."[15]

• Incongruity

Using words to draw a picture of the impossible can also add some humor. Arthur "Bugs" Baer wrote: "An empty cab drove up, and Sarah Bernhardt got out." The sentence could have been merely incongruous; or it could have been Baer's way of criticizing the French actress.

• Getting it All Wrong

One of Robert Benchley's benchmarks was his posing as an authority — and getting it all wrong. It is a device less useful to the article writer than to the fiction writer, but because it can help the writer satirize, say, self-help books and technical writing, perhaps it deserves at least passing mention here.

Bill Landers, a sales representative and a sometimes PR man, dabbles in this kind of humor. One of his essays, never published, dealt with "The Passing of Gas." Before showing that the internal combus-

[15] H. Allen Smith, *The Compleat Practical Joker*, Doubleday & Company, Inc., Garden City, N.Y., 1953, p. 135.

tion engine was doomed, Landers first described how an engine works:

> The most important part of the American car is the tailpipe, which protrudes from beneath the rear bumper. It is through this tunnel that air is sucked into the motor part and combines with the gas to produce fumes. It should also be mentioned here that before reaching the motor part the air must pass through a device called the "muffler." This gadget is designed to warm the air that might be sucked in on cold days and bring it to a compatible temperature with the gasoline.

It almost sounds reasonable

When some Americans objected to the length of time institutions kept their flags lowered following the death of Martin Luther King, Landers worked up a formula "to achieve national grieving without overdoing it or underdoing it." The flag would be lowered to various heights and for various lengths of time depending on the worth of the individual. A "blue ribbon commission" would assign ratings.

Landers saw some difficulties in his scheme. "Since it is unquestionably going to crowd the pole when a number of important people pass on at about the same time, a pole schedule will have to be established." Hearing of the idea, Ron Abell, Portland writer, concurred. "The flagpole gap must be closed." Abell wondered what to do with the flag "upon the decedence of someone who has made no dent whatsoever in our national life. . . ." Abell thought the flag probably should remain at the top of the pole, "and a windbreak should be created around it so that it will not even flutter." For the death of a leader "good and noble," Abell suggested that the flag be lowered *totally*. "By this I mean that it could be removed from the pole and buried in the ground." For the death of "those among us who exist only by the Christian tolerance of several million of their neighbors," the flag should be "carried to the top of Mt. Everest and flown from a 3,000-foot flagpole."

Abell further suggested that the distance down the pole should be determined by dividing the individual's *own estimate* of his contribution by his *actual* contribution. For instance: "Mr. Nixon. . . has estimated his value to our national heritage as, let us say, 100 units. The commission, however, makes a finding. . . that his true contribution. . . has been one unit (perhaps an inflated figure). Dividing. . . ." You get the idea.

Getting sentences in the wrong order can also do the job. Wrote Marc Connelly in a letter to Frank Sullivan: "Guess who I just had a drink with at the bar. Corey Ford. Give up?"

CHAPTER 10

Titles, Openings, Closings

Come up with a good title for your article, an intriguing opening paragraph or two, and a satisfying closing paragraph, and get them so they work together in harmony — and you solve a major part of your writing problem. This chapter will examine the three and suggest approaches to writing them.

• THE TITLE

That the title does not do justice to the article may not be the fault of the writer. Many of the problems with titles can be traced to the editor.

One problem concerns the difference between the title as it appears in a blurb on the cover and the title as it appears inside the magazine. The two may not agree. The reader often cannot find the article the cover has promised.

Another problem concerns the predisposition of the editor. An influential alternative newspaper preparing a series of features for an issue examining a big-city daily asks this author to contribute a feature on the paper's design and format. All the other features turn out to be highly critical; *this* feature finds flaws but carries a theme saying that, all things considered, the paper is as well designed as most. The headline supplied by the editor: "Design at Best Won't Save Poor Content."

Another problem concerns the editor's insistence on playing up a famous writer in the title of the article in addition to giving the writer a byline. This from *Advertising Age:*

CREATIVITY COMES BEST
FROM 'EXTRA-ENVIRONMENTAL MAN,'
NOT STUCK WITH PAST, SAYS GOSSAGE
By Howard L. Gossage

Another example, from *Ad Ass't:*

THE HUMOR OF ED RENFRO'S DRAWINGS
By Ed Renfro

Surely the late Howard Gossage and the still active Ed Renfro found the double mentions awkward.

Still another problem concerns the magazine's reluctance to break away from a formula in creating its titles. You can parody some magazines purely on the basis of the titles they run. *Mad* once ran a table of contents page for something called *Popular Scientific Mechanics*, with such titles as "Road Tests Show Rolls Royce Is Well Made," "Drill Press Converts to Lawn Mower," and "Rebuilding a Crushed Car — For Those Who Followed Last Month's 'Rebuilding a Garage.'" Readers of the mechanics magazines, at least at that time, could recognize the titles as being close in form to what their magazines offered each month.

But many magazines, especially today, are open to innovation in title writing, and one of the great contributions the freelancers can make is in this area of journalism. The editor may reject the title, but it is there, just in case.

Mort Weisinger, who helped found the Society of Magazine Writers, now the American Society of Journalists and Authors, says that "a catchy, clever title is the greatest asset for the beginning writer as well as the professional."[1] The first article he wrote, about the Inquiring Photographer for the New York *Daily News*, sold to a magazine because of its title, the editor told Weisinger years later. "When it arrived, it went right into our slush pile," the editor said. "But the title was so provocative, the reader pulled it out and passed it upstairs." The article dealt with the brashness of the Inquiring Photographer as he stopped people on the street and asked them sometimes embarrassing questions. Its title:

AMERICA'S NOSIEST MAN.[2]

[1] Mort Weisinger, "Titles That Talk," *The Writer*, August 1975, p. 12.
[2] Although magazines run titles in all-lowercase or caps-and-lowercase, this chapter will use all caps to better display them.

So important is the title that you may put off writing the article — put off even doing the research — until a good one occurs to you. Often the title is the article. When you look around for an article idea, you look around essentially for a title. Starting with a title, you have your theme laid out before you. You resolve to put nothing down in the article itself that does not fit the title and contribute to the theme.

Let's say you plan to do an article on beards. Reginald Reynolds' *Beards* (Harcourt Brace Jovanovich) has started you thinking. If you can come up with a title right away you can decide the approach to take. What about "The Stubble I've Seen"? All right; you decide to do the article in first person, using a light touch. The emphasis will be on the first awkward days when beards form.

Whenever a good title occurs to you, write it down and file it away as an article possibility. In a Public Broadcasting Service program on selecting clothing, the announcer at the end says that, if the advice offered on the program were followed, people would find that clothing is "more fun than a fig leaf." Not a bad title for an article, you decide; it has both rhythm and alliteration.

But coming up with a title may involve more than merely recognition; it may involve a conscious hunt, conducted after the article is underway. You will look for a good title while you conduct your research. You will study your market to see what kind of titles your editor seems to prefer. You may end up making a list of various titles, then eliminating those that don't work.

• The Two-Way Title

The reader can take some titles two ways. If both ways are right, fine. *National Review* gave this title to a column on "coffee-table books":

THE GROANING COFFEE TABLE

Did *National Review* mean that the books were bad? Or did it mean that the books were heavy and expensive? Probably both.

A title like the following, over a *New York Times Magazine* article by John Culhane, could just as well suggest meddling editors as crusading editorial cartoonists:

THE CARTOON KILLERS THRIVE AGAIN

The article, it turns out, deals only with the cartoonists, applauding their contributions to building an informed electorate.

More successful in its two-way meaning is the two-sentence title the New York *Times* put on an "Arts and Leisure" section feature about a Woody Allen comedy:

WOODY ALLEN IN A COMEDY ABOUT BLACKLISTING?
DON'T LAUGH

• Headlines and Titles: The Difference

Working as a reporter for a newspaper, you would not write the heading — let's call it the headline — for your feature. That's a job for the copy editor. A reporter cannot know how long the headline will be. Newspapers tend to standardize their headlines. This is necessary because of deadline pressures and page-layout restrictions. Whoever writes the final headline writes it to fit a given space. Lowercase letters each count as one unit, and capital letters each count as one-and-a-half units — with some exceptions. The headline writer is as much a counter of letters as a creator of phrases.

Some magazines, if they deal with news rather than feature material, use headlines similar to those used by newspapers. Trade journals fall into this category. "Successful Salon Owners Offer Guideposts to Better Salon Management," goes a headline for a *Modern Beauty Shop* piece. "New Spring–Summer Hairstyles to be Announced in Los Angeles" goes one in *American Hairdresser.* But in the same issue of a trade journal carrying news-like items with newspaper-like headlines, you may find features with titles similar to what you see in general magazines.

Even if what you submit as a freelancer is to go into the regular news columns of the newspaper, or onto a page in a magazine where newspaper-like headlines appear, it is a good idea to put some kind of title on the first page of your manuscript. The title will tell the editor what your piece is about. It will also help the headline writer see what to play up.

So what is a title and how does it differ from a headline? Unlike a headline, a title does not have to follow any set of rules. It doesn't have to have both a subject and a predicate (although it can have both); it doesn't have to be written in present tense (although it can be). And there is no limit on the length, unless the editor happens to have a prejudice against long — or short — titles.

A title can be no more than a one or two-word label. Or it can be a whole sentence. Or more.

What did *The Atlantic* call its article about dwarfs?

DWARFS

And what did *Holiday* call an article on gambling?

I HOPE I BREAK EVEN BECAUSE I NEED THE MONEY

A title can combine elements of title-writing with elements of headline-writing. From Larry L. King's article in *Sport* about a Baltimore quarterback who was good enough to make the fans forget Johnny Unitas:

JOHNNY WHO? BERT JONES TAKES OVER IN BALTIMORE

Anything goes except the overly familiar.

• The Title That's Trite

Back in 1939 E. M. Forster brought out *Two Cheers for Democracy*, and ever since, writers and editors have been giving two cheers for people and movements they support, but support with some misgivings. The "Two Cheers for ——" title may be the most popular in American magazines. Each year sees dozens of variations like:

TWO CHEERS FOR KENNEDY   (*The Nation* for an editorial giving him the support in 1960 it would rather have given to Adlai Stevenson)

* * * * *

TWO CHEERS FOR THE PRESS   (T. S. Matthews in *Saturday Review*)

* * * * *

TWO CHEERS FOR THE NATIONAL GEOGRAPHIC   (Anne Chamberlin in *Esquire*)

* * * * *

TWO CHEERS FOR MR. FORSTER   (*The New York Review of Books* for a review of a study of Forster's works)

Wilfred Beckerman in 1975 published this book with St. Martin's Press: *Two Cheers for the Affluent Society*. And then there is Jack Newfield's title for his article in *The Nation* seeing some — but not much — good in the flower children.

ONE CHEER FOR THE HIPPIES

It should be clear that, if you want to put an original title on your article you should avoid one beginning with "Two Cheers."

Almost as numerous have been the "Where There's Smoke" titles appearing since the Surgeon General's report on cigarette smoking.

- ## Titles from the Standpoint of Content

In writing a title, think of the assignment from the standpoint of both content and form. The content of the title should reflect the content of the article. The title should tell just enough about the article so that the reader can decide whether or not to read it but not enough so that he won't *have* to read it.

If your article finds some good in an unpopular cause or picks away at something most people would regard as worth preserving, by all means reflect this in your title. Not many people will defend the spoils system in politics. The very name is pejorative. So, for *The Washington Monthly*, Charles Peters comes up with:

A KIND WORD FOR THE SPOILS SYSTEM

You might want to intrigue the reader by saying something unlikely in your title.

THE HORSE THAT SAVED A SCHOOL

That was the title John O'Connor (or his editor) gave an article in *Good Housekeeping*. The article told of the Au Clair School for autistic children, Bear, Delaware, and its money problems, which were solved when school authorities bought, reared, and raced Silk Stockings, a harness-racing horse. It was a good example of a local story good enough to interest a national audience.

Numbers — even odd numbers — sometimes add appeal to a title. There is a ring of authenticity about them. "Nine Ways to Save Money at the Grocery Store" probably has more appeal than "How to Save Money on Groceries," although a "how" in a title should not be underrated.

- **The How-to Title** They may not be clever, but you can't fault how-to titles. Almost every magazine uses them because nearly every magazine runs how-to articles.

You would not want to hide the fact that what you're offering the reader is how-to information, but a how-to article does not necessarily need the words "how to" in a title. Just naming the activity may be enough. The more specific you can be in a how-to title the better.

HOW TO STAY SLIM AFTER LOSING WEIGHT   (*Ebony*)

* * * * *

HOW TO CONDUCT A FRANCHISE BUSINESS   (*Success Unlimited*)

* * * * *

HOW ONE URBAN COUNTY FIGHTS NOISE POLLUTION   (James A. Hilcken in *American City & County*)

* * * * *

BUILD YOUR OWN SUPER-TOURER   (Frank Berto in *Bicycling!*)

* * * * *

LOOK YOUR PRETTIEST DURING PREGNANCY   (*Good Housekeeping*)

* * * * *

GROWING BETTER HOUSEPLANTS   (*Good Housekeeping*)

• **Who, What, Where, When, Why, How Titles.**   One system for coming up with titles involves going to the traditional questions to be answered in any news story — the five "W"s and the "H" — and picking one as your base.

A *Who* title names the person around whom your personality sketch or interview article is built.
A *What* title presents some outstanding fact.
A *Where* title names a place described in a travel article.
A *When* title fits a historical piece.
A *Why* title fits an argumentative piece.
A *How* title, unlike a How-to title, goes over an educational — not a mechanical — piece, like one *McCall's* ran by Mark Rasmussen. Its title:

HOW SUN MYUNG MOON LURES AMERICA'S CHILDREN

- **The Superlative Title.** Another possibility is to base your article on a superlative and feature it in the title. Chester Kyle came up with this one for *Bicycling!*:

THE WORLD'S FASTEST HUMAN

Mort Weisinger believes strongly in the superlative as a title ingredient. Some examples from his long list of credits:

MEET THE HIGHEST I.Q. IN AMERICA

* * * * *

THE ODDEST BETS IN HISTORY

* * * * *

I'VE GOT THE WORLD'S MOST MYSTERIOUS DISEASE
(An as-told-to article by a victim of multiple sclerosis)

- **The Question Title.** You may find your title in a question. Just make sure you choose a question your particular readers want the answer to.

SHOULD MEN WEAR JEWELRY?   (*Ebony*)

* * * * *

IS YOUR DOG A GYPSY?   (Ann Lawrence in *Girl Talk*)

* * * * *

IS THIS ALL THERE IS TO MARRIAGE?   (Lilly Gioia in *Guideposts*)

"The typewriter's question mark looks like an inverted hook," observes Mort Weisinger, "and it has enabled me to hook dozens of editors."

Be sure to include a question mark. But there are some titles that can go as either questions or nonquestions. Your title could be either "What's in a Name?" or "What's in a Name," for instance, depending upon whether you perceive your title as asking or telling.

- **Titles from the Standpoint of Form**

Any literary form goes. A title is often a figure of speech. *Pioneer*, a magazine published by United States Borax & Chemical Corp., gave this title to an article on what alcoholism costs U.S. citizens:

TWO-BILLION-DOLLAR HANGOVER

A title can even take the form of a multiple-choice question, which could fit, say, over an article about the nature of exams in college.

You can take a name peculiarity and play with it in the title. Say you have a Psmith you're writing about. You can see that you get another "S" word in your title and then put a "P" in front of it. For a Kenneth Crawford column in *Newsweek* dealing with the declining fortunes of the Ku Klux Klan, the magazine chose this as a title:

KURTAINS FOR THE KLAN

Editors' preferences in titles change. At one time the colon title was left pretty much to the thesis or book writer, but increasingly it has appeared in the magazines.

NEWARK'S KENNETH GIBSON: A MAYOR'S MAYOR
(*Ebony*)

* * * * *

DIVORCEES: THE NEW POOR   (Alice Lake in *Good Housekeeping*)

* * * * *

GUEST SPEAKERS: HANDLE WITH CARE   (Jean Mater in *The Rotarian*)

Although somewhat dated, the double title, its units joined by an "or," appears occasionally today. It usually introduces an article written with a light or sarcastic touch. From Mary Vespa's article in *Ms.*:

A TWO-YEAR OLD IN FALSE EYELASHES
or
HOW TOMORROW'S MISS AMERICAS ARE MADE

- **The Appropriate Title.**   The inspiration for your title may come from the nature of the material your article deals with. To construct the heading for a feature on movies that made it — and didn't make it — in 1975 (small towns didn't take to many of them), the New York *Times* adapted *Variety* magazine's style:

WHY STIX NIX BIG PIX

TV Guide leaned on the speech mannerism of the late Ed Sullivan to write a title for an article on the platform shoes worn by TV stars:

R-R-REALLY BIG SHOES

For a piece about 11 classics in pornography that were to be published in this country, the defunct *Fact* chose this title:

MOVE OVER, LADY CHATTERLY

For a feature on TV censorship, the New York *Times* chose:

HOW THE GOSH-DARN NETWORKS EDIT THE HECK OUT OF MOVIES

For an article about the strong-willed leader of the Erhard Seminars Training, *New Times* chose:

THE FÜHRER OVER EST

• **Putting Rhythm in Your Title.**   Your reader has a better chance of remembering your title if it has some rhythm. *The Christian Century*, for a piece examining Jacques Barzun's *House of Intellect*, took a song title, added some rhythm, and came up with:

THIS OLD HOUSE OF JACQUES BARZUN

A title can even carry a bit of rhyme.

THE NECKER CHECKERS   (*Newsweek* for an article on supervision of dorm visitors on campus)

• **Humor in Titles.**   A little hilarity can't hurt.

ARE SWISS SUBMARINES BETTER THAN OURS?   (B.E. Tabarlet in *Saturday Review* for an article about the U.S. Navy)

* * * * *

CAN HOWARD COSELL'S MOUTH FILL ED SULLIVAN'S SHOES?   (Cover blurb in *Police Gazette* at the time Cosell launched his short-lived Saturday-night variety show on TV)

• **The Pun.**   The pun is the most prevalent form of humor found in article titles.

The Camelback Inn, Phoenix, back in the early 1960s had been criticized for anti-Jewish, pro-John Birch policies. When columnist Inez Robb attacked the far right in a speech, she was asked to leave the inn. *The Nation,* in an editorial, suggested that the inn could look for further criticism; to quote the editorial's title, this last episode might well be:

THE STRAW THAT BROKE THE CAMELBACK

Some other pun titles:

HOME IS WHERE THE MART IS   (Feature on garage sales in the Indianapolis *Star Magazine*)

* * * * *

FUNERALS: A DYING TRADITION   (William R. MacKaye in the Washington *Post*'s *Potomac* magazine)

* * * * *

IS RAPID TRANSIT ON THE RIGHT TRACK?   (*Mainliner*)

* * * * *

INSTRUCTION JUST FOR THE YELL OF IT   (*National Observer* for a feature on a cheerleaders' clinic)

* * * * *

ON THE CHAMPAGNE TRAIL   (*New York* for an article analyzing brands of champagne)

But the double meaning has to make sense two ways. Here's one that didn't work very well, from *Columbia Journalism Review:*

NEW WRINKLES IN FORECASTING

The article was about an old weather forecaster being replaced by a young one. It was not, then, a matter of new wrinkles replacing old. It was a matter of *no* wrinkles replacing wrinkles.

- **Alliteration.**   A title also can have some alliteration.

LATINS ARE LOUSY LOVERS   (Helen Lawrenson's classic in *Esquire*)

* * * * *

SOUP, SOAP, AND SALVATION   (Article on the Salvation Army in the defunct *Cascades,* published by Pacific Northwest Bell)

When you use alliteration, it is wise to use just a little. Perhaps only two words would start with the same letter, and the words in the title would be widely separated. A little alliteration goes a long way.

The composer-lyricist Stephen Sondheim (he did the lyrics for *West Side Story* and the music and lyrics for other Broadway musicals) recalls that his counterpoint teacher called alliteration "the refuge of the destitute." "That's my attitude toward alliteration in a lyric. Any time you hear alliteration, get suspicious. . . . For example, when you hear 'I Feel Pretty' in *West Side Story* and the girl sings 'I feel fizzy and funny and fine,' somebody doesn't have something to say."[3]

- **Contrast and Irony.**   Some contrast or irony within the title helps.

    THE HIGH COST OF NOT SPENDING   (*The Reporter*)

    * * * * *

    AN ODD PROPOSAL TO RESTORE EVEN TEMPERS   (*New York*)

    * * * * *

    THE RIGHT TO BE WRONG   (Oregon *Journal*)

    * * * * *

    FRANK PERDUE: THE TOUGH MAN BEHIND THE TENDER CHICKEN   (Louise Melton in *Buffalo Spree Magazine*)

- **The Takeoff.**   Lou Shannessy Smith of La Crosse, Wis., in a letter-to-the-editor of *The Writer*, complained that every time she came up with a good title she found that someone else had already used it. Only half seriously she suggested: "Maybe it would be smarter just to parody successful titles, instead of cudgeling the poor old brain in an effort to be original. Like 'Winny the Few' for a horse story. Or 'By Law Reprossessed' for an article on finance companies. Or an 'unforgettable character' piece on doctors, called 'Medicine Folk.' "

Actually the parody title may now be the most popular title in the magazines. It can take off from almost anything: a book title, a song title, a TV program, an advertising slogan, a popular expression — just so the point of takeoff is a familiar one to the readers of the magazine where the title is to appear.

[3]Quoted by Craig Zadan in "Listening to Stephen Sondheim," *New York*, Nov. 11, 1974, p. 76.

The defunct *Reporter* magazine, for the title over an article about Norman Vincent Peale, took off from one of Peale's book titles, coming up with this:

SOME NEGATIVE THINKING ABOUT NORMAN VINCENT PEALE

The Rev. Mr. Peale, with his positive thinking, used to be a favorite target for criticism. Adlai Stevenson, comparing Peale to the Apostle Paul, said: "I find Paul appealing but Peale appalling."

Some other title takeoffs from book titles:

YOU'RE OK BUT I'M STILL THE BOSS   (John L. Kirkley in *Datamation*)

* * * * *

THE LITTLE RAILROAD THAT COULDN'T   (*Business Week*, for an article about the bankrupt Jersey Central)

* * * * *

IN LUKEWARM BLOOD   (Stanley Kauffmann in *The New Republic*, for an unfavorable review of *In Cold Blood*)

* * * * *

THE CRIME OF PUNISHMENT   (*Saturday Review*)

* * * * *

FUTURE SCHLOCK   (*The Nation*, for a critical review of *Future Shock*)

A book title that inspired too many takeoffs was *Everything You Always Wanted to Know About Sex.* . . . Every magazine you picked up for months after the book made its splash had an "Everything You Always Wanted to Know" title. One of the good ones appeared as a cover blurb for *New York*, August 3, 1970. The art showed a nude woman holding out two ice-cream cones so that they formed a sort of bra. The blurb:

EVERYTHING YOU ALWAYS WANTED TO KNOW ABOUT ICE CREAM BUT WERE TOO FAT TO ASK

Song titles or lyrics can also inspire article titles. For an article suggesting that Secretary of State Henry Kissinger was "changeable as a chameleon," Robert Sherrill, in the defunct *Lithopinion,* chose as his title:

I WONDER WHO'S KISSINGER NOW?

New York, to head an item about Catholic Church officials putting pressure on Bloomingdale's to stop promoting and selling Jesus Jeans, used:

LEANING ON JESUS

Takeoffs from TV programs:

WILL THE REAL WARREN BEATTY PLEASE SHUT UP
(*Esquire*)

* * * * *

WILL THE REAL HUBERT HUMPHREY PLEASE SIT DOWN?
(*The Progressive*)

A takeoff from a radio program of the 1930s and 1940s:

ONE MAN'S FAMILY   (*The New York Times Magazine* for an article about the Charles Manson group)

The following takeoff would be appreciated only by those who remember a classic late 1920s Carl Rose cartoon in *The New Yorker*:

I SAY IT'S SPINACH

It went over an article in *The Progressive* in which Kenneth Turan criticized movie critics who want all movies to be made for intellectuals.

Here are some takeoffs from popular expressions. That the expressions are trite does not detract from the titles. The takeoffs sanitize the triteness.

FROM RUGS TO RICHES   (*Monsanto Magazine*, for an article about a successful carpet cleaning company)

* * * * *

THANK GOD IT'S THURSDAY?   (*Time*, for an item on the four-day week)

* * * * *

LET THEM EAT COOKBOOKS   (*New York,* for a column on cookbooks flooding the country while food shortages exist)

* * * * *

WHAT TO DO UNTIL THE HUNTING SEASON COMES
(*The American Legion Magazine*)

Are you ready for this one? *The National Observer* came up with it for a feature about Jimmy the Greek:

ODDS, TO A GRECIAN, EARN

• The Blurb

So much for the creative aspects of title writing. Doing a takeoff, coming up with a good pun, feeling the rhythm of what you write, even working up some alliteration — these activities can be fun. Now comes a more grimy aspect of title writing: blurb writing.

Have you noticed that most magazines run a longer title in connection with the regular title? That longer title is called a "subtitle" or, more commonly, a "blurb." This kind of blurb is different from a cover blurb; the cover blurb is really only a title. This blurb is an elaboration of the title. It helps explain the title. It does not merely *restate* the title.

If the title sacrifices some clarity in an attempt to be clever, a blurb is all the more important. You should get into the habit of writing a blurb for each of your titles even though your magazine market does not run blurbs.

An editor, on first seeing your article, does not have the advantage the reader has. The reader sees the article as it is laid out by the art director; the nature of the display type and the quality of the art help set the mood. The editor sees only the manuscript. It may take a blurb to get the editor ready for what is to follow. And if the magazine does run blurbs with its articles, your blurb may eventually get into print.

A blurb can go above or below the title, depending upon the preference of the editor. Many magazines use both styles in a single issue. Here is an above-the-title blurb (and the title) from an issue of *Parents' Magazine* (Bernard Bard, author):

> The shocking decline of student scores at all grade levels has led to widely diverse attempts at educational reform. But before we can correct the problem, we need to be sure we know

WHY OUR SCHOOLS ARE FAILING

Here is a title-first setup from the same issue (Cecelia M. Dobrish, author):

CAN VALUES REALLY BE LEARNED AT SCHOOL?

If the answer is yes — as these programs indicate — then the schools can play a vital role in reinforcing parental standards.

In the following title–blurb combination (Cherry K. Turnage, author, in *Good Housekeeping*), you might expect to find quotation marks around the question. But the editor may have felt that the change from big type in the title to smaller type in the blurb made it clear enough that it was a child's question followed by a mother's explanation.

MOMMY, WILL I BE BLIND?

My heart broke when my four-year-old son, Mark, asked me that. It took two years and several operations before I could give him his answer.

Many writers have a problem coordinating the title with the blurb. *Catholic Digest* provides an example:

No matter what the Russians say, you cannot

LEARN WHILE YOU SLEEP

The title seems to issue a command for the reader to do something the combination title-and-blurb seems to say can't be done.

Esquire for years led all other magazines in the flair of its titles. Unlike other magazines, it put as much creative effort into the blurb as into the title. Actually, the combination added up to one long title.

WHO'S AFRAID OF THE WARREN REPORT?

Elementary, my dear Warren. Everybody. And here's why. . .

The blurb may be absolutely vital to the title. From *Esquire* again:

WHY JOHNNY CAN'T FLUNK

"Dear Mom and Dad: Once again I have took all the money you sent me for beer and spent it on term papers. . ."

The defunct *Together* needed a lead-in blurb to fully explain an ironic title:

"You shall love your neighbor as yourself" — until he or his children or pets happen to displease you, or you are tempted to gossip. Then you may find that you. . .

LOVE YOUR NEIGHBOR, BUT NOT VERY MUCH

The New York Times Magazine, for an article on picking names for children on the basis of what names mean, used a combination in which the blurb (above the title, in this case) was as title-like as the title itself.

Cyril is sneaky, John is straight

THE GAME OF THE NAME

A blurb can be shorter than the title itself. From *Psychology Today:*

GERALD FORD vs. HUMAN NATURE: FIGHTING INFLA-TION WITH BUTTONS AND SLOGANS

Good luck

• Typing Your Title

The editor and art director will decide how the title will be displayed, but if you submit a long title that you know will carry over into two or more lines, you should make an attempt in your typing to start new lines only at logical breaks. Keep phrases together.

Even though the magazine will run your title in caps-and-lowercase letters, or in all-lowercase letters, you should type your title in all caps and center it on the page. Leave a little space above and below it. If you include a blurb, type it as you would the body of your article, in all-lowercase, but give it wider margins to set it apart. Don't let the editor think the blurb is the opening paragraph of your article.

Your byline, also centered, goes under the title–blurb combination. Again, leave space above and below it.

• Your Title's Chances

Even if you come up with a spectacular title, you face the strong possibility that it won't be used. Perhaps the art the editor and art director come up with negates the thrust of the title. The editor works out a new title, then, to make it agree with the art. Or maybe your title happens to be similar to some others the editor already has ready for an issue; the editor wants variety. You can't know what the other titles will be when you write yours.

Sometimes you will agree that the editor's new title is better than the one you submitted.

• THE OPENING

Many article writers feel that the beginning of an article is its most important part. If they can't immediately capture and hold reader interest, they know that what appears later in the article will remain unread. Just as important, if a writer can't sell an editor in the first few paragraphs, the article will not see print. Editors do not have time to read thoroughly every freelance manuscript coming to them. Through experience they have discovered that a manuscript with a weak beginning is not likely to deliver anything of interest on later pages. Reading the first few paragraphs is enough.

As a writer, then, you start looking for lead ideas during your research phase. In the writing phase you may spend as much time on the opening as you do on the body of the article. But you do not necessarily write the opening first. You may start with the article's interior, watching all the while for some emphasis that belongs up front. Wade Nichols, when he was editor of *Redbook*, told an author who was having trouble with his article opening: "If you can't find a lead, maybe you should abandon the article. There's something wrong with it."

If you can come up with a good opening right away, you may find that the remainder of the article just naturally falls into place. A good lead, arrived at early, can do as much for the writer as for the reader. Edward Gibbon, the British historian, said that once he got the first sentence the way he wanted it, the writing of *The Decline and Fall of the Roman Empire* went along smoothly.

A lead, so far as an article or a feature is concerned, is not necessarily just the first paragraph; it may consist of several paragraphs. But the first paragraph, usually, is the most important. And if it is true that the last sentence of any paragraph is the most important sentence in that paragraph, it follows that the last sentence of the first paragraph may be the most important sentence in the article. Give it special attention. Check out some last sentences of first paragraphs in current articles to see whether you can detect techniques that would be useful to you.

Here are some last-sentences-of-first-paragraphs taken from the writing of Dan Wakefield:

The wild old Village has reached respectable middle age; tough old Tammany is fast approaching respectable senility. ("The Village and the Tiger")

* * * * *

In fact, my local rooming-house life in the quiet community only made me itch all the more. ("Promised Lands .")

* * * * *

But the question forever nags — "Is this it?" ("Is There a 'Literary Life' Before Death?")[4]

Perhaps the most successful magazine article ever published was "— And Sudden Death," the piece J. C. Furnas did for *Reader's Digest* for August 1935.[5] By 1935 the *Digest*, which was established in the early 1920s, had a large and enthusiastic audience; "— And Sudden Death" gave the magazine another big boost in circulation and prestige. It also called attention to a national tragedy — highway accidents — in a most dramatic way. The article came about because editor-publisher DeWitt Wallace, just then in the process of changing his magazine from strictly a reprint magazine to one that featured both reprints and original articles, was moved by a garage mechanic's vivid description of several recent local automobile accidents. Wallace got in touch with Furnas, who was then working on an article for the *Digest* on traffic problems, and told him to play up the need for safer driving. Furnas did, and the resulting article, grim and a bit shocking, got wide attention.

The promotion department of the magazine sent proofs out to 5,000 newspapers and other publications inviting the media to reprint the article after the *Digest* ran it. Editors from all over the country did

[4]You can see these sentences in context in Dan Wakefield's *Between the Lines,* The New American Library, New York, 1966.

[5]See Chapt. V of James Playsted Wood's book, *Of Lasting Interest: The Story of the Reader's Digest,* Doubleday & Company, Inc., New York, 1958.

reprint the article, in whole or in part; people began talking about it. It appeared eventually in comic-strip and motion-picture form. Some state officials got reprints for distribution to traffic offenders and license applicants. James Playsted Wood, in his book about the *Digest,* reports that "Within three months [after the publication of the article] *The Reader's Digest* distributed 4,000,000 reprints . . . to more than 8,000 companies, clubs, civic groups, and other associations which requested them, giving the article greater circulation than any other magazine article before or since." Wood even gives the *Digest* article part of the credit for a reduction of one-third in the ratio of traffic deaths to miles driven in the following six years.

What kind of writing could make a piece of nonfiction on a rather common subject so effective? Let's take a look at the opening (the quote is from the article as it was reprinted June 1959 in *Together,* with figures updated):

> Publicizing the total of motoring injuries — over 1.3 million disabled in 1958 with 37,000 deaths — never gets to first base in jarring the motorist into a realization of the appalling risks of motoring. He does not translate dry statistics into a reality of blood and agony.

There is a hint here that the next few paragraphs are likely to get down to cases, as indeed they do, but not before some amplification of the first paragraph.

> Figures exclude the pain and horror of savage mutilation — which mean they leave out the point. They need to be brought closer home. A passing look at a bad smash or the news that a fellow you had lunch with last week is in a hospital with a broken back will make any driver but a born fool slow down at least temporarily. But what is needed is a vivid and sustained realization that every time you step on the throttle death gets in beside you, hopefully waiting for his chance.[6]

Now the author is digging in. He's switched from third to second person. And he's used a rather frightening figure of speech. In subsequent paragraphs he uses such phrases as "a mangled body on a slab waxily portraying the consequences of bad motoring judgment," "the flopping, pointless efforts of the injured to stand up," "the steady, panting groaning of a human being with pain creeping up on him as the shock wears off," "a hysterical woman with her screaming mouth opening a hole in the bloody drip that fills her eyes and runs off her chin."

[6] "Hopefully" is used correctly here.

Furnas's opening is inviting in that it accepts the reader as an equal with the writer, putting them both in a position of looking at the problem and worrying about its solution. There is no hint at first that the reader himself is part of the problem. There is no preaching.

In his opening paragraphs, the author talks with the reader about the other guy. The author assumes — or pretends to assume — that the reader is already well aware of the enormity of the problem.

• Putting Yourself in the Reader's Place

In writing your opening, try to put yourself in the reader's place. Ask yourself: what reward does the opening promise to deliver? Is that reward great enough — is it immediate enough — to encourage the reader to stick with the article to its end?

If the readers of *The Christian Reader* knew Nancy Orlecki Ham personally, maybe she could capture their attention with this beginning for her "Down on the Farm" article:

> Fall was the busiest and grandest time at our farm in Alberta, Canada, 35 years ago. There was work for everyone: all twelve of us kids plus Mom and Dad supervising and working side by side. I don't recall any complaints about the dawn to dusk labor. . . .

But most readers, surely, would pass by to another article. What do they care about grand times and no complaints 35 years ago in Alberta?

• Kinds of Openings

Only in the opinion magazines and the literary quarterlies can you get away with the casual openings used by the nineteenth-century essayists. As a writer today you cannot assume that your reader is already interested in your subject. You must create that interest, and the opening is where you do it.

You may find yourself using the same kind of opening article after article because it seems to work for you. But you should try other openings to see if you can find one that works better. In fact, you should try several different openings for any one article you write.

Sometimes writing an opening becomes a matter of outguessing an editor. Your intent may be to produce the kind of opening the editor seems to prefer, judging from the kind that appears most frequently in the magazine. On the other hand the editor may be tired of seeing the same kind of opening, article after article, and may welcome one that stands out from the others.

The kind of article you write, the audience you envision, and the material your research yields should dictate the kind of opening you choose. There are many to choose from. In considering the different kinds of openings, bear in mind that not every opening fits exactly into a category. Some openings are one of a kind. Many openings combine aspects of two or more of the openings described in the following paragraphs.

- ## The Narrative.

> They threw me off the hay truck about noon.

This is James M. Cain's start for *The Postman Always Rings Twice,* a lusty novel (for then) written in the early 1930s. Cain was a master of the narrative technique. His novels, also strong in dialogue, moved swiftly to their no-nonsense conclusions, and they lent themselves nicely to later scripting for the movies. The narrative opening is to be expected in a Cain novel or any novel or short story that gives the reader plenty of action.

The narrative opening is to be expected in an article, too. From a narrative opening a writer can move to a generalization or to some statistical material — material too heavy to unload on the reader at the beginning.

Of the various ways to begin an article, a narrative probably is the most popular. Few readers can resist a good story. It isn't just the narrative article that lends itself to a narrative opening. An essay — even an essay on a serious topic — can take such an opening.

Benjamin Stein in "Whatever Happened to Small-Town America?" an essay-article in *The Public Interest,* starts off with three long paragraphs of narrative recounting an episode on *The Rockford Files* TV program. Then this fourth paragraph (not reproduced here in full):

> This characterization of the small town as evil and threatening to innocent city dwellers is now a staple of contemporary American mass culture. But the small town wasn't always seen that way. Over a relatively brief time, cultural attitudes have changed virtually 180 degrees. . . .

Caroline Totten uses a narrative to begin her "Suddenly You're a Victim" article in *Essence*:

One evening Jane Miller sent her husband Jim to the local store to buy a gallon of milk and a bag of potato chips. Shortly after he left, it began to rain, and she began to worry. He hadn't taken a raincoat or an umbrella, and he'd probably get soaked and catch cold again. About 45 minutes passed. She checked on their sleeping twins, then returned to the kitchen and set the coffee pot to perking. Where was he? she thought. Just as she sat down and opened a magazine, the doorbell rang. It was a policeman.
"Are you Jane Miller, wife of James Miller?"
She nodded.
"I'm Officer McBride," he said. "May I come in?". . .

After three more paragraphs of conversation in which Mrs. Miller learns that her husband was killed after walking into a robbery-in-progress, the author switches from narrative to information.

At that moment the Miller family joined the ranks of thousands of innocent victims who suddenly come face to face with violent crime. Recent statistics indicate that. . . .

Jane O'Reilly's narrative opening for her "Making the Holidays a 'Peak Experience' " article in *New York* is as much description as narrative. It goes like this:

It must be Christmas because yesterday I got a Yuletide newsletter from someone I went to school with. Mimeographed, with hand-drawn holly leaves around the edges. I get a few of these annual wrap-ups every year. They begin "Dear Friends," which presumably includes me, although I can't remember having any friends when I was growing up in St. Louis. Perhaps I remember inaccurately — I would have preferred having friends — because the letters arrive, correctly addressed and mailed early with the proper postage. My sister still mails things to the place I lived five years ago, but these Christmas messages arrive directly, ignoring my fifteen years of wandering and two name changes.
The one I got yesterday reads:
Dear Friends,
It's hard to believe another year has passed! . . .

• **The Shocking Statement.** Almost as popular as the narrative opening is the shocking-statement opening. You spring some idea or fact on your readers to astound them, promising details later in the article. You hope your readers' curiosity prevents their leaving you for an article farther back in the magazine. In any article you are in effect competing with other writers for the limited amount of time readers can spend with the magazine. A shocking-statement opening is a competitive opening.

How is this for an example? It comes from Garry Wills's "Hurrah for Politicians" article (a shocking title) in *Harper's Magazine*.

> Politicians have many virtues that ignorant people take for vices. The principle ones are: (1) compromise of principle; (2) egotism; (3) mediocrity.

You begin to see his point when you get to his theme sentence a few paragraphs later. "People do not like to be ruled by their superiors. They will settle for their equals, but prefer their inferiors."

• **The Description.**   Perhaps the hardest opening to bring off is the one that offers one or several paragraphs of description. With this kind of opening you take a chance that only the literary-minded reader will stay with you. Of course the description can be more instructive than literary. It can tell what it's like to work at some job, to travel to some place, to try some treatment, to undergo some trial, to experience some pleasure.

The best descriptive openings involve figures of speech. Andrew Kopkind in *New Times* starts off an article on Renee Richards and sex changes with this picture:

> It was one of those oppressive mid-Atlantic afternoons in August, when just going outside is like walking into somebody's mouth.

After a few more sentences of description, Kopkind goes into a narrative in which Richards goes up to her opponent after a tennis match to exchange pleasantries.

For his descriptive opening on a *New York* piece written at the time Vice President Ford was about to ascend to the Presidency, Richard Reeves takes off from an expression made popular by a radical writer earlier in the century:

> I have seen the future and it scares hell out of me.

D. Keith Mano, in "America's Number-Two Conservative Spokesman" in *New York*, shows how to use description to start off a personality sketch. His subject is William A. Rusher. This is about half of the first paragraph:

> The voice is an engine. Between sentences it seems to idle, in neutral and ready, *mmm, graaarh*. At times William A. Rusher will speak of himself in the third person, as if he didn't really presume to be William A. Rusher. The teeth are stocky and powerful: whoever Rusher is, you wouldn't want to be bitten by him. At 51 he appears farm-boyish, with Clark Kent glasses and skin so fair it could probably manage freckles. . . .

In "A Big Boom You Never Hear," an article in the St. Petersburg (Fla.) *Times* Sunday magazine, Dick Bothwell uses description to get readers interested in fish raising:

> There they hang in their silent world of crystal — living glints of translucent color, all pearl and gold; red, blue and green.
>
> For an instant they pause, staring with that amazed expression imparted by the round black eyes. Then the flick of a tail, the twitch of fins and off they shoot in a trail of bubbles, only to pause and meditate again.
>
> Goldfish, tropical fish — the silent pets with the exotic names: Black Moor, Comet, Fantail, Kissing Gourami, Angelfish, Rosy Barb, Red Wag Sword.
>
> Tiny things, most of them, less than an inch long. Yet these streamlined gill-breathers, the first animals with backbones, represent a billion-dollar business [in 1966] in these United States — a business getting bigger by the minute.
>
> For example: Did you know that 25-million families in the nation own goldfish, which makes it the No. 1 pet? Did you know that guppies and other tropical fish make up Florida's largest air freight export item? . . .

Richard Selzer, a rare physician who writes with style,[7] begins (and continues) an *Esquire* article on "Skin" with description. We come into the article in the middle of the second paragraph:

> See how . . . [the skin] upholsters the bone and muscle underneath, now accenting the point of an elbow, now rolling over the pectorals to hollow the grotto of an armpit. Nippled and umbilicated, and perforated by the most diverse and marvelous openings, each with its singular rim and curtain. Thus the carven helix of the ear, the rigid nostrils, the puckered continence of the anus, the moist and sensitive lips of mouth and vagina.
>
> What is it, then, this seamless body stocking some two yards square. . . ?

- **The Generalization.**   Most beginning writers think first of the generalization as a way to start. Unfortunately, the generalization in their hands — or in anybody's hands — is not very stimulating. The reader has probably heard it often. "The divorce rate today is higher than ever before — and growing." "Most Americans vote against something rather than for something." "Today's generation of students raised on television rather than books. . . ." That sort of thing.

Here's a generalization opening from a religious magazine:

> World Communion Sunday has lost much of its novelty and excitement. . . .

Here's another — from Pat Stanton's "New Paths for Bikers" in *The Sohioan,* a company magazine for Standard Oil of Ohio.

[7]See his collection of essays, *Mortal Lessons,* Simon and Schuster, New York, 1977.

Americans generally used to regard bicycles as children's playthings to be cast aside as soon as one became old enough to drive a car.

No more. Millions upon millions of adults across the nation have rediscovered the sheer fun of pedaling a two-wheeler. At the same time, they are profiting from the substantial health benefits that bike riding offers.

From the standpoint of style, you can't fault the writing. It's just that the two paragraphs show no evidence of research, no sign of new thinking on the subject. It isn't until the third paragraph that the reader learns something new.

In 1972, for the first time since World War I, more new bicycles than new cars were sold in the United States. . . .[8]

Given a light touch, the generalization becomes more acceptable as an opening. Here's an *Esquire* staff writer starting out "The Grateful Dad," a feature on Father's Day gifts:

After a yar of skirmishing along the frontiers of the generation and sex wars, your average male chauvinist-pig old man deserves at least a day of rest and a few tokens of esteem to quiet his nerves. Fortunately, June 20 is his day and the stores are prepared with some splendid gear, as you can see. In the picture opposite . . .

For most articles it is probably safest to start off with some specifics and then move to a generalization.

• The Informative Paragraph.

More than 30,000 vehicles a day travel over a railroad crossing that bisects a major intersection in Oklahoma City, Okla. But high-density polyethylene panels have smoothed out the bumps much to the delight of motorists, the railroad and the city.

The preceding lead paragraph appeared in "Rx for Ailing Railroad Crossings," an article in *American City & County*. Elected or appointed officials in other parts of the country, reading such an article, could pick up ideas from it for taking care of railroad crossing problems in their own cities or counties. The article illustrates that fact that what appears to be a purely local story can interest readers in many locations. Such readers have little time for literary flourishes. The sooner the article gets down to cases the better.

[8] Why this article in an oil company magazine? The fourth paragraph provides your answer. "Responding to this trend, Sohio last year [1974] began offering full-size 10-speed bikes for sale to credit-card customers through its mail-order merchandising operation. . . ."

Paragraphs of pure information make good openings for articles in trade and professional journals.

- **The Summary.** Closely related to the information-paragraph opening is the summary opening. The difference is that the information paragraph simply reports facts. The reader must read on to see what the facts portend. The summary paragraph puts the entire article into one introductory paragraph. Only the reader who wants details need read on.

  Like the information-paragraph opening, the summary opening works best for articles written for trade or professional journals. Of all the different article openings, the summary opening comes closest to matching the opening — or lead — of a news story in a newspaper. Typically, the news-story lead, sometimes in a single paragraph, answers who, what, where, when, why, and how questions.

- **The Direct Address.** In the direct-address opening you take an advertising copywriter's approach. Your opening becomes a "Hey, you!" or "Now hear this!" kind of thing. You would write this kind of opening in real or implied second person. The direct-address opening would strike some editors and readers as too obvious, but others might appreciate its no-nonsense approach.

  Richard Register in "Here Comes the Sun," an early article on solar energy in *West,* opens with direct address.

  > Okay, ecology fans, all you people who voted for Proposition 9 because you thought it meant well — it's tough question time: if fossil fuels polute and nuclear power plants threaten to zap you with blasts and poisons, how are you going to heat your houses, run your electric trash recyclers, and read the Sierra Club newsletter after dark? Stumped? Go outside and look straight up. With any luck at all, you'll see the answer — at least, the answer proposed by a growing number of scientists and environmentalists who are suggesting that we replace our dirty and dangerous power plants with a safe, clean source of energy: the sun.

- **The Quotation.** Newspaper editors — some of them — don't like quotation leads because a quotation often is not representative. It is selective. It does not, then, do an adequate summary job. But as an article or feature writer you should not be bound by this prejudice. Your opening does not have to summarize. A quotation can be a good way to begin. It can also be a good way to end.

The question is: Do you want to give over to someone else the honor of launching or wrapping up your article?

If you can come up with something just as good, put the opening in your own words. If not, don't be afraid to bring in someone else to help you.

You may want to dramatize your opening quotation by giving it a different typographical treatment from the remainder of the article. Type it narrower than the paragraphs that follow, then, and leave some extra space. The editor will decide whether to set the quotation in italics or boldface type.

On a separate line you can name the quote's originator, preceding the name with a dash.

• **The Question.**   No doubt it can do the job, but the question opening is perhaps the least imaginative opening you can come up with. It is overused. And, badly phrased, the question opening can be an embarrassment. A question opening is often condescending.

The value of the question opening lies in the transition it sets up for the paragraph immediately following the question. If the question seems worth exploring, the reader moves easily into the followup paragraph.

In a *Popular Mechanics* article on "Men in White for Ailing Autos," reprinted in *Catholic Digest,* E. D. Fales, Jr., takes no chances that his question will skip by the reader. He phrases several. His lead goes like this:

> Can those new diagnostic centers for automobiles really tell you what is wrong? Should you consult one before you buy a used car? Can they find troubles a dealer can't find? If there is trouble in your present car, can they do a better job than your corner mechanic? Or are all those dynamometer rollers and gauges, oscilloscopes, stethoscopes, and electric meters put there just to impress you?
>
> I spent several weeks visiting diagnostic centers. . . .

• **Humor.**   If you intend to infuse your article with humor, the place to start is in the opening. Any of the kinds of humor mentioned in the previous chapter can work.

The pun appeals to many writers.

> Finding a good psychiatrist in New York is enough to drive you crazy.

That was Carol Rinzler's opening sentence for her "How to Find a Psychiatrist" article in *New York.*

Parody is another favorite opening. It can be useful in establishing the right mood for an article. The subject matter of the article suggests the style to use.

From *Time*, for a feature on the late (now, but not then) publisher Bennett Cerf, well known to *Time* readers as a panelist on the *What's My Line?* TV program:

> And now, panel, for the mystery guest. Masks in place? Good. He is salaried. He works for a profit-making organization. He deals in a product. It is smaller than a breadbox. On the side, he is a TV personality, a lecturer, and a writer of sorts. Also a show-biz nut, a pal of stars, a party trooper and a shameless punster. But he cleverly directs all these other activities toward the promotion of his product, the reward for which would fill a large breadbox with something like $375,000 a year.
>
> Actually, there is no mystery here. Bennett Alfred Cerf, 68, is an open book. Board chairman of Random House, he is the nation's best-known book publisher — better known than many of the authors he serves. . . .

Readers recognized the style as coming from the moderator of the program.

Sundancer, publication of Hughes Airwest, started off a guide to the dams at Las Vegas this way:

> In the beginning there was the Colorado River. And the federal government saw that it was good, except for the floodwaters. And the federal government said, "This river shall be dammed and the floodwaters shall be contained along the Arizona–Nevada border." So it came to pass that a structure was erected across the waters of the Colorado, and it stood seventy stories high and two football fields deep at its base. And on the 30th day of September, 1936, the federal government rested, saying, "We shall call this structure Hoover Dam." And lo, the multitudes were amazed and proclaimed Hoover Dam "The Eighth Wonder of the World."
>
> No wonder. Even now, some 40 years later, Hoover Dam is still the highest dam in the Western Hemisphere. . . .

The writer apparently saw — or pretended to see — a similarity between the creativity of God and the creativity of the federal government. So he phrased his opening in Biblical language.

• **Enigma.** Some writers manage to hold onto readers by being enigmatic. They puzzle their readers to the extent that the readers have to stay with them to figure out what the writers are getting at. Ted Mahar, in his movie column in *The Oregonian* on the resurgence of the motion picture industry, began like this:

The bad news first: It kinda looks like we're in a recession.

But — ah ha! — there's also good news: it kinda looks like we're in a recession.

The point Mahar was making (taking liberties with "like") was that people go to the movies more often during a depression or recession than during good times.

And you have to get deep into his column before you understand Mike Royko's opening paragraphs about a famous cartoonist beaten up in 1975 for taking pictures.

CHICAGO — As Bill Mauldin was getting his face punched and his groin kicked, I'm sure he didn't know that something wonderful was happening.

But it was. The beating of Mauldin, who is a friend of mine, was one of the finest events to occur in Chicago for many years. The sound of his nose breaking was sweet music.

Before anyone thinks I'm a sadist, let me explain why I feel that way.

The explanation was that the guy who attacked Mauldin thought he was attacking an ordinary middle-aged man with a camera instead of the country's foremost political cartoonist. Mauldin's photographing of illegal parked cars belonging to public officials attending a party thus got much more notice than it would have received otherwise.

Royko tried to imagine the consternation at the party when the officials learned that the victim was Mauldin. Finally, after 25 paragraphs:

All those nameless people who can be freely punched in the nose, pushed around, kicked, stomped, walked on — thousands of them all over the city. But this one had to be Bill Mauldin.

That's what I mean about something wonderful happening. The powerful think nothing of pushing around the powerless. But this time the powerless wasn't.

And what a weekend it must have been in the households of the Daley Clan and the Flanagan Clan. The phones must have been ringing off the hooks. . . .

• **The Surprise.** Another way to start is to fool your readers — temporarily. Make them think you are saying one thing when in reality you are saying something else. Spring a surprise at, say, the third paragraph, as Patricia O'Brien does in one of her personality sketches for her Chicago *Sun-Times* "Women with Power" series.

She's the quintessential independent woman. She started by working 48 hours a week as an ammunition tester in an Illinois factory while going to college, graduated Phi Beta Kappa, picked up a master's degree in business from Harvard University, married, had six children, wrote seven books, served as vice president of the National Federation of Republican Women and is now [in 1976] going to law school full time — while traveling back and forth across the country giving speeches.

She's got the kind of style that makes feminists applaud and gives housewives an attack of the I'll-never-amount-to-anything blues.

A Midwest version of Betty Friedan? Hardly. This liberated woman is Phyllis Schlafly, one of the Grand Ogres of feminism. And her power base is her stunningly effective national campaign against ratification of the Equal Rights Amendment.

Or fool readers into thinking they are reading about the present when in fact they are reading about the past. Earl and Miriam Selby use this approach in a lead article in *Reader's Digest:* "How One State Fights to Stay Livable." "Up and down Oregon's Willamette River, untreated sewage poured in from every bordering town and city," the opening paragraph began. The paragraph ended by pointing out that citizens, impatient with their apparently unconcerned legislature, passed an initiative measure by a 3-to-1 margin telling the politicians "to get on with the job of giving the Northwest's dirtiest waterway a scrubbing."

The second paragraph went like this:

Such a script may sound like something out of our recent past. In fact, those events took place 37 years ago — evidence of how long Oregonians have been fighting to keep their state livable.

Jon Nordheimer in the New York *Times* constructs his opening by putting his surprise into a sentence fragment and using it as his second paragraph, the better to dramatize it.

There is a rebirth of interest in the Hawaiian hula.

By male dancers.

In ancient Hawaii women were forbidden to dance the hula and it was performed only by men at religious ceremonies.

Now young Hawaiian men are learning the dance as part of a new wave of interest in the authentic culture of the islands before it was invaded by sailors, tourists and movie merchants.

• **The Teaser.**   You have two problems with the teaser opening. One is to make sure the suspense you build and the phrasing you choose entices rather than discourages the reader. A single paragraph of teasing is about as far as you should go. The other problem is one you can't very well solve as a writer. It involves the art and display worked out by the editor and the art director. The reader may already know what you are up to by the time you begin your lead paragraph. This is not to say that you should avoid the teaser opening, — only that you should bear in mind its limitations. You are safest with it in an all-type magazine without opening-spread displays.

This teaser opening was for "Sweet and Sour," an article warning of the dangers of sugar consumption written by John Pekkanen and Mathea Falco for *The Atlantic:*

> It has come to be called "white gold." Some people claim it is addictive, and many doctors and researchers believe it poses a dire threat to our national health. It has created a black market. Many rock music stations play songs which glorify it. On the average, each and every one of us consumes nearly two pounds of it a week. Lest there be any remaining mystery as to what it is, it is sugar.

• **The Comparison.**   Bruce Handler, who as a student in Magazine Article Writing at the University of Oregon sold his first article, on jogging, to *This Week,* now is Brazil correspondent for *Newsweek* and the Washington *Post.* He uses the comparison opening in "Flying High in Rio," an article in *The New York Times Magazine:*

> And at about the same time President Ford was telling North Americans that "the state of the Union is not good," President Ernesto Geisel was telling Brazilians that "1975 will mark a promising new phase in the upward movement of our country toward its high destinies. Inflation is under control. There is no unemployment. Good harvests have been forecast from north to south. Industry continues to expand."
>
> At the same time that General Motors and Ford were laying off North American workers and offering big rebates to clear out inventories of unsold cars, their Brazilian subsidiaries were advertising for workers in the newspapers, anticipating increased consumer demand.

Barbara Kerr of *The Oregonian* takes two paragraphs of description to build some contrast at the start of her feature on Rosemary Casals.

Through the years, much has been made of tennis player Rosie Casals's temper: She swats balls at her opponent's head, yells at the umpire, makes obscene signals to unruly spectators, and is said to have never smiled during a match.

Off the court, however, she displays a rare but apparently workable combination of honesty and politeness. Above all, she seems serious, solidly on course toward two basic goals: "I want to be good and make the money."

- **Unorthodox Handling.** In some magazines there is room for the unorthodox opening. Jerry Bledsoe in *Esquire,* for his "Down from Glory" article about the astronauts (where are they now?), starts out like this:

> I should like to begin with Bob Voas, of whom you have probably never heard. As a kid, growing up in a Chicago suburb, Bob Voas read all the Buck Rogers comic books. He was. . . .

Another possibility: You can create the illusion of coming in on the story after it has already started. Patricia O'Brien, using "So" as her opening word, does this in a feature for the Chicago Daily News Service following the death of Jackie Kennedy Onassis's husband in 1975. What was Mrs. Onassis going to do now? There was much speculation in the press.

> So now it's time to dissect Jackie Kennedy Onassis, cutting out each fault, each arrogance, each greedy act, laying it all out on the table so the world can see: See? See? She isn't perfect at all.

- **THE CLOSING**

Unlike the traditional news story constructed so the editor can lop off the last paragraph or two to make the story fit, an article or feature needs a final touch to make readers know they are at the end and to make them feel good about staying with the author until then.

For one thing, the article or feature is longer than the typical news story. The momentum it creates calls for some braking action. To change the figure of speech: the ending, as someone has suggested, should be like a cup of coffee after a good meal.

Max Gunther, in *Writing the Modern Magazine Article*, says that an ending should be "satisfying" but admits it is nearly impossible to say what *makes* it satisfying. "If an ending gives you this feeling [of satisfaction], it has done its job. It is an ending that feels like an ending; it comes down with a nice hard final thump; it completes the unit that the article started out to be."

In many cases you would want your closing to summarize. But you do not have to be obvious about it. Certainly you do not want to begin your last paragraph with "In conclusion," or "To summarize:".

If you close down with a call for some kind of action, lead up to it. Don't put that call all in one final paragraph. Whatever kind of closing you choose, don't let it appear to be tacked on. Integrate it with the body of the article.

As with the title and opening, you would be thinking about a good closing paragraph or paragraphs early in your article's development. You might even write the closing before you write the remainder of the article.

But the closing should conform to the theme or mood of the article. If your article is basically serious, you would want a serious closing. If it is lighthearted, you would want to conclude with a humorous touch. To make sure that his readers understand that he is only fooling in his "How to Write a Thesis without Really Thinking" article in *Phi Delta Kappan,* Kenneth McIntyre ends on this note:

> Don't forget to write a page of acknowledgments, in which you should implicate your supervising professor and any other accomplices, as well as your typist and even your wife, "without whose loving assistance, encouragement, and forbearance this thesis could never have been written." Don't bother to mention me, even if this article has been helpful. I have enough troubles of my own.

Stan Federman, writing a personality sketch for *The Oregonian* about a blind piano tuner who also runs a five-piece combo, ends on a light note. It is an appropriate ending considering the fact that his subject was a man who didn't take himself seriously.

> He calls the group Rip Edwards and the Henweighs. He claims the name came to him in a shower one night ("I get some of my best ideas in the shower").
> Henweighs??? What's a henweigh?

"Oh, about two and a half pounds," he laughs with the look of a man who has been waiting for you to ask that very question.

Sometimes the way to end is with a gimmick. *National Review* ends a short item quoting two unfavorite politicians like this:

Zzzzzzzzzzzzzzz.

The nature of the subject matter can suggest the gimmick. Cleveland Amory, devoting part of one of his "Curmudgeon-at-Large" columns in *Saturday Review* to *The Nothing Book*, a best seller with only blank pages, ends with this sentence:

And we wish we had a funny ending for this piece. We have, however, done the next best thing. We have left you two blank lines.

The space separating that item from the next item in his column (three picas, if you want to know) is considerably more generous than usual.

David Sendler in "Pre-mortems," an article in *Lithopinion*, deals with self-written epitaphs. He quotes any number of them. One is Dorothy Parker's:

Excuse my dust.

Another is H. L. Menken's:

If, after I depart this vale,
you ever remember me
and have a thought to please my ghost,
forgive some sinner
and wink your eye at some homely girl.

In the spirit of his quotations, Sendler closes down his article like this:

Finally, an article's epitaph:
  The End.

With the public's preoccupation these days with the mass media and their inner workings, some writers take their readers into their confidence, showing how their articles evolve. The article itself becomes the subject. This is an approach that can easily get out of hand, but if you use it, carry it through to the end. Here's how Don McKinney ends an article in *True* on "Nonfiction: How the Pros Write It":

> To sum things up, I won't sum things up. That part of an article always bores me. If you want to know what I said, go back and read it again.

• Kinds of Closings

Earlier in this chapter you considered 15 ways of opening an article: The Narrative, The Shocking Statement, The Description, The Generalization, The Informative Paragraph, The Summary, The Direct Address, The Quotation, The Question, Humor, Enigma, The Surprise, The Teaser, The Comparison, Unorthodox Handling. You could almost consider the list as a list of closings, as well. Most of the kinds of openings can also serve as kinds of closings. Especially useful are The Narrative, The Description, The Information Paragraph, The Summary, and The Surprise. And let's add a new category: The Tie to the Opening. We'll take it up first.

• The Tie to the Opening.
To use this kind of closing you plant a fact, idea, or story at the beginning of the article, forget it as you move to the middle, then look back on it at the end.

Joseph Epstein uses this kind of closing for his "Professing English" article in *Commentary*, arguing against the premise that teaching correct English usage is elitist. In the early part of the article he had referred to the acceptance of the split infinitive as symptomatic of the problem.

> Which brings me back to the split infinitive. In alerting students to its existence in the world I suppose I can be accused of wishing to train good capitalists. The split infinitive, questions of usage, the study of prose rhythm and of the principles of argument, none of this, it is true, is going to bring about the socialist revolution — an event I, for one, await with no impatience. What it does do is to give students and their teachers a feeling of beginning afresh, an opening into all the possibilities of human expression that the last twenty years in English studies have done so much to destroy.

- **The Narrative.** Now that you have read the opening to *The Postman Always Rings Twice*, perhaps you would like to read the ending.

First, some background: The hero is about to be executed, not for an earlier murder, for which he is guilty, but for the accidental death of his girlfriend accomplice. A touch of irony. All right; here's the hero talking (the novel is written in first person):

> Here they come. Father McConnell says prayers help. If you've got this far, send one up for me, and Cora, and make it that we're together, wherever it is.

The narrative closing works for an article as well as for a short story or novel. Used at the end, though, the narrative should be shorter than when used at the beginning. The narrative serves as a sort of riding-off-into-the-sunset ending, with the point of the article already made in preceding paragraphs.

William K. Zinsser, after just about deciding that widespread use of saltpeter to curb sexual desire is a myth, ends his article (mentioned in the preceding chapter) with a trip to the druggist to check the mysterious substance. Was it as easy to detect in food or drink as one of his interviewees said? He put a small amount in a cup of coffee. Then:

> Shakily I lifted the cup and took a sip. It tasted terrible. I started to take another swallow, but some invisible force — some primal instinct that came from I know not where — pushed my hand back to the table. I took the cup out to the kitchen and poured the coffee down the drain. A man can't be too careful.

- **The Description.** The descriptive closing, less common than other closings mentioned here, requires literary skills. Roberta Taussig provides an example from a feature she did for the Bluffton (Ohio) *News*. Her subject was a summer art class. Students had been sprawled on the grass sketching a church building.

> At which point art period ended, and the artists, herded along by art assistant Kay Motter, walked back to school, boards and drawings under their arms.
>
> Left behind, the church, now thoroughly drawn and sketched, stood impassively in the cool sunshine, and the lawn, flattened in artist-shaped patches, began the slow work of straightening itself back up.

• **The Informative Paragraph.** Where space is at a premium, and where the article serves to inform, the last paragraph works as hard as any other paragraph to impart information.

Ted Morgan uses numbers to draw a contrast if not to point out an irony in his article, "Oz in the Astrodome," appearing Dec. 9, 1973 in *The New York Times Magazine*. His subject was the then 15-year-old Guru Maharaj ji. Some 15,000 to 20,000 persons had attended the Millennium there after much international ballyhoo. The article's end went like this:

> Volunteers began to dismantle the stage and roll up the red carpeting that covered the Astroturf. By contrast, the Divine Light Mission had 8 hours to clear the stadium, so that the Astrodome people would have time to get it ready for the Sunday football game between the Cleveland Browns and the Houston Oilers. By noon, the Astrodome's "Earthmen," dressed in orange, were vacuuming the field, and soon 37,230 football fans watched the Browns beat the Oilers, 23 to 13.

Giving the exact score for a routine football game, and ending the article with that score, helps show the insignificance of the big meeting the article reported on.

Mark Goodman, in *New Times*, salutes George Blanda upon his being released by the Oakland Raiders in 1976. "George Blanda became an improbable knight-errant in black-and-silver armor to the lame, the halt, the sclerotic and the just plain out-of-breath, an ornery, grizzled beacon announcing to his followers that, no matter what their bosses and their children and their TV sets drummed into their brains, life in America did not have to end at 40." Goodman concludes on this note:

> But it does have to end sometime. The Oakland Raiders announced only weeks before his 49th birthday that George Blanda had been placed on waivers again; this time there was no reprieve. He pointedly said goodbye to only a few teammates, threw his golf bags in the back of his car and stormed off. His records will stand forever: 342 games played and 2,002 points scored in 26 seasons. And if the stoutest men in Blanda's violent world cursed him and hated him and dueled in blood and pain with him under somber Sunday skies, it will also be recorded that not one of them had whatever it takes to play pro football until he was, by God, 49 years old.

A remarkable ending when you consider that in that one paragraph is some news, some narrative, some statistics, some opinion, a tribute. The "by God," which interrupts the flow in the last take, helps convey the writer's strong feeling.

• **The Summary.**   This is the obvious — and sometimes the best — way to end. You expect this kind of ending on a scholarly or technical piece. But you find it on other articles as well.

William Barry Furlong uses a summary to end his article in *The New York Times Magazine* on Mark Fidrych, the flakey Detroit Tigers rookie pitching sensation. Fidrych, Furlong argues, is more than a fad. We come in on Furlong after the last paragraph has started:

> He is an experience — existential, romantic. He is almost an act of faith in an age of doubt, a happy display of innocence in a time of cunning. He won renown by seeming to talk to baseballs. But whether or not baseballs got the message, one thing is clear: the people did.

Furlong had already established the fact that fans had warmed up to Fidrych. The ending therefore is not tacked on. It follows naturally the paragraphs that precede it.

• **The Surprise.**   Once in a while you may choose to end on a note that may be in the right mood but that is completely out of character in the mode of expression. Nora Ephron uses such an ending for her "A Few Words About Breasts" article in *Esquire*.[9] In the body of the article, Ephron tells of the agonies and absurdities of growing up small-breasted; about buying a Mark Eden Bust Developer, sleeping on her back for four years, and splashing cold water on her breasts every night because a well-endowed actress in an interview said that was what she did. Ephron also talks about bathing suits with built-in busts. ("That was the era when you could lay an uninhabited bathing suit on the beach and someone would make a pass at it.")

The beauty of this paragraph you are about to read is that the final

[9] You can see it — and other great articles — in the magazine's 40th anniversary issue, October 1973. The issue is available in book form: *Esquire: The Best of 40 years*, David McKay Co., New York, 1974.

word is so unexpected. In 1972, when the article orginally appeared, we did not see it often in print. And Ephron does not use language like that anywhere else in the article, making its appearance at the end all the more dramatic.

One last explanation to put this paragraph in context. Ephron's preceding paragraphs admit that the 1960s and 1970s instilled a better attitude among men and women about breasts. And the paragraph just before the last paragraph mentions women who tell Ephron that, really, growing up in the 1950s with big breasts had been more a problem than a blessing. "They couldn't sleep on their stomachs. They were stared at whenever the word 'mountain' cropped up in geography. . . . They had a terrible time of it, they assure me. I don't know how lucky I was, they say." Then:

> I have thought about their remarks, tried to put myself in their place, considered their point of view. I think they are full of shit.

Mostly the surprise ending involves content rather than form. And you see it most frequently on short features used by newspapers for change of pace on pages heavy with news.

• Three Kinds of Closings to Avoid

Handled right, any kind of a closing can work. But three kinds continue to give writers trouble and annoy readers. One is the pat-on-the-head closing, in which the writer gives the reader a friendly last word or two:

> Good luck!

With an exclamation mark yet. A civil remark to make when the instruction is offered in person, but in print a "Good luck!" offered seriously strikes some readers as condescending. (If good luck really did attend to all the persons who read a how-to-do-it, the writer might find the resultant competition so intense he would curse the day he ever gave away his secrets.) Not that you don't want to offer the reader some encouragement at the end. Of course you do, if improving his well-being has been the purpose of your piece. But you can good-luck him in more useful terms.

JoAnne Alter really says "Good luck!" in the last paragraph of her "Little-Known Ways You can Earn Extra Money at Home" article in *Family Circle*, without the words (but with the exclamation mark). The paragraph followed a warning against "'work-at-home' schemes that yearly exploit tens of thousands of women looking for ways to earn some extra money."

> The best and most satisfying way to earn money at home is to use your time, talents and creativity to benefit yourself, not some promoter. There are legitimate opportunities aplenty for making good money at home. All you need do is take advantage of them!

The second closing to avoid is the one that goes like this:

> For further information, contact. . . .

This kind of closing makes your piece sound too much like a piece of puffery turned out by a PR organization.

The third kind of closing to avoid — it is closely related to a "Good luck!" closing — is the "Amen" or "I'll drink to that " closing, with or without an exclamation mark. Unlike the "Good luck!" closing, which follows a how-to piece, the "Amen" closing follows an opinion piece. It is an agreeable way to end only if handled imaginatively, as in the *National Review* gimmick example cited earlier. Too often it consists of a couple of ordinary or even trite words tacked on as a separate paragraph, adding nothing to the reader's understanding but serving to dilute the force of the real last paragraph.

A writer for the Eugene (Oreg.) *Register-Guard* ends a feature on Oregon's former Gov. Tom McCall like this:

> Overall, Tom McCall is as feisty as ever, apparently brimming with good health and his characteristic good humor. He misses being governor, but is genuinely unsure about whether he wants to jump into a major political race again, at the age of 65 in two years. But, as one observer during his League [of Women Voters] speech last Wednesday said, "He sounds more like a candidate than an elder statesman."
>   True enough.

How much does the last line add? Wouldn't the ending, a summary, work just as well without it, even though the real ending is someone else's direct quote? Isn't "elder statesman" or "than an elder statesman" a better thought for the reader to walk away with than "True enough"?

The writer gets in one last lick here, no doubt, to compensate for the fact that someone else ends the article for him. Or it may be that after spending so much time on the feature the writer can't accept the fact that the job is done.

• THE BIG THREE IN CONTEXT

A way to end this chapter is to reprint a short article to show how title, opening, and closing work together to develop a theme. The article happens to be a column written by the author for *IABC News*, a monthly for company magazine editors published by the International Association of Business Communicators. Like many columns, this carries a running title, "The Look of the Book,'" with a special title each month narrowing in on the subject. Note how a planted idea in the beginning comes up again at the end.

THE TYRANNY OF DESIGN

Not quite two years ago *New York* magazine ran an article by Linda Abrams called "Living with a Fussy Man." It started out with "Living with an art director isn't easy" and proceeded to chronicle a list of complaints from various women who had experimented with so precarious an arrangement.

The basic problem, it turned out, had to do with decor. An art director is "obsessively involved with his environment." The non-art director in any kind of living arrangement ends up, as one wife expressed it, "feel[ing] like a guest in my own home." One complainant said that whenever she arranged some flowers, her art-director husband would walk into the room and promptly rearrange them.

George Lois, the advertising art director who used to do the *Esquire* covers, is quoted as saying: "When I come home from work, the first thing I do is hug my wife and the second thing I do is go around the apartment and rearrange everything so that it is placed perfectly, the way I want it."

"The home to an art director is a giant layout with endless possibilities," Ms. Abrams wrote. "Not only is he interested in what the furniture looks like, but also the shower curtains, picture frames, door knobs, dishes, Christmas cards (an important symbol of taste that everyone sees), and appliances.

"Better a toaster should be a Braun than a G.E. — the G.E. may be more functional, but the Braun is better designed."

She added: "Dining room tables look like they've been set with a T-square and every corner is a still life waiting to be photographed."

Words used to describe art directors in Ms. Abrams's article seemed to fall mostly in the "egotistical," "rigid," and "meticulous" categories. About all that emerged on the credit side of living with an art director was that at least he "will never leave his socks on the living-room floor."

As one who likes to identify himself with art directors, I found the article unsettling. I confess to most of the transgressions there catalogued. I have this feeling that a chair not quite at a right angle to the wall causes lower-back pain. I get the impression that food served on Danskware not only tastes better than food served on ordinary earthenware but probably is more nutritious as well.

I have the usual Eames chair in my studio, of course, and never mind that it was designed for a five-foot-eighter rather than a six-footer. Who needs support for the back of his neck as he lounges?

For more than twenty years I put up with a wafer-thin Olivetti Lettera 22 (in light olive) that hopped all over my Jens Risom desk as I met, just barely, my various writing deadlines. Only recently have I mustered the courage to disrupt the visual lineup in my studio by bringing in a clunky 1920s Underwood No. 5, the only machine ever produced that, with its sprightly touch, converts the task of typing into a form of recreation.

My choice of a watch narrowed down to the Movado "museum time-piece" with its plain black face interrupted only by a small gold ball where the "12" is supposed to be. Breathtaking in its stark beauty. But ask me the time, and all I can tell you is that it is either before noon — or after.

My fountain pen is a matte-finish chrome-and-black Lamy 2000, a stunning artifact but almost impossible to hold onto as you write because of the cone-shaped tip and because two metal clips, there to hold the cap in place when the pen is at rest, dig into your fingers.

An art director puts up with all this because he cannot help himself. His feel for design becomes a disease. The tyranny of design is that it compromises the sound judgment of those whose lives it touches.

The art director's DTs (design tyrannies) follow him from home to job. An art director at one of the glamour magazines, in a previous, more innocent decade, used to airbrush out the navels of swimsuit-clad models and paint them higher up on the torsos where, he was confident, they really belonged. God had His strengths, but what did He know about design?

The art director has come a long way in magazine journalism since those experimental days in the 1920s and 1930s when the slicks began assigning the page-layout job to experts instead of word-oriented editors or people in the back shop. Today, when the art director speaks, the editor listens. On some mastheads, the art director ranks right up there next to the editor. On some magazines, the art director has a say on content as well as form. It is not unusual for a manuscript to be accepted or rejected on the basis of how well it lends itself to illustration, the art director being in on the decision. It is not unusual for copy length for a manuscript to be dictated by an art director concerned with how nicely the columns will line up.

A measure of the art director's influence on magazines today can be seen in the depressed state of the gag cartoon, an art form perfected by *The New Yorker*, which continues to act as our best cartoon showcase. Elsewhere, though, the gag cartoon barely survives. . . . In the impressively designed company magazines, gag cartoons have fallen from favor. And all because art directors find them intrusive on the page.

Perhaps some unpleasant encounter with an art director led J. B. Handelsman to this masterful idea: The cartoon shows Saint Peter standing at the gates of heaven talking to a worried-looking man on the outside. In back of Saint Peter is an art director (you can tell he's an art director by his hair style and the mod clothes). Says Saint Peter to the man outside: "I'm terribly sorry. The art director thinks your ears are too big."

The company magazine editor keeps in mind the tyrannies design brings as he collaborates with his in-house or consulting art director. While bowing to the art director's superior design training and feel, the editor nevertheless does not — should not — accept without question every dictate on type and picture choice and placement. He remembers, for instance, the art director's pitch for a typeface last year that gets only scorn from the same art director this year. Fickleness is part of the tyranny.

There is one question that the editor, in fairness to his reader, must keep in readiness for the art director bent on some new design approach.

The question is "Why?"

Why that type rather than this one?

Why that kind of art?

Why that cropping?

Without at least that much participation in the design of his magazine the editor becomes a guest in his own home.

CHAPTER 11

NEWSPAPER FEATURES

While some magazines list "feature editors" in their mastheads and call short nonfiction pieces "features," the word really belongs to newspapers. It is a versatile word, serving both as a verb and as a noun. As a verb, "feature" means "play up," as in "feature the old man in your story." As a noun, it means about what "article" means in the magazines. It can also refer to a syndicated column, a puzzle, a comic strip, an editorial cartoon — anything going into news or editorial columns other than straight news stories and editorials.

"Feature" is a word that has given editors and teachers problems for years, says Prof. Neale Copple, who heads the journalism school at the University of Nebraska. "All they have to do is mutter the magic word, 'feature,' and the reporter changes hats.

"Suddenly, his imagination comes alive. He works at being interesting. He writes brightly. He writes lightly. He writes humanly about human beings. Ask yourself if that's not the way every decent story should be written. If featurizing means making a story readable, then it is part of all well written stories. If it means making human beings out of the people in the news, then substitute it for 'humanizing' and let's go on with it. Humanizing or featuring is a tool of depth reporting."[1]

Prof. George A. Hough, 3rd, of Michigan State University says that "Features deal with qualities of human nature and situations which we all understand because they are the kind of things that happen, or

---

[1]Neale Copple, *Depth Reporting: An Approach to Journalism*, Prentice-Hall, Inc., Englewood Cliffs, N.J., 1964, p. 17.

"When I want a Jimmy Breslin touch I'll *hire* Jimmy Breslin!"

could happen, to anyone. The feature exploits our interest in other people and reminds us that we all share a common experience."[2]

Prof. Mitchell V. Charnley of the University of Minnesota observes that a feature contains "material selected for presentation primarily because of some element other than . . . timeliness. . . ." Timeliness can play a part in a feature, he adds; but it doesn't play a major part.[3]

Spencer Crump, chairman of the journalism department of Orange Coast College, concludes that "There is . . . no way of categorizing feature stories by standards agreeable to all journalists. Even those working side by side on one newspaper probably would give various definitions."[4]

[2]George A. Hough, 3rd, *News Writing*, Houghton Mifflin Company, Boston, 1975, p. 123.

[3]Mitchell V. Charnley, *Reporting* (Third Edition), Holt, Rinehart and Winston, New York, 1975, p. 302.

[4]Spencer Crump, *Fundamentals of Journalism*, McGraw-Hill Book Company, New York, 1974, p. 133.

• FEATURES AND ARTICLES: THE DIFFERENCES

Features in newspapers and articles in magazines share more similarities than differences, and the differences that do exist vary a great deal, depending upon which newspapers and which magazines are used in the comparison. But in general, features differ from articles in these ways:

1. Features are shorter because (1) most of the nonadvertising space in newspapers must go to news, and (2) newspaper readers, diversified as they are, expect a little coverage of a lot of things.
2. Features use shorter paragraphs because some newspapers still run narrower columns than magazines run. A long paragraph set to a narrow measure looks longer than a paragraph set in a normal width.

Too many lines without an identation can discourage readers. Note how Edgar Williams breaks up a long paragraph of direct quotation in this Philadelphia *Inquirer* feature on ordination of women:

> "Ever since childhood," Judith Heffernan said, "I've had this drive to become a Catholic priest. For a long time it seemed an impossible dream. But now —"
>
> But now?
>
> "Now I can see it happening. The way things are moving along, I can see myself being ordained before my 50th birthday."

Williams's "But now?" not only nicely breaks up a quotation, but it also tells the reader an interview is going on. Furthermore, it helps prevent the feature from turning into a series of same-size paragraphs, something that happens too often in newspapers.

3. Features appeal to readers in general. Magazines build their audiences out of persons with specialized interests. A newspaper feature may have to do a little more backgrounding than a magazine article on the same subject would do.
4. Features deal mainly with local matters.
5. Features are not above celebrating the trivial. When fifth-grade teacher John Gardner of Garden Grove, Calif., tried in 1976 to establish a world record for the number of women and girls to sit on his lap (one at a time), AP moved Laurinda Keys's feature over

Figure 11.1 Chuck Hilty, conducting a "People" column of odds and ends for the St. Louis *Post-Dispatch*, needed some art for a short item, rewritten from wire service copy, about a woman who plays a piano backwards. Words alone could not describe what the woman really did. And no photograph was available. So Hilty called on staff artist Paul Stoddard, who produced this clarifying yet light-hearted pen-and-ink sketch.

its wires to newspapers everywhere. It was not a piece of writing to make the pages of a magazine, except perhaps for a brief "personals" mention or an anecdote in a bigger article on the lengths people go to to earn mention in the *Guinness Book of World Records*.

6. Features can cater to the interests of small segments of the total audience. In contrast, with as few as half a dozen articles making up an issue of a magazine, each article must carry some appeal for all the subscribers.

7. Features can ride on the material gathered from a single source.

8. Features focus less on causes, trends, and ideas, and more on events.

9. Written against a tighter deadline, features rely more on direct quotes than articles do. Reproducing quotations takes less time than paraphrasing them and putting them into some kind of perspective.
10. Needing to crowd a lot of material into little space, features can't always offer strong transitions between sentences and paragraphs. And features usually do not show the strong organization articles show.

Again, these are only generalizations. They do not accurately describe the nature of features published by some newspapers. And in some cases they describe what happens to show up in newspapers, not what editors would like to publish.

• FEATURES AND NEWS STORIES: THE DIFFERENCES

"The feature reporter casts a wide net in search for facts, sometimes pulling in and using things a news reporter would consider frivolous," says Prof. William L. Rivers of Stanford University. "The feature writer's report provides a reading experience that depends more on style, grace, and humor than on the importance of the information."[5]

"The difference between news and feature stories is largely one of intention," says Professor Emeritus Curtis D. MacDougall of Northwestern University. ". . . unorthodox journalistic rhetorical methods, customarily associated with feature writing, may be used to improve ordinary news stories in which the writer's purpose is to be informative about overt happenings. On the other hand, a feature article emphasizing human interest may be composed according to the standard rules for formal news writing."[6]

Sometimes a straight news story becomes a feature in spite of itself, as in Frank J. Prial's front-page New York *Times* story for Dec. 6, 1975. The lead went like this:

A New Yorker who played the role of a thief on the television show "To Tell the Truth" was arrested and charged with being a real thief after a Dutchess County policeman recognized him on his home screen.

[5]William L. Rivers, *Free-Lancer and Staff Writer: Newspaper Features and Magazine Articles* (Second Edition), Wadsworth Publishing Company, Inc., Belmont, Calif., 1976, p. 39.

[6]Curtis D. MacDougall, *Investigative Reporting* (Sixth Edition), Macmillan Publishing Co., Inc., New York, 1972, p. 490.

Not only do features overlap news stories; they also overlap investigative or interpretive stories. MacDougall suggests that "Becoming proficient as a feature writer is excellent preparation for interpretive reporting and writing of more significant happenings in city, state, nation, and the world."[7]

The less often a newspaper comes out, the more likely it is to prefer the feature to the news story. Weekly newspapers tend to devote a larger proportion of their newsholes to features than daily newspapers do, especially if you count the materials supplied by public relations organizations. While daily newspapers subscribe to both wire services and feature syndicates to supplement what their own staffs produce, weeklies subscribe only to the syndicates, some of which offer stories, comics, puzzles, and other material designed for the weeklies' less big-city-oriented audiences.

• WHO WRITES FEATURES?

Freelance writers produce many of the articles appearing in magazines. Staff writers (reporters) produce most of the features appearing in newspapers.

Feature writers enjoy some advantages over article writers. Although, like any writers, they must put up with some editing, they write with a virtual certainty that what they turn over to their editors, whether it is great or just passable, will be published. They can count on regular pay checks. But on a newspaper, writers may be expected to turn out straight news stories as well as features. Only on the larger papers, usually, can writers specialize in features. As feature-writing specialists they would not then be assigned to beats. They would generate many of the stories they work on.

The feature writer on a newspaper is likely to be the writer with a vivid imagination, a sense of humor or at least a light touch with words, and a feel for the bizarre as well as for the bazaar. Freaks of nature, for instance, continue to draw the attention of feature writers across the nation, and as growing season begins, those writers may find themselves taking on the added function of "onion editor." An "onion editor" takes down details offered by breathless citizens that they have raised a carrot that looks like the President or a tomato that

[7]Curtis D. MacDougall, *op.cit.*, p. 505.

"I hear you're working on a feature on air pollution."

resembles a bunch of grapes or that they have found some kind of animal that seems out of character. One feature writer wishes he had retained the newsperson's traditional and celebrated skepticism. On April 19, 1976 Douglas Ilka of the Detroit *News* did a feature about the discovery of Siamese twin toads, "A one in a million biological occurrence." "The little toad's front legs grow into the top of the front legs on the larger toad," Ilka explained. He had been careful enough to check his story with a biology professor who told him over the phone: "I have heard of it happening with frogs but this is the first time I have heard of twin toads." A photograph of the finder, one

Vince Sadzinski, holding his toads, accompanied the story. One toad appeared to be riding on top of the other.

Jeffrey Hadden took over the story the next day with a new development. The twin toads, it turned out, were, er, "merely a harbinger of spring" engaged in "the timeless process of populating their corner in Warren [near Detroit] with more toads." Left overnight in a bucket of water, the toads had separated, leaving a layer of eggs.

Columnist Pete Waldmeir added his comments the following day under the heading, "Mother Nature's Wonder Just an X-Rated Show." "The office know-it-alls, as you might expect, were merciless in their ridicule of the [original] story," he reported. "For my part, . . . I think the story was delightful.

"Warts and all."

A feature can generate enough interest to make other staff members on a newspaper decide to get in on the act. When the "Siamese twin toads" reported on in the Detroit *News* turned out to be two ordinary toads engaging in the rites of spring (see the account in this chapter), editorial cartoonist Draper Hill approached the story from the standpoint of the toads, who had reason to object to all the publicity. (*Cartoon courtesy of Draper Hill.*)

"It's something about an invasion of privacy."

Even the paper's new editorial cartoonist, Draper Hill, got in on the act. On the day of Waldmeir's column, he showed a couple of angry toads on a lawyer's desk (you could tell one of the toads was a female because she had long eyelashes) with a puzzled lawyer looking up at his secretary, who explains: "It's something about an invasion of privacy."

Typically on a newspaper, the feature writer is able to see things in major — and trivial — events that escape the notice of ordinary observers or even veteran straight-news reporters. Chuck Hilty, putting together a "People" column from wire service dispatches for the St. Louis *Post-Dispatch*, came up with a short item about a jail inmate who escaped while playing basketball. Keep your eye out for him, Hilty told his readers. "He's wearing a pair of blue jail trousers, cowboy boots and may be bouncing a basketball." He had climbed up on a roof to retrieve the basketball and then kept on going. This was Hilty's last line: "Police still haven't caught up with him to assess the biggest penalty for traveling that a basketball player has ever received."

Don't get the idea that a feature story has to be an entity bereft of social consequences. Consider: An AP reporter hears of a man imprisoned for murder for 64 years, the last 59 of them without a visitor or a letter, and so he writes a feature. The feature brings more than 3,000 letters, including one from the man's niece, who had never met him. She flies from her home in San Leandro, Calif., to near Chester, Ill., where her uncle is, and convinces a parole board that the man, then 84, should be released to her custody. She looks after him until 1976, when he dies — at 97.

Like a writer for a magazine, a writer for a newspaper can develop a specialty. David Shaw, a feature writer for the Los Angeles *Times*, for eight years dealt with a wide variety of subjects, many of them controversial, spending from three weeks to three months on a feature, traveling far from Los Angeles when necessary, turning in pieces ranging from 4,000 to 6,000 words (sometimes newspaper features, especially when run in installments, turn out to be longer than magazine articles). In 1974 he narrowed in on a subject: the media, including his own. His new features, often highly critical, generate more controversy than many of the earlier pieces.[8]

---

[8]David Shaw, "Newspapers Can Dish It Out, But Can They Take It?" *New York*, Nov. 15, 1976, p. 63.

Writing for a newspaper — whether producing news or features — provides a good background, often, for a magazine job. For instance on AT&T's slick *Long Lines* magazine, each of the staff members (as of 1977) worked originally for newspapers; Dana Eisele as assistant city editor of the Kansas City *Star*; Mike Miller as a reporter for the Easton (Penn.) *Express*; Lorrie Temple as religion editor for the Wichita *Beacon*, urban affairs writer for the Seattle *Post-Intelligence*, and staff writer for AP; and Michael L. Zeaman as reporter-copy editor for the *Daily Oklahoman* and copy editor for the Los Angeles *Times*.

• FEATURE POSSIBILITIES

The feature writer's interest in people makes the personality sketch a popular form for newspapers. Whenever new appointees or elected officials take office, they are ripe for personality sketches. Readers want to know something about them — what to expect from their reigns. But people don't have to be important to merit space. They may be only interesting or merely typical.

With the wave of nostalgia sweeping the country, local-history pieces and biographies of past leaders become important. Older readers, especially, appreciate features like this. Some of these readers will provide the necessary information.

The publication of a book by a local author is always meat for a feature. Los Angeles *Times* columnist Richard Buffum in 1976 constructed a column around a writer/cartoonist of nearby Newport Beach.

> I met Marv Myers walking along Marine Ave. on Balboa Island over the weekend. He was alone. Nobody walks along Marine Ave. alone. They eat frozen bananas and stare into shop windows in groups. Marine Ave. is togetherness.

After that beginning, Buffum reported that Myers was smiling even though he was alone. Something was "terribly wrong." Myers had an explanation: even though his women friends were no longer speaking to him and his men friends were afraid to be seen with him, he was enjoying brisk sales of *How Not to Catch a Man*, a self-published book dedicated to what Myers calls the "lively flock of women who helped me write this book — most of them unknowingly."

> The point is that Marv is completely responsible for the horrid comments he makes about women in his book. . . .

"Women are grabbing it off the stands, and sometimes ripping it in half," he said. But they're buying it and avoiding him. That's why Marv was smiling and alone. . . .

Buffum reprinted several paragraphs of tongue-in-cheek advice from the book and then suggested he could add some advice of his own, giving some examples. And he ended his column with this:

But I won't [add to Myer's advice]. I like to walk down Marine Ave. with my wife. It's no fun to eat frozen bananas alone.

The feature writer examines news events for their effect on the lives of readers. When a teacher's strike hit Pittsburgh in 1975, Vince Gagetta, for the *Post-Gazette*, wrote a feature suggesting ways 62,000 idled students could "keep academically alert and intellectually stimulated." The tips, directed to parents, came from local educators whom Gagetta interviewed.

Another possibility is the same-day feature that takes off from a straight-news story. Such a feature is called a "sidebar." It may go on the page with the news story; it may go on some other page.

A similar feature is the one that provides a local angle for a national story originating in another city. The writer interviews local authorities or people at random for their opinions, or describes what is happening locally and contrasts it to what is happening elsewhere.

With the increased leisure time most newspaper readers enjoy, where to go, where to eat, what to see, and how-to-build or -grow-it features become popular. With more rights groups organizing to exert their various pressures, reporters find additional sources for features.

Often the feature writer makes something out of an annual event that the editor, more out of a sense of duty than anything else, thinks should have attention. It may be the county fair, registration week at the college, the opening of the Christmas buying spree at the stores, or the first signs of spring.

The adventurous reporter will live his own feature, subjecting himself to physical and mental gymnastics and then reporting his reactions to readers. The readers enjoy the adventures vicariously. Before he left newspapering to start his own bookstore, Mike O'Brien, for the Eugene (Oreg.) *Register-Guard*, often played a George Plimpton role for readers. Once he tried being a trapeze artist. His story started like this:

When a mild-mannered reporter from the Register-Guard discovers himself dressed in tights, standing on top of a ridiculously small platform that's far higher up in the air than he has ever had any desire to be, and when he discovers further that he's in front of 2,000 to 2,500 onlookers, the question that comes to his mind is:

"What in bloody blue blazes am I DOING here?"

O'Brien took a couple of paragraphs to tell how he got there and then wrote:

If most of my previous aerial experience hadn't been limited to slipping on icy sidewalks and falling down stairs, the situation wouldn't have been so absurd.

There were three other "aristocrats of the circus" (Ringmaster Parley Baer's phrase) up there on the platform with me.

There were several differences between them and me.

Probably the most notable was the fact that the gals, Kim and Dorothy, and the guy, Rusty, looked good in tights.

That is not to say that I looked bad in tights. Actually, if you like the looks of a garden hose disfigured by random lumps, you'd have been quite taken with my appearance.

The other primary difference between me and these three members of the Flying Artons was to become obvious as things got underway. This was that they knew what they were doing. . . .

The story went on to recount his awkward efforts before falling safely into the net.

Another time he decided to take part in a playoff with a grandmaster at chess who was taking on 45 opponents at one time. O'Brien lost so quickly that, considering his $5 entry fee, he figured each move cost him $1.67.

A number of persons came up to talk to him after the match. O'Brien concluded his story on this note:

Probably the worst blow was dealt by a woman who was trying to be kind.

"Congratulations for staying as long as you did," she said. "I understand a person can get clobbered in as little as three moves."

"I did."

"Oh, I thought it was five," she said, backing away.

And I folded up my board and stole off into the night.

A stunt as a clown turned sour, because the professional clown who talked him into it turned out to be a character O'Brien lost respect for. The professional clown suggested the stunt to cheer up youngsters at a local hospital. But it developed that he was more interested in the publicity than good works. In his feature, O'Brien said he should have expected as much.

On his first trip into the Register-Guard to set things up, he brought along no less than five different tear sheets from other newspapers around the country, all of which detailed precisely the same stunt — and all of which featured prominent pictures of . . . [him].

Still, the idea seemed worth pursuing, so O'Brien allowed himself to be made up as a clown, and he accompanied the real one on the hospital calls. What turned O'Brien off was his companion's quick dismissal of the youngsters and the constant calling for a photographer.

It was a different kind of feature O'Brien turned out later that day. It criticized the clown as much as it detailed the adventure. The *Guard* gave the feature this headline: "A Very Unfunny Visit to a Hospital." It was a story the professional clown probably did not include in his presentation to the newspaper in the next town where the circus played.

The bigger the newspaper, the better the chance that a feature can go into general-interest matters. Ken McKenna, in the New York *Daily News,* did a 1,100-word feature on "Goofing Off: A Not-So-Fine-Art." He reminded readers that goofing off involves not showing up for work as well as not working hard while there, and added that doing only what you are asked to do and no more is also a form of goofing off. He offered statistics, quoted authorities, cited books, brought in anecdotes, gave case histories, and ended with someone else's quote:

". . . Most people fundamentally are not happy goofing off."

With the article went a cartoon illustration of a business executive flying paper airplanes into a waste basket and a boxed sidebar containing 260 words about a secretary, Cindy J., who didn't find her job satisfying. The combination of the three filled a full tabloid page.

It would be a mistake to assume that every newspaper feature must be written in a clever style. Like some news stories, some feature stories write themselves. "If the facts are interesting, unusual, or amusing, there is no need to interlace the story with excessive adjectives or write in a superheated style," says Prof. M. L. Stein, head of the journalism department of California State University of Long Beach. "The best written features are handled with restraint."[9]

Some features take on the serious assignment of explaining social movements and economic conditions. Few subjects these days are too

[9]M. L. Stein, *Reporting Today: The Newswriter's Handbook,* Cornerstone Library, New York, 1971, p. 98.

controversial for the feature writer to handle. On some newspapers, the feature writer can come down hard on one side or the other.

• WHEN TIME STANDS STILL

When you see a lead in your newspaper like this:

> SALT LAKE CITY — Firemen today were investigating the cause of a fire which yesterday destroyed . . .

or like this:

> PULLMAN, Wash. — Oregon's Ducks held their 12th straight track victory over Washington State today.

you know a reporter tried hard to find a "today" angle for a story that should have been written the day before. Newspaper style dictates that somewhere in the first sentence the reporter answers the question "When?" even if the newspaper is embarrassingly late with its coverage. Sometimes the story is big enough to merit coverage several days in a row. Finding a "today" angle for it each day can tax the best reporter.

But feature writers worry little about "When?" They can come onto their stories the second day or later and tell them enthusiastically, feeling no need to hide the fact of lateness. Scooping the competition does not interest these writers. They may not have to worry about deadlines, either. What they write may go into a bank against which the editor draws when colums of straight news need feature items to enliven them.

Feature writers on newspapers and with the wire services may get their training by updating the obits of persons destined to get full news and feature treatment when they die. To use a pre-written obit, an editor need only type out a new lead.

• HUMAN INTEREST AND COLOR

A feature usually is rich in human interest and color. In some newsrooms, "human interest story" or "color story" means "feature story."

A story has human interest when it involves cheesecake, sex, violence, good fortune, tragedy, cuteness, youth, old age, or animals.

The story tugs at the heartstrings or causes the reader to identify with or withdraw from the hero, villain, or victim.

A story has color when it offers details of setting and action that readers might have observed had they been there or that they may have missed while there.

Supplying color, as Charnley sees it, "depends on careful selection rather than on photographic detail. It grows out of the writer's decision on basic theme — gaiety, confusion, noise, banality, anguish, — and his choice of supporting specifics. It must not include distracting nonessentials."[10]

• ARTISTRY IN FEATURES

No doubt the writing in newspapers has improved in response to competition from other media, and the "new journalism" has helped break down some of the repressive rules in the newsrooms. But good writing could be found in newspapers back when they were our chief source of information and entertainment. It may be a little flowery by today's standards, but Bob Considine's emotional story about the second Joe Louis–Max Schmeling fight is instructive. As you read this opening for his International News Service story, remember that Louis had lost the first match in 1936, two years earlier, and that there were racial overtones here, with Schmeling coming from Nazi Germany with its attitudes of Aryan superiority.

> Listen to this, buddy, for it comes from a guy whose palms are still wet, whose throat is still dry, and whose jaw is still agape from the utter shock of watching Joe Louis knock out Max Schmeling.
>
> It was a shocking thing, that knockout — short, sharp, merciless, complete. Louis was like this:
>
> He was a big lean copper spring, tithtened and retightened through weeks of training until he was one pregnant package of coiled venom.
>
> Schmeling hit that spring. He hit it with a whistling right-hand punch in the first minute of the fight — and the spring, tormented with tension, suddenly burst with one brazen spang of activity. . . .[11]

In the old days — and to some extent today, too — the sports pages of the newspapers provided much of the writing flair. Perhaps the

[10]Mitchell V. Charnley, *op cit.*, pp. 314–315.

[11]Reprinted in Louis L. Snyder's and Richard B. Morris's *A Treasury of Great Reporting*, Simon and Schuster, New York, 1949, pp. 532, 533.

most memorable lead ever written came from Grantland Rice following a Notre Dame–Army football game.

> Outlined against a blue-gray October sky, the Four Horsemen rode again.
> In dramatic lore they are known as Famine, Pestilence, Destruction and
> Death. These are only aliases. Their real names are Stuhldreher, Miller,
> Crowley and Layden. They formed the crest of the South Bend cyclone be-
> fore which another fighting Army football team was swept over the prec-
> ipice at the Polo Grounds yesterday afternoon as 55,000 spectators peered
> down on the bewildering panorama spread on the green plain below.

A more recent example of a good lead comes from an AP story published on the day of Jimmy Carter's first radio call-in show in 1977:

> Things to do today:
>   1. Wash the car.
>   2. Shop for groceries.
>   3. Call the President.

Then the writer got into the meat of the story: that this was the first
time a President had involved himself in such a program, that Walter
Cronkite would be there with him, that CBS was producing and paying for the program, and that chances of actually getting through to
the President were minimal.

• TRITE FEATURES

Fortunately, many newspapers have abandoned the practice of coming up each year with clever ideas for calling readers' attention to all
the special days and holidays. Their readers on St. Patrick's Day, for
instance, no longer have to face stories printed in green ink, carrying
Al Johnson bylines with "O"s in front of the last names (By Al
O'Johnson) and leads that begin, "Shure and begorra . . ." Perhaps we
have an Irish managing editor of the Seattle *Post-Intelligencer*, Ed
Stone, to thank. In 1962 he delivered to the readers of *The Bulletin of
the American Society of Newspaper Editors* "A Modest Proposal for the
Abolition of St. Patrick's Day" that pointed out:

> The newspaper cliché that the Irish are a happy-go-lucky race is as utterly
> in error as anything could be. In actual fact, the Irish are a melancholy race,
> steeped in pessimism, with their prevailing gloom periodically relieved by
> moments of exaltation.
>   Their faults and their virtues probably are pretty much on a par with
> those of other nationalities and races and why there should be a special day

set aside for their outpouring of sticky sentiment supposedly in their honor is beyond reasonable explanation. . . .

• OVERREACHING FOR A FEATURE ANGLE

It is tempting to overreach for a feature angle. An *Oregonian* reporter does it for a front-page feature on torn-up streets:

> If a guy named Joe Cantel ever runs for a city office in Portland in August, he's a cinch to get more than enough votes to win.
>
> This is because during August each year the city street crews get "mole fever" and rid themselves of the virus only by digging holes and tunnels in downtown streets.
>
> Road repair barriers — imprinted with "Cantel," the name of their man-ufacturer — surround each of the holes. Any Cantel candidate would be getting more free advertising than his combined opposition could buy.

There followed a cataloguing of streets and intersections where traffic was being stalled and rerouted. The last three paragraphs:

> And don't try to turn left off Burnside. The diggers have signs all over the place warning not to do that.
>
> Keep going straight to avoid getting hit by a truck loaded with torn-up pavement.
>
> But remember, if Joe Cantel ever runs for office, he's a good man.

This example comes from a campus newspaper:

> Wednesday might be remembered by some as "D-Day" at the University of Oregon.
>
> After a lengthy D-bate, the U of O faculty Wednesday D-cided that re-storing the D wouldn't D-grade the university's grading system.
>
> But the faculty D-layed until next month any action on the mechanics of adding the D to the grading system.
>
> The University's grades have been limited' to A, B, C and N (no-pass) since 1970 when the D was dropped. . . .

The overreaching becomes more objectionable when it plays un-fairly with lives. Under the headline "Sugar Ray is Loser, Wife Wins the Purse," the New York *Daily News* offered this beginning to a news story:

> Former world middleweight champion Sugar Ray Robinson made another comeback try, this one in Manhattan Supreme Court yesterday. He made a few feints from the witness chair, but when it was over, Sugar Ray was still down for the count.

The beginning writer tends to overreach, too, in matters of style. This from a campus newspaper:

> Sporting the svelte tongue thàt aided in precociously establishing his lofty position, Boyd chanced to quote Thomas Jefferson in the course of his arguments for ROTC.

• FEATURES FROM OUTSIDE

Much of the feature material in a newspaper comes from outside, and not directly from freelancers. It comes from the wire services, including AP and UPI, and from feature syndicates, like King Features and United Feature Syndicate. Newspapers pay for wire-service copy and syndicate material on the basis of their circulations.

Wire-service feature writers operate as newspaper feature writers do in that style matters are standardized, but they operate as article writers do in that what they write must have national or at least regional interest. Wire-service writers are regular employees. Some features distributed by the wire services were written originally by writers attached to newspapers.

Writers for the feature syndicates operate under a contract, or, in some cases, they submit work as freelancers.

Some feature material comes from PR sources and costs newspapers nothing. It is possible to work full time as a feature or article writer for a PR organization or department.

• FREELANCING TO NEWSPAPERS

Newspapers with locally edited magazine sections represent the best newspaper markets for freelancers, although the pay does not match what national magazines offer. These sections appeal particularly to freelancers who have trouble coming up with ideas that interest a national audience. Newspaper magazine sections, like newspapers themselves, prefer a local angle for features.

Because some newspapers have trouble interesting advertisers in these sections and because of the availability of syndicated magazine sections like *Parade* and *Family Weekly*, the base of the local sections is often unsteady. Some of them start off as legitimate magazines with original content but end up carrying mostly canned material and TV program schedules and notes. But the *ANPA Public Affairs Newsletter* in June 1976 reported that "More newspapers are publishing more Sunday magazines. This year 477 newspapers are publishing 590 magazines with their weekend editions. In 1975, there were 560 Sunday or weekend magazines published by 467 newspapers. Ten years ago, there were 453 Sunday or weekend magazines published in 358 newspapers." That the number of magazines in each case outnumbers the newspapers publishing them can be traced to the fact that some newspapers publish more than one. One magazine might be general-interest; another might deal with homes and gardens.

The newspaper market for freelancers does not confine itself to the magazine section. Newspapers occasionally buy features from freelancers for regular news columns. The secret of selling is to know which editor to approach. Titles and duties vary from newspaper to newspaper, but generally the city editor makes decisions on material involving the city or its immediate surroundings; the county or state editor makes decisions about material covering the fringes of the newspaper's circulation area. Sports or special-section material would go directly to the editors involved. Newspaper editors operate rather independently of each other and are not likely to pass material on to other editors. A freelancer's business with one of these editors is likely to take place in person rather than through the mails.

A newspaper seldom worries about exclusive rights. You can resell your feature to the newspaper in the next town, provided the second paper doesn't circulate in the first paper's territory. Of course, you would let the second editor know the feature had already run elsewhere.

In recent years, newspapers with circulation of 50,000 or more have established op-ed pages across from their editorial pages to carry the overflow from the letters columns, to present the work of additional columnists and cartoonists, and to publish opinion pieces by freelancers. So freelancers in some cities now have a newspaper market not only for features going into a magazine section but also for R.O.P. features (features that can fit anywhere in the "run of the paper"), and for features that read like editorials.

• FREELANCING FROM NEWSPAPERS

Not only is it possible to freelance *to* newspapers: it is possible to freelance *from* newspapers. Some newspaper staff writers, to supplement their incomes, to gain additional experience or national exposure, or to reach for a freedom of expression they feel they may not have on their newspapers, produce articles in off hours and submit them to magazines. Newspapers are more willing now to let their reporters do this, provided the moonlighting does not interfere with their performance at the office or preempt the research gathered on company time. Steve Neal, a reporter for the Philadelphia *Inquirer*, says that the only freelancing discouraged by his paper is freelancing to publications in competition with the paper, like *Philadelphia Magazine* or *The New York Times Magazine*. "Our editors encourage contributing to our own magazine and to national publications. Also, book-reviewing is encouraged."[12]

The reporter turned freelancer may find it possible to go more deeply into a subject than when writing about it for a newspaper, and to develop angles not appropriate for the newspaper's family audience. Neal, who does personality sketches for his newspaper, likes to do personality sketches — about the same people — for the magazines. "The great advantage in doing a magazine profile over a newspaper profile is having more space," he reports. "A newspaper profile can seldom be in excess of 1,000 words. A magazine piece can be anywhere from 2,500 to 5,000 words. With increased space, the subject's character and motivations can be further developed. The writer also has greater freedom to inject his opinion into the article."[13]

Even so, the feature appearing in a newspaper often bears a striking resemblance to the article appearing in a magazine. If the feature deals with a subject of interest to people outside the newspaper's circulation area, there is no reason why the feature, adjusted somewhat to meet the needs of the new audience, and the article, pruned to meet space limitations, couldn't trade places.

[12]Letter to the author from Steve Neal, Nov. 10, 1976.
[13]*Ibid.*

CHAPTER 12

Not by Words Alone

As a freelancer or staff writer for a magazine or newspaper, you need to know something about art. Your sale or placement of a piece of writing may rest on its illustrative potential and maybe even on your ability to use a camera.

To sell to the small, specialized magazines, especially the trade journals, you often have to supply photographs. Even the magazines that ordinarily assign professional photographers to take pictures at the direction of an art director after a manuscript has been accepted like to see writer-contributed photographs. In the words of Editor Art Spikol of *Philadelphia Magazine*, "they lend credibility to the subject." As editor of a company magazine, where almost certainly you would do all the writing, you probably would do the picture taking, too. As a reporter on a small newspaper and possibly even a medium-size daily, you might both take notes and snap pictures while out on a story.

All a single chapter on photography and art can do is point out some of the problems and pass along a few bits of advice. Many recently published books, including a few cited in this chapter, can give you more detailed guidance. John Hedgecoe, in *The Book of Photography* (Knopf, New York, 1976), offers unusually comprehensive coverage of the topic with plenty of illustrations.

• KINDS OF ART

Art destined to be reproduced in a magazine or newspaper falls into two categories: line art and continuous-tone art. Line art includes any-

Figure 12.1 Using fast-speed film, Stephan E. Burkhardt, editor of *The Consultant*, publication of Abbott-Northwestern Hospital Corporation, Minneapolis, captures the interest and concentration of a group of hospital executives at a hearing before the State Board of Health for permission to proceed with consolidation and renovation plans. The photograph ran on the front page of the publication to illustrate a story announcing the granting of the hospital's request. The natural poses and the natural lighting bring artistry to what could have been a very routine shot.

Figure 12.2 Another meetings shot, taken with fast film, using ordinary room light. It was one of three photographs illustrating a story in *The Visiting Fireman*, bi-weekly publication of Fireman's Fund Insurance Companies. The story described special training sessions set up by the company to familiarize staff members with a new computerized information system. Photographer William F. Lawler nicely captured the concentration of the persons who were there listening and taking notes.

thing made with black markings on white paper, particulary pen- or brush-and-ink drawings. Continuous-tone art includes photographs as well as paintings. If you add washes (water-color grays) to a line drawing, as artists do for some of the cartoons they do for *The New Yorker*, you change the line art to continuous-tone art.

Whether line or continuous-tone, all art must go through a photographic process so that plates can be made available to the printer. In the printing, line art looks just as it looked in its original state, although the platemaker may have reduced or (rarely) enlarged it. Continuous-tone art undergoes more of a change. The platemaker uses a glass "screen" to capture the grays and convert them to black dots. In the process the continuous-tone art becomes a "halftone." In the magazine or newspaper, a halftone consists of nothing but black dots arranged to create the illusion of grays. The printed photograph, then, is something quite different from the continuous-tone print made on photographic paper from the original negative.

Figure 12.3   One of a dozen photographs for an article on research associates and assistants at the University of Oregon Health Sciences Center, this one concentrates its focus on a mouse held by Dr. Marlene Wilson. Had photographer Susan Pogany kept both the researcher and the mouse in sharp focus, the photograph would have been hard to read. Notice how nicely the white of the mouse's whiskers contrasts with the blackness of Dr. Wilson's hair.

Figure 12.4 Only a view from the air could show fully the shape of the Trojan Nuclear Plant near Rainier, Oregon. Afternoon sun helped create the three-dimensional effect. Portland General Electric Company arranged with Jan Fardell of the Longview (Wash.) *Daily News* to take the photograph. *Northwest Public Power Bulletin* ran it.

For this reason, the photograph the editor starts out with had better be crisply focused with a good range of tones, from very dark to very light. It is inevitable that what is reproduced in the magazine or newspaper will be inferior to what the platemaker starts out with.

The finer the screen, the better able the platemaker is to hold onto the detail of the photograph. But a fine screen requires printing on good quality paper. One reason magazines were able to offer readers better halftones than newspapers could was that magazines were printed on smooth stock. When newspapers finally switched from letterpress printing to offset lithography, they were able to improve picture quality. Offset allows for fine-screen printing on newsprint-quality stock.

• Illustrations

While photographs can illustrate, the mass media reserve the word "illustration" for art produced by persons who draw or paint rather than persons who use a camera. And while writers who produce art usually

Figure 12.5(a and b) Photographer Jan Fardell shot the interior of the Trojan Nuclear Plant with existing light. The figure occupies the "optical center" of the picture, a spot slightly above the real center and a bit to the left. Note that the lines of perspective lead to the figure. The looseleaf book in the foreground helps identify the scene. Tom Santee, editor of *Northwest Public Power Bulletin*, needed a vertical photograph, so he cropped what he had to make the picture at the left. That the photograph could take such cropping made it particularly valuable to the editor.

Figure 12.6 Sometimes a posed shot, head-on, is the best way of showing people involved in a story. This photograph illustrated a feature about Joe Mocny (above, left) and his wife Donna, owners of a barbeque restaurant. Photographer Duncan McDonald arranged his subjects (the owners and, at right, the chef they hired) to include steps to the restaurant and the sign marking the establishment. The rather formal arrangement made possible easy reading of the small sign. *(Photo by Duncan McDonald.)*

Figure 12.7 Another shot showed owner Joe Mocny demonstrating to employees how to flip barbequed ribs. (*Photo by Duncan McDonald.*)

HOLD
IT!

Figure 12.8 Art Spikol, executive editor of *Philadelphia Magazine*, uses his own cartoon to illustrate one of his columns for *Writer's Digest*. The column, called "Nonfiction," dealt this time with "Push-Button Journalism." In listing Spikol's accomplishments as an advertising art director and creative director, magazine art director, and magazine editor, *Writer's Digest*, in a legend under the column, said he "did all of this while going blind, with one hand tied behind his back."

use a camera rather than a drawing board or easel, a few paragraphs about illustrations may be useful here.

Think of illustrations as pencil, chalk, or ink drawings; oil, acrylic, designer-color, or water-color paintings; maps, charts, graphs, and tables; collages. Editors tend to use illustrations only for short stories, photographs for articles. But sometimes articles require illustrations. Humor pieces, for instance, benefit from cartoon illustrations. Travel pieces benefit from maps. Technical pieces benefit from charts, graphs, and tables.

Editors make their own arrangement for illustrations after an article is accepted, but if you are capable of turning out professional-quality drawings or paintings, go ahead and submit them with your article. Think of how much trouble you could save an editor who finds in the mail a package of material, complete, ready to mark up and send to the printer! But be prepared to have your art rejected even if your writing is accepted. Most editors are not ready for package submissions, unless the art consists of photographs.

Louise Melton, a Framingham, Mass., cartoonist and writer, keeps her two occupations virtually separate, selling cartoons and illustrations to magazines as varied as *New Woman, Playgirl, Mechanics Illustrated, True Story, Rural New Yorker, Stag, Rotarian, Modern Medicine,* and *Evergreen Review* and articles to publications like *TV Guide, The Christian Science Monitor, Arizona,* the Providence *Journal,* and *Dynamic Maturity.* "I almost never illustrate my own work," she says. "I have found editors oddly chary of combination writer/cartoonists (Jules Feiffer notwithstanding)." I guess . . . [doing both drawing and writing] smacks of amateurishness. That doesn't mean I've given up trying. I have some features out now which I have great hopes for. . . ."[1]

Art Spikol says, "It's rather uncommon to get illustrations along with stories — I don't remember it ever happening when I was able to make use of the illustrations. I think I might have been offered illustrations twice in the last two years."[2]

Student Barrett Tillman enclosed some cartoon illustrations with his article to *Air Progress* on pilots' superstitions. The magazine bought the article (he went on to sell some sixty articles to several magazines on various aspects of aviation and is working on his second book) and

[1]Letter to the author from Louise Melton, August 20, 1976.
[2]Letter to the author from Art Spikol, Sept. 20, 1976.

Figure 12.9 Natural-light photography helps frame small-town postmaster Al Cavanaugh in the window at the back of his 100-year-old store at Mist, Oregon. The posters outside show up just enough to be recognized as posters but not enough to detract from the subject. Photographer Jeff Clausen used the photograph to illustrate a personality sketch in the magazine he edited, *Northwest Timber*, published by Crown Zellerbach Corp.

took enough note of the sketches to assign them to a professional cartoonist, who used them as models for his own sketches.

If you do submit illustrations, arrange to have Photo-Mechanical Transfers or Velox prints made from them first. More faithful to the originals than mere office-machine copies, PMTs and Velox prints can go to the editor in place of your originals, or they can stay behind as insurance in case your originals are mishandled or lost.

If you know that your drawings are not good enough to reproduce but you are convinced that drawings, not photographs, are what your article needs, submit rough sketches that can be used as guides for a professional artist. Explain in a covering letter that the sketches are not meant for reproduction. Nevertheless, it is wise to use a pen or

Figure 12.10 A photograph doesn't always need a center of interest. This photograph by David James Thompson, used to illustrate an article on turkey farming in Crown Zellerbach's *Northwest Timber*, offers readers an interesting pattern of nearly same-size turkeys behind a wire fence of nearly uniform rectangles.

marker rather than a pencil, and draw neatly and clearly (if awkwardly). Where you know your drawing does not communicate adequately, write a description in the margin and point, with an arrow, to the spot that needs improvement.

Photographs too poor to reproduce but clear enough to see can also serve an artist as reference material.

• Photographs

Thirty-five-millimeter cameras with built-in light meters and semiautomatic settings make it almost impossible to fill out a 20- or 36-exposure roll of fast film without getting at least a few pictures worth publishing. But more important than impressive equipment to the part-time photographer is a good picture sense.

Figure 12.11 To combine a window shopper with the merchandise at a shop at Cannon Beach, Oregon, photographer David James Thompson for Crown Zellerbach's *Northwest Timber* magazine, shoots from inside the store. This way, the photographer is able to show both facial expression as well as merchandise. The backlighting helps emphasize the shape of the items on sale.

An understanding of the principles of composition helps. Good composition results from careful selection and arrangement of the elements to be shown in the photograph. Normally, you would keep the number down, and you would allow one element to dominate the others. You want only one center of interest in a picture. But don't put it in the middle. Instead, move it up or down or over slightly to one side. If your subject is moving or if its shape tends to point, have it move or point *into* rather than out of the picture.

A photograph should make a single point or have a single theme. But "just as musical compositions sometimes succeed without a dominant theme, on their tonal and rhythmic values alone, photographs too may succeed without a center of interest, on their tonal or rhythmic values alone," says Prof. Marvin J. Rosen of California State University at Fullerton. "When a photograph succeeds through its use of textures, or through rhythmic repetitions of pictorial elements, usually those become the central or dominant idea. The picture is then 'about' these textures or rhythms."[3]

Don't feel that everything in your photograph has to be in focus. That kind of picture can look cluttered. Instead, try focusing on something in the foreground, letting things behind appear fuzzy; or focus on something in the distance and let unimportant items up close appear fuzzy.

You might want to frame your shot by shooting through a grove of trees, focusing on an item some distance from the camera. For example, if you want the figure of a man to show up clearly, shoot him against a plain background. You do not have to back him up against a blank wall to do it. You can silhouette him against the sky by moving your vantage point, shooting from below. You don't have to shoot all your pictures at normal eye level. Worm's-eye and bird's-eye views can strenghthen your composition.

For most of your shots you will want to move in close. But don't encourage your subject to look straight into the camera. Encourage him to conduct himself as he would if no camera were present. Don't be afraid to stage some of your shots. If you missed the action, ask your subject to repeat it.

You will discover that timing is all important to your capturing any action. If you click your shutter at the beginning or end of a golf stroke, for instance, you can suggest more action to the viewer than if you click half-way through. A dribbled basketball clicked at the moment it hits the floor looks like a medicine ball.

When photographing an inanimate object unfamiliar to your publication's readers, show it in scale. Put it in context with something readers will recognize.

But more important than any of these considerations is the message of the photograph. Is what it says relevant to the article it illustrates? Does it add a dimension, or is it merely decorative? A photograph that is artistically and technically faulty may sell to an editor because it helps the reader understand better what the article is trying to say.

Make sure you coordinate your photographs with the text. Don't let them say one thing, your text another. Pictures can lie. Don't allow a photograph to catch the subject in an uncharacteristic pose, making your carefully worded description a sham so far as the reader is concerned.

[3]Marvin J. Rosen, *Introduction to Photography*, Houghton Mifflin Company, Boston, 1976, p. 146

Figure 12.12. A child life therapist, Lurinda Mollahan, visits three-year-old Troy Shrum, victim of a traffic accident who was recovering in the hospital at the University of Oregon Health Sciences Center, Portland. The child was still quite ill, bedridden, and unable to talk, but he and his therapist communicated playfully by making faces at each other. To get the right picture, to be used to illustrate an article about therapists working in the pediatric ward, Susan Pogany, managing editor and photographer for the center's *News* magazine, took many shots, settling for this one because it "seemed to capture the warm, trustful relationship they had developed." To supplement the natural light, Pogany aimed an overhead bed light toward her subjects and shot at 1/60th of a second with a "fairly wide open" aperture.

Figure 12.13 The contact sheet showing the shots Susan Pogany took for her photograph appearing in the *News*. While the pictures may look about the same, subtle differences made the choice difficult. Pogany settled for Number 29, the first picture in the fifth row, and made an 8 x 10 glossy print, cropping it only slightly at the left.

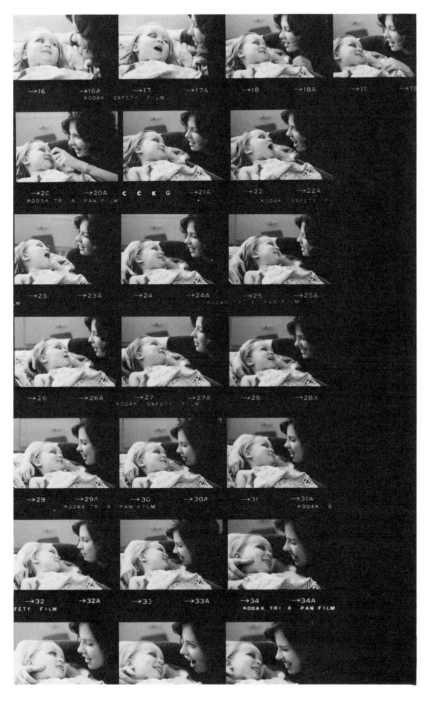

Figure 12.14 An example of the stock art available to writers and editors in *Quaint Cuts in the Chap Book Style*, one of many books in the Dover Publications Pictorial Archives series. The artist is Joseph Crawhall, chapbook artist who did woodcuts in England in the 1800s. Drawings from books in the series can be used without further payment to the publisher.

• Stock Photos and Art

Some markets are willing to accept stock photographs you can obtain from various public and private organizations. Government agencies maintain public information departments that supply photographs as well as facts to writers and editors. So do chambers of commerce, trade associations, and large companies. Often all these organizations ask is a credit line and return of the photograph after use.

You also have access to private picture agencies that, for a fee, offer stock photographs on almost any subject you can think of. But usually, editors rather than writers deal with the private picture agencies. Some of them specialize, as Culver Pictures, Inc., does with its several million historical photographs and prints.

The trouble with stock photographs, no matter the source, is that you may not find exactly what you need and you may choose a photograph that has already appeared in print. Your readers — some of them — may have seen it. On the other hand, you get professional-quality work, either free or at a price you couldn't beat if you went out after custom work.

Figure 12.15 This farmhouse at Round Hill Farm, an exhibit farm in Allegheny County, Pennsylvania, was built in 1838. Round Hill's job is to "teach the thousands of visitors the importance of agriculture and illustrate the ties that bind all men to the land for basic existence." To show the farmhouse in its proper setting, Joseph B. C. White, writing about Round Hill for *Soil Conservation*, a publication of the Soil Conservation Service, moved back and up a hill. This is a modified bird's-eye view. The figure in the foreground leads the reader into the picture and adds some scale. The Soil Conservation Service and many other government agencies make photographs like this available to writers and editors.

Picture agencies also represent a market for your own photographic work. Read their requirements as set forth in the annual *Photographer's Market,* a companion volume to *Writer's Market.*

To illustrate your article, you also have access to various collections of stock artwork. Dover Publications, New York, offers probably the best buys in stock art. It publishes dozens of inexpensive collections of pieces taken from the public domain. You can reprint this material without further payment to anybody. Of course, you are not likely to find many contemporary subjects in such collections.

• THE WRITER AS PHOTOGRAPHER

You may surprise yourself with your success at picture taking. The art involves some of the same judgments needed in writing. Clifton C. Edom, Professor Emeritus, University of Missouri, observes that "a person who learns to write achieves a discipline which carries over into his photography. He learns how to select the important elements and how to present them." But, he warns, to take pictures you "must have the sensitivity of a poet and the tough skin of a Marine Corps sergeant."[4]

Barry Lopez has enjoyed almost as much success with his photography as from his writing. The beauty of doing your own photography, he says, is that the two — copy and art — develop simultaneously. Each fits the other. In fact, Lopez's story line has often been dictated by his photographic thinking.

If you don't take pictures for publication, you can still use a camera as you use a tape recorder: to take notes. The "notes" would remind you of the appearances of people, buildings, and scenes.

• Cameras to Use

The move from the Speed Graphic to the twin-lens reflex camera to the 35-mm camera to, finally, the 35-mm SLR, along with the availability of Tri-X film, has made picture taking for publication more convenient and the photographer less conspicuous; 20- and 36-exposure rolls of film encourages photographers to take plenty of

[4]Clifton C. Edom, *Photojournalism*, Wm. C. Brown Company Publishers, Dubuque, Iowa, 1976, pp. 62, 63.

pictures on each assignment. And if they can't cock and click the shutter fast enough, photographers can use motor-driven cameras that make it possible to take pictures in split-second sequences. It was a motor-driven camera — a Nikon F — that captured the widely published series of pictures of a young mother and child falling from a fire escape in 1975, a series that earned the photographer a Pulitzer but brought some unfavorable response for capitalizing on tragedy.

Easily the most popular camera among photojournalists and photographers working for the magazines is the 35-mm SLR, available in a multitude of brands. SLR stands for "single-lens reflex." The camera's one lens allows both viewing and picture taking. What you see is what you get. (A twin-lens camera gives you a view slightly different from what you snap.) Some freelancers find that the Olympus OM-1 or OM-2 is ideal because it is about a third smaller and lighter than other SLRs and yet has the features most photographers want.

With their interchangeable lenses and superior viewing capabilities, SLRs "are the most flexible of cameras, though mechanically they are the most complex and must be cared for" says photographer Joel Siegel. "A fine camera, after all, is an incredibly complex — and beautiful — piece of equipment."[5] But the older-style cameras still meet the needs of some photographers.

A twin-lens 2¼ x 2¼ (the Rolleiflex is the best known) has the advantage of yielding larger negatives than a 35-mm, which means that you have a better chance of avoiding graininess in your blowups. And working from a basic square, you have a better chance, when ordering 8 x 10s, of going either to a horizontal or vertical. With a 35-mm, you start out with either a horizontal or a vertical; trying to make a vertical out of a horizontal, or vice versa, could be more of a problem. But the twin-lens 2¼ x 2¼ has a disadvantage in that you have to hold the camera low to focus it; you do not have the maneuverability. Another disadvantage is that with some 2¼ x 2¼ cameras you can't interchange lenses. With a 2¼ x 2¼ you have to get your variety by changing your position.

Even the Polaroid camera has its uses in publication work. Its advantage is that it makes a print available within seconds. And it is possible to rig such a camera to pre-screen the print so that it can be pasted down with columns of type and shot by the platemaker as

---

[5] Joel Siegel, *West*, Los Angeles Times, Nov. 22, 1970, p. 24.

Figure 12.16 It takes a fast shutter speed and some extra light to get this kind of an indoors shot. The player is All-American Ronnie Lee, who went on to a professional career with Phoenix. That Lee is high off the floor and off balance gives the picture its action. That the other players form a sort of triangle around him give the picture its strong composition. That the scoreboard shows in one corner helps put the picture in context. The crowd in the background adds texture to the picture. *Courtesy of the University of Oregon Athletic Department.)*

Figure 12.17 The last leg of a 440-yard relay event at a state track championship meet. The batons have just been passed. To capture the action, Duncan McDonald knelt and shot up at the runners, producing a worm's-eye view. He used a long lens, fast shutter speed, and Tri-X film. Note the interesting configuration the shadows make. That three of the runners are caught with both feet off the ground adds to the action.

though it were line art. But for most editors, Polaroid prints do not carry enough tonal range, and the photographer finds it difficult to make duplicate prints and enlargements.

If the lighting is just right and you don't have the problem of subject movement, *any* camera, including an Instamatic, can give you a picture good enough to reproduce.

If high artistry is not important to you but maneuverability is, and yet you want a camera that has a good lens and some versatility, you might want to consider one of the pocket 35s: an Olympus 35 RC, say, or a Rollei 35 miniature. You sacrifice the interchangeable-lens option, and in the original Rollei 35 miniature you have no rangefinder (you have to estimate distances), but here's what you could do with this pair: you could put color film in one and black and white film in the other, and you still would have little to haul around. The Rollei fits in your shirt pocket. The slightly larger Olympus 35 RC has an optional automatic feature. The negatives for either are full-size; you don't have to put up with half frames. Under ordinary lighting conditions, you get good, clear prints of reproducible quality.

Light availability will help you decide what shutter speed and f-opening to use. The more light you have, the faster your shutter speed and the higher your f-opening number.

Whether or not your subject is moving will also affect your choices. In general you will use shutter speeds of $1/250$ or faster when you want to capture moving subjects. Even if you use a slower shutter speed, you can capture the movement by making sure it is coming toward or away from the camera rather than across its field of vision. If it moves across, you can still capture it by "panning" the camera — moving it slightly with the moving subject.

Sometimes you want some blurring. Blurring can contribute to the feeling of speed. In that case you would use a slower shutter speed.

The higher the f-opening number, the greater your depth of field. If you want a lot of your photograph in clear focus, go with an f/16 or f/11 setting. If you want more selective focusing, go to a lower f-setting.

Of course you have to coordinate your shutter speed setting with your f-opening setting. Your light meter will help you make your decisions. Your settings become more complicated as you move to other than standard lenses.

• Lenses to Choose

You may resist using them at first, but eventually you'll find interchangeable lenses a necessity. A wide-angle lens will enable you to capture more width without stepping back too far from your subject. A telephoto lens will allow you to take close-ups without actually moving closer to the subject.

The telephoto lens foreshortens the space, cramming more into your picture than you could get otherwise. Wishing to show the clutter of signs on a tawdry street entering a town, for instance, you would make your point more dramatically than if you used an ordinary lens.

As you become more familiar with your camera and its accessories, you will be able to move back and forth more readily among regular, wide-angle, and telephoto lenses, and you will be able to improve your photographs through use of filters and supplemental light sources.

• Photographing in Color

When you move to color, your job becomes more difficult because you have one more dimemsion to consider. As much as shape, placement, and texture, color affects your composition.

You may want to adjust what your picture includes so that it concentrates on one or two colors instead of offering a rainbow of colors. Some of the best full-color pictures reproduced in magazines appear to be done in monotones. At any rate, one color should predominate.

Many photographers prefer to work with Kodachrome color film, with its warmer colors, but it is not as fast as Ektachrome, with its cooler colors. If reds are important to your shooting and you have plenty of light, you will go with Kodachrome. If blues are important and you have less light, you will choose Ektachrome.

If your market runs full-color photographs, submit transparencies or slides, not color prints. Some editors prefer 2¼ × 2¼ transparencies, as from a Rolleiflex or a Hasselblad (an SLR camera), because they blow up better than 35-mm transparencies do.

Reproducing color photographs adds considerably to a publication's printing costs. Instead of one printing impression, the publication needs four. A few newspapers, printed by the letterpress process, get by with three impressions for their full-color photographs, but the photographs look washed out and weak.

To avoid the costs of full-color photography, smaller magazines sometimes turn to duotones: photographs printed in two colors, one of the colors being black. To do this, the magazine takes an ordinary black and white photograph and makes two plates: one for the black ink and one for the color ink. This is a matter decided on by the editor. It does not affect the writer/photographer who submits black and white prints for publication.

• Processing

Your big problem in photography may be processing. Unless you do it yourself, you probably will never be satisfied with the results. The problem starts with the developing of the film. Brian Lanker, Pulitzer prize-winning photographer now with the Eugene (Oreg.) *Register-Guard*, says that, if you can't do your own full processing, you should at least develop the negative yourself and then turn it over to a processer for prints. Commercial processors tend to overdevelop negatives.

Whether or not you develop your own negatives, if you go outside for processing you will probably try several firms or individuals before you find one who takes the proper interest in your work and charges prices you can afford. Rather than order separate prints of each frame you may be better off ordering contact-print sheets. Using a magnifying glass you can pick out the prints that show the most promise and then ask for blowups.

Editors like to see full-frame prints on glossy, smooth, or resin-coated paper. Do not submit prints on rough textured paper.

"The editor knows he's dealing with an amateur when he gets an 8 x 10 print with an even quarter-inch border all around," Lander says. A full-frame print would put more border at one dimension than the other, because a 35-mm frame does not quite fit the 8 x 10 proportions. To show the editor he's getting full frame, Lanker advises a black frame all around. You would still leave white space on the outside so that the editor can make his crop marks.[6]

• WORKING WITH PHOTOGRAPHERS

As an alternative to taking your own pictures, you can make arrangements with a local photographer to take them for you. You may find one who, like you, would be willing to work on speculation. The photographer's pay comes once the article is sold. You could ask your market to pay for the article and photographs separately. Or you could pay the photographer outright, before the article is sold. What you pay depends upon your bargaining power. Obviously you can't afford to pay much if, for instance, your market pays you $50 for the

[6]Interview with Brian Lanker, Oct. 18, 1976.

package. Listings in *Writer's Market* may give you some idea of what editors pay separately for photographs.

If you work with a photographer, spell out clearly what you want, perhaps by submitting rough sketches, but allow some flexibility. At least let the photographer work out the mechanics. You will find that some photographers are merely shutter snappers; others are artists of great sensibility whose picture sense will bring you usable shots you did not envision.

• WRITING CAPTIONS

Newspapers call them "cutlines," magazines call them "captions." They are necessary lines going under photographs, putting them in context, naming names, and explaining what the camera cannot. Even though some photographs, used for mood or theme purposes, go without captions in the magazines, you should write captions for all your pictures. Let the editor decide what to leave off.

Howard Chapnick, president of Black Star, a large photograph agency in New York which buys from freelancers, says, "Captions are a necessity! Agents, picture researchers, and editors are constantly frustrated by the sloppy unprofessionalism of some photographers. Captionless pictures are useless unless they are symbolic and nonspecific. Simple good sense dictates that sales should not be lost for lack of caption information."[7]

As an outsider you would probably supply more caption for each picture than the editor could actually use. Your two- or three-sentence caption would boil down to a sentence or two, or even a sentence fragment. Some magazines still doctor their captions to make the last line come out even with the other lines. That should not be your concern as a freelancer.

When you illustrate your article with photographs of people, don't merely type their names out and think you have written captions. Even for a close-up shot — a mug shot — give your editor a couple of sentences of information, and don't repeat what you've said in the body of the article. If the person in the picture is quoted in the text,

[7]Howard Chapnick, "The Free-Lancer and the Picture Syndicate," chapter in Clifton C. Edom's *Photojournalism*, Wm. C. Brown Company Publishers, Dubuque, Iowa, 1976, p. 251.

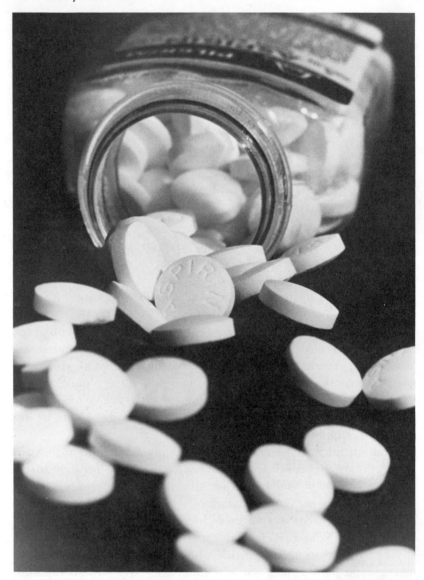

Figure 12.18 "Americans have come to view aspirin as a cure-all drug. Millions of these little pills are consumed each year, making them the nation's most indiscriminately used drug." That was the caption for this photograph taken by Susan Pogany for *University of Oregon Health Sciences Center News*. The arrangement of the pills into a circular but natural pattern was important to the composition here. The focus that allowed only one of the pills to say "aspirin" helped avoid a clutter of words. It was also important to arrange the bottle so that no particular brand was evident.

you may want to add a quote in the caption. You will probably have several quotes left over from your research.

The Pennzoil Company's *Resources*, in an article by E. L. Harris, Jr., runs a full-page, full-color photograph of a ship used to haul sulphur, with several other photographs, including two mug shots. One of the mug shots is closely cropped, the face only partially shown. A man in a cap is looking at an expanse of sea. The caption goes like this:

> Captain Bud Winchester has been at sea since 1943 and captain of the *Marine Duval* since 1972. "This is what I've worked for from the start," he says. "I'm satisfied to stay here, to keep the company happy, the customer happy."

The other mug shot moves back a bit to show a man holding a cup of coffee, pausing to look out the window. The caption for this photograph goes like this:

> Chief mate Gerrard Carroll makes his morning check of the five sulphur tanks, noting temperature and steam pressure. One of the youngest chief mates in the American Merchant Marine at 29, he hopes one day to captain a sulphur vessel.

Because captions often get only last-minute attention, writers, in their hurry to put their packages together, sometimes settle for phrasing they would never use in the bodies of their articles. They turn to cuteness when substance is not there. Hence the inevitable "The naked truth about" caption for a picture of a child missing his pants or "The long and the short of it" caption for a picture showing a tall and short man gawking at each other.

This is not to say that you can't occasionally resort to the light touch. Even the New York *Times* gives in to the urge. Under a front-page photograph of the then mayor, shown running, the paper carried this line: "Keeping fiscally, er, physically fit: Mayor Beame doing daily stint of jogging at Carl Schurz Park. . . ."

The big problem is to avoid stating the obvious. If your photograph shows the "body of an unidentified woman wrapped in gray blanket and sheet, bound with rope," lying there in the woods, don't end with this sentence, as one newspaper did some years ago:

> Foul play is suspected.

You should confine each caption to a single topic. Don't do as one newspaper did when it ran an AP Wirephoto picture of then FBI director Clarence Kelley and his bride-to-be. It was one of those picture-and-cutlines items that newspapers run without an accompanying story. The newspaper gave it this caption:

KELLEY TO WED — FBI Director Clarence Kelley has aired plans to wed Shirley Dyckes (left), Washington, D.C., schoolteacher and ex-nun. President Ford has said he will not fire Kelley for accepting gifts.

The director had been in the news for accepting gifts, but that problem had nothing to do with his impending marriage. The second sentence in the caption, then, becomes something of a *non sequitur*.

Ordinarily you would write your caption in present tense. Here's Toni Kosover's *Family Circle* caption for a picture showing a woman exercising with a man assisting.

If you want to stay trim, it certainly doesn't hurt to be married to the owner of an exercise studio. Here Sue Lorence works out under the watchful eye of husband Larry.

Here's a caption in New York Telephone's *State Region News* under a picture of a man lifting another by his shoulders:

Central office supervisor Al Cresser (left) shows how he applied "bear hug" to Larry Cormier's diaphragm. It saved his life.

Don't bother with an identation for the first sentence. Most magazines don't use paragraph identations for captions.

Type each caption double-spaced on a separate 8½ x 11 sheet. Either key the sheets to the photographs or tack the sheets to the photographs with Scotch or masking tape. If you tack the sheets to the photographs, do it in such a way that the editor can read the caption while looking at the photograph. You can fold the sheets so that they cover the photographs, typed sides facing inward. The editor would simply flick the sheets down to read them.

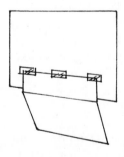

At the end of each caption put, in parentheses, the name of the photographer, whether it is you or someone else, with a "Photo by" in front. If the photograph was given you by a public or private organization, for use with your article, type "Photo courtesy of . . ." If the same name appears at the end of all your captions, the editor may decide to run a single credit line on the opening spread. All he has to do then is cross out your parenthetical credits; but the information is there on each photograph if he needs it.

• SUBMITTING ART TO THE EDITOR

When you are submitting an article to a market new to you, you may want to hold onto the art, especially if it consists of transparencies, until the editor expresses an interest. When you do submit it, pack it with a piece of chipboard or corrugated cardboard to keep the art from bending. Keep your fingerprints off the surfaces, of course, and avoid marking on the backs. The pressure from your writing instrument will dent the front surfaces, and the dents will show up as black marks in the reproductions. Never join photographs to each other or to their captions with paper clips. Paper clips dent, too.

Some editors are willing — in fact, they would prefer — to look at your contact-print sheets to pick out those shots that should be blown up to usable size. They may ask for sheets *and* negatives, with the thought of taking care of the processing in their own plant.

Editors appreciate occasional photographs with excessive even-tone backgrounds or foregrounds — areas that can be used for surprinting (producing a black image) or reversing (producing a white image) a title or caption.

Submitting full-frame rather than cropped prints gives editors a chance to do a little editing to better fit the art to the page. With full-frame prints, editors have an easier time cropping horizontals to verticals and verticals to horizontals; this is sometimes necessary to make photographs fit. If you don't like having your well-composed photographs cropped, include in your selections to editors both horizontals and verticals.

You don't need model's-release forms for your photographs provided they are used for editorial and not advertising purposes and provided they do not ridicule the persons shown. To illustrate some

Figure 12.19 Because photography is so much a part of Duncan McDonald's freelance work, he features two of his photographs on his business card.

Figure 12.20 A photograph with only a small part of its area carrying an image can be useful to a magazine editor. The blank area, whether light or dark, can be used to carry type. For this full page in *Northwest Timber*, a company publication of Crown Zellerbach Corp., editor Jeff Clausen uses a photograph by photographer Jim Hallas, bleeding it to the edges and "reversing" type in the black area. The hint of a log truck at the top going down a road at night is enough to establish a mood for the article, written by the editor. "It's dark," the article begins. "The normally green trees tonight are deep black silhouettes outlined against a southwestern Washington sky. . . ."

How's the night life at Cathlamet?

**Please don't be too critical if Melvin Just and
Henry Blankenship can't see the forest for its trees.
They, and other CZ night loggers, do have an excuse.**

It's dark. The normally green trees tonight are deep black silhouettes outlined against a southwestern Washington sky.

Photographer Jim Hallas and I are riding with Don Hepler up narrow, winding, gravelled Williams Creek Road in Hepler's orange company pickup somewhere near Naselle on CZ's Cathlamet Managed Forest. Countless stars surround a half moon, but it's still very dark.

Almost prophetically, Don mentions having seen a herd of 80 elk the night before when two bucks bound across our headlight beam, gracefully leap a short fence and disappear into a thick stand of hemlock.

"Wow!" is all a startled Hallas can say while I, watching Don calmly puff his pipe with not much reaction to having seen the deer, deduce that night loggers must take these animal sightings in stride—perhaps much like a city commuter sees his daily traffic jams.

The pickup sporadically bouncing up a steepening hill, Hepler be-

gins talking about the pros and cons of night logging work. Hallas cradles his Nikons like an over-protective father while I try to record readable notes on an unsteady scratchpad.

"It's really different at night out here," explains Don, a Cathlamet assistant night woods foreman. "You go to work when most people are heading home for the evening. The weather's usually worse, there's no sun and you get home for the late-late movie. But somehow you get used to it all."

Suddenly the stillness of the night is broken by the roar of a Skylok grapple yarder 800 yards across a steep canyon filled with felled timber. Don advises we're somewhere near Nemah, not far inland from the ocean. Four 1,000-watt multi-vapor lights atop the yarder boom are shining at us and at three similar lights mounted on a portable tree farmer on the road directly ahead.

This place would look, from a distance, like a football stadium, only here there are but two people, a couple of machines and lots of logs.

No O. J. Simpsons in this neck of the woods.

Henry Blankenship gives a wave from some 75 feet off the road to the right. A night hooktender for the past two years, he precariously maneuvers amongst fallen logs and brush on a steep hillside. A thin man of 25, Henry leaps and bounds around the hill like a deer. Hallas and I enthusiastically, but sometimes clumsily, attempt to keep up with Henry for some pictures and a short interview. Tough work.

"It was strange at first out here," Henry admits, "but now it's just like most any other job. The biggest problem is seeing. These lights do the best job they can, but sometimes a log just disappears. It gets cold, wet and windy out here, but I don't have much control over that. There are good and bad points about any job, you know."

Across the canyon, grapple operator Melvin Just returns the grapple to the brush. Henry spots a log and begins talking Melvin onto it via a two-way radio. "Down, down, right, articles it may be necessary in the photographs to present a cross section of the population. As a photographer you will try to find people that fit into this cross section.

In your cover letter you may want to call your editor's attention to qualities in your photographs not immediately apparent. You may want to suggest further art possibilities. But you would not submit a suggested layout. The editor's art director takes care of that. Be content to turn over to your editor a well-typed manuscript and a set of fully captioned 8 x 10 glossies. The editor will take it from there. The additional negotiations you have with your editors will provide the subject matter for the concluding chapter.

CHAPTER 13

Working with Editors

Unless you edit the newspaper or magazine you write for, you face the possibility of your work's being rejected or altered on its way to the reader. Even if you are your own editor, you are not quite free to say whatever you wish. Libel laws and other regulations inhibit you. The owner of the medium or its board of directors represents another constraining force.

But it is the editor — the "gatekeeper" in the jargon of the communications scholars — whom most writers correctly see as their biggest hurdle to publication. There is first the problem of convincing the editor that the article should be run; there is then the problem of putting up with or arguing against changes the editor wants made. "Some writers are skittish, like young colts," reports Larry Dietz, senior editor of *New West*. "Others are merely slothful. Still others appreciate a firm hand on the reins and a touch of the whip on the flanks. Each must be handled differently."[1]

Writing for some magazines, the writer gets little if any editing. *Esquire*, for instance, operates — or has operated — on the principle that a writer good enough to appear in the magazine is good enough to appear without alteration. That is not the case at *The New Yorker*. Brendan Gill tells of pressure the accomplished writer feels when his copy is to go through the unrelenting checking and questioning process of the editors there. Grave doubts set in. "Poor devil, he will type

[1]"Between the Lines," *New West*, Aug. 30, 1976, p. 5.

out his name on a sheet of paper and stare at it long and long, with dumb uncertainty. It looks — oh, Christ! — his name looks as if it could stand some working on."

• THE EDITOR'S JOB

A person does not have to be a good writer to be a good editor, any more than a critic has to be a director to pan or praise a film. Nobody ever accused the late Harold Ross, an ex-newspaperman, of graceful writing, yet for *The New Yorker* he gathered together and watched over the most talented and exciting group of writers ever to contribute to a single magazine.

"This does not indicate a lack of merit but merely that the material does not fit their needs at this time. . . ."

Editing involves talents and abilities quite different from those needed by a writer. Although many editors gained their positions following successful writing careers, perhaps for the very publications they now head, not all writers would want the higher role. As ex-freelancers, they would not appreciate the 8-to-5 aspects of a desk job; they would abhor the preparation of budgets; they would not be able to manage people, especially writers with tender psyches (sometimes the tenderness verges on neurosis). Editing also involves copy-editing and rewriting of others' manuscripts. Not all writers are suited for this work, either. *(like me!)*

The editor's job varies greatly from publication to publication, depending partly on the publication's size. On small magazines, editors spend as much time writing as editing. Not only do they rewrite material coming in from freelancers; they originate and write articles on their own. On company publications, editors often serve as one-person staffs, writing everything that goes into print. Large publications with several top editors sometimes anoint outside writers with an editor's title, like "contributing editor," possibly in lieu of generous payment for pieces — titles are cheap enough — but most certainly because an "editor" title confers status "writer" does not.

Don't expect title uniformity among publications you write for. As either a staff writer or a freelancer, you could deal with an editor-in-chief, editor, executive editor, managing editor, assistant editor, articles or features editor, or, on a newspaper, with any of these plus several others, including a city editor. As a freelancer contributing to magazines, look first on the masthead for an articles or features editor and send your work to that person by name. If you find no such editor, look for a managing editor, an executive editor, or an assistant editor.

Directed to a large magazine, your manuscript no doubt would stop at the desk of a first reader or assistant before going on to the editor you address it to. It is the job of the first reader or assistant, someone, probably, who has graduated recently in liberal arts or English from an Eastern college, to weed out impossible manuscripts and send the few remaining ones to a more senior editor. Even when you sell that editor, acceptance may hinge on the manuscript's reception at a meeting of the editorial board.

On a small magazine, all the buying decisions could rest with one person. A surprising number of magazines are run by single individuals or by staffs of only two or three persons.

• WHY EDITORS REJECT ARTICLES

An editor can find any number of reasons for rejecting an article, among them these:

1. The idea or theme of the article does not hold enough interest for the magazine's readers.
2. The article offers no information or insights not already understood by the readers.
3. The editor ran an article on the same subject within the past two years or already has a similar article scheduled for an early issue.
4. The article scolds or preaches rather than alarms or excites.
5. The style is stilted. The article reads like a term paper. The writer fails to use anecdotes. The writer doesn't tell a story.
6. The writer has trouble with grammar and usage. The manuscript would require too much editing.
7. The manuscript appears to be libelous.
8. The editor is overstocked, or the editorial budget for the year is nearly depleted.
9. There is nothing wrong with the article as such; it simply is directed to the wrong market.

• THE ART OF REJECTION

Dr. Samuel Johnson is said to have informed a writer: "Your manuscript is both good and original; but the part that is good is not original, and the part that is original is not good." Ruth Kirk, thumbing through a mid-1800s issue of *Hutchings California Magazine*, found a column, "Answers to Contributors and Correspondents," with rejections right there for all to see. One writer, addressed only by initials, was told: "If we had a very large hay press with which we could condense your manuscript to one quarter its present volume it might be admissible." Another was told that a second-hand sewing machine using black thread on white cloth could turn out "a far more intelligible manuscript than that which you sent us."

But editors in the main, especially today, try hard to be civil. A favorite clause goes like this: "Unfortunately, your material doesn't meet our needs at the present time." Whatever writers learn from their editors, they learn, usually through printed rejection slips. Some magazines stock two kinds: one that says no more, really, than "Thanks for letting us see this material"; and one that sounds more sincerely regretful and even invites further contributions. A writer who comes quite close to selling may get an original typed letter signed by the editor.

Knowing that writers long for some kind of personalized attention, a few magazines work out multiple-choice printed rejection slips, and editors, before slipping manuscripts into their return envelopes, check off the reasons for rejection.

Don Gold, managing editor of *Travel & Leisure*, thinks it unlikely that editors will ever give up the jargon of rejection. Writers, he says, don't want the real truth about their "deathless prose. It would be too painful." In a playful mood, he puts forth a "modest proposal" that writers who want the truth should include with each submission their own printed multiple-choice rejection slips for editors to mark. The slips could include such items as "This is dreadful, unpublishable and an affront to civilization. Burn it."; "With my problems, I can't concentrate on your manuscript. Don't nag me now."; and, most realistic of all reasons, perhaps: "I don't like this, and I don't know why."[2]

• The Editor as Villain

Elbert Hubbard, a late-nineteenth-and-early-twentieth-century author and editor, said that an editor is "a person. . .whose business is to separate the wheat from the chaff and to see that the chaff is printed." Mark Twain and, later, Adlai Stevenson made similar observations, and many writers no doubt feel the definition holds today. Suspicious that editors don't even look at the manuscripts coming in, writers have been known to connect inside pages with tiny hairs or pieces of Scotch tape; when the manuscrupts come back with their seals unbroken these writers know they have been unfairly treated. Fearful that editors will steal their ideas, beginning writers wonder about copyrighting their material before sending it in.

But editors don't need to read through entire manuscripts before seeing that they are unsuited for publication. First pages often tell enough. And if the ideas are good but the writing bad, editorial

[2]Don Gold, "Rejection Slip," *The New York Times Magazine*, Aug. 22, 1976, p. 87.

"It's her first typed rejection letter signed by an editor. . . ."

budgets allow payment for ideas alone. That similar ideas show up later in the magazines in most cases can be traced to coincidence rather than cupidity. Writers often come onto similar ideas independently and simultaneously. Anyway, writers already own common-law copyrights on what they write. Statutory copyright comes only upon publication, and editors arrange that. If a publication does not copyright its contents, writers can make independent arrangements upon acceptance of their manuscripts.

Writers have stronger cases against editors over the rough handling given rejected manuscripts and the unreasonable amount of time some editors take to make up their minds. Too often the manuscripts have to be retyped before being sent out to new markets; and good ideas are dead by the time writers get their manuscripts back. A week of two should be time enough for editors to make a decision to accept or reject a manuscript.

Highest on the list of editor offenses are unnecessary changes made by editors that give writers a style not their own, or alter writers' meanings. Getting a $150 check for an article about an indoor climbing wall for rock climbers was not enough to mollify Clay Eals for the editing done to his writing. "I'm not saying my version was the best that could have been written on this story," he says. "But they sure changed the style to a backwoods, hokey kind of writing."[3]

> George Mattox is asking rock climbers to come in out of the rain.
> Mattox runs a shop on the downtown mall [at Eugene, Oreg.] that features the unlikely combination of smoking accessories and outdoor wear and equipment.

turns into this when published:

> There's this guy out in Eugene, Oregon, who can move mountains.
> He's not some mystic or guru. He's not even a civil engineer.
> His name is George Mattox and he runs a smoking accessory/outdoor equipment shop in downtown Eugene. . . .

Eals saw some phrasing in succeeding paragraphs he most certainly would not use: "And it isn't old miracle-worker George himself . . ." "You see, the . . ." "A K-2 it's not. . . ."

He was most surprised to find direct quotations altered. His "'That's why people can come back and come back' " became " 'That's why the same people keep coming back again.' "

When another writer, Jack Sack, found that reference books contradicted each other on a geographic question he had about Europe, he decided to visit the places and write an article about them to correct the inaccuracies. When his article came out, he found that his editor had changed his facts because they did not agree with a reference book the editor consulted! "Now I make a habit of absolutely insisting that editors not make any changes unless they check them with me," he told Andrea Kotula, who was preparing an article for *Writer's Digest*. "I'm very amenable to editing — people will suggest something and I'll do it — but I just want to know what it is before it appears in print."

"The rarest and best luck a writer can have is to find a first-class editor," says Nat Hentoff. "But editing for style and to make things clearer is quite different from taking things out or, in some horren-

---

[3]Letter to the author from Clay Eals, Jan. 28, 1976.

dous cases I know about, adding things, so that the author doesn't see them until the piece appears in print."

Sometimes you have to protect yourself against editors by restructuring a sentence before your manuscript goes out. For instance, you would have trouble getting this sentence by some editors: ". . . is one of those persons who believe . . ." It would probably come out "corrected" to read: ". . . is one of those persons who believes . . ." So you would write this instead: ". . . numbers himself among those persons who believe . . ."

When your manuscript includes a proper name with an unusual spelling, like "Willson," it is a good idea to put a "correct" or "cq" over it to tell the editor you know it to be right. (Newspaper copy editors often place a row of dots below a word whose authenticity seems open to question.)

• The Editor as Ally

On the other hand, few published writers can say they have never benefited from changes made by alert editors. Writers get too close to their manuscripts. What seems clever at the writing turns out to be only cute when seen later in an impartial reading. Words or facts that seem right to the writer turn out to be miserably wrong, in spelling or in meaning, under the editor's eagle eye.

Almost all writers can use help in smoothing out grammatical and spelling problems, and some writers benefit from more extensive changes made to improve a manuscript's clarity and style. Even editing an article for length can make it more compelling. Some writers welcome the changes because they know that they are needed.

When changes are minor, the editor makes them without consulting the writer, and few writers complain about that. When they are major, the editor may return the manuscript to the writer with instructions for revising. In some cases the editor makes the changes and lets the writer see the alterations either on the copy-edited manuscript or on galley proofs.

• UNDERSTANDING EDITORIAL NEEDS

The secret to getting along with editors is to understand that their points of view have to be broader than those of writers. Like writers, editors want to serve readers, but with unified publications, not just individual pieces of writing. Editors make their decisions on the basis of the impact complete issues of their magazines make on readers.

The problem becomes more complicated on company publications published for public relations reasons. One of the reasons many company publications do not welcome contributions from freelancers is that freelancers cannot be expected to understand company policies and their restrictions on editorial content. Company magazine editors almost always have to rework manuscripts from outside to bring them into line with policy. Some editors warn outside writers on assignment that what is wanted is "research"; when the material comes in, the editors pick out what they want and write it in a way they know will satisfy the overseers. One arrangement used by a magazine on the West Coast — the editor doesn't want the magazine named for fear he will be inundated with hungry writers — is to pay the writer $75 a day plus expenses for the *research*; the magazine's staff does the writing.

Knowing company policy becomes more difficult for freelancers who, dealing with various editors, flit from one to the other, sometimes in person, sometimes by mail, sometimes by phone, selling, cajoling, agreeing on slant, and maybe in the end going ahead with projects they have only slim hopes of selling. To take one example: Barry Lopez's schedule over a period of a few months while he was working on a book. With two or three articles about winches sold to *Popular Science*, Lopez on assignment did one more, a "straightforward, bread-and-butter piece" for the magazine's *Motorcamping Handbook 1975*. "An article like this really has no recognizable style — it could have been authored by anyone," Lopez says. With it went a chart describing the advantages and uses of winches — "a time-consuming project, but the sort of thing *PS* likes — and expects." For *Travel & Leisure* he did a " regional," tough to write because you have to fill an assigned space. "The idea. . . [for the article] originated in a query letter . . . and was later discussed with an editor in New York. It was such an abstract idea I finally said I would just go and do it — but I felt confident that I knew exactly what they wanted." For the struggling *Pacific Wilderness Journal* he did a piece on cottonwoods "because I feel very strongly that a freelance writer who's good should contribute to local publications regardless of payment. I like cottonwoods, have been collecting notes on them for a while." For *Audubon* he did an article about night — "a vague idea I had which was catalyzed in a conversation with Les Line, the editor. I went home and read — which is a typical approach — until I felt comfortable that I had marshalled the data to support my gut feelings." And for *North American Review* he capitalized on some of his research for a book by writing about wolves in association with photographer John Bauguess. It was an unusual article in that the author worked out the layout, which packaged the text and photographs into sections called "Begin," "Continue," and "Finish."[4]

Other writers may find enough success with one or two publications to concentrate their attention there. "When I find an editor who likes me, I stick with him," says Louise Melton.

• FACING EDITORIAL TABOOS

In some respects restrictions for writers loom larger now than before. Libel decisions in the past two decades allow more to be said, but new attention by the courts to the right of privacy threatens access to some sources for writers. The 1976 revision of the federal copyright law to bring it into conformity with international copyright regulations leaves less material in the public domain. Writers feel freer to use profanity but face taboos on what they can say about various social groups. Nobody dares offend these groups. Editors grow timid.

Many groups are less willing now to take verbal abuse, and some are quick to resort to organized pressure against writers and their editors. A joke, read without benefit of the sardonic smile on the writer's face, can backfire in print, as Herb Caen found when, in a San Francisco *Chronicle* column after the elections of 1976 (in which a state proposition to allow greyhound racing failed, as well as a proposition to extend farmworkers' power to organize and bargain), he concluded with a "fearless forecast":

> For next year's election, the forces behind Props. 13 and 14, both of which lost, will pool their resources for a ballot measure to legalize the racing of Mexicans.

Two days later, after a public outcry and demands made upon the *Chronicle* to change its ways, Herb Caen apologized, saying the "joke"

---

[4]Letter to the author from Barry Lopez, May 25, 1976.

"was supposed to have been a satirical jab at the subtle racism behind the defeat of 14." But he added:

> On the other hand, no apologies are offered to the non-Mexican "progressives" who couldn't wait to phone or write their "shocked outrage" at such "arrant racism." (Where, by the way, were these self-righteous troublemakers on the many occasions when I have written positively about Cesar Chavez's efforts to aid the farm workers?) . . . If these hypocrites and phonies are looking for bigots, they may consult the nearest mirror.

• References to Women

Possibly the most troublesome area in usage these days centers on women: how to refer to them and how to make sure they are fairly represented.[5] On many publications and in many publishing houses, for instance, "man" or "mankind" no longer seems inclusive enough. When Marvin Harris revised his anthropology textbook, *Culture, Man and Nature*, he found it wise to retitle the book: *Culture, People, Nature*.

In her "Alternating Currents" column in *Rolling Stone*, Ellen Willis argues that "If a culture uses the same word ['man'] for 'humanity' and 'male person' and a different word for 'female person' it is not unreasonable to suspect that the culture associates humanness with maleness. And if one then examines the culture and notes that for most of its history, married women were legal nonpersons, and women generally were denied the most basic political and economic rights, suspicion becomes certainty."[6]

Some publications will not tolerate an emphasis placed on women's looks. Benjamin De Mott in *The Atlantic* tells of an experience with one publication (not *The Atlantic*). Checking proofs of an article, he found that a copyreader had inserted the word "handsome" in front of a man's name. When De Mott complained, an apologetic editor wrote back: ". . . it's the Sabotage. . . . They hit you, that's all, the libbies in the office. They do it all the time now. They rewrite. One sexist remark deserves another." De Mott's offense had been a sentence earlier in the article in which he referred to a woman as "a beautiful . . . and articulate Manhattan matron."[7]

---

[5] See Casey Miller and Kate Smith, *Words and Women: New Language in New Times*, Doubleday, New York, 1976.

[6] Ellin Willis, "Tongue Twisted," *Rolling Stone*, Nov. 4, 1976, p.30.

[7] Benjamin De Mott, "Culture Watch," *The Atlantic*, August 1975, p. 86.

When AP and UPI in late 1976 revised their joint stylebook after 20 years, "the most controversial question to come before the style committee," according to UPI general news editor Bobby Ray Miller, "was courtesy titles for women." The committee decided to eliminate "Miss,""Mrs.," and "Ms." from sports-wire copy but to retain the titles for news-wire copy. "Ms." would be used when women, married or single, requested it. On first mention in a story, the woman's full name would be used, without a "Miss,""Mrs.," or "Ms."

And *The New York Times Manual of Style and Usage*, published in 1976, called for some changes in references to women. ". . . we should avoid words or phrases that imply that The Times speaks with a purely masculine voice, viewing men as the norm and women as the exception." But the *Times* did not go for "Ms." nor would it condone "chairwoman" or "chairperson" in place of "chairman." Until 1976, the New York *Times*, on first mention of a woman in a story, used her husband's name with a "Mrs." in front; hence, "Mrs. Robert Collins." Now it's "Betty Collins" first, then "Mrs. Collins" subsequently.

The Chicago *Tribune* uses "Ms." only for features dealing with feminists, while the Centralia–Chehalis (Wash.) *Daily Chronicle,* to name one other paper, avoids "Ms." altogether because, as it said in an editorial, "In our judgment, the combination of the letters 'Ms.' represents neither an abbreviation of a word nor a socially acceptable form of address. The term simply isn't accepted by the majority of the people of this nation."[8]

Confusion over this one matter is so great that on a single newspaper, "Ms." may be used for stories in one section but not in another.

Magazines are more willing than newspapers to use "Ms." or last-names-only on second mentions of women. But many newspapers use "Ms." when women request it of reporters interviewing them. Some newspapers are now using last names only for second mentions of women.

An advantage of last-names-only or "Ms." treatment of women is that the writer no longer has to stop to look up marital status. It was proper in the past to refer to married as well as unmarried actresses as "Miss," even when your story dealt with an actress and her children,

---

[8] Quoted in "Stylebook Revisions Ask Help on Ms.," *Editor & Publisher*, Aug. 30, 1975, p. 36.

but you never knew how to handle second mentions of, say, women writers or women in other professions. How could you even find out whether or not they were married?

Of course you pay a price in precision when you drop Miss and Mrs. distinctions. Marital status adds one more dimension to your description. Some writers would argue that what we need is not the elimination of the distinction but an adding to it: a new courtesy title for men to permit marital distinctions there. And when you use last-names-only for second mentions and your article or feature deals with a married couple, how do you distinguish between Graham and Graham? Using "George" and "Carol" would strike some readers as being too familiar.

• He/She Problems

The times even dictate the pronouns allowed a writer. On some publications the generic "he" has fallen into disfavor. A "he" becomes a "he or she," a "him" becomes a "him or her," and a "his" becomes a "his or hers." Subject to this kind of editing, a manuscript written under the naïve assumption that "he" covers everybody may end up like this after editing:

> An impossible deadline may proscribe an artist's producing an ad with any real flair, but never mind: after it has had its few days in the magazines and newspapers, the campaign over and another one launched, the ad quickly recedes from his or her consciousness, perhaps not even to yellow as a clipping in his or her samples file. Nothing to remind him or her of his or her folly.
>
> He or she may not always get off so easily.
>
> One day someone will ask him or her to design a trademark or other item equally enduring. Let him or her then settle for a first inspiration, and years later the trademark will haunt him or her from. . . .

At any time before the 1970s, and for many publications even now, you would settle for the generic "he," "him," and "his" here. But if your own inclination or your editor does not permit it, you would have to do some rephrasing. Here are some of the solutions:

1. Use "him or her" at the beginning and then, for the remaining pronouns *in the series of sentences* use the generic "he," "him," and

"his." In a later series, you would start the process anew. (This answer still will not satisfy some editors, and it does introduce an inconsistency.)

2. Use male pronouns for one series, female pronouns for the next. (But the alternating may really eliminate one sex each time from the mind of the reader who otherwise accepts the generic quality of "he".)

3. Start off with the plural form — use "artists' " for "artist's" and then "their" or "they." This is the most satisfactory solution, but it does limit your phrasing flexibility.

4. Use the second-person "you" as much as possible. Say "You can find your way around the city by . . ." rather than "A person can find his or her way around the city by . . ."

Carol L. O'Neill and Avima Ruder solve the problem in their book *The Complete Guide to Editorial Freelancing* by identifying freelancers as "she" "since the majority are female and the pronoun is handy." But the writers use "he" for authors and editors. "We hasten to acknowledge the numerous 'he' freelancers and the many 'she' editors and authors."[9]

An illustration of the confusion comes from a *New York Times Magazine* article on Nashville by Patrick Anderson, who, in an anecdote, has Toosie, a nightclub operator, "womaning the cash register," but later he writes about the country music fan's insatiable need "to hear his or her favorite music."

Several new pronoun constructions have been offered: like *(s)he* for "he or she" and even *himer* or *herm* for "him or her." Some writers and editors use a slant line in place of an "or," hence *he/she*, *him/her*, and *his/her*. No doubt some editors would like to change those around to *she/he*, *her/him*, and *her/his*.

Illiterate persons have no trouble with "he or she" because, in their ignorance, they use "their" as a pronoun for both singular and plural nouns.

No doubt those who push for these changes in the language will win out, because as more and more young writers use the newer forms, the purists who prefer the traditional forms will appear, rightly or

---

[9]Explained by Carol L. O'Neill and Avima Ruder in a footnote in *The Complete Guide to Editorial Freelancing*, Dodd, Mead & Company, New York, 1974, p. 1.

wrongly, to be "sexist" to those readers who have grown up with the newer forms.

If this seems like a lot of fuss about an insignificant matter, be assured that you will surely face the problem if you write for some segments of the print — or broadcast — media. Textbook publishers, not wanting to offend any group for fear of losses in adoptions, are particularly sensitive to charges of "sexism in language." Magazines edited by or for women are sensitive, too, and so are other publications which do not wish to be labeled "sexist" by the activists in this area and by others who are concerned.

• KEEPING IN TOUCH

Writers who live at a distance from New York find it helpful if not necessary to fly in to the city occasionally to touch base with editors. The writer's goal is not only to return with some assignments but also to make arrangements to be called when an article is needed on a subject the writer specializes in.

"Without contacts you can't be a [published] writer," says Barry Lopez, a Finn Rock (Oregon) writer who appears regularly in from 15 to 20 magazines. Lopez who tends to specialize in nature topics, lately has turned to book writing. Research for a book on wolves for Scribner's led to additional sales to *Harper's, North American Review, Forum*, and *Ms*.

Is living in remote Finn Rock, across the country from the publishing industry, a handicap? It is, and it isn't, he says. He no doubt misses some assignments because he isn't nearby when the editor needs somebody. On the other hand, an editor needing an article dealing with the Northwest doesn't have to worry about air fare and extra expenses. "Ms. Crawford, get me that writer out in Finn Rock, Or-e-gawn." To keep his contacts alive and maybe to pick up some new assignments, Lopez flies to New York twice a year and makes the rounds.

Although his articles represent much revising and polishing (Lopez's writing has been compared to Annie Dillard's), it is not his *writing* that editors are interested in so much as his *thinking*, Lopez believes. Lopez is a writer with firm convictions and a deep interest in "man and his natural world." That is not quite the same thing as being an environmentalist. "That's too political. And politics don't interest me," he says. Editors think of Lopez when they want pieces that are more literary than political.[10]

It helps to develop contacts not only among editors but among other people who have contacts with editors. John Thomas, a free-lancer who sells mostly to local markets, was the name that occurred to the director of the University of Oregon News Bureau when *Sports Medicine* called for help in locating someone to do an article on new research into jogging's effects. The magazine called the University because Bill Bowerman, ex-track coach there, was involved. For his work, Thomas earned $200, plus additional fees and expenses for his photography.

• USING AGENTS

Does having an agent help in dealing with editors? No doubt it does. But few agents want to handle one-time sales to magazines. It can take as much effort to place an article as to place a book manuscript. At 10 percent of what the article earns, an agent can't make enough to cover the time involved.

Even when writing a book you may have trouble lining up a legitimate agent. You have to show promise as a money-maker. You may find it easier to sell your book manuscript directly to a publisher than to persuade an agent to take it on. But if you can line one up, an agent will not only find you the right publisher from among the several hundred doing most of the business, but also negotiate a more favorable contract for you, earning you additional monies that would more than cover the 10 percent of royalties (the fee an agent would charge). Furthermore, agents representing book authors often help place their articles in order to spur sale of the writer's books.

• WRITER'S RIGHTS

Out there in their cubby-hole offices are editors who hold onto manuscripts for months without responding, who lose manuscripts, who

[10]Interview with Barry Lopez, May 24, 1976.

soil them before returning them, who butcher them in print, who fail
to pay even on publication, who close down their magazines still owing
money to writers. One editor, to avoid payment to this author, ran
one of his short articles, complete with illustrations, in a letters-to-
the-editor column.

Fortunately, such editors are in a minority and such treatment is
rare. The writer's magazines and newsletters help by singling out
bad-apple editors and their magazines and warning readers about
them. And writers whose livelihoods depend on what they sell have
organized into various groups to bring pressure on editors for faster
decisions, better pay, subsidiary rights, and other considerations. In
some cases, freelance writers have joined with staff writers and reporters to achieve common goals. Among the many freelance writers' organizations are these:

American Society of Journalists and Authors (formerly Society of
Magazine Writers), 123 W. 43rd St., New York, N.Y. 10036.

Authors Guild, 234 W. 44th St., New York, N.Y. 10036.

Authors League of America, 234 W. 44th St., New York, N.Y.
10036.

National League of American Pen Women, Inc., 1300 17th St.,
N.W., Washington, D.C. 20036.

Almost every group of specialized writers, like business writers, dog
writers, football writers, outdoor writers, medical writers, and travel
writers, have their own organizations. Some organizations serve both
writers and editors. *Writer's Market* lists more than 50 national writers'
organizations, in addition to numerous local and state writers' clubs.

If you are interested in causes and want to contribute your writing
talent to some nonprofit organization, Writers in the Public Interest,
17 Myrtle Drive, Great Neck, N.Y. 11021, might be able to advise you.

• THE PAYOFF

What freelancers earn for their work is determined by scales set up by
editors, although some writers are able to negotiate with editors to

earn more than what is offered. A writer who contributes regularly to a magazine probably earns more than what the magazine says its rates are. Payment varies from a penny or two to ten cents or more per word, with payment for photographs figured separately (a few dollars to several hundred per print). Short articles or articles appearing in major magazines may bring writers as much as a dollar a word. An article published in a slick, general-interest magazine can bring $1,000, $2,000, or more, plus travel expenses. An article in an in-flight magazine brings between $100 and $500. An article in the typical trade journal brings from $50 to $200. A lot of magazines pay less. Some pay by the column or printed page rather than by the word. An editor once told freelancer Ron Abell that he should be thankful the publication didn't pay well. By paying so little, the editor argued, the magazine was able to stay alive, and Abell would always have a market.

Some struggling young magazines or literary quarterlies pay only in extra copies of the publication. Some publications rely on their readers to contribute material as a public service. *The Pacific Sun*, an alternative weekly published in Marin County, north of San Francisco, put together a volunteer task force from among its readers to develop investigative features. The system has a disadvantage to the editor, in that members of that task force do not know the sources, but it has an advantage, in addition to money saved, in that the members bring a freshness to the coverage. "The task force is letting us do the kinds of stories we could not do before," says editor Don Stanley. "With our small staff and budget we lacked the resources to really dig into the facts behind the issues."[11]

Magazines that can't pay much sometimes make up for the deficiency by offering the writer special courtesies. *The Nation*, whose pay rates are negotiable, sends contributors forms asking for names of friends, journalists, opinion makers, and others to whom marked copies should be sent. The policy "also generates interest in the magazine to nonsubscribers" suggests Steve Neal, a contributor.[12]

Too many magazines still use the pay-on-publication ruse. That means they can "accept" an article, then hold onto it for months or even years waiting for a propitious time to run it. That time may never come, and the author may never be paid.

[11] Andrew Radolf, "Volunteer Reporters," *Editor and Publisher*, July 10, 1976, p. 12.
[12] Letter to the author from Steve Neal, Nov. 10, 1976.

The best publications pay on acceptance, thanks to pioneering practices of the old *Saturday Evening Post*. You still run the risk of the article's not being run, but at least you have your money.

Major and even lesser magazines sometimes pay a "kill fee" for an article that is commissioned or simply encouraged but in the end not purchased. The "kill fee" will be considerably less than regular payment. Ron Abell, working on an article that would have brought him $500, ended up with $100 when his editor decided against the piece. With the "kill fee," the writer then is free to peddle his article elsewhere.

Once in a while an article appearing in a magazine draws a letter from a book publisher inviting the writer to do a book-length manuscript on the subject. Or the article may be picked up by an anthologist and run in a book with similar articles. That means an honorarium added to the original payment. But, considering the amount of time involved in conceiving, researching, writing, and marketing an article, the pay for the freelancer is not substantial. There are no tangible fringe benefits, either. No paid vacations.

But there are other rewards, not the least of which are your contacts with people while you are researching your article and the contact with people afterwards. Often you will hear from readers thanking you for your advice, agreeing with what you've said, adding information you may have missed (maybe you can do a followup article), or quarreling with you on your facts, ideas, and conclusions. Some editors publish reader response to articles and expect writers of articles to provide response to the response, which is also published. If you know you are right, you will put your adversary down gently; if you are wrong, you will admit it.

Then again, your article may appear and you will hear nothing. No one will write, even to complain. Even so, you can be sure you reached people. Even when they are affected by what they read, people ordinarily don't get in touch with writers or even notice their names. But knowing that you have passed along useful information, done some entertaining, and possibly even changed some minds makes writing and placing an article or feature worth all the effort.

ASSIGNMENTS

1. For your newspaper, do a personality sketch of a local character or official or celebrity.

2. Go through a copy of a daily newspaper and look for ideas for articles. Read local as well as wire-service stories. Read the editorial page and the special sections in the paper. Look at the ads. See if you can find at least ten possible ideas — they may, at this point, be nothing more than subject areas — that you can further develop into articles for national markets.

3. The chapter on markets carries a nine-point program for analyzing magazines as markets. Pick out a magazine you want to write for, and using the program, analyze that market. (Note that the program asks for three ideas you might want to develop for articles for the magazine.)

4. D. Keith Mano has described the *National Enquirer*, considering its large circulation, as "probably the second most important conservative publication in America." What could he mean by "conservative" in this context? And what publication would be the *most* important conservative publication in America? Coming up with an answer to that second question (or to a related question: What is the most important *liberal* publication in America?), do the necessary reading and research to write an article on the subject. What could be a market for such an article? And what would be its slant?

5. Pick one of your ideas and write a query to an editor, by name, trying to get a commitment.

6. Pick out an article in a current issue of a popular newsstand magazine and one in a specialized magazine and, in a single paragraph, state the theme of each. Be explicit.

7. Pick out one of the books on article and/or feature writing — it could be this one or one named in the bibliography — and write a review (no more than three typed pages) for one of the writer's magazines (assume it runs full-length reviews), a daily newspaper (assume the book is written by a local author), or *Journalism Quarterly* (know that your professor-readers will be making decisions on whether to adopt the book for their classes).

8. Pick out a book published in the past year — fiction or nonfiction — and read as many reviews of the book as you can. Do a paper contrasting and evaluating the reviews. But read the book yourself to prepare for the evaluation.

9. Go to one of the magazines that have well-organized filler-publishing programs — a magazine like *Reader's Digest* or *Catholic Digest* —, study the several filler categories, read the instructions in the magazine for submitting fillers, and write one for the magazine you choose. Your problem, in most cases, will be to keep the filler short enough.

10. Go to one of the publications that have set up departments to publish longer fillers — publications like *Newsweek* with its "My Turn" feature or *Redbook* with its "Young Mother's Story" feature — and write a contribution to fit.

11. Go through any published article and see if you can figure out what sources the writer went to for the information in the article.

12. Do outlines of two already published articles in a single magazine, and see if you can find any similarities in the organization.

13. Writing about music can really test your ability to handle description. Assume that, for your local newspaper, you have the assignment of covering a music concert. You can consider the feature a review, if you wish, but by the time the paper publishes it, let's assume, the concert group will have moved on to another town. You're covering a one-night stand. For your "concert," use an LP record. If it is a real recorded concert, so much the better. You can pick a rock group, country-and-western group — any kind of group you wish. Be subjective in your description of the music but remember the audience you are writing for. For this assignment only, you may make up some facts about the audience to round out your feature; but the made-up facts should sound reasonable. No more than three typed pages, total.

14. Pick out an already published article or feature that you think is poorly written — and rewrite it. Don't bother doing additional research. But, if you find a hole in the information, indicate in a parenthetical remark what additional material you would put there. Hold onto any of the original phrasing and structure that you think works. This is just an exercise. You would not attempt to market your final product.

15. Find an episode or long anecdote in a published article and retell it, but in a much shorter form. Use your own words, but quote where necessary. Work in some kind of credit for the original author. Do not embellish. Your retelling should be considerably shorter than the original.

16. Find some statistics in a textbook or book of statistics — preferably statistics presented in tabular form — and present them (or some of them) in more readable form. See if you can "humanize" the statistics.

17. Find an article opening that you like, and write three *different* openings. Do the same thing for the ending. See if you can come up with openings and closings as good as — or better than — the originals.

18. Pick out a newspaper feature and explain how the writer could expand or change it to make it into an article for a national magazine. Name the magazine it might be submitted to.

19. Find an unillustrated article or feature you think has illustration possibilities and describe at least three photographs that could be taken to be used with the article.

20. Settle on an idea that seems promising, pick a market, and begin work on your major article or feature. Work out the theme, write a tentative title (this will help you stick to your theme), and begin your research. When you have enough material from your research, begin your writing. Make sure you serve the needs and cater to the interests of your readers.

Bibliography

Alexander, Louis, *Beyond the Facts: A Guide to the Art of Feature Writing*. (Houston: Gulf Publishing Company, 1975.)

Anderson, Margaret J., *The Christian Writer's Handbook*. (New York: Harper & Row, 1974.)

Armour, Richard, *Writing Light Verse and Prose Humor*. (Boston: The Writer, 1971.)

Aronson, Charles N., *The Writer Publisher*. (Arcade, N.Y.: Charles N. Aronson Writer Publisher, RR 1, Hundred Acres, Arcade, N.Y. 14009, 1976.)

Ashley, Paul P., *Say It Safely* (5th ed). (Seattle: University of Washington Press, 1976.)

Babb, Laura Longley (editor), *Writing in Style*. (Boston: Houghton Mifflin, 1975.) (Features from the Washington *Post*.)

Behrens, John C., *Magazine Writer's Workbook* (2nd ed). (Columbus, Ohio: Grid, Inc., 1972.)

Bird, George L., *Modern Article Writing*. (Dubuque, Iowa: Wm. C. Brown Company Publishers, 1967.)

Boggess, Louise, *Writing Articles That Sell*. (Englewood Cliffs, N.J.: Prentice-Hall, 1965.)

————, *Writing Fillers That Sell*. (New York: Funk & Wagnalls, 1968.)

Borland, Hal, *How to Write and Sell Nonfiction*. (New York: The Ronald Press Company, 1956.)

Brady, John, *The Craft of Interviewing*. (Cincinnati, Ohio: Writer's Digest, 1976.)

Brennecke, Ernest, Jr., and Clark, Donald L., *Magazine Article Writing*. (New York: The Macmillan Company, 1944.)

Burack, A. S. (editor), *Writing and Selling Fillers and Short Humor*. (Boston: *The Writer*, 1967.)

———, *The Writer's Handbook*. (Boston: The Writer, Inc., 1975.) (One hundred chapters — articles that appeared originally in *The Writer*. Includes a listing of 2,500 markets.)

Casewit, Curtis, *Freelance Writing: Advice from the Pros*. (New York: Macmillan, 1974.)

Cavallo, Robert M., and Kahan, Stuart, *Photography: What's the Law?* (New York: Crown Publishers, Inc., 1976.)

Christian Writers Institute, *Handbook for Christian Writers* (6th ed). (Carol Stream, Ill.: Creation House, 1974.)

Clement, Clarice, *How to Become a Nationally Syndicated Newspaper Columnist*. (Chicago: Arcadia Books, P.O. Box 5263, Chicago, Ill. 60680, 1976.) (31 mimeographed pages of routine advice.)

Dickson, Frank A., *Writer's Digest Handbook of Article Writing*. (New York: Holt, Rinehart and Winston, Inc., 1968.)

Dillon, Mary, *Writing Magazine Articles Today*. (Boston: The Writer, 1977.)

Douglis, Phil, *Communicating with Pictures*. (Chicago: Lawrence Ragan Communications, Inc., 407 S. Dearborn St., Chicago, Ill. 60605, 1977.)

Duffy, Thomas G., *Let's Write a Feature*. (Columbia, Mo.: Lucas Brothers Publishers, 1969.)

Dygert, James H., *The Investigative Journalist*. (Englewood Cliffs, N.J.: Prentice-Hall, 1976.)

Fontaine, André, *The Art of Writing Nonfiction*. (New York: Thomas Y. Crowell Company, 1974.)

Gardner, Helen, *The Business of Criticism*. (New York: Oxford University Press, 1969.)

Gehman, Richard, *How to Write and Sell Magazine Articles*. (New York: Harper & Brothers, 1959.)

Giles, Carl H., *The Student Journalist and Feature Writing*. (New York: Richards Rosen Press, 1969.)

————, *Writing Right – To Sell.* (New York: A. S. Barnes & Company, Inc., 1970.)

Greene, Theodore Meyer, *The Arts and the Art of Criticism.* (Princeton, N.J.: Princeton University Press, 1966.)

Gunther, Max, *Writing the Modern Magazine Article.* (Boston: The Writer, Inc. 1968.)

Henry, Omer, *Writing and Selling Magazine Articles.* (Boston: The Writer, 1962.)

Hinds, Marjorie M., *How to Make Money Writing Short Fillers and Articles.* (New York: Frederick Fell, Inc., 1967.)

Holmes, Marjorie, *Writing the Creative Article.* (Boston: The Writer, Inc., 1969.)

Hunt, Todd, *Reviewing for the Mass Media.* (Philadelphia: Chilton Book Company, 1972.)

Jacobs, Hayes B., *Writing and Selling Non-Fiction.* (Cincinnati, Ohio: Writer's Digest, 1967.)

Kernaghan, Eileen, *et al., The Upper Left-Hand Corner: A Writer's Guide for the Northwest.* (Seattle: Madrona Publishers, 1975.)

Knott, William C., *The Craft of Non-Fiction.* (Englewood Cliffs, N.J.: Reston Publishing Co., Prentice-Hall, 1974.)

Kostelonetz, Richard, *The End of Intelligent Writing.* (New York: Sheed and Ward, 1974.) (Deals with the antiestablishment press.)

Kurtz, David L., and Spitz, A. Edward, *An Academic Writer's Guide to Publishing in Business and Economic Journals* (2nd ed). (Ypsilanti, Mich.: Bureau of Business Services Research, Eastern Michigan University, 1974.)

MacCampbell, Donald, *Writing for Publication.* (New York: The World Publishing Company, 1966.)

————, *Don't Step on It – It Might be a Writer.* (Los Angeles: Sherbourne Press, 1972.)

Mathieu, Aron M. (editor), *The Creative Writer* (2nd ed). (Cincinnati: Writer's Digest, 1973.)

Maxon, Hazel Carter, *Opportunities in Free Lance Writing.* (New York: Universal Publishing and Distribution Corporation, 1964.)

Metzler, Ken, *Creative Interviewing.* Englewood Cliffs, N.J.: Prentice-Hall, 1977.)

Milton, John, *The Writer-Photographer*. (Radnor, Pa.: Chilton Book Company, 1972.)

Morris, Terry (editor), *Prose by Professionals: The Inside Story of the Magazine Article Writer's Craft*. (Garden City, N.Y.: Doubleday & Company, 1961.)

Neal, Harry Edward, *Writing and Selling Fact and Fiction*. (New York: Wilfred Funk, Inc.)

Newcomb, Duane, *How to Make Big Money Free-lance Writing*. (West Nyack, N.Y.: Parker Publishing Company, Inc., 1970.)

———, *A Complete Guide to Marketing Magazine Articles*. (Cincinnati, Ohio: Writer's Digest, 1976.)

Nicol, Eric, *One Man's Media – and How to Write for Them*. (Toronto: Holt, Rinehart and Winston of Canada, 1973.)

O'Neill, Carol L., and Ruder, Avima, *The Complete Guide to Editorial Freelancing*. (New York: Dodd Mead & Company, 1974.)

Oppenheimer, Evelyn, *Book Reviewing for an Audience*. (Philadelphia: Chilton Book Company, 1962.)

Palmer, Florence K., *The Confession Writer's Handbook*. (Cincinnati: Writer's Digest Books, 1976.)

Patterson, Helen M., *Writing and Selling Feature Articles* (3rd ed). (New York: Prentice-Hall, 1956.)

Raffelock, David, *Writing for the Markets*. (New York: Funk & Wagnalls, 1969.)

Reynolds, Paul R., *The Writing and Selling of Non-Fiction*. (Garden City, N.Y.: Doubleday & Company, 1963.)

———, *A Professional Guide to Marketing Manuscripts*. (Boston: The Writer, 1968.)

Rivers, William L., *Writing: Craft and Art*. (Englewood Cliffs, N.J.: Prentice-Hall, Inc., 1975.)

———, *Free-Lancer and Staff Writer: Newspaper Features and Magazine Articles* (2nd ed). (Belmont, Calif.: Wadsworth Publishing Company, Inc., 1976.)

Rockwell, F. A., *How to Write Nonfiction that Sells*. (Chicago: Henry Regnery Company Publishers, 1975.)

Roer, Bernice, *How to Write Articles*. (St. Louis, Mo.: The Bethany Press, 1963.)

Romero, Donald George, *A Handbook on Professional Magazine Article Writing*. (Columbia, Mo.: Lucas Brothers, 1975.)

Rose, Camille Davied, *How to Write Successful Magazine Articles*. (Boston: The Writer, Inc., 1967.)

Schapper, Beatrice (editor), *Writing the Magazine Article: From Idea to Printed Page*. (Cincinnati:Writer's Digest, 1970.)

Schell, Mildred, *How to Make Money Writing Magazine Articles*. (New York: Arco, 1974.)

———, *Wanted: Writers for the Christian Market*. (Valley Forge, Pa.: Judson Press, 1975.)

Schoenfeld, Clarence A., *Effective Feature Writing: How to Write Articles That Sell*. (New York: Harper & Brothers, 1960.)

Scott, Jack Denton, *How to Write and Sell for the Out-of-Doors*. (New York: The Macmillan Co., 1962.)

Shaff, Albert L., *The Student Journalist and the Critical Review*. (New York: Richards Rosen Press, 1970.)

Sherwood, Hugh C., *The Journalistic Interview* (rev ed). (New York: Harper & Row, 1972.)

Singer, Samuel L., *Reviewing the Performing Arts*. (New York: Richards Rosen Press, 1974.)

Swain, Dwight V., *Tricks & Techniques of the Selling Writer*. (Garden City, N.Y.: Doubleday & Co., 1965.)

Thomas, W. H. (editor), *The Road to Syndication*. (New York: Fleet Press Corporation, 1972.)

Turner, Robert, *Some of My Best Friends Are Writers But I Wouldn't Want My Daughter to Marry One*. (Los Angeles: Sherbourne Press, 1970.)

Williams, John A., *Flashbacks: A Twenty-Year Diary of Article Writing*. (New York: Doubleday and Company, 1973.)

Williamson, Daniel R., *Feature Writing for Newspapers*. (New York: Hastings House Publishers, 1975.)

Writer's Market. (Cincinnati: Writer's Digest.) (Published annually.)

Youngberg, Norma, *Creative Techniques for Christian Writers*. (Mountain View, Calif.: Pacific Press Publishing Association, 1970.)

Zinsser, William, *On Writing Well: An Informal Guide to Writing Nonfiction*. (New York: Harper & Row, Publishers, 1976.)

Index